Rabbi and Minister

LIBRARY OF LIBERAL RELIGION

RELIGION WITHOUT GOD
by Konstantin Kolenda

HUMANISTIC JUDAISM
by Rabbi Sherwin T. Wine

THE MASK OF RELIGION
by G. Peter Fleck

OLD TALES FOR A NEW DAY
edited by Sophia Lyon Fahs and Alice Cobb

RABBI AND MINISTER
by Carl Hermann Voss

Carl Hermann Voss

Rabbi and Minister

The Friendship

of Stephen S. Wise

and John Haynes Holmes

Prometheus Books

1203 Kensington Avenue

Buffalo, New York 14215

Published by Prometheus Books
1203 Kensington Avenue, Buffalo, New York 14215

Library of Congress Catalog Number: 80-7453
ISBN 0-87975-130-4

Printed in the United States of America

To Christians, Jews, and men of all faiths who stand
shoulder to shoulder as brothers in the struggle
for human dignity and freedom.

ALSO BY CARL HERMANN VOSS

THE UNIVERSAL GOD: *The Eternal Quest in Which All Men are Brothers*—An interfaith anthology

THE PALESTINE PROBLEM TODAY: *Israel and Its Neighbors*

THIS IS ISRAEL: *Palestine—Yesterday, Today and Tomorrow* (with Theodore Huebener)

RABBI AND MINISTER: *The Friendship of Stephen S. Wise and John Haynes Holmes*

STEPHEN S. WISE— SERVANT OF THE PEOPLE: *Selected Letters*

A SUMMONS UNTO MEN: *An Anthology of the Writings of John Haynes Holmes*

LIVING RELIGIONS OF THE WORLD: *Our Search for Meaning*

QUOTATIONS OF COURAGE AND VISION: *A Source Book for Speaking, Writing, and Meditation*

EDITED BY CARL HERMANN VOSS

THE BITTER CHOICE: *Eight South Africans' Resistance to Tyranny*
by Colin and Margaret Legum

THE MODERN MEANING OF JUDAISM
by Roland B. Gittelsohn

MIRRORS OF MAN IN EXISTENTIALISM
by Nathan A. Scott, Jr.

VIOLENCE AND DEMOCRACY
by Jonathan B. Bingham and Alfred M. Bingham

DAVID FRIEDRICH STRAUSS AND HIS PLACE IN MODERN THOUGHT
by Richard Cromwell (Foreword by Wilhelm Pauck)

Contents

Preface   13

Prologue: In the Beginning (1907)   17

PART I. Stephen Samuel Wise: Out of Zion (1874–1906)

1. THE GOLDEN DOOR   27

2. "CHAI" MEANS EIGHTEEN—AND LIFE   34

3. BASEL, LOUISE, AND THE NORTHWEST   40

4. EMANU-EL REJECTED   53

PART II. John Haynes Holmes: Puritan in the Blood
    (1879–1906)

5. DREADING TO LEAVE AN ILLITERATE MINISTRY   63

6. DANVERS AND DORCHESTER   68

PART III. Wise and Holmes: Tribunes of the People
    (1907–1920)

7. YOUR YOUNG MEN SHALL SEE VISIONS   79

8. A SOCIAL GOSPEL   93

9. I, THE LORD, LOVE JUSTICE   101

10. TO PUBLISH GOOD TIDINGS   108

CONTENTS

11. IF I FORGET THEE, O JERUSALEM   127

12. WHY DO THE NATIONS RAGE?   138

13. A HOUSE OF PRAYER FOR ALL PEOPLE   151

14. AS OF RIGHT AND NOT ON SUFFERANCE   162

15. THE LABORER IS WORTHY   171

PART IV. Between Wilson and F.D.R. (1921–1932)

16. WHAT DOTH THE LORD REQUIRE OF THEE?   187

17. WHO IS THE GREATEST MAN IN THE WORLD?   198

18. HE HATH HOLPEN HIS PEOPLE ISRAEL   209

19. RIGHTEOUSNESS AS A MIGHTY STREAM   220

20. DESPISED AND REJECTED OF MEN   231

21. LEARN WAR NO MORE   243

22. THEY SHALL REPAIR THE RUINED CITIES   251

23. ALL WE LIKE SHEEP DID GO ASTRAY   261

24. A LITTLE MAN IN THE BIG CITY   271

PART V. Along the Autumnal Slope (1933–1949)

25. THE YEARS OF THE LOCUST   285

26. AND DARKNESS FELL   299

27. HAMAN REDIVIVUS   312

28. PERFIDIOUS ALBION   323

29. GANDHI'S INDIA   330

30. LET MY PEOPLE GO   337

31. THE LION AND THE LAMB   345

32. THE LAST PURITAN   352

CONTENTS

Acknowledgments and Sources   361

Writings of Stephen S. Wise   377

Writings of John Haynes Holmes   378

Index   381

Foreword

When *Rabbi and Minister: The Friendship of Stephen S. Wise and John Haynes Holmes* was first published in 1964, it received praise from all sides.

Reinhold Niebuhr of Union Theological Seminary in New York City said, "I hail this comprehensive story of two giants in the religious life of New York for almost fifty years as a significant contribution to our religious and social history. Dr. Voss has given us new light on the mood and the method of 'The Social Gospel' of which both men were gifted exponents." His colleague, Paul Tillich, described the book as "deeply moving," observing that "the nearness of the author to the persons and the events, his narrative style, the vividness of his reports, the warmth of his valuation, even when critical, his ability to show the religious ideals and tensions of this period, both in Protestantism and Judaism—all this makes the reading of this book a profound spiritual experience."

Their friend and neighbor, Father George B. Ford at Corpus Christi Roman Catholic Church, asserted that "no definitive life of Rabbi Stephen S. Wise and Dr. John Haynes Holmes could more fully and persuasively convey the consuming passion of these two nonconformists, incomparable religious leaders during the first half of this present century."

The former Prime Minister of Israel, David Ben-Gurion, expressed his gratitude for "such a beautiful and useful book...an excellent piece of work."

In presenting this paperback reprint of *Rabbi and Minister* at the beginning of the 1980s we find ourselves in full agreement with these comments and point to the book's timeliness, for it presaged the interreligious cooperation and growing ecumenism of our day. At the same time it emphasized the continuing imperative to attain justice in the social order, to highlight the emergence of Israel after the horrors of the Holocaust, and to defend its freedom and survival.

We commend this book to the clergy and laity of churches and synagogues alike and would note with approval the other books in Dr. Voss's triad about these two great men, *Stephen S. Wise: Servant of the People—Selected Letters* and *A Summons Unto Men: An Anthology of the Writings of John Haynes Holmes.* The words and works of Wise and Holmes live on for us in these pages.

ALFRED GOTTSCHALK, *President*
Hebrew Union College-Jewish
Institute of Religion

JAMES LUTHER ADAMS,
Professor Emeritus
Harvard Divinity School, Cambridge, MA

EDWARD E. KLEIN, *Rabbi*
Stephen Wise Free Synagogue
New York City

DONALD SZANTHO HARRINGTON,
Minister
The Community Church of New York

Spring, 1980

Preface

RABBI AND MINISTER deals with Stephen S. Wise and John
Haynes Holmes and their joint endeavors in a turbulent period
of world history—the decade before the United States entered
World War I, the War, the Russian Revolution, the postwar
twenties, the rise of Fascism, the New Deal, the Second World
War, the upsurge of nationalism with special reference to India
and Israel, and the advent of the Cold War.

A happy destiny brought them both to New York City in the
winter of 1907 and launched them on parallel pilgrimages. In
that year Stephen Wise and John Haynes Holmes entered upon
their ministries; and an affinity of interests generated a friendship
that lasted forty-two years, ending with the death of Stephen
Wise. Their relationship was remarkable not only for what they
joined in achieving, but also for the interplay of two completely
different personalities whose mutual affection and admiration did
not prevent sharp, even basic, differences on vital current issues.
Both men were colorful, dynamic, provocative, and the way
they dealt with the problems of their times has enduring relevance for the problems of today—indeed, of any day.

However they might vary in their views on public affairs, their
goal was always the same: to attack injustice wherever they saw
it, to champion freedom, equality, and justice in every form.
They sought "to build the Kingdom of God on earth," as it had
been clearly defined for them in their Judeo-Christian heritage.
As they saw it, religion could make the human more divine and
transform men's cruelty and deception into mercy and honesty,
hatred into love. They sought and maintained freedom of the
pulpit and they used that power to fight for civic righteousness,

the rights of labor, justice and equality for all races and creeds, the independence of India, the fulfillment of Zionist aspirations, the abolition of war. No worthy cause found them indifferent: they challenged injustice, cruelty, lack of honor, and censured those responsible no matter how powerful they might be. Together they led the forces of public decency to rout corrupt government in New York City.

Wise and Holmes, controversial figures in the world of thought and action, connoted to most men the ideal of dignity and eloquence in the pulpit, joined with personal courage and integrity. They gave both commitment and leadership in great struggles. To our chaotic time, when lethargy gazes passively at evil, they demonstrate the value of what Dr. Johnson called "the good hater" and the power of the good fighter. Their un-self-conscious identification with the loftiest aspects of the causes for which they fought will never be outdated.

All these impressions ignore the personal side of their natures. Each man had a deep humanity, a great tenderness, and an infinite compassion which were revealed in his intimate relationships with family and friends. Holmes was, perhaps, more restrained in the expression of his feelings; Wise's whole life was a spontaneous outflowing of love for those near to him. Complex as were their personalities, their own friendship grew deeper with time.

I write of them with warmth and conviction, because I have known them in their personal lives as well as in their public actions. I worked with them and enjoyed their friendship. I first heard of them in the 1920s from my father, the late Rev. Dr. Carl August Voss, in Pittsburgh. In the next decades in New York, I listened to their sermons and watched both men, in their independent pulpits, make liberal religion a force for social and political reform; I heard them speak from pulpit and platform to large audiences which responded to their fervor, their logic, their sincerity. *Rabbi and Minister* is a testament of faith in them and their labors, an attempt to acknowledge something of what they meant to our society during the first half of the twentieth century.

This book is not intended as a definitive biography of the two men. Such a work would require many volumes. Furthermore, the autobiographies, *Challenging Years* by Stephen S. Wise and *I Speak for Myself* by John Haynes Holmes, give a full account of their careers; they include many incidents which were omitted from this book to save space and avoid repetition. This is a portrait of an historic and unique friendship, a record of remarkable collaboration in many common causes. It therefore highlights some, but understandably not all, of their efforts in their individual ministries.

CARL HERMANN VOSS

Saratoga Springs, N.Y.
January, 1964

Prologue: In the Beginning (1907)

The first of a series of meetings looking to the completion of the plans of the Rev. Dr. Stephen S. Wise for the founding of a free synagogue was held in the Hudson Theatre, in West Forty-fourth Street yesterday morning, and was attended by an audience that filled the theatre.

—NEW YORK TIMES, January 28, 1907

The Church of the Messiah, New York, has extended a unanimous call to Rev. John Haynes Holmes, Dorchester, Mass., to fill the place made vacant by Dr. Minot J. Savage's resignation last February, as minister in association with Rev. Robert Collyer.

—THE UNITARIAN, January, 1907

ON THE LAST SUNDAY OF JANUARY, 1907, a tall, broad-shouldered man in his early thirties walked onto the stage of the Hudson Theatre in New York City to lead a religious service in English and in Hebrew. Neither in architecture nor in atmosphere did the theater in the Times Square district resemble a place of worship. The bare stage and garish chandeliers were hardly an appropriate setting for a worship service. The congregation that morning was no less unusual. It consisted of Orthodox, Conservative, and Reform Jews, avowed atheists and free thinkers, socialists and single taxers. A few were wealthy but many were poor. They had come in response to the invitation of the young rabbi, Stephen S. Wise, and to hear him preach on "What Is a Free Synagogue?"

17

Stephen Samuel Wise was already well known, not only in Jewish circles but also in the Christian community. Men spoke highly of him; they admired the power of his speech and the compelling strength of his presence. Even those who disagreed with his social liberalism and ardent Zionism granted him respect. Jews and non-Jews knew of his courageous ministries on both East and West Coasts and his widely publicized rejection a year earlier of overtures from the most fashionable, wealthy Reform congregation in America, New York's Temple Emanu-El. They were aware that Wise, merely by announcing his availability, could have become a leading candidate for any synagogue of Conservative or Reform Judaism in search of a rabbi; but he had preferred an unexplored path: the founding of a new religious organization in the city of New York.

His Free Synagogue was to be no "indirect or circuitous avenue of approach to Unitarianism, no society for the gradual conversion of Jewish men and women to any form of Christianity," but would remain "loyally, unswervingly, uncompromisingly Jewish in its ideals, in its free and democratic organization, to reassert the democratic ideal of Israel, and to present the teachings of Judaism in the light of today added to the light of yesterday." Its motivation would be reverence for, but not bondage to, the past. Judaism, said Wise, was "*Wahrheit im Fortschritt*," which he translated freely to mean "Truth on the march!"

Most of the people present realized that Wise's Free Synagogue would be at variance with Jewish religious customs of the time. Because of this they listened all the more intently as he described its dominant purpose as the desire "not to innovate but to renovate, not to destroy but to reconstruct, and to democratize anew the spirit and form alike of the present-day synagogue."

Wise's detractors had sarcastically suggested, "Hire a hall!"— and he had done so. His defenders, generously represented in this audience, welcomed whatever heterodoxy lay in his religious and political views, especially in his zealous Zionism. Believing in him, many had offered to help. Wise had enlisted the support of sympathetic friends; even those who were members of long-established synagogues in the city did not hesitate to aid him, promising more help if he were successful.

To those, on the other hand, who thought the rabbi mannered and self-centered, and something of a demagogue, the choice of a playhouse for his synagogue services seemed ironically appropriate. Did he not seem conscious of his splendid physique? Was he not aware of the impression he made as he tilted the fine head condescendingly or inclined it in deference? Here on the stage of the Hudson Theatre, he chose arch phrases, indulged in resounding rhetoric, used classical quotations, composed clever aphorisms.

Those who agreed with him, however, were enthusiastic about his battles against wrong and injustice, and against the foes he daringly named. Even at this early date, Wise had gathered a sizable following who revered his religious fervor and liked his flair for oratory. What others called faults, they regarded as strength. To such disciples, Stephen Wise was not, as his critics claimed, a poseur. Dramatic? Yes. Powerful and impressive? Without question. But he was no mountebank. He was indisputably a man of courage with the audacity of a Hebrew prophet.

As Wise listed the basic tenets of the projected free synagogue —"pewless and dueless, a free and unmuzzled pulpit, . . . a free and unhampered presentation of Jewish teachings"—he seemed to enjoy his role as a rebel against conventional organized religion. He believed with Ralph Waldo Emerson: "Whoso would be a man must be a non-conformist," and with the prophet Isaiah: "Do not preach smooth things."

When this first service was over, not all the audience left. Some moved up onto the stage and eagerly asked when this Free Synagogue would be organized.

Delighted by this swift reaction to his appeal, yet aware that such enthusiasm might be short-lived, the young rabbi answered with restraint, asking his audience for patience and for their assistance. The project seemed to be successfully launched.

II

Exactly one week later, on February 3, 1907, another brave start took place in New York City. Under more promising auspices a twenty-seven-year-old clergyman began his ministry in the well-established Unitarian Church of the Messiah at Park

Avenue and 34th Street. After the preliminary scripture readings, prayers, and hymns, he mounted the steps to the elevated pulpit above a gold-carpeted platform in the Byzantine sanctuary. Along the depth and across the breadth of the imposing dark-paneled interior he peered through his pince-nez. Then looking resolutely into the questioning eyes of his new congregation— totaling about a hundred that morning—John Haynes Holmes began to preach on "The Church and the New Age."

He looked back on the nineteenth century as "the most wonderful century in all the history of mankind." Was it possible to find words to describe the wonders of "the old, worn-out superstitions that were destroyed, the decrepit traditions that were shattered, the wealth of knowledge that was unearthed, the boundless store of truth that was revealed"?

Between the years 1800 and 1900 had occurred, he said, the most astounding revolution of religious thought in Christian history. The Reformation of the sixteenth century was, in contrast, merely a shift of emphasis from an infallible church to an infallible Bible—and had been neither a revolution nor a reform. Now a new dispensation was at hand. Owing to the "higher criticism" of the Bible and the revolution of society as a new doctrine, he foresaw "the establishment of the Kingdom of God upon the earth, the coming of which was proclaimed by the Master many centuries ago. Now is the march begun toward that Kingdom Whose sovereign is God, Whose ambassador is Christ, Whose subjects are the sons of humankind, Whose laws are Righteousness and Peace and Love. Now is at hand that 'one divine, far-off event toward which the whole creation moves.'"

Not only the dream of Tennyson but the faith of Emerson was to be fulfilled: "Every man will be an authority unto himself, and the revelation from God, as it comes to his own heart, will be the religion of his life." As the tyranny of creeds was abolished and each man chanted the credo written on the tablet of his soul, not as taught by priests or churchmen, there would be an eternal era of good feeling, the end of all bitterness and strife, bigotry and ill will.

He described the time "as plainly a situation of confusion and dissension and uncertainty, yet moving toward an outcome full of hope and inspiration" and he allied himself with "those liberals who are right in seeing that the revolution of the past and the confusion of the present are immediate forerunners of the brighter day."

Christianity, destined for elevation to a new level of power and influence, would enjoy a dominance over the hearts of men such as it had never known before. A new theology would supplant the old, so irrational and unprogressive. This new theology would fit the facts of human experience, for "the scientific method of observation and deduction has at last entered the field of religion and is working out a new system of religious thought upon strictly scientific principles, founded upon the everlasting truth of fact."

Newspapers of the preceding days, February first and second, carried no announcement of a new minister at the Church of the Messiah. On Monday morning, February 4, the New York *Times* described in detail other events in the world of organized religion: President Nicholas Murray Butler's part in the dedication service of St. Paul's Chapel at Columbia University; Dr. Charles Parkhurst's sermon at his Madison Square Presbyterian Church in opposition to Mrs. Mary Baker Eddy's "Christian Science"; and Stephen Wise's second Sunday morning address in the Hudson Theatre, "The Service of the Preacher to His Age." But there was not a line about Holmes.

The omission was odd, for the Church of the Messiah was both prominent and influential. Its former ministers—Orville Dewey, Robert Collyer, and Minot Savage—had been men of high caliber and were often quoted by the metropolitan newspapers; and the church itself had a distinguished history. At its dedication in 1826, one of the members, William Cullen Bryant, wrote a hymn of dedication; and William Ellery Channing, Nestor of American Unitarianism, came from Boston to preach that man was inherently good, society potentially redeemable, and God basically benevolent. Through the next eighty years, the congregation followed Channing faithfully. These Unitarians, a doctrinally emancipated group of Christians, maintained their belief that science need not be hostile to religion and that the theory of evolution could be an aid, rather than a deterrent, to explain Creation and probe the mysteries of life and death. Their Christianity looked to love as the remedy for social ills and as an ethic for all mankind. In its inclusiveness of belief, it held that other religions possessed significant insights into the nature of Divine Reality.

The 1907 congregation of the Church of the Messiah knew little about the aspirations or potential of this personable young man; and the world outside was not yet aware of him, for his circle of followers was limited. The congregation appeared to have been favorably impressed in November, 1906, when Holmes preached as a candidate. A few members admitted to some doubts: Holmes was such a young man and his only experience had been less than three years as minister in the Boston suburb of Dorchester. True, he had from the beginning seemed enthusiastic and, at the reception following the service that autumn morning, had been swift with answers to questions. He obviously had a keen mind and a remarkable memory. Then, too, he had a gracious manner. In the pulpit, he gave the impression of vigor and strength.

Their call to him had been unanimous. On this midwinter morning three months later, they felt the same stimulating, exciting quality in his preaching. Holmes had an inner fire which made him a logical successor to the meteoric Minot Savage. A prophet's passion impelled him. With dark hair above a scholarly face distinguished by aristocratic features, he was earnest of mien. His resonant voice, with its Harvard accent, carried conviction.

Both the congregation and Holmes knew he had passed one test. Now there was another. He had to prove his fiber as he began this ministry in a great metropolis of enormous wealth and vast poverty, of splendid avenues and sprawling slums. In 1907, New York's three and a half million citizens had only recently been appalled by new revelations of political corruption. They were soon to be shaken by the stock market's tumble and a resultant panic. The congregation had begun to be concerned about the role of the church in this New Age Holmes described so vividly—an era of scientific advances, labor conflicts, imperialist rivalries, and men's yearning for justice.

At the same hour, some ten blocks to the north and four blocks to the west, Stephen Wise developed his theme of a free pulpit in an age of transition.

III

Both Wise and Holmes looked to the past for guidance; but they wanted also to see ahead, assay the world's problems, and appraise America's potential. Toward these ends, the two men moved with sure direction and along parallel paths.

It was not until the late spring of 1907 that they met at a meeting of the Liberal Ministers' Club in the City Club on West 44th Street. From that day the rabbi and the minister were fast friends and comrades-in-arms. Their ministries to New York City and to the world at large were of Jew and Christian bent on making religion relevant to an era of social change. A unique kinship of mind and heart bound them in indissoluble friendship. Their accord caused Holmes on many occasions to say of Wise, as did the Friar in Lessing's *Nathan the Wise:*

> Nathan, you are a Christian.
> Yes, I swear
> You are a Christian—better never lived.

And Wise to say to Holmes:

> Indeed, the very thing that
>   makes me seem
> Christian to you, makes you a
>   Jew to me.

I. Stephen Samuel Wise: Out of Zion

(1874–1906)

> *Out of Zion shall go forth the law and the Word of the Lord from Jerusalem.*
>
> —ISAIAH 2:3

1. The Golden Door

. . . *Give me your tired, your poor,*
Your huddled masses yearning to breathe free,
The wretched refuse of your teeming shore.
Send these, the homeless, tempest-tost to me.
I lift my lamp beside the golden door!
                                         —EMMA LAZARUS, 1883

STEPHEN WISE, unlike John Haynes Holmes, was no stranger to Manhattan. When Wise brought his wife, Louise, and their children, James and Justine, from Portland, Oregon, in the fall of 1906 and founded New York's Free Synagogue the following year, he returned to a city he had known since early childhood, to the island of Manhattan among whose million inhabitants he had grown from adolescence to manhood, attended college, pursued rabbinical studies, and served in his first rabbinate.

New York was not, however, his native city, for Stephen Wise was born in Budapest, Hungary, on March 17, 1874. The coincidence of his birthday with Saint Patrick's Day delighted him all during his sixty-nine years of residence in a city of so large an Irish element; each spring, he joined with Irish friends and neighbors in celebrating the great day.

In keeping with the growing custom of Anglicizing foreign names, his father, Aaron Weisz, had adapted his last name to an American spelling. He discovered, soon after his arrival in America, that Weisz, pronounced "Vice," was hardly an appropriate name for a rabbi.

Stephen saw New York for the first time in the summer of 1875. He was seventeen months old, when he and the three

27

other children—Ida, Wilma, and Otto—came to America with their mother, Sabine de Fischer (Farkashazy) Weisz.

To prepare the way and expedite their transition, the father, Aaron, had preceded them in 1874. Nine years earlier, on the day of Lincoln's assassination in 1865, he had received his Ph.D. from the University of Leipzig and had told his fellow students that someday he would go to live in the land of Lincoln. Now he had fulfilled that vow. Soon he established himself as the rabbi of Rodeph Sholom Congregation and purchased a small house on East 5th Street.

The family settled quickly into a busy, pleasant life, just a block from the school the children soon began to attend. Their home was unpretentious, but whatever it might lack was amply compensated by the parents' love for the children.

Wealth and position had been left behind. Aaron Wise could have had an assured rabbinical career in Austria-Hungary, for he was the son of Joseph Hirsch Weisz, Hungary's Chief Rabbi. Sabine was the daughter of Baron Moritz de Fischer, founder of Hungary's porcelain industry and maker of the famed Herend porcelain. All this the family gave up without regret for an unknown life in the New World which posed challenges Aaron had long sought.

As the Chief Rabbi and his wife, Sarah, stood on the platform of the station in Budapest in 1875 and waved farewell to Sabine and her four small children, the old couple wept, sensing this would be the last time they would see their daughter-in-law and grandchildren. Indeed, their son and his family never returned; nor did the grandparents ever come to America, despite the repeated urging of Aaron who had saved enough from his modest salary to buy steamship passages. A few years later, the Chief Rabbi died. His widow left Budapest for the Holy Land where, after a decade as a legendary "Mother in Israel" in the Jewish community of Jerusalem, she too passed away. Her lifelong prayers were answered, for she was buried on the westward slope of the three-thousand-year-old cemetery on the Mount of Olives facing the Holy of Holies.

Aaron Wise could do no more than regret that his parents did not come to New York; he and Sabine now had to look to the years ahead, provide for their children, and make them a part of American life. During the next twenty-one years until his death in 1896, Aaron raised his family in a growing metropolis through which poured as many as a half million immigrants each year, some to stay in the city and its suburbs, but more to move out across the nation in search of jobs and homes. Many travelers who had known him in Hungary came to pay their respects to Aaron Wise. Often the rabbi's house sheltered for a night, a week, or longer if necessary, immigrant families who had just arrived from Europe.

As he grew up, Stephen was impressed by the sagas of these refugees from the Old World who told of their escape from Czarist Russia or imperial Austria-Hungary, whether by bribes, the help of friends, or a *ness*—a miracle. He would linger at the dinner table and listen to the discussions about trends toward a socialist society or the more promising future for Jews in America, the power of despotism in eastern Europe or the growing military might of Imperial Germany. Later in the parlor, where family daguerreotypes were displayed on the mantelpiece and marble-top tables, and where freshly laundered antimacassars were neatly pinned to the backs of high, uncomfortable chairs, Stephen would stretch his lanky form before the fireplace to watch the flames and postpone awhile the three flights' climb to his bedroom for study hours. He and his brothers and sisters— now numbering seven, for Ella, Joseph, and James were born in America—would hear from their father and his friends of their hopes in this land of liberty. He sensed the anxiety and relief in these refugees of the 1880s and 1890s who came by the tens of thousands to land at Castle Garden and received help from a tiny staff of the Hebrew United Charities; and he felt within himself the compassion expressed by a neighbor, Emma Lazarus, who read to him a sonnet she had written in 1883 about the Statue of Liberty and its meaning to immigrants.

As he saw newcomers swept into the turmoil of the city, Stephen began to understand that the liberty they welcomed had to be won anew by them and by everyone in this new land and, when won, constantly defended. He learned this lesson early. The intense convictions about democratic rights and responsibilities that later carried him into battles for these values of the American heritage were forged in spirited arguments at home. From an early age he remembered how the older members of the family discussed the disputed electoral struggle between Samuel Tilden and Rutherford B. Hayes for the Presidency. When he was ten, the campaign of James Blaine against Grover Cleveland excited his imagination; and a sharp image was etched in his memory by the parades on Broadway of the Cleveland men carrying flaming torches and huge placards opposing Blaine with slogans of "Rum, Romanism, and Rebellion."

The problems of government in this growing city interested him. In his home, only a short distance from the headquarters of Tammany Hall, he heard many times of the exposé of the Tweed Ring's graft in the early 1870s.

His father, patient with a precocious son, explained these complicated issues to him. Aaron Wise, informed and sympathetic to socialist theories, aware of the economic and political forces at work in the land, encouraged the family debates. In the generation following the Civil War capitalism flourished unrestrained. No longer were affairs of state determined by selectmen of New England or cultured planters in the South, but rather by those whom some writers called the new "Lords of Destiny" and the "Robber Barons": Jay Cooke and Jay Gould, Cornelius Vanderbilt and Andrew Carnegie, and the elders of the Rockefeller and Morgan clans.

Labor was, however, not to be thwarted; it clamored for bread —and roses too. Marxism had not yet gained a foothold, and Populism was to feel its strength only after the droughts and crop failures of the late 1880s. There had already been a bloody railroad strike in 1877 and in 1886 the bombs of the Haymarket Riot struck terror in the hearts of the upper classes. The Molly Maguires sprang up, but were discredited by their violence and eventually withered away. The Knights of Labor flourished for a while, but soon lost their hold on the workingmen. The American Federation of Labor gave promise of leadership, however, and steadily gained influence and power. "The class struggle" was not now an intellectual pastime of the ivory tower. It was a harsh reality in the marts of this maturing America.

America had burgeoned. Here was an incredible land, rich in resources, both natural and human. Few took thought of the morrow. Forests were destroyed, prairies laid waste, and rich topsoil carried to the sea by turbulent streams. Depressions increased in swiftness of cycle and depth of depredation. Poverty, disease, and crime festered in the cities.

Into this melee there came movements to make men responsible for the character of civilization. The sprawling American giant needed both restraint and direction, and men talked of applying religion to the world. At this point in history, Stephen Wise grew to manhood.

At times highly strung, always impressionable and responsive, Stephen was at first somewhat slow in learning. Once started in the process, his curiosity spurred an absorptive mind. By the age of eight, he had mastered German, which was spoken at home, and the Hebrew of his father's synagogue. He began to read the great German writers Lessing, Schiller, and Goethe. Soon he became familiar with the Hebrew prophets, source of the passion for justice which moved his father, as it had his father before him, and now surged within himself.

Then he made the English language and its literature a major interest. He turned to Shakespeare and Ben Jonson, Milton and Locke, Matthew Arnold and Wordsworth, committing to memory many sonnets, parts of plays and essays. His writing and his speech, both private and public, always reflected the cadences of these classics.

Stephen's physical strength, unusual in a boy of his age, was partly native endowment and partly due to his love for wrestling, running, and climbing, sports in which he excelled. The neighborhood had no playgrounds; the asphalt pavement could be a baseball diamond, but the traffic of carriages, drays, and delivery wagons interrupted the game too often.

Walking over many miles of city streets was a major recreation. The lad hiked through a city where side streets were often dirty and neglected, lighted at night by gas lamps, jammed by day with horse-drawn wagons, where the main avenues were noisy with cable cars, and elevated railways swayed with the weight of steam engines and clattering cars. He strolled along the North and East rivers of the great seaport, where ships from many lands brought to the docks more than two-thirds of America's imports. Often he watched longshoremen hoist on deck and load into hulls the industrial goods which comprised more than half of the country's exports.

Yet Stephen, though stalwart and seemingly assured, was uncertain and diffident. Plagued by a feeling of inadequacy he would turn to his father and confess to timidity and insecurity.

Aaron Wise, who treated Stephen more as a younger brother than as a son, answered with characteristic kindness: "When you feel life is too much for you, remember to say: 'Always do what you are afraid to do.'"

The boy did not forget. When he entered the College of the City of New York he braced himself to meet on an equal level students older than himself and professors prepared to give short shrift to a fourteen-year-old lad. He plunged into the study of Greek grammar and Latin constructions. He read Ovid and Virgil, Aeschylus and Sophocles, Plato and Aristotle, exulting in a newly felt power as he translated classics into English.

Young Stephen surprised his teachers, for he turned out to be a serious student. He mastered impressive areas of philosophy and history, economics and government. He showed a passionate craving to study and work on the problems that had absorbed the ancients.

To broaden his interests and learn from great scholars, he transferred in 1891 to Columbia University for the last year of undergraduate work. Specializing in Greek and Latin and following the guidance of his friend, Richard Gottheil, head of the Department of Semitics and son of Temple Emanu-El's rabbi, he graduated a year later with honors. He was now eighteen years of age and a Bachelor of Arts.

Determined since earliest childhood to become a rabbi, Stephen faced a problem in the final stage: Where should he go for further study? Should he enter the Jewish Theological Seminary? This seemed an unwise move, for he inclined toward a more liberalized interpretation of Judaism; and the Seminary represented the Conservative wing, which was also a reaction against Orthodoxy but not quite as attractive to Stephen. Cin-

cinnati's Hebrew Union College, under its president, Isaac Mayer
Wise, founder of American Reform Judaism, was no more appealing to him, for it was still a new school and did not provide
the breadth of learning he and his father deemed necessary.

A pattern had been set for a number of years with Stephen
Wise studying the Old Testament and post-Biblical books in
Hebrew under the direction of his father; he had received additional instruction from Alexander Kohut and Gustav Gottheil,
each of whom was delighted that so young a lad could compre-
hend so swiftly. Now it seemed right for him to broaden this
program by going abroad. Aaron Wise decided therefore to send
his son to study with Adolf Jellinek, Chief Rabbi of Vienna, and
later to England to work with Adolf Neubauer at Oxford.

2. "Chai" Means Eighteen—and Life

> Mr. Stephen S. Wise, though still . . . a very
> young man, is endowed by nature with all
> those gifts that go to make the eloquent pulpit
> orator and is certainly destined to take a
> prominent position among the young rabbis
> of this country. —AMERICAN INSTITUTE, 1892

WITHIN A FEW DAYS after his graduation from Columbia University in 1892, young Stephen Wise boarded a steamer for Bremen and from there went by rail to Vienna. Each day of the journey he marveled anew at this return to the Old World and his good fortune in being one of the rabbinical students gathered at Adolf Jellinek's villa in Baden-bei-Wien.

Wise now worked with Jellinek, who led him through the maze of his own rabbinical duties, directed him in advanced studies, explained "The Science of Judaism" ("Wissenschaft des Judenthums") of which he was the master, and interpreted trends in European politics. He introduced the young American to commentary and exposition, and encouraged him in research projects at the university and state libraries. On occasion he allowed Wise to stand with him before the Ark in the Great Synagogue of Vienna and to preach from the pulpit he had made famous.

Stephen had great admiration for this rabbi with the kind face now creased with age, the cultured, witty teacher who spoke persuasively about the "community of Israel," which bound him by mystic ties to fellow Jews everywhere. Soon Wise was promoted to private secretary and confidential aide and took longhand dictation of letters and articles. Late each afternoon the seventy-two-year-old Jellinek and the eighteen-year-old Wise conversed in German as they walked along Vienna's spacious Ringstrasse, down through the busy Kaerntnerstrasse, and out to lovely Schoenbrunn Palace.

Wise's funds were limited, and he had to move on to carry out his plans for a stay at Oxford. He requested that, by the summer of 1892, Jellinek ordain him to the rabbinate. The Chief Rabbi examined Wise in rabbinical lore, Biblical history, post-Biblical writings, and practical details of synagogue life and found him ready for the rabbinate. With Jellinek's blessings upon him, Stephen, now a true Teacher in Israel and awed by his newly won place in an ancient tradition, left Vienna for Paris; without pausing he continued to England and, after a brief stay in London, went to Oxford for further study.

Oxford offered all his father had told him it would—and more. Each morning he left his "digs" and, thrilled by the cluster of Gothic towers, walked down High Street toward the University. Regularly he met his preceptors. Adolf Neubauer, the Biblical scholar, was in residence. Wise attended his lectures and received tutorial guidance. In the Bodleian Library, he pored eagerly over hundreds of dusty, crumbling manuscripts stored in the Biblical, rabbinical, and Arabic archives. In these ancient rooms, he was intoxicated with learning and wished he could devote a lifetime of study to the Hebraic heritage.

When he crossed the Atlantic to America in the early winter of 1892–1893, hours of inner interrogation agitated him: Now ordained, should he accept a pulpit? Or continue studying toward a doctoral degree? Perhaps both?

On his return to New York in November, circumstances made the decision. Both the parish ministry and graduate studies awaited him. His ability as an exceptional preacher soon became known, for he preached an anniversary sermon to his father's Rodeph Sholom Congregation in the fiftieth year of its founding. The young Stephen Wise already had a manner and a presence that lent dignity to his sermons.

Wise was not tempted to forsake organized religion, although attracted by idealistic goals in the secular world. He had chosen

the rabbinate, and there he would work. He was excited by the
steady growth of the American labor movement, especially of
Terence Powderley's Knights of Labor. He was repelled by the
repressive measures used against the workers in the Pullman
Strike of Chicago and the Homestead uprisings in western Pennsylvania, and he was outraged by the attacks on Illinois' governor,
John Altgeld, in the aftermath of the Haymarket assassinations.
Wise had, however, no doubts about his choice of vocation, no
intention of becoming either a labor organizer or social reformer.
These interests he could further in the ministry and remain a
rabbi, speaking his mind in the pulpit.

In the spring of 1893, the trustees of Congregation B'nai
Jeshurun invited him to become assistant to Rabbi Henry F.
Jacobs. Now it was almost as though he were again in Vienna
with Jellinek, for Rabbi Jacobs was both mentor and guide to the
nineteen-year-old youth; but the interval was brief, because the
saintly Jacobs died in the autumn. The grief-stricken congregation considered asking Wise to accept the post of senior rabbi.
Although some members protested he was too young, an over-
whelming majority elected him.

He worked intensely now. In the early morning hours, dressed
in his Prince Albert coat and stiff shirt, he walked quickly to his
synagogue study on the southwest corner of Madison Avenue
and 65th Street. First he gave himself to planning services, ar-
ranging organizational events, preparing weekly bulletins, sched-
uling and teaching confirmation classes, making sick calls, seeing
visitors and callers, and representing the congregation at meetings of charitable organizations in the Jewish community. Then,
often foregoing lunch, he hurried across town to Broadway and
took the horse car to Columbia University for his graduate
courses in Arabic, Syriac, and Sanskrit. Under the guidance of
Richard Gottheil, he focused his research on Solomon ibn
Gabirol's *Improvement of the Moral Qualities,* an eleventh-cen-
tury Jewish ethical treatise written in Arabic. He began to translate the work into English and to write an extensive commentary,
a project that appealed to him because it combined scholarship
in Semitics and the wisdom of an honored Jewish sage.

In the midst of his studies and this first rabbinical post, two major events of his personal life shook him to the core. In 1894, the elder Wise was stunned by the news of his mother's death in Jerusalem. The cablegram arrived on the eve of his and Stephen's departure on a long-planned trip to visit her in the Holy Land. They canceled their journey and Aaron Wise observed the traditional week of mourning.

Only two years later, in March of 1896, a few hours after preaching his Passover sermon, Aaron Wise suffered a heart attack and died. There was sadness in all New York at the death of Rodeph Sholom's rabbi, and the newspapers—English, German, Hungarian, and Yiddish—told of the loss in front-page stories.

The unusually close father-son relationship had been central to Stephen's life and its severance was the deepest sorrow he had ever known. Aaron Wise had been to Stephen a living example of many virtues: the unremitting diligence needed to master English, a new language; forbearance and charity to cope with jealous colleagues in the ministry; an abhorrence for *"die Sklaverei der Kanzel,"* the enslavement of the pulpit; kindness and generosity to all who needed help; and a love of Zion, that desolate land of Palestine, which Aaron, along with a few other visionaries, believed could with God's help be revived and restored to His People.

The father's death created added responsibilities. Stephen, now only twenty-two, took care of his mother, his younger brother, and his younger sister. His days were busy—at home, in the Jewish community, at Columbia University, in his graduate seminar, but especially at Congregation B'nai Jeshurun. Not content only with the stirring substance of his sermons, Wise now perfected their structure. He wrote and rewrote many times, committing them to memory. When, on occasion, he was called upon "to say a word" at public meetings, whether in English, German, or Hebrew, it was likely to be the right word.

As a rabbi, he ministered with tenderness to the sick and the dying. He confirmed children, officiated at weddings and funerals, heard his people's problems, brought courage to the timid and frightened. Such pastoral fidelity led the members to love and trust him.

A rabbi, Stephen Wise constantly reminded himself, should be more than preacher and pastor, scholar and teacher. He must be one who "speaks for God"; and, in the pattern of the prophets of old, Stephen Wise's social passion grew strong. To his congregation he explained socialism. He expounded the "single tax" proposals of Henry George, with reservations but with sympathy. He advocated equal suffrage for women, pressed for the abolition of child labor, demanded the elimination of the sweat shop, sought the eradication of slums, and warned of the perils of a high tariff.

He sided with labor in the Brooklyn streetcar strike of 1894, upheld the right of conductors and motormen to organize in a union and bargain collectively, and protested the killings in that conflict. His sermon "Strikes and Strikers," inspired by his investigation of the controversy, was delivered, as he liked to recall, "to the horror of the dear nice orthodox people in the congregation." The president of the synagogue said to him, "What do you know about a strike? We want religion, not strikes." In that hour, he declared an independence that he never lost over the next half century and that possessed a unique force.

His Judaism was a variant from the past. No longer able to accept the Orthodox Judaism of seven generations of rabbis in the family's ancestry, he turned more and more to Reform Judaism. He had already begun a transition from Conservative customs, paying less attention to dietary laws and considering the separation of sexes in the synagogue to be unimportant. He gave up the yarmulka, or skullcap, and added English in the reading of scripture and prayers.

Wise's belief that a spiritual leader must carry the message of prophetic Judaism into all of life—social, political, and economic—derived in part from the Jewish tradition of the *Magid* [the preacher] but was also greatly influenced by the nineteenth-century movement in Protestantism known as the "Social Gospel." He had come to know the leading spokesmen and their writings, which demanded the application of religion to every phase of the common life. He owned all of Theodore Parker's published works, marking the margins, underscoring sentences, and writing reactions on the end papers; the Abolitionist preacher was to him a supreme example of the prophetic preacher. Eagerly he read each new book by such "Social Gospel" spokesmen as Josiah Strong, Washington Gladden, and Lyman Abbott; regularly he exchanged letters with them. The language and thought used by Wise in the pulpit and on the platform were as much that of "Social Gospel" Protestants as of the Hebrew prophets. To some extent he became the child of his ebullient age and declared that democracy was the hope of the Western world; but significantly he stressed that it had to be undergirded with the precepts and power of vital religion. To this objective he gave himself, as the Deuteronomist urged, with heart and soul and strength.

3. Basel, Louise, and the Northwest

If you will it, it is no legend.

—THEODORE HERZL, 1896

AFTER FIVE YEARS of carrying on a successful ministry in New York City and studying toward his doctorate at Columbia, Stephen Wise experienced one of the most decisive events of his life. In the summer of 1898, he attended his first Zionist Congress and joined in the political movement to secure a publicly recognized, legally assured national home in Palestine for the Jewish people.

A new stage in his thought had come with the publication of *The Jewish State*, Dr. Theodor Herzl's tract, in 1896. As he read this small book with a monumental message, he heard his late father's voice: "The land of the Book belongs to the people of the Book." With high hopes he followed newspaper accounts of the proceedings of the historic First Zionist Congress that Herzl and Max Nordau convened in the spring of 1897. As a consequence, he joined in founding the Federation of American Zionists on July 4, 1898, and accepted the Honorary Secretaryship, a post with many duties but no remuneration.

Desiring to join with Zionists from other parts of the world and hoping to meet Herzl, Wise attended the Second Zionist Congress in Basel. Some of the expenses he defrayed by serving as correspondent for the New York *Journal* and *Harper's Weekly*, reporting the sessions with vivid descriptions and obvious partisanship. These Zionists, he wrote for his American readers, included "great men who were great Jews, great Jews who were great men." The Basel Congress of 1898 made him aware of the power of a people now suddenly conscious of their destiny.

Wise not only learned about Jewish refugees who had fled terror in the Pale of eastern Europe, but he also came to know Jews of every country. Their hope of a restored Zion was as impressive to him as their ability to discuss it heatedly, intelligently, and lengthily in these sessions.

The most dramatic, compelling figure was Theodor Herzl, who, as Wise said, "stood before men like a king and would have stood before kings like a man." Wise never forgot the moving moment of adjournment after an all-night debate. Dawn was about to break over the city. Herzl, framed on the podium against the widespread window of the Basel Casino, spoke the concluding words as the rising sun shed a roseate glow over him: "Zionism is not only a mournful necessity, but a glorious ideal. May it succeed! And may nothing deter us from the work we have undertaken, nor destroy anything before an enduring movement is created. We are on the march. The moral march of the new Jew has begun. Where will it lead us? Let us hope: to better days."

When Herzl invited Wise to become the American Secretary of the Zionist Movement, he gladly accepted. In addresses throughout the East and Midwest, in editorials for the Zionist Department of the *American Hebrew*, in articles for the European journal of the Movement, *Die Welt*, he urged the Zionist solution of a Jewish national homeland. Steadfastly he countered the contention of the anti-Zionists that Zionism was parochial and particularistic, that it ran counter to the American dream of "the melting pot" and jeodardized acceptance of the Jew in American life.

In those years at the close of the nineteenth century, Zionism was neither fashionable nor popular. "No man in his right mind, especially an intelligent young rabbi intent on advancement, should support the Movement," one of his friends warned him. But Wise had no use for such discretion, and continued to plead the cause at every turn.

Most Reform rabbis echoed Isaac Mayer Wise of the Hebrew Union College who condemned "the whole plan as a dream of romantic and impractical minds." The Central Conference of American Rabbis affirmed that "America is our Zion and Washington our Jerusalem," and anti-Zionists soon found themselves

faced with the anti-Semitic inference that Jews boasted of controlling the nation and claimed Washington as their headquarters. Meanwhile, Wise and his fellow Zionists plodded ahead;
Herzl's "hope of better days" seemed long deferred.

Letters came to him from all over the country—Cleveland,
Baltimore, Boston, Knoxville—written in English, German, Yiddish, Hebrew, asking for copies of *Die Welt* and rejoicing with
Wise and Richard Gottheil in the news that "Zionism, in general,
is gaining ground."

To Henrietta Szold, daughter of a Baltimore rabbi, Wise wrote
to ask if she, as secretary of the Jewish Publication Society, saw
any likelihood of that organization's publishing Zionist literature.
She replied regretfully: "So far as I know the temper, equally
of the Zionist and the non-Zionist members of the Committee, a
strong indisposition would manifest itself."

The year 1899 had even greater significance for Stephen Wise
because during it he met his future wife. He had not yet succumbed to the campaign of many a doting mother who considered her daughter his answer to the Biblical query, "A good
wife who can find?"

In January, 1899, a cousin of the Waterman family died; and
the family asked Louise Waterman to notify the rabbi of their
loss. There was no telephone available and she had to convey
the news personally, walking from her home on East 68th Street
to the rabbi's home not many blocks away. She was announced to
him and waited in the parlor. In a few moments, the rabbi came
down the stairs and entered the room. As far as Wise was concerned, the courtship began that day. He called frequently, wrote
long letters, and with persistence pressed his suit. Louise felt
attracted, for Stephen was a powerful suitor. But to marry a
rabbi! This had never crossed her mind.

Organized religion was not unknown to her. The Waterman
family, notably Uncle Leopold, had been Reform Jews of renown
in New Haven, and her father, Julius, had maintained a nominal
membership in New York's Temple Emanu-El, primarily for
family burial privileges in its cemetery; but like her brother and
sister, Leo and Jennie Waterman, Louise preferred the Ethical
Culture Society, where she enjoyed hearing Felix Adler lecture

in lucid, nontheological language about practical ways of leading the Good Life.

Stephen soon discovered that Louise shared many of his social ideals. She had read and understood the Stoics Marcus Aurelius and Epictetus, the Transcendentalists Emerson and Thoreau. She admired the Christian socialism of Frederick Maurice and Charles Kingsley, and was familiar with the evolutionary theories of Charles Darwin, Herbert Spencer, and Thomas Huxley. Her social consciousness was tangibly expressed by work in the University Settlement where she taught painting.

Steadily he courted, visiting her during working hours at the Settlement or during her evenings of painting in the "studio" at home.

The Waterman family began to worry: Was she really serious? Did she plan to marry this rabbi, this immigrant of Hungarian descent? Incredible—for a Waterman of German-Jewish lineage from Bayreuth and Nuremberg! Why not someone of Bavarian parentage? Why not a lawyer or a banker? To make certain Louise really knew what she was doing, Leo and Jennie, her brother and sister, insisted she go abroad and view her romance in perspective. Her trip to Europe at her family's insistence that summer, and his to the West, would take them six thousand miles from each other; then each could judge objectively.

As always when he traveled, saw new sights, met interesting people, and had a chance to think without the pressures of his ministry, Wise regained whatever zest he had lost. Along the way West, he gave Zionist speeches so convincing that they moved many, even in such anti-Zionist centers as San Francisco and Portland, Oregon.

When Wise spoke at Portland's Temple Beth Israel, the people extended him an invitation to succeed their rabbi who planned to retire within the year. Wise accepted and arranged to begin his work in August, 1900.

At the very turn of the century, on the last day of 1899, Louise promised to marry him.

Leo and Jennie finally gave their consent, too, but not before Felix Adler had obtained for them an estimate of Wise from Thomas Davidson, one of Wise's closest friends and head of the

Breadwinners' College at Croton-on-Hudson. Professor Davidson, scion of Scottish Presbyterians and a scholar in Christian philosophical theology, wrote:

> My dear Prof. Adler:
>
> I was very sorry to miss you the other day, and am so now, all the more that you had a special object in coming. Now I have your note, which I will do my best to answer, though an answer is not easy.
>
> The fact is, I am so fond of Stephen Wise personally, that I cannot, perhaps, be trusted to judge him impartially. I have known him for the past six or seven years, and my respect and affection for him have grown all that time. He is loyal in his personal relations, and socially attractive. I cannot think of him as doing a mean thing. When roused, he is an eloquent and powerful speaker, with a delightful sense of humor.
>
> He is still young—only twenty-seven, I think—and may have some of the faults of the young and inexperienced, delight in sense of power and perhaps desire for popularity, though the last is not especially prominent.
>
> He is distinctly a stirring man, original and forcible, with great schemes in his mind. I always leave him with the sense that I have been facing a brisk, bracing wind.

As for his "delight in sense of power and desire for popularity," Wise had already confessed in a letter to Louise a fortnight earlier: "I am a man of temperament . . . nervous, cross, petulant, irritable, selfish, vain, and even envious, with one miserable, unpardonable, besetting weakness, an unrighteous ambition which deadens the best within men in public life—love of fame, applause, popularity. Will you not show me, by your teaching and example alike, self-denial, self-effacement, self-forgetfulness? Will you not help me and save me from myself? God knows I never was more earnest in my life!"

Not until November could Stephen and Louise be married, for several major projects were still incomplete. Louise encouraged him amid his unfinished commitments.

Encouragement came from others too, especially from Richard Gottheil, who, in February, 1900, introduced Wise at a large Zionist meeting in Cooper Union. Mindful of the historic coincidence that, almost forty years to the day, Abraham Lincoln had delivered his famous Cooper Union Address on that same platform, Gottheil likened Wise to Lincoln, a man who led his people to victory in the midst of seeming defeat. Gottheil also lamented Wise's imminent departure for Portland and told the audience this might be the last time Wise would be heard in New York for some years to come.

Wise caught the cue and said the cause, not he, was important. No single individual's plans for his own life could be considered significant. For all of them, Zionism was of supreme importance: "Of Israel and Zion one thing is true. They can conquer. God is our leader, and with the General of the Heavenly Hosts to lead, who will say that we go not to victory? In the old Greek games, the man who won the race was not he who went fastest, but the one who bore a lighted torch to the end of the course. We Zionists have entered a race. The torch will be won, not because we are fastest, but because that lamp is a light unto the world. It will never be extinguished. Come, brothers, the lamp is in your hands. Run the race and may God give you the victory forever!"

When the Zionists gathered in June for their Third Annual Convention in New York, Wise was able to report on behalf of his Propaganda and Publications Committee that its work had progressed well. There were 135 societies all over the nation, a total membership of more than 10,000. He ventured a prediction that soon an official organ would be established and a Zionist book concern founded.

He shared the hope of the delegates that Dr. Theodor Herzl might visit America. But Herzl, weary from intensive travels and fruitless efforts to pacify a movement riddled with factions, never came.

Wise kept up a steady correspondence with Herzl after their first encounter in 1898. Sometimes Herzl's letters were typed on the lined paper of the Zionist Bureau in Vienna; at other times they were handwritten. All were simple, direct, and full of intense feeling, according Wise trust and affection. Constantly, they asked for information about developments in America and "the success of your propaganda journeys."

Wise was chosen one of twenty delegates to represent the Federation of Zionists at the 1900 Congress in London and at the Central Actions Committee in Vienna; but he declined because soon he was to take up his new duties in Portland.

In late July, 1900, he left for the Northwest. He rode the Northern Pacific to Portland, traveling to a part of the country far from all he had known and loved for a quarter of a century. On the journey to Oregon he discovered the generosity and openheartedness of the people who were to help him in his new life. During the one-thousand-mile stretch between Minneapolis and Helena, he was seized with an acute attack of appendicitis. Through the night, the conductor tended him with care; and his fellow passengers comforted him. Finally, in the hospital at Helena, the medical staff gave him expert attention. The Jews of the city, when they heard of the rabbi's predicament, brightened his stay with flowers, fruit, and friendly visits. Best of all, his brother Otto came swiftly from San Francisco. While in Helena, Stephen Wise wrote to his fiancée, Louise Waterman, that if he died, he wanted as his epitaph:

> Servant of God,
> Defender of Israel,
> Lover of Humanity.

Fortunately, no operation was necessary; and the arrival in Portland was delayed only a few days.

In Portland, which at that time had been a municipality for less than half a century, Stephen Wise found a boom-town metropolis. Its population of 45,000 in 1890 had doubled in the following decade. Strategically situated on the Willamette River just twelve miles from the confluence with the Columbia River and only one hundred miles from the Pacific Ocean, Portland was a seaport for ocean-going ships. Here was a social laboratory in microcosm, with social problems quite similar on a small scale to those of the New York he had just left. Wise sensed the power of the gambling interests and their opposition to reform movements. He appraised the effectiveness of the few social agencies then available and decided the synagogue must play an important part in battling against social evils.

Of greatest urgency was his rabbinical work. On Fridays, Wise attracted his congregation to Sabbath Eve services at the Temple by addresses on "Present-day Problems in Ancient Settings." He had the usual round of rabbinical instruction: the confirmation class each Saturday morning, a children's service on the first Sunday of each month, the Study Circle of the Altar Guild on the last Sunday of each month, the Council of Jewish Women each third Wednesday of the month; and biweekly addresses to the Religious School of the Temple. He trained a new cantor, learned to know the congregation, and became acquainted with the non-Jewish community in the rapidly growing city.

Now he turned to another item on his agenda, the most important event of his life: marriage to Louise. In early November of 1900, shortly after his first observance of the High Holy Days with the new congregation in Portland, he returned to the East for the wedding. At the reception following the ceremony the officiating rabbi, Kaufmann Kohler, a leader of Reform Judaism and a longtime friend of the Waterman family, advised Louise: "My dear, you have married a promising young man who will, I am sure, go far. But he will accomplish much more if you can cure him of his *meshugass*, this lunacy of Zionism. To rid him of that will be the greatest service you can do him—and yourself."

Louise had no intention, however, of following Kohler's advice. Already a convert, she considered Zionism her cause, too. Eighteen months before, as she was about to leave for Europe, Stephen had given her a tiny Magen David pin, blue and gold enamel with a six-pointed star, adopted as the emblem by the Movement. To the surprise of her friends and the dismay of her family, she wore it everywhere, and would, she informed Kohler, continue to wear it. Now on the fourth finger of her left hand was a ring that bound her for life to Stephen; and she would aid him in everything he supported, including Zionism.

With Louise at his side, Stephen Wise's life in the Northwest seemed idyllic despite heavy duties in his congregation, the city, the state, and along the West Coast. Louise, like Stephen, felt drawn to the Northwest and its stalwart people, tall mountains, great forests, and rushing streams. She loved Portland, where roses bloomed the year round.

Her joy in this new life and her pride in Stephen's ministry were shared in long letters to her sister, Jennie Waterman. On May 14, 1901, she wrote: "Today is our wedding anniversary—six months—and we are happier than on the first 14th, if possible. This morning I found on my table a lovely bunch of roses with this card—please keep the card for me. Stephen and I are together all day long, and a rarer nature I have never known, so equable, good, kind, and yet strong. We are very, very happy."

And a year later: "I am told that his address last night was fine and the men were most enthusiastic. An old gentleman told me that Stephen was already the most important Jew in Oregon —in time would be in the United States! High praise—I do not care very much. He is good and tender and earnest and true, and that is all I want."

He was indeed the most important Jew in Oregon. In actual fact, he was more important than the well-known president of his congregation, Solomon Hirsch, who had been Minister to Turkey under President Benjamin Harrison.

Hirsch used his diplomat's skill to convey to his rabbi some complaints of the congregation. The Temple members, Wise wrote his brother-in-law, Leo Waterman, were "inclined to be 'small.'" He explained: "They mutter and grumble because of my long vacation. The burden of the arraignment is that I hold myself aloof from my people and appear to have no personal interest in them. My teachings are too heterodox, especially for Mr. Hirsch. I did nothing to prevent the many inter-marriages [between Jews and Gentiles]. Furthermore, I gave too much time to lecturing to non-Jews, little to my own people."

Yet to Wise, if not to some of his congregation, his activity among non-Jews was a major factor in his ministry. He organized an interfaith movement and, as Chairman of the Religious Committee for the Lewis and Clark Centenary in 1905, planned the program over many months.

His leadership in social reform was manifested by his appointment by the governor in 1903 as one of the first Commissioners of Child Labor in Oregon. He took seriously this unpaid post, pressing for the abolition of child labor in the state.

He spared no one in his denunciations of this and other social evils. He scored the gamblers and slot-machine men who looked upon "an Open Town as good and profitable for the city." When Wise thundered against gambling in Portland, he had an attentive audience. Evidence of his outspoken ministry is this paragraph in a letter to his wife, then visiting relatives in the East: "If the pulpit be morally impotent, it shall not be for lack of my zeal or my courage. Yesterday, Charles Kohn telephoned, ostensibly to inquire about my health. After a moment, he said he had heard of the subject of my sermon today: 'Business is terrible, why must *you* always be the leader? If things go on this way, the members of the Temple won't be able to pay their dues, etc.' And this from my *best* friend. Observe the veiled threat, the intimidation. I will give him my answer tonight—I'll be damned sooner than be silent."

He attacked opponents of a new city administration, and helped elect Portland's mayor. He then declined the new mayor's invitation to join the cabinet, for a clergyman, he maintained, should not hold a paid public office.

Wise's love for scholarship, awakened at Columbia, nurtured in Vienna and at Oxford, did not abate. His knowledge of the languages he knew as a child—English, German, and Hebrew—had been supplemented by work in Latin and Greek at college and then by postgraduate studies in Syriac, Sanskrit, and Arabic. When his Ph.D. dissertation was published by Columbia University in the *Series of Oriental Studies* in 1902, he dedicated the first copy:

> To you, Louise, my wife, my love, my sweetheart, my precious angel,
>
> from your
> Stephen

And in the lower right hand corner, he noted numerals inscribed in her wedding ring as a reminder of their favorite verse in Psalm Thirty: "Thou didst turn for me my mourning into dancing. Thou didst loose my sackcloth, and gird me with gladness."

The translation of Solomon-ibn-Gabirol from the Arabic whetted his appetite for more. The care he devoted to his Ph.D. thesis made scholars aware of his talents; and when the Jewish

Publication Society planned a new translation of the Bible, Wise
was included among the men to whom invitations were sent.
Solomon Schechter and Cyrus Adler, heading the Publications
Committee, instructed Henrietta Szold, secretary of the Society,
to assign Wise the Book of Judges. On this he worked during
his years in Portland, and his translation has remained to this day
a solid scholarly contribution.

Family life was important too. Following the birth of James
Waterman Wise a year after their arrival in Portland, Wise sent
weekly bulletins to the relatives in the East. After some months
he could report: "My little loafer, 23 lbs., 2 feet 4½ inches, is
doing famously, and by the time you get to see him on the
'Krabbeldecke' [crawling spread], I expect him, Huxley-like, to
know the biological history of every animal thereupon stitched.
At seven A.M. he starts up his 'Open-heir Concerts,' simply mono-
logueing vocally and conversationally."

Two years later, a daughter, Justine Waterman Wise, was born
to them: "The little angel smiles the livelong day and awakens
but once in the night for a meal, which I prepare without delay."

Stephen and Louise planned for the four of them to take a
vacation trip to New York after the High Holy Days in 1903.
Stephen warned Uncle Leo and Aunt Jennie: "We have been
wrong in portraying our son to you as a little angel. Now he
really is—*sometimes*. But he is a Zoroastrian dualist, half Ahura
and half Mazda, and not infrequently, to revert to Anglo-Saxon
terms, young Nick gets the upper hand. Some people are mean
enough to hint that he is spoiled. If so, you have my parental
authorization to unspoil him in October or November."

The trip to the East that autumn was really more than a
vacation. He was tired and exhausted and felt the need to get
away to think and plan for the future. He decided to take his
family with him to Europe.

The stay abroad coincided with the meetings of the Zionist
Actions Committee in Vienna in early 1904, and Wise attended
as an American delegate. Again he met Herzl, still determined
and inspiring but weakened by repeated heart attacks, saddened
by constant setbacks.

Wise later described one of their last encounters: " 'Vise'—he couldn't say 'Wise'—'How old are you?' I said, 'I am just thirty years.' 'You are a young man; I am an old man.' And the 'old man' was only forty-two; but the Jewish people had broken his heart. Then he turned to me and said: 'Vise, I shall not live to see the Jewish State, but you will live to see the Jewish State.' "

Shortly after Wise returned to the United States, word came that Herzl, crushed by rebuffs on every side, had died. "Complete confidence and unending friendship," as Herzl put it in one of his last letters to Wise, had united the two men.

After Herzl's death, Wise told his Portland congregation:

> He was one of the rarest of men, dreamer and doer alike. "*Wenn Ihr wollt ist es kein Maerchen.*" ["If you will it, it is no legend."] To charge him with having been an irresponsible dreamer is wickedly and cruelly libelous. The pygmies, plodding and un-prophetic, looked upon this giant, gazing at the distant horizon, and they cried aloud, "Irresponsible dreamer!!"—For us he died. His cause shall be our cause; for it will we live and labor.

Wise's European travels and the period of rest had brought new insight into his work and a fresh outlook for the years ahead. He had gone back to Portland, still puzzled and disappointed by the resistance in his congregation but resolved to complete his contract, perhaps to stay even a year more. Then he would make plans.

"For the present I must be patient and bide my time, but it is hard. I shall not stay long," he wrote to his brother-in-law. "If I were not weighted down with debts—in a word, if I were five thousand to the good, instead of being twelve thousand to the bad [Wise had assumed the debts of a relative]—I would leave tomorrow and take my chances. Free to go anywhere. I do not think I would have to wait long for a 'call.' " He still could not understand the lethargy and indifference of Temple Beth Israel, "for I have worked hard and think I have done my duty."

He continued to do his duty: spoke frequently; organized on many fronts; wrote often, especially for the new *Jewish Encyclopedia*; and read widely—new exciting books about the "Social

Gospel"; Leonard Huxley's two-volume biography of his father, Thomas Huxley (a birthday gift from Leo); essays by Kingsley, Maurice, Emerson, and Parker.

It was not long before Temple Emanu-El invited him as a guest preacher. Fifteen different rabbis had been asked to take part in, as one wit called it, "an oratorical contest." Each was to occupy the pulpit and give guest lectures at assigned times throughout the year. Wise confirmed his own dates and prepared to leave for the East in the late autumn of 1905.

4. Emanu-El Rejected

> *I want to see him surrounded by sympathetic*
> *followers in any small hall and be himself.*
> *Simple beginnings have before this led to great*
> *results in the world of religion and ethics and*
> *they will again.*
>
> —LOUISE WATERMAN WISE, 1906

STEPHEN AND LOUISE WISE talked often of Temple Emanu-El as a possibility for him. Family and friends in the East encouraged their hopes. He had all the necessary qualifications. The influential members—including the Schiffs, the Warburgs, the Seligmans, and the Guggenheims—and the quite sizable endowment might make possible a ministry of power, although Wise was dubious about the freedom of utterance and of action which he considered essential.

His younger brother, Joseph, considered Stephen a logical choice and urged him to act with more energy, to exert a bit of influence. Wise spurned his advice and, in a note to Louise, said, "No one but you will ever believe that I would not lift a finger to become rabbi of Emanu-El. I will preach for them; they must do or leave undone the rest. I know you would have it so. I would scorn myself if I descended to solicitation or electioneering on behalf of that which will come unsought or not at all."

Now, in December, 1905, the position seemed to be within his grasp. They were on their way to New York where Wise would be a "candidate," a word he disliked, for he would prefer to be chosen without rivals.

Immediately after the first address, "The New Conscience,"

James Seligman, president of Temple Emanu-El, brought several trustees to the Waterman home on East 68th Street to meet with Wise and discuss the vacant post and a possible call. Louis Marshall, a New York attorney and Honorary Secretary of Emanu-El, served as chairman of the conference.

The committee cordially greeted the thirty-one-year-old rabbi and asked him for his reactions and suggestions. Wise held in his hand two small pieces of paper with brief reminders of the matters he wanted to discuss and the stipulation he felt he must make. First, he paid tribute to Gustav Gottheil and added that any man would feel honored in being considered as a successor to the great rabbi. Wise asked then that there be a un-animous recommendation by the trustees, and, if possible, un-animity on the part of the congregation. He requested one term of office—three or perhaps five years—and, if that were successful, then an indefinite period.

Further, he intended to participate in the reading of every service, with the understanding that the Sunday morning service be his with Dr. Joseph Silverman, Co-Rabbi, to co-operate. But, he added, all invitations for guest preachers were to be issued by him—with, of course, concurrence of the Board. He was to preach three times a month, messages designed not only for Jews but for non-Jews as well, with the proviso that a program of services, forums, education classes, and social service would be carried on in a newly established division "downtown" among the tenements of the Lower East Side. Ultimately, he anticipated, the Temple was to become a free synagogue, that is, having no rented pews. As the rabbi, he would attend meetings of the trus-tees and eventually be granted membership on the Board.

So far the committee were unperturbed by his clearly defined, quite specific requests. A rather positive, determined young man, they thought; but they liked his forcefulness.

During Wise's remarks, his eyes moved searchingly from face to face as he tried to gauge the reaction of these men observing him so quizzically. Would they grant him the freedoms he desired? Would they allow him to create a really free and inde-pendent synagogue? He felt this was a decisive moment of his life; yet his voice was calm as he proceeded.

He would like to institute a Sunday series of lectures and invite university presidents: Charles William Eliot of Harvard, Arthur Twining Hadley of Yale, Nicholas Murray Butler of Columbia, and Jacob Shurman of Cornell; bring in leaders from the fields of law, medicine, journalism, teaching, politics, letters, and commerce to discuss the ethics of their callings; present authorities on comparative religions: Charles Cuthbert Hall of Union Theological Seminary, Kaufmann Kohler of the Hebrew Union College in Cincinnati, and Solomon Schechter of the Jewish Theological Seminary in New York. Let each give his interpretation of religion and religions.

Nor did the committee members hesitate here. The idea was new but not radical or dangerous. Wise seemed to them an energetic young man with original ideas and the executive ability to put them into operation. True, he was demanding more powers than those usually accorded a rabbi of Emanu-El; but, on the whole, they felt some complacency in their own liberal attitude. There was no objection to this suggested program.

Then Wise put them to the test. He was about to demand of these shrewd, practical men a liberty of speech and action such as they had not conceived.

"If I accept," he continued steadily, "I must have an absolutely independent pulpit, not dominated or limited by the views or opinions of the congregation."

Marshall was instantly alert. "The pulpit of Emanu-El has always been and is now subject to the control of the Board of Trustees!"

At that moment Wise looked up and saw Louise standing in the shadowed hallway beyond the parlor door; she was shaking her head as though to say, "This you cannot do!"

"If that be true," Wise answered quietly, "there is nothing more to say."

He put the tiny notes in his pocket, buttoned his coat, and started to rise.

"Wait," said Mr. Moses. "Just what do you mean by a free pulpit?"

Wise faced them resolutely and, as he later recalled the crucial moment, said, "This is what I mean. In Oregon I have been among the leaders of a civic reform movement in my community. I would want to do the same in New York no matter whom it affected. Mr. Moses, if it be true, as I have heard it rumored, that your nephew, Mr. Herman, is to be a Tammany Hall candidate for a Supreme Court judgeship, I would oppose his candidacy in and out of my pulpit.

"Mr. Guggenheim, as a member of the Child Labor Commission of the State of Oregon, I must say to you that, if it ever came to be known that children were being employed in your mines, I would cry out against such wrongs.

"Mr. Marshall, the press states that you and your firm are to be counsel for Mr. Hyde at the Equitable Life Assurance Society. That may or may not be true; but, knowing that Charles Evans Hughes' investigation of the insurance companies in New York has been a very great service, I would speak in praise of his report and in condemnation of the crimes committed by the insurance people."

Wise faced their first quick reactions of consternation, resentment, even amusement: "This is my conception of a free pulpit, gentlemen. You will wish to discuss it."

He walked from the room.

Feelings ran too high for the committee to make a decision, and the matter now came to a standstill. Seligman and Daniel Guggenheim took Wise for a long walk along Fifth Avenue and urged him to reconsider; they assured him he need not take Marshall's statement about the trustees too seriously.

Jacob H. Schiff joined the group and insisted: "Take it, rabbi, take it. Of course they'll want to restrict your sermons, but you take the job anyhow. After you're elected, you can tell them to go to hell—and I'll back you up."

Wise would not, however, alter his stand and later that week returned to Portland. Soon he received a letter from Louis Marshall, reaffirming the board's position about the "freedom" of Emanu-El's pulpit.

This Wise considered a challenge. On January 5, 1906, he wrote his famous "Open Letter" and addressed it to the Trustees of Temple Emanu-El. He used it as the basis for his sermon the following Friday evening at Beth Israel and then released it to the press, long before it reached the addressees in New York City. He stated that it had become his duty to send it. "The steadily waning influence of the church and synagogue is due in no small part, I hold, to the wide-spread belief that the pulpit is not free."

He then repeated, "If I am to accept the call to the pulpit of Temple Emanu-El, I do so with the understanding that I am to be free and my pulpit is not to be muzzled."

He defined his conception of the function of the preacher: "The chief office of the minister, I take it, is not to represent the views of the congregation but to proclaim the truth as he sees it. How can he serve a congregation as a teacher save as he quickens the minds of his hearers by the vitality and independence of his utterances? How can a man be vital and independent and helpful, if he be tethered and muzzled? A free pulpit, worthily filled, must command respect and influence; a pulpit that is not free, howsoever filled, is sure to be without potency and honesty. A free pulpit may sometimes stumble into error. A pulpit that is not free cannot powerfully plead for truth and righteousness."

There was understandable irritation on the part of Emanu-El's trustees because Wise was so precipitate in using the "Open Letter" as a sermon in his own pulpit while they had read it for the first time in the New York *Times*.

Louise's letters to Jennie, during the winter and spring of 1906, reflected the bitterness of the dispute and her own conviction that Stephen could do no wrong. She defended her husband whose motives had been impugned: "I am certain of Stephen's future. It will be the greater for his present aloofness. To have Stephen known, as I have known him—and know him— is all I ask."

Less than a week after the "Open Letter" to Louis Marshall, Wise submitted to the trustees of Portland's Temple Beth Israel his resignation as rabbi, effective at the end of June. If they desired, he would remain until the High Holy Days that autumn. The decision was final, and he planned to return to the East.

Wise was determined to settle again in New York. He considered the city a pivotal area of the nation's social and political liberalism and the center of America's cultural life. It was also the core of Jewish life, religiously and ethnically, and the focal point of Zionism in American Jewry. Moreover, he longed to see again his friends in the Liberal Ministers' Club; he was sure they would understand his plans for a free synagogue. Only a handful of rabbis across the land had written to him in these recent weeks of the Temple Emanu-El fracas, but he was not afraid to stand alone.

Many months before, he had told Mr. Wolfe, Hirsch's successor as president of Beth Israel, of his plan "to start a new and free and living synagogue movement in New York if I am not called to Emanu-El." In a letter to Leo Waterman, he had foreseen his subsequent declination of Emanu-El: "Even if I am called, I will very probably decide not to become assistant keeper of the morgue; but I plan to end my work in Portland within the year."

Mr. Wolfe had been shocked by Wise's resignation and begged Wise to reconsider. He tried to dissuade him. The Temple could not do without him: "The congregation will do everything you ask for if only you stay—and far more too. We shall raise your salary, and although you say you will not accept more pay, the Board will overrule you."

When Wolfe met Louise one day, he pleaded, "Dr. Wise does not realize what he is giving up. He is not our rabbi. He is the leader of the whole Northwest. Tell us some way to keep him. There is nothing we will not do."

Why not a petition signed by every prominent man and woman in Oregon? Wise, when he heard of it, rejected the proposal. It would make the leave-taking more difficult.

Letters, many from Christians, asking him to remain, came to Wise from all sections of the state. Portland's leading lawyer, Ralph Wood, told the closing session of the Beth Israel Forum: "Most men's places can be filled in this world, but not Stephen Wise's. He has brought new ideals to Oregon, but the void he will leave can never be filled."

In his final sermons Wise unfolded plans for the project he would begin three thousand miles away: "The founding of the Free Synagogue, to which from this hour the life of your rabbi is to be dedicated, will be the abiding proof of such loyalty to the synagogue as will not lightly suffer it to lose the high place singled out for it by the compelling destiny of the God-choosing people of Israel. The free synagogue will justify its name, for it will be free to all, hospitable to the poor and rich, inclusive alike of the non-Jew and the Jew."

One additional thing he wanted to make clear: He would not forsake Judaism. The Free Synagogue would not be "a way out

of Judaism but a way unto and forward with Judaism." Wise
wanted to give his people leadership, but they also needed
prophetic teachings: "The Lord hath shown thee, O man, what
is good. For what doth the Lord require of thee, but to do
justly, love mercy, and walk humbly before thy God?"

In Micah's single sentence lay the source of Wise's spiritual
drive. To him, a theist, God was no archaic concept. On the
Rock of Israel, the God of Abraham, Isaac, and Jacob, would he
build this new temple.

Louise was not sure she knew what Stephen meant when he
spoke about the Jewishness that made his people so precious to
him or when he referred to prophetic values in Judaism; but he
must be right, she insisted to Jennie in her letters.

Their immediate moves were uncertain: "Stephen has yet
hardly made very definite plans—but thinks at first of merely
engaging a hall and speaking on Sunday mornings in order to
explain his views and become known in New York."

Definite plans could be formulated later. At this moment he
defined objectives. Wise knew what he wanted: the chance to
warn Liberal Judaism it was in danger of becoming "an unvital
sect of the Jewish faith, at the periphery of Jewish life rather
than at its inmost core . . . in need of a rebirth of that vision
of God without which Israel cannot and ought not to be, a revival
of deepest, solemnest emphasis on that sovereignty of righteousness in the universe, which implies the reaffirmation of Israel's
prophetic insistence upon social justice and social righteousness
here and now."

There was no need to stay in Portland and fight that battle,
he told the people of Beth Israel: "I leave you because you do
not need me. The battle for freedom has been won, won without
having been fought."

And yet, had it been won? Just before his departure for the
East, the Board of Trustees amended the constitution of Temple
Beth Israel. From now on the rabbi would cease to be a member
of the Board. Wise was astounded and protested earnestly, almost
bitterly.

"But, rabbi," the trustees argued, "don't you realize that this
motion is a compliment to you?"

Wise countered: "Gentlemen, I see I have wasted six years

in Portland. You are undoing all I have tried to create, everything I've struggled to inculcate in you, my congregants. I cannot in conscience ask any man to be my successor unless this resolution is rescinded. I must insist that my negative vote be recorded in the minutes of this meeting."

When the resolution was carried with but one dissent, his, he said, "I will not be in Portland on the day of the Annual Meeting at which this resolution must be carried by a two-thirds vote; or if I am, I will fight it body and soul."

Then to Louise on that sad September night, he wrote the words, "My year of work begins with this slap in the face—how it almost robs me of all zest and heart. The thing is trifling, but the spirit, alas, universal—the disdain and contempt of the congregation's hired man. I hate it. It almost drives me out of the ministry."

The mood passed; and now a melancholy moment of a different sort came as he prepared to say good-by. The congregation thronged the Temple every Friday night in these final weeks, and they still importuned him to stay. This was a lifetime job. He could have a staff of assistants, another secretary, a higher salary, longer vacations, a new home, and whatever else he wanted.

His heart was heavy that Friday night of the farewell sermon: "I have never done anything, and can never again do anything, which costs me more than to speak the word of parting tonight. Had I consulted pleasure and profit instead of responsibility and obligation, had I assessed personal advantage higher than public duty, I would not be leaving you tonight, for I have had everything here to make my ministry happy and prized. It is hard to give up my ministry among you, for I am only a man; and I love Beth Israel and Portland and Oregon."

He could forsake the Portland congregation, as well as his leadership and prestige in the Northwest, only because he knew his destiny lay in New York City: "There Jewry is the largest in America, in the world. To it belongs the hegemony of Israel the world over. If in New York the battle for freedom of the pulpit, for the freedom and the moral supremacy of the Synagogue can be won, such a victory may mightily influence for good the destinies of American Israel."

II. John Haynes Holmes:
Puritan in the Blood

(1879–1906)

Puritanism springs from the very core of the personal conscience—the sense of duty, the sense of responsibility, the sense of guilt, and the repentant longing for forgiveness.

—RALPH BARTON PERRY
(Puritanism and Democracy)

5. Dreading to Leave an Illiterate Ministry

After God Had Carried Us Safe to New
    England
And Wee Had Builded Our Houses
Provided Necessaries for Our Liveli Hood
Reard Convenient Places for Gods Worship
And Setled the Civill Government
One of the Next Things We Longed for
And Looked After Was to Advance Learning
And Perpetuate It to Posterity
Dreading to Leave an Illiterate Ministry
To the Churches When Our Present Ministers
Shall Lie in the Dust
      —SEVENTEENTH-CENTURY INSCRIPTION
      OVER JOHNSON GATE, HARVARD YARD

NEW ENGLAND AND THE PURITAN TRADITION, not New York and its amalgam of races and cultures, were the formative factors in the younger years of John Haynes Holmes.

The Holmes family came from England to Plymouth in 1620, settling in Duxbury and remaining in that area through the seventeenth, eighteenth, and nineteenth centuries. His mother's ancestral clan, the Haynes family, immigrated to Boston in 1635 and lived in the city and adjacent towns.

Although their immediate families were rooted in the Boston area, Marcus Morton Holmes and Alice Haynes moved to Philadelphia soon after their marriage early in 1879. There, on

November 29, their first child was born and named for his grand-father, John Haynes.

Morton found the new job in Philadelphia unsatisfactory. In fact he was dissatisfied with every job he tried; and, in 1884, he took his wife and the children, four-and-a-half-year-old John and the year-old Marion, back to New England to try another line of work, that of a wholesale dealer in furniture. They lived for a time in Everett, and then permanently in Malden, within easy traveling distance of Boston for concerts, plays, and lectures on the occasions when their small household budget allowed, or for the Holmes and Haynes families' celebrations of holidays.

John, Marion, and the newest child, Hector McIntosh Holmes, grew up in a house distinguished by inadequate heating and plumbing, yet remembered for ample space and friendly neighbors. John did not begin public school until he was seven; his mother at first thought her boy too bright to need the earliest years of schooling, but the delayed start may have been caused by his father's meager income which left little for children's needs. For years, Alice Holmes despaired of her husband's uncertain job prospects and saved money by making suits for her boys. After school John went the rounds of his newspaper route; even before his teens, he began a personal library of choice books with the profits.

At fifteen, he entered Malden High School, where his achievements quickly convinced the teachers he should go on to college. Unfortunately he was headed in the wrong direction, for he had chosen the commercial course in the expectation of working in the music publishing firm, the Oliver Ditson Company, owned and managed by his grandfather, John Cummings Haynes.

The principal and a teacher soon corrected that error. One gentle spring evening they visited the family. In the mellow light of a parlor specially dusted and freshly aired for the occasion, they persuaded the surprised parents, and John, that he should give up commercial studies and begin college preparatory work, to enter Harvard after graduation. All agreed, and the switch was made. John took extra studies, widened the range of already extensive reading in the classics and history, declaimed in the Literary Society, and wrote copiously for *The Oracle*, a student publication. Three years later, he was graduated from Malden High School with highest honors and passed his entrance examinations for Harvard.

Finding sufficient money for college posed a stiff problem; but financial aid came from Grandfather Haynes, who paid the tuition fees, and his parents, who provided the little they could. Relief came a year later, when Holmes won the first of a series of scholarships for board and room for the next five years.

His years at Harvard were divided evenly between the College and the Divinity School. Financial necessity forced him to compress the usual four years of undergraduate work and three years of graduate study into a six-year period. By his junior year he had won his Phi Beta Kappa key and was ready to graduate from the college, but preferred to postpone receiving his *summa cum laude* Bachelor of Arts degree until 1902, so that he might graduate with his classmates.

From his sophomore year Holmes had known that graduation meant entry into the ministry. He was in great measure motivated by the example of Theodore Parker, the work of Minot Savage, and the presence in Boston of great preachers.

Theodore Parker's relationship to Grandfather Haynes was a major influence. As a young man John Cummings Haynes had been one of the Boston men who resolved in 1845: "That the Reverend Theodore Parker shall have a chance to be heard in Boston." As Treasurer of the Twenty-Eighth Congregational Society, Haynes helped to give Parker his platform, first in the gloomy Melodeon, and then in the commodious Music Hall. Forty years later, Parker, though dead, lived in his memory and his grandson's mind.

Minot Savage was then minister of the Church of the Unity; and when John stayed weekends at the affluent Haynes home, his grandfather took him to hear Savage. Now there was a man to admire—author of nineteen books, hymn writer, poet, leader in American Unitarianism, and magnetic orator.

At the church on Hollis Street, in a sanctuary filled long before the service, they would watch Savage emerge dramatically from behind the pulpit and stand on the edge of the platform to preach for an hour with not a scrap of paper before him.

Savage might present basic tenets of Unitarianism or discuss what he thought were errors in Roman Catholicism, expand on the marvels of modern science or assert the rights of the laboring classes.

What an array of facts and sweep of oratory! The older John never knew it, but young John, listening so intently to Minot Savage, wished he might someday speak as swiftly and surely, explain new ideas with such confidence and similarly sway an audience.

After the service, the two would go to the literature table in the narthex and invest a quarter or half-dollar in a pocketful of nickel publications, Savage's latest sermons printed each week from stenographic notes of previous Sundays and sold by the thousands across America. On the walk home, Grandfather would compare Savage with Parker, itemizing contrasts and parallels between the two men, judging them the greatest preachers he had ever heard.

They listened to princes of the pulpit in that hub of New England's universe: Phillips Brooks and George Gordon in their cathedrals of Trinity Church and Old South, opposite each other on Copley Square; Edward Everett Hale and Charles Gordon Ames in their citadels of the Unitarian faith, South Congregational and the Church of the Disciples. At other times, old John, Morton, and young John might hear a visitor in Boston, perhaps Muzumdar, from India, meditating on the Church Universal, or Robert Ingersoll, the rationalist, challenging orthodox Christianity. The three would talk of John's great-grandfather, a Universalist preacher long remembered for his religious liberalism and defense of the dispossessed. They would attend vesper services and hymn-sings in the Unitarian and Universalist churches of their neighborhood.

At Harvard, John responded to President Charles W. Eliot's high character, found inspiration in courses by George Pierce Baker in rhetoric, Albert Bushnell Hart in history, and George Herbert Palmer in philosophy. Oddly enough, he never studied with Kittredge or Copeland in English literature, William James or George Santayana in philosophy, but always attended their extracurricular lectures. In the Divinity School, he took courses under Francis Greenwood Peabody, George Foot Moore, and Kirsopp Lake, leading professors of their time in social ethics and preaching and in the origins of Judaism and Christianity.

Holmes would have nothing to do with collegiate athletics; they were a bore. He preferred to join the Debating Society or act in the Elizabethan revivals of his fraternity, Delta Upsilon. More enjoyable for him than sports was the several miles' walk from Cambridge down to the Public Library in Copley Square where he could browse in the Theodore Parker collection of 14,000 books. Like Parker a half century earlier, the twenty-year-old Holmes would read a page at a glance, a serious work in several hours, a weighty tome in a day; and, poring over volumes marked in the margins with Parker's Greek and Latin comments, he agreed with Thomas Wentworth Higginson's report to his fellow trustees of the Boston Public Library that the Parker Library "was the work of a man possessing a more omnivorous passion for books than almost any of his contemporaries in this country." Holmes also had a hunger for books of his own. He hoped some day to allay it.

In the Divinity School he read the great books of the day: Adolf Harnack's *What Is Christianity?*, Auguste Sabatier's *Religions of Authority and the Religion of the Spirit*, Francis Greenwood Peabody's *Jesus Christ and the Social Question*, and so many others he could not keep count. He discussed these books with his friends on long afternoon walks in the tree-lined streets of Cambridge, along the winding banks of the Charles River, or far into the night in their rooms in Divinity Hall. He now knew at first hand the writings of the Transcendentalists with whom Theodore Parker had worked: Ralph Waldo Emerson and Henry David Thoreau, Margaret Fuller, George Ripley, and Orestes Brownson, all of them spiritual heirs of Goethe and Kant, ardent believers in "The Over-Soul," and proponents of a more equitable society.

Holmes' affection for Harvard was unbounded. Proud of his Bachelor of Arts and Bachelor of Sacred Theology degrees, he loved the College and its Divinity School for their rich traditions, eminent professors, and magnificent libraries, but most of all for his cherished friendships of those six years.

6. Danvers and Dorchester

In these days came John . . . preaching.
—MATTHEW, 3:1

HOLMES PREPARED for the ministry not only in classrooms and libraries but also in places that gave him practical experience. No sooner had he chosen his vocation in 1899 than he found a teaching post in the Sunday School of the Unitarian Church in Cambridge where Samuel McChord Crothers, an essayist and lecturer, was minister. A year later Crothers asked young Holmes, then twenty-one, to serve as the Sunday School superintendent. In the cramped parish house of the Cambridge church, Holmes selected teaching materials, recruited teachers, and conducted worship services for the church school at noontime. During the eleven o'clock service in the sanctuary he listened appreciatively to the lyrical prose of Crothers, who was to Holmes the exemplar of a ministry marked by moral fervor and intellectual courage.

By 1902, when Holmes completed his first year in the Divinity School, he had a scholarship to be earned by work as a student preacher; the Dean's office chose the Unitarian Church of Danvers as his student parish. His first Sunday as an apprentice preacher, June 5, 1902, remained a vivid memory because of the cordial reception given his sermon and a matching warmth by the weather. The theologue wore the typical preacher's regalia of tall hat, cane, and kid gloves, Prince Albert coat and pin-striped trousers, stiff shirt and starched collar, buttoned patent-leather shoes and silk socks. As a result he was soaked with perspiration. His sermon, "The Realities of Life," was a success; and the congregation asked him to be their regular minister. For

68

the next two years he shared his latest learning from Divinity Hall with his fewer than fifty parishioners on their crude benches in the tiny hall where a New England admonition, "Redeem the Time," encircled the large clock on the rear wall.

On occasion Holmes had a visitor from Brooklyn, Madeleine Hosmer Baker. They had met during his first year at Harvard and became engaged the next summer, 1899. The unusually attractive Madeleine went with him and the Haynes relations each year for a two-month vacation in Maine. The family's perpetual benefactor, Grandfather Haynes, brought the entire clan to a small hotel he rented at Seal Harbor on Mount Desert Island.

The courtship flourished during Christmas and Easter vacations and letters flowed constantly between Brooklyn and Cambridge. With a restraint as commendable as it seems incredible, John and Madeleine planned in 1899 to be married only after graduation, ordination, and installation, which would be 1905, or more likely 1906.

The days did not drag for Holmes as he filled every minute with books, music, plays, and lectures. In undergraduate days— as during the next half century—he read everything he could lay his hands on; and he retained the knowledge, even then preferring history and biography to theology and Biblical lore. A musician of talent and taste, he attended many concerts and operas in Cambridge and Boston. An actor at heart, he saw as many plays as he could afford, admiring most of all Sir Henry Irving.

Already a preacher of marked ability, he looked forward each month to Divinity Hall visits by the leading clergymen of the day, a custom inaugurated by Ralph Waldo Emerson in the 1830s. These informal meetings with outstanding ministers enabled the students to cross-examine them on their methods.

Of all the monthly guests, Edward Everett Hale, the editor and writer, was the most popular. This leading liberal religionist of the day spoke to the needs of these young men seeking direction in a puzzling world. In some strange way Hale seemed to have answers for all their problems and had no pretense about himself. Like a giant visitant from another world, he towered above them and looked at them with burning eyes in a shaggy head, resembling a classic bust of Homer, and, with a mighty voice, roared as though from Sinai.

The most exciting visitor, however, was the dashing Minot Savage of the Church of the Messiah in New York City. One evening Holmes asked Savage to share with them the secret of his remarkable extempore preaching, but the students received no answer. Holmes would not give up and questioned him again. Savage was considered a master of this technique and Holmes wanted to know: "What is the formula?"

How could Savage tell them that in reality his gift was of the spirit? At last Savage relented and swiftly said: "I like to see a man who shoots without a rest," that is, without any visible or tangible aids, hence, no manuscript, no outline, not even little reminder notes.

In 1904, two of the most important events in Holmes' life occurred: the ordination-installation service in a full-fledged pastorate, and marriage to Madeleine.

The first led inevitably to the second. The patient pair, after a five-year engagement, now hoped to be married the following Christmas if, by good fortune, the Divinity School graduate found a vacant pulpit in the autumn or early winter of 1904. Suddenly, in the opening weeks of 1904, Holmes was asked to become minister of an awesomely titled institution, The Third Religious Society and Third Congregational Church of Dorchester. In this small, one-hundred-year-old parish on the outskirts of Boston, Holmes preached to an established congregation, proud of their role in the struggle for religious liberalism and conscious of a historic place in the rise of Unitarianism.

On a blustery Wednesday evening in early March, 1904, he was impressively ordained and installed in a single service of double purpose. The Dorchester congregation heard Samuel McChord Crothers preach the sermon, William Wallace Fenn of the Divinity School present the charge to the minister, and Rush Shippen of Washington, D. C., give the right hand of fellowship. They sang hymns written by Theodore Parker and Minot Savage.

The family whispered among themselves that this was the first time Grandfather Haynes had entered a church in eight years,

for Minot Savage's resignation from the Church of the Unity in
Boston in 1896 and departure for New York's Church of the
Messiah had left the old man embittered and disillusioned. John
Cummings Haynes was silent in wonder that the stripling who
bore his name should now be an ordained minister and in charge
of a church. By the grandfather's side sat Morton and Alice
Holmes, marveling at what God and they had wrought with their
first-born.

The second signal event of the year, Holmes' marriage, took
place three and a half months later. In his characteristic way of
crowding days with important commitments, Holmes preached
in Dorchester in the morning of Sunday, June 26, and prepared
for the trip to Brooklyn. In midafternoon of a steaming day, he
met his best man, Roger Lee, and the four ushers at South Station. They all boarded the grimy train for the six-hour run to the
old Grand Central Station in New York and transferred, dishev-
eled and sooty, to the subway for Brooklyn. By five o'clock on
Monday afternoon, the party had revived and was resplendent in
wedding attire in the stately Church of the Saviour (Unitarian)
in Brooklyn Heights. John and Madeleine were married by her
pastor, John P. Forbes. After the wedding reception in the Baker
home on Garden Place, the couple escaped to a resort known as
The Woodlands near Roxbury, New York, and, after a two-week
honeymoon, returned to Dorchester to settle in a room rented to
them by a parishioner. When this proved unsatisfactory, they
rented a house of their own.

The years 1904, 1905, and 1906 sped swiftly by as Holmes
studied, wrote, and preached, all the while strengthening his
Dorchester Church. For long hours each morning in his secluded
study he continued the intense reading program begun in his
Harvard years and found ammunition for sermons he fired, like
Savage's, in rapid volleys without a "rest." Like Savage, he was
a skilled marksman and hit his target unerringly.

These sermons revealed that basically Holmes was an indi-
vidualist. Twenty years after Josiah Strong had written *Our
Country*, Holmes could read and agree with the well-known
Congregational minister that Americans must stretch their "hands

into the future with power to mold the destiny of unborn millions" and could echo Tennyson's hope that the world moved inexorably toward the day when

> The war-drums throb no longer, and the battle-
> flags are furl'd
> In the Parliament of man, the Federation
> of the world.

He accepted Strong's belief that "Americans may reasonably look forward to a time when they will have produced a civilization grander than any the world has known." Strong's imperialism could be forgiven if one believed, as did Holmes, that the Anglo-Saxon world represented and promulgated the two great ideas of civil liberty and a more spiritual Christianity.

Holmes had already read all of Herbert Spencer, whom he considered "the greatest thinker since Aristotle"; and now, with enjoyment, he re-read many of the long volumes. He delved deep into the writings of John Fiske whose Christianity, rid of doctrines and dogmas, would be, he hoped, the true religion of the new day.

With Spencer and Fiske as texts, glossed by Darwin and Huxley, Holmes preached the theory of evolution. Such preaching was not a radical departure from the conventional, for evolution had been long accepted by liberal religionists and had never been a controversial issue among Unitarians; it was nevertheless new to many in his growing audiences of 1904 to 1906.

He urged his people to read *Looking Backward*, the two-decades-old novel that was still popular, and to envisage with Edward Bellamy an ordered society of household appliances, consumer goods, and creature comforts for all. He was enthusiastic about Henry George's *Progress and Poverty* and agreed with him that the ills of the social order were caused by a monopoly of land; the "single tax" was a part of his social thought, more because of Henry George's noble spirit, however, than because of the soundness of the suggested solution.

As he roamed far in history and economics, sought facts and figures to strengthen his indictments of social inequities, and shared hopes for a planned society, he became more and more a disciple of the "Social Gospel." Religion must be "applied," the churches concerned with social change, and ministers prepared to pass moral judgments on the evils of racial discrimination, economic greed, and international war.

John Haynes Holmes may have been influenced in part by Josiah Strong and his Congregational colleagues Lyman Abbott and Washington Gladden; but the prime sources of his inspiration were the basic books of liberal Christianity and its social outlook written by Francis Greenwood Peabody. Peabody, his favorite teacher in the Divinity School, was a key figure in the Unitarian movement of that day; and to the Peabody influence he was indebted when he gave a commemorative sermon for the one hundredth anniversary of the birth of Abolitionist William Lloyd Garrison on December 10, 1905, and, ten months later, preached on "The Black Man of the South," a sermon suggested by the massacre of Negroes by white men in Atlanta.

As a Unitarian, Holmes gave lectures to his congregation at least once a year on what were then the denomination's central tenets: the fatherhood of God, the leadership of Jesus, salvation by character, and progress onward and upward.

Each spring he suggested that his parishioners attend the Annual May Meetings of the American Unitarian Association in Boston and hear addresses by Savage, Peabody, Samuel A. Eliot, President of the A. U. A., and his father, Charles W. Eliot, president of Harvard.

His Dorchester parish of that period boasted of two members, Elizabeth and Ellen Channing, who were direct descendants of William Ellery Channing. It was the Elizabeth Channing Branch of the Women's Alliance that engaged a local printer in 1906 to publish Holmes' first book, *The Old and the New*, a series of sermons on Unitarian views of the Bible, the Church, heaven, hell, salvation, prayer, and revelation.

In the eyes of the orthodox and the Calvinists, the Methodists and Baptists of the community, these sermons were heretical; but to Holmes and his quite considerable following they were Christian, for they centered on the historical Jesus. The other Christians in town, devout believers in the Divine Christ, as the Son of God, looked upon the Unitarians as a breed apart.

Holmes prepared his sermons with such care that even on rainy Sundays his congregation remained large. To his parish Holmes gave himself with enthusiasm. Faithfully he made his rounds of pastoral calls; each year he checked the list and made sure he had reached the entire congregation.

It was a glorious, happy time. He loved his work and adored his family. His first child, Roger, arrived most inconveniently on a Saturday afternoon, the day Holmes reserved as sacrosanct for final preparation of his Sunday sermon. For once this day was disrupted.

Not only intent on giving faultless sermons and worship services to his congregation, John Haynes Holmes also gave meticulous attention to every parish matter. His perfectionism caused such tensions within himself that he nearly collapsed in the spring of 1906. To regain strength he withdrew to a near-by farm and remained in seclusion for several weeks.

The presence of the infant Roger in the household may have helped wear him down; but it is possible he was even more disturbed by conditions that led him to insert this item in the "Weekly Calendar" of April 22, 1906:

> PERSONAL NOTICE.—I regret the necessity of making public announcement to this Society, through the Calendar, that I am greatly in need of assistance in my Sunday School work. Several new teachers must be secured at once, if the work of the school is not to suffer injury. I have no hesitation in saying that the greatest need of our Society at present is in the Sunday School, and that this need must be satisfied at once if the school is to maintain efficiency. I shall be glad to talk with any persons who are willing to enter upon this important work, and shall hope for an immediate response to this appeal.

He stumbled along with the Sunday School and never found the help he needed.

Certainly disturbing was the small town's gossip, not that usually relating to a man's private life, for his was impeccable, but rather talk about the religious liberal whose thoughts seemed dangerous to the conservative-minded. His spirits were lifted, however, by exciting news in the fall of 1906. Word came to him that he was being considered for the vacant post as junior minister to Robert Collyer at the Church of the Messiah in New York City. When he received the invitation to preach a trial sermon, he accepted without hesitation and arranged for the first Sunday in November.

As they waited in the anteroom of the New York church for the signal to enter the sanctuary, Robert Collyer watched Holmes pace back and forth and sensed the young man's anxious tension. Walking slowly to his side, the eighty-three-year-old Collyer embraced him and asked, "Are ye nervous, laddie?"

Holmes could scarcely respond. He nodded—"Yes."

Then Collyer placed his enormous hand on Holmes' shoulder and said gently, "Don't ye mind. They be just folks out there, just like your own at home. Ye'll do your best, I know."

After his first few words, Holmes felt the warmth of the audience and did do his best. The congregation responded favorably. After a month of doubt and expectancy, Holmes met with the pulpit committee at the Hotel Touraine in Boston. They extended a call and he agreed to come in February.

When Holmes brought Madeleine and Roger to New York, he carried with him a gift which was part of the Theodore Parker heritage. The day before they left, he had gone into Boston to say good-by to Grandfather Haynes. The old man had taken from the bookshelf his most precious possession, the Bible with Parker's two inscriptions: "The Property of the Religious Society at the Melodeon, February 16, 1845"; and, after the purchase of a successor Bible: "To Theodore Parker from the Society, November 21, 1852." The next entry was a notation of the gift to "Deacon J. C. Haynes by the Society" after Parker's death in 1860. Now young John saw old John write in quavering script: "Presented to John Haynes Holmes, by his grandfather, John C. Haynes, February 1, 1907."

John Haynes Holmes felt the need of the Parker spirit, for the problems at the Church of the Messiah were many: a small, conservative membership; a traditional pew rental and ownership system; eighty-eight years of proud tradition; attendance of less than a hundred each Sunday; and a meager endowment, of which an East Side tenement was a part. Now it was Holmes' turn to face these problems.

In that early February of 1907 Holmes walked about the
neighborhood of his new church. He saw four-story brownstone
residences on 34th Street and looked south on unbroken rows of
red brick houses along Fourth Avenue. Opposite the church
stood the Princeton Club; two blocks to the south, the car barn.
In the back streets lay areas of deterioration, slum sections. The
horses and carriages, hansom cabs, and Fifth Avenue stage-
coaches were the major means of transportation for the growing
population, and worsening traffic made it difficult to get around
the city.

Each Sunday morning John Haynes Holmes, dressed in tall
hat and frock coat, entered the church and greeted well-to-do,
respectable parishioners—the men with their own "shining tiles"
[high, stiff hats] and frock coats, the women with large hats
and long skirts. He felt their friendliness toward him, the untried young minister; but he wondered if he could meet the
demands of this staid, old-time Unitarian church.

III. Wise and Holmes: Tribunes of the People

(1907–1920)

Taught by no priest, but by our beating hearts:
Faith to each other, the fidelity
Of men whose pulse leaps with kindred fire
Who in the flash of eyes, the clasp of hands,
Nay in the silent bodily presence, feel
The mystic stirrings of a common life
That makes the many one.

—GEORGE ELIOT (Poems)

7. Your Young Men Shall See Visions

*Your old men shall dream dreams, and your
young men shall see visions.* —JOEL, 2:28

WITHIN FIVE WEEKS of the first service in the Hudson Theatre,
Stephen Wise began a branch of the Free Synagogue on the
Lower East Side and rented the main auditorium of Clinton
Hall for meetings on Friday and Sunday nights. Hundreds of
younger people, encouraged by Lillian Wald and the staff at her
Settlement House on Henry Street, gave Wise an enthusiastic
response. These young Jews had found Orthodoxy insufficient
and preferred his combination of Reform Judaism and social
liberalism. In the Downtown Branch, as it soon came to be
called, Wise held synagogue services on Friday evenings and
conducted a Social Problems Forum on Sunday evenings. In
both Downtown and Uptown Branches the audiences wholeheartedly approved of Wise's "free Judaism":

> First, freedom of the pulpit; second, abolition of any distinc-
> tion between rich and poor as to pews and membership privi-
> leges; third, a direct, full participation of the synagogue in all
> social services required by the community; and fourth, a com-
> plete identification not only with the Jewish faith, but also with
> the faith and future of Israel as a people.

The Uptown and Downtown branches of the Free Synagogue
were formally organized in mid-April of 1907 when more than
one hundred men and women gathered in the Hotel Savoy.
Among them were such strong backers as financier Henry

79

Morgenthau, publisher Charles Bloch, attorneys Joseph Levine and Max Steuer, and representatives from some of the leading families in New York Jewry: Seligman, Lewisohn, and Straus. Morgenthau, as Acting Chairman, and Bloch, as Acting Secretary, announced a signed membership list of 192 and pledges for a 1907–1908 budget of $9,300. Stephen Wise was unanimously elected Rabbi, but only on the condition he specified that he would receive no salary for the first year.

Emil Hirsch, Rabbi of Temple Sinai in Chicago and Wise's guest of the evening, was so carried away by the enthusiasm of the meeting that he asked "for the privilege of being regarded by all of you as a nonresident assistant rabbi of the Free Synagogue." Hirsch noted that several other Jewish communities in America vouchsafed freedom to their rabbis but not New York. There was therefore all the more need for "an uncompromising free Judaism in this city." The newly organized Free Synagogue would "develop into a splendid organization under the magnificent leadership of Dr. Stephen S. Wise."

Wise was very practical and concrete that night. He outlined their needs: a meeting place more suitable than the Hudson Theatre, ample room for an office staff and a lending library, a religious school for the children and young people. Larger sums of money would be needed in the following years, no matter how straitened his people's circumstances during the economic lag of 1907.

In his Minister's Letter to the congregation in September, Wise wrote that the Executive Committee of Fifteen had rented the unused building of the Church of Eternal Hope (Universalist) on West 81st Street between Columbus and Amsterdam avenues and announced services to usher in the New Year and to observe the Day of Atonement. For the first Sunday service after the High Holy Days Wise invited as the speaker Professor Thomas G. Masaryk, who was to become the spiritual and political father of the Czechoslovak Republic. Masaryk and other guest speakers, like social workers Jane Addams and Jacob Riis, and religionists Edward Everett Hale and Walter Rauschenbusch, helped implement the preamble to the Free Synagogue Constitution: "Its pulpit shall be free to preach on behalf of truth and righteousness in the spirit and after the pattern of the prophets of Israel."

To the annual meeting in the spring of 1908 Wise disclosed that at the end of the first year the membership roll stood in excess of 300. His plans for the future required a 100 per cent increase in budget. The amount was pledged. Henry Morgenthau cried delightedly: "Look at this lusty infant; and after listening to the statistical recital of what has been accomplished, we must all admit that our Minister has accomplished wonders!"

Wise's success soon brought a tart reaction from Samuel Schulman, Rabbi of Temple Beth-El: "The way to start a free synagogue is to cultivate a voice, place a pitcher of ice water on a stand, and marry an heiress."

The report of this comment only made Wise smile. His good humor was untroubled by the remark. Louise was less resilient and not so forgiving. Several days later Louise and Stephen were strolling along Fifth Avenue and met Schulman. Louise was silent; but her husband greeted him cordially. The two men talked a while. As they were about to part, Wise pulled a cigar from his vest pocket and gave it to Schulman. A few minutes later Louise asked, "How could you do that, Stephen, after the way he spoke about us last week?"

"Well," answered Wise cheerfully, "you see, my dear, that was last week."

Schulman, like Louise, was also unforgiving. All during his active career he sniped at Wise. He and many like him were unhappy about the way in which Stephen Wise dramatized issues and secured headlines across the nation.

Rabbis throughout the country began, however, to write Wise to congratulate him. Young students shared their intentions of entering the rabbinate because of his inspiration. Soon he began to be fired with a plan to supplement the Synagogue's program with a training project to teach young rabbis. For the time being he was too busy to develop the idea. He had too many other things to do, not the least of which was to prepare sermons and lectures that underscored the need of organized religion's passing judgment on the issues of the day.

His concerns ranged from the rights of labor to woman

suffrage, from discrimination against Jews to the oppression of the Negroes. These addresses reflected his social and economic liberalism: "Is Charity Bankrupt?" and "Reform and Reformers." The content was at once both scholarly and provocative, and rarely was the audience disappointed.

Finding an hour of respite from his office on West 81st Street, Wise would walk in Central Park. There he would jot down thoughts that came to him as he, a tall, powerfully built man, dressed in frock coat and striped trousers and carrying a large black hat, strolled along the walks. When he returned to his study, he would dictate from these slips of paper and toss the typed notes into a drawer or a file on the subject, and from the full folder, he would later outline his address.

Wise's personality was the indispensable ingredient for the enjoyment and understanding of his sermons and speeches. The man's fire and conviction bolstered the spoken word. Mounting the platform or ascending the pulpit with vigorous gait and standing upright before a vast audience in a crowded hall, he made the atmosphere electric. The tension mounted, as he waited for the rustling to cease; and his tall, solid form dominated the audience.

To his detractors the performance bordered on the demagogic. He seemed too dramatic and relied unduly on forensic powers, his sincerity diminished by studied rhetoric, his charm marred by exaggerated gestures and stilted mannerisms; but under it all, they had to concede, there was an exaltation.

The many intimate references to himself, his wife, his father, his children, and his famous friends were such a part of his speaking that friends accepted and welcomed them; but his opponents deprecated the personal allusions. His followers grew ever more numerous, however, and looked upon him as the reincarnation of Jewish leaders of centuries before: a Joshua, a Bar Kochba, a Judah Maccabeus.

Amid his many activities, Wise still managed to devote time to study. He snatched two to three hours early in the morning, for he needed little sleep and, with ideas buzzing in his brain, arose at five in the morning. He would read and write before the household was awake; and at night would again take up his reading, the heavier the book, the better. The notes he made in those days, in a notebook just large enough to fit in the palm of his hand, included quotations from Sainte-Beuve, Browning's *The Ring and the Book*, William James' *The Will to Believe,* John Morley's *John Stuart Mill*, Stubb's *Life of Charles Kingsley,* Lord Bryce's *Studies in Contemporary Biography*, and Trevelyan's *Life of John Bright.*

In his first two years in New York, Wise did not find it easy to have the time and quiet needed for study and reflection because their home was temporary and living arrangements inadequate. When the Wises arrived from Portland in the early autumn of 1906, the four of them moved into the spacious Waterman home at 46 East 68th Street, which had been left to Louise, her brother, and her sister by their father. Louise's brother and sister, Leo and Jennie Waterman, planned the household so that Louise slept on the second floor, Jim and Justine and their nurse on the third floor, and Stephen on the fourth.

For two years they lived in this fashion. The children often eluded their nurse to invade committee meetings or intrude upon a wedding ceremony. The telephone rang constantly as Wise began the Free Synagogue in two widely separated areas of the city, the Lower East Side and the Upper West Side, and maintained a heavy schedule of public speaking that continued for the next forty years.

Leo and Jennie rejoiced in having Louise and her family home again, but their orderly and conventional way of life was constantly disrupted. Stephen and Louise wanted to create their own home for themselves and the children. They needed and wanted to feel free to make their home one in which there would be a freer spirit and one to which they could bring people of all types. Soon they found a place they liked and Louise used a part of her inheritance to buy a house on West 90th Street where they lived comfortably for the next three decades.

A few months after his own arrival in New York, John Haynes Holmes paid a courtesy call on his new friend Stephen Wise in the brownstone house of the Watermans. As he recalled it, he rang the bell and in an instant heard children dashing down the hall to the door. They opened it with a rush while their nurse tried to restrain them.

The six-year-old boy asked, "Who are you? And what do you want? Did you come to see my Daddy or my Mummy?"

The four-year-old girl said, "Daddy, you silly! He's the only one around here who's important."

The nurse apologized and was about to take the children away when behind her appeared their father who scooped up a child in each arm. He gave the younger to Holmes and said, "May I present Justine Waterman Wise?" As Holmes took Justine in his arms, the little girl planted a moist kiss on his cheek and said, "I'm to call you 'Uncle John,' Daddy says. So there, Uncle John," and kissed him again.

"This is James Waterman Wise," said his father as he held tightly to the small boy who solemnly shook hands with his father's friend.

As the nurse took Jim and Justine with her, the two men went into the living room and were soon joined by Mrs. Wise. In the course of their conversation, Holmes told how, when he and his wife and the baby arrived in New York, they went first to a residential hotel on Madison Avenue, but were now planning to move to Yonkers and rent a house owned by his Grandfather Haynes. The church had no parsonage; and since members had begun to move out to the suburbs, it was no longer necessary to live near the church as had Robert Collyer and Minot Savage, his predecessors. They would need this extra space because they were expecting another child (their daughter Frances, born in 1908). Holmes planned to commute by subway each day; but he had trouble finding a place to study, for he had little quiet at home and no office in the church.

Wise was astonished that no study was available to Holmes in the Church of the Messiah. Holmes explained that the Trustees wanted the church shut during the week and used only on Sunday. He had been compelled to rent a small office in the Johnson Building at 28th and Broadway. He still hoped for a study in the church where people might come to see him.

He described the difficulty he had in getting to know the

members of the church, partly because they were so widely scattered, but mostly because New Yorkers never seemed to be "at home." When he did come to pay a "parish call," they would look at him as though he were an intruder. At that time, and thereafter, he was convinced "of the utter impracticability of work of this kind."

He told Stephen and Louise Wise of some of the other problems which beset him. In the first place, the membership of the church was really unknown, for the membership book had been lost. He and his church officials had been trying to assemble a list of authentic members and had come up with 107 names. There were 37 pew holders and the remainder rented pews on an annual basis. The majority of these people, Holmes wryly noted, "were mostly Unitarians and some were Collyerites." When Minot Savage abruptly retired in 1905, a large contingent on the periphery of the church drifted away. Of those who remained, he said, far too many believed only in the typical Unitarian credo of "The Fatherhood of God, the Brotherhood of Man, and the Neighborhood of Boston."

He described the education program of the church as lacking in both teachers and pupils. A new education committee had met to make "a thorough examination of the situation," but the results were meager and the future of the Sunday School uncertain.

He listed for them the several new projects he had evolved to arouse interest in the church: a confirmation class for new members, both young and old; a study class in comparative religions; a discussion group on the basic teachings of Christianity; committees to deal with child labor, temperance, peace, and slum removal; a Robert Collyer Men's Club; a lending library; a Messiah Dramatic Club; and a Social Service League. It had been a disheartening, discouraging process. If the audience had not grown larger each Sunday at the eleven o'clock services, he would have considered his efforts futile.

As Holmes said good-by to the Wises, he and Stephen planned to exchange pulpits in the near future so that each might preach to the other's congregation.

Holmes, like Wise, had the power of speech. His preaching

encompassed the entire world. There were universal qualities in his thought and catholicity in his concern. As a New Englander, an heir of the Transcendentalists, and a child of the Enlightenment, he was aware that science was in the ascendant and revolution more than mere theory.

The congregation of the Church of the Messiah was accustomed to the Biblical cadences and Elizabethan phrasing of Robert Collyer who, in semiretirement, still preached every eight or ten weeks. In Holmes' cascading oratory there was, however, a change of pace. The young man was persuasive and personable. His sermons were direct and simple, his illustrations contemporary and familiar. Poetic quotations came from Victorian poets like Browning and Tennyson, and such Edwardians as William Watson and Wilfrid Wilson Gibson. His prose was swiftly moving and it was a rare occasion when he resorted to a manuscript. The only items on paper he carried into the pulpit were quotations he wanted to have exact; otherwise he spoke without notes.

Holmes believed in the cyclonic approach. The moment he entered the pulpit or stepped on the platform he began to speak rapidly and powerfully so that no one would be lulled into a daydream. A correspondent to *The Unitarian* reported that, when, in January, 1908, Holmes addressed the New York Unitarian Club, he spoke "with glowing and eager eloquence, brushed aside all consideration of the incidental issues of manner and ecclesiastical habit, and set the ideal of Emerson and the spirit of Theodore Parker as the pattern for today."

His theme: "The modern preacher must speak the message of his own soul confidently and unreservedly; must preach for righteousness without fear and without equivocation, meeting today's issues of social and civic wrong with direct application of the great principles of Christianity as Parker met the issues of human slavery and civic wrong of his time."

His first target was the church. Nineteen centuries had been given the church to establish its efficacy and worth, and it had failed miserably. He inveighed against a church which dealt with "moonshine, not with realities." He accused the Christian church of resembling an "old man in his second childhood . . .

chattering and mumbling the silly and meaningless reminiscences of a long past youth . . . utterly oblivious of the actual facts of the present time." He was convinced that "the Christian church is holding no vital place and doing no vital work in modern life, but, like one of the old stone forts of the Revolutionary era in Boston Harbour, is only a relic of a bygone age." All this he hoped to change.

Historical sermons on anniversaries of the Church of the Messiah and the American Unitarian Association were only a means to an end: to make the church and churches more relevant to the times.

His sermons on the Bible concerned a book he loved dearly and knew well; but he did not hesitate to point out the many absurdities and inconsistencies in its pages. He spoke of the Bible as a human document, created by men and not by the hand of God, a charter for human freedom and eternal evolution toward higher standards in society and self.

Holmes wanted to bring to his congregation as much new knowledge as possible. This was the era of new thoughts, the age when men believed they could change their world and, in changing it, find themselves transformed as well. Give light and the people would indeed find their own way. Make sure they read books, more and more books. Then men would see that the human race had suffered long enough; and at length would come the glorious day, "as prophets long foretold" and hymn writers now could sing, the long-awaited time when men would be reprieved from oppression and injustice. If human slavery could be wiped out, widespread illiteracy eradicated, and disease lessened, why then could not war and poverty be erased from the earth?

If scarcity had been the hallmark of the past, was there not now before them a future of potential abundance enabling men and women to bring their children into a world of plenty? The Golden Age of which seers and saints, poets and prophets had dreamt was, if not on the horizon, certainly not far beyond the horizon. Why could not the Kingdom of God be achieved on this earth with more rational planning, more will power, and more human striving? He believed that sermons on Christianity and socialism, on the centenary of Darwin's birth and his theory of evolution, on the centennial anniversaries either of the birth or death of such great men as Wendell Phillips, Leo Tolstoy, and Theodore Parker, would awaken people to the new learning and make them feel the need of liberation from the past.

He did not hesitate to equate the goals of the church with those of movements working for a better world. He construed the objectives of organized religion and of secular idealism as being the same and therefore asked that the church and society become one. Thus he tended to avoid the thorny problems of separation of church and state, basic issues of the Protestant Reformation, and paid scant attention to the finiteness of man.

His preaching rarely left anyone unmoved. He had a richness of allusion, used striking similes and metaphors, and invoked appropriate historical parallels. When aroused by some injustice, as he was most of the time, he seemed to many more powerful than William Jennings Bryan or Robert Ingersoll. To his friends and enemies alike, he was clearly the best extemporaneous speaker they had ever heard. Swift, incisive, and compelling, he attracted the audience's attention at the very outset and never lost it.

Another side to his preaching was pitched to a lower key when he engaged in literary exposition or expressed the mystical side of his faith. Prayer was to him a reality, "the little lever, by one turn of which the spiritual life of God may be diverted from the storage batteries of man's spirit into every remotest particle of human life."

The deeply mystical spirit and reverent note were always apparent; but in his effort to be timely, Holmes was sometimes too much so and therefore not timeless enough. The Eternal did not shine through. To those who wanted a minister to come to grips with the personal issues of life only, he seemed to give disproportionate emphasis to social problems. To a much larger group of people, however, he appeared to be prophetic, one who spoke "on behalf of God."

Such constant speaking and writing were not done without preparation. All week long, in the midst of his myriad duties, he thought about next Sunday's subject. He scribbled notes at the breakfast table in the house the family bought in 1908 on Garden Place in Brooklyn. He added more ideas to a note pad balanced on his lap during the twenty-five-minute subway ride to 34th Street and Park Avenue. He wrote sentences on the back of envelopes as he waited for a committee meeting to begin some evening. His reading, done at snatched intervals during a crowded week, added substance. Thursday was devoted to hours of searching for illustrations and strengthening his arguments.

The final preparation was reserved for Saturday which he set aside entirely for rest and reflection. Early in the morning he climbed to a tiny room on the top floor of the house where there was quiet. The children were not permitted to disturb him there. He took no telephone calls and allowed no interruptions. Carefully he laid out the week's accumulation of notes on the bare pine table. Swiftly he made a final outline and just as quickly memorized its major points. Lying on the simple cot in the corner, he mulled over the material and pictured how he might present the theme. He had been told that Minot Savage preached Saturday afternoon drafts to his daughter; but Holmes chose to preach silently to himself, as he lay on the cot and stored strength for the next day. On Sunday morning his sermons showed that he was rested and ready.

On Monday, he transferred to paper the sermon of the previous day. By Wednesday he read the printer's proof; and on the following Sunday morning, the sermon was available for five cents per copy in the foyer of the church. Each year he chose the ten best, had them bound in red leather, and placed the book on his library shelf.

In his second year in New York, Holmes took stock and assessed both gains and losses. The church had been brought together, the membership rolls re-formed, and many new members accepted.

He was not satisfied with merely the one service on Sunday morning and told his congregation: "At our regular Sunday morning services I am now attempting to do what it is impossible to do at any single gathering of our people. I am attempting, in a period of time limited to one hour and a half in duration, to lead our people in a sincere and devout worship of God—to preach to them upon those subjects of the moral and spiritual life which, by long habit and wise tradition, are deemed most fitting in a Christian pulpit—and also to turn our people to the consideration of such contemporary questions of political, industrial, and social reform as we are now coming to see cannot long be neglected by the church, if the church is to serve society as it properly should."

The accomplishment of these purposes in a single service was "manifestly impossible . . . a work, fragmentary in character . . . unsatisfactory to both minister and people." He cherished a dream of ideal Sunday services in an ideal church, not just one service, but three public services each Sunday: "the morning service . . . much like our present morning services—with anthems, responsive readings, hymns, prayers, and a sermon dedicated to the serious and exhaustive treatment of the great fundamental questions of theology, ethics and religion"; then an afternoon service, not over an hour in length and liturgical in character, devoted to the single purpose of worship, with the church darkened as in a cathedral and the service musical, highlighted by scripture readings and the historic prayers of Christendom, and a ten-minute address dedicated entirely to the uplift and comfort of the soul; and finally in the evening, a service popular in nature: "with militant choir music and spirited hymn singing, the main feature of which would be an address by some well-known speaker on some subject of large public interest with discussions with the audience, adoption of resolutions, etc." This evening service would be an extension and enlargement of his Good Citizenship Class to place the Church of the Messiah in line "with every worthy movement for the betterment of the social conditions of city, state, and nation."

If financial aid were made available, the church would no longer be a place for merely entertainment or instruction, not solely a medium for an individual to seek salvation in an ark of safety and an asylum of refuge, but "an organization inspired by trust in God and dedicated to the bringing in of God's Kingdom upon earth." To accomplish this objective he needed three thousand or perhaps even as much as four thousand dollars; but the church budget allowed no such sum and he found no members generous enough to provide it.

These goals, sought so earnestly, he described in enthusiastic addresses to many audiences. Denominational correspondents in *The Unitarian* and the *Christian Register* termed his presentation "a most ringing forth-setting of our essential faith." His people at the Church of the Messiah thought so too and tried to respond accordingly, but not with the zeal and means that Holmes desired.

To many in his own church and in other churches his sermons answered all objections and covered all arguments. His delivery seemed like a flaming torch to give light in every corner of life. To them his body and spirit were at one in his preaching; his gestures seemed never to break the spirit but were an integral part of the whole performance.

Not all his hearers, however, considered him the answer to Isaiah's "Whom shall I send and who will go for us?" In 1908, when Holmes gave a two-hour-long address at the Middle Atlantic Conference of Unitarian Churches in Troy, New York, on "Unitarianism and the Social Question," he was criticized for having been "profuse and ponderous." His rhetoric was "fervid, too stringent and too stinging, unduly socialist and extreme." One opponent called his analysis of society "a despairing onslaught." A sympathizer hoped his "leadership would prove as intelligent as it is fiery, as broad, comprehensive and constructive as it is strenuous." Some of his contemporaries felt that Holmes lacked "discrimination" and wanted "real revolutionary socialism." Another complained because "our earnest friend has a vehemence of tone, an exaggeration of statement."

Holmes would not, however, be deterred. Aided by Alson Robinson and Arthur Weatherby, he and William Peck of Needham, Massachusetts, founded the Unitarian Fellowship for Social Justice in 1908; and at its 1909 meeting in Templeton, New Hampshire, Stephen Wise spoke.

Wise also wanted people freed from bondage to creeds and doctrines. He urged leaders of Protestantism to join with his followers in Judaism and liberate religious institutions for larger tasks, especially for the reformation of society. To do this they must clarify for their audiences new knowledge, circulate fresh ideas, and struggle for the extension of freedom in intellectual, social, and political spheres.

Both Wise and Holmes now began another association which was to last until the end of their active careers; they became almost annual lecturers at the newly organized Ford Hall Forum in Boston. The Forum, founded by George W. Coleman in February, 1908, and directed by David K. Niles, soon became one of the most liberal and provocative in America. Meetings were held each Sunday evening from October through April and began with a half-hour inspirational program of music and readings; then the speaker would elaborate on a controversial subject in such a way as to bring discussion and, it was hoped, disagreement from the audience.

In this fashion both men spoke throughout the country, frequently for Emerson's definition of f-a-m-e: "Fifty and my expenses," but more often for expenses only. They preached the Word, which, for them, meant urging their listeners to seek more justice for men and women everywhere.

8. A Social Gospel

The new social purpose, which has laid its masterful grasp on modern life and thought, is enlarging and transforming our whole conception of the meaning of Christianity.

—WALTER RAUSCHENBUSCH, 1910

As a UNITARIAN, Holmes subscribed to no formal creed and thus stood apart from the evangelical Protestantism of Christianity. He did not call Jesus "the Christ," nor did he believe, as the name of his church implied, in Jesus as the "Messiah." When he invoked the name "Christ," he referred to Jesus as a unique figure in religious history, the culmination of Hebraic prophecy and the epitome of the Judeo-Christian tradition. All men were imbued with the spark of the divine, but the Nazarene preeminently so. Never did he consider Jesus the "Son of God," whose appearance on earth was the sole incarnation of the Almighty, the only Person through whom God revealed Himself. "Saviorship" was to Holmes an obsolete theological term; and the Galilean, he contended, had been betrayed by those who called him "Savior." Jesus was to be honored as a heroic servant of humanity, an eternal contemporary, who made all the children of men "sons of God."

Jesus' teachings were not without parallel in this or any other age, Holmes reminded his congregation. He urged them to recall Marcus Aurelius, "noblest Roman of them all, one of the few almost perfect characters of history." Was he not an approximation of the Christian ideal? "With the single exception of Jesus, perhaps Socrates, it is probable that this wise ruler and saintly man holds a place second to none in the affection and reverence of humanity."

Quite un-Christian, in Holmes' eyes, were many of Jesus' followers across the centuries. They kept alive an institution, the church, that incorporated the very evils Jesus condemned: chains of dogma, barriers of hate, miasmas of superstition, opposition to learning; yet, he conceded, "all things considered, there is no other movement in human history which can be compared with Christianity as a civilizing influence—and none to which we are more directly indebted for the most beneficent of the institutions of organized society, of which we are today the happy heirs and guardians. Nor, from the standpoint of that truth which is stranger than fiction, is there any tale of greater marvel and miracle than that of the origin, growth and universal extension of the Christian Church."

The church could measure up to the ideal by listening to the urging of Henry Demarest Lloyd not only "to preach Christ but do Christ . . . judge civilization not by the six-million dollar Cathedral on Murray Hill but by the children in the back alleys." Holmes therefore led his parish in aiding the program of the Warren Goddard House, a social settlement in East 33rd and 34th streets that fulfilled the slogan of the Settlement House Movement: "Not alms but a friend." Its head residents were Mary Kingsbury Simkhowitch and Edith Kendall. Despite his full schedule, Holmes served as a board member; helped guide the staff, paid and volunteer; and secured relief funds for hundreds of neighborhood families during the unemployment months of 1907 and 1908. The workers were impelled by the settlement house ideal that had fired the hearts of hundreds to leave comfortable homes, luxurious clubs, and quiet classrooms, work in city slums, and, as Jane Addams said when founding Chicago's Hull House in 1887, make "the Christ become incarnate once more in many a gentle and heroic heart to seek and save those which are lost."

Poverty, Holmes explained to the Goddard House staff and his congregation in those early years, was a product of social conditions; only when the environment was changed would poverty be banished. If the individual's shortcomings were blamed as important contributing factors, such limitations still failed to explain the misery of man. The suffering individual had little control over adverse conditions; these could be changed only by society. The application of justice and the total reform of society were necessary. Charity organizations and settlement houses would now have to shift their base of operations and become centers of agitation for social reform.

But this was just the beginning: in seeking justice, men and women would be practicing the only true charity, that is, "to seek the establishment of the Kingdom of God in the world without, and thereby its easier and more immediate establishment in the world within!"

"Social service" was the term usually applied to the thrust of organized religion on behalf of social justice; and it ran parallel to the reform movement which Theodore Roosevelt strengthened as he took planks from the platform of William Jennings Bryan's Democratic Party and Eugene V. Debs' Socialist Party. McClure's published the findings of the leading Muckrakers: Ida Tarbell, Ray Stannard Baker, and Lincoln Steffens. Social novelists, led by Upton Sinclair, Frank Norris, and Jack London, awakened the public to deplorable conditions in the packing industry and the railroads. The labor movement, especially the American Federation of Labor under the leadership of Samuel Gompers, made headway. Successful efforts to conserve natural resources were led by Gifford Pinchot and Jacob Riis. Campaigns against food adulteration and a movement to prohibit the liquor traffic were under way. The franchise for women and the blight of child labor became focal points of discussion by responsible citizens. Laissez faire no longer reigned unrestricted and governmental controls had already taken effect. As he began his term of office, President William Howard Taft tried to slacken these currents of reform but found himself carried along by them despite his lack of enthusiasm.

All this puzzled Robert Collyer. At a convocation of the Hackley School at Tarrytown one Sunday afternoon in 1909, Collyer and Holmes were seated on the veranda talking. Suddenly, Collyer turned and asked, "John, what are the members talking about when they say that you are a socialist?"

Holmes then explained public ownership of utilities and of the major means of production. He described the objectives of socialization of natural resources. He hoped that through socialism each might be aided according to his needs and rewarded according to his ability.

There was a long pause. Collyer shook his head and said, "I don't understand it, John. I don't like it." Then the old man smiled and said, "But if you like it and believe in it, preach it for all you're worth."

With such encouragement Holmes preached a sermon on "Christianity and Socialism," distinguishing between socialism as a system of economics and socialism as "a spirit, an ideal, an inspiration . . . a religion." He looked upon "the pure idealism of socialism, the love, sympathy, good will, the political, industrial, and spiritual brotherhood of man, as the religion of Jesus, of him whom I call Master." Its goal: "The Kingdom of love and good will and peace for which that Master lived and died." Its faith: "The faith in man and in man's future which sustained the Master in life and which sustained even in death."

His sources of authority were many: he quoted Walter Rauschenbusch and Jack London; William Morris and John Ruskin; George Bernard Shaw and H. G. Wells. He referred to John Spargo's book, *The Spiritual Significance of Modern Socialism* and, for precedent, to the formation of the "Christian Socialist Fellowship" with six hundred ministers of thirty states and twenty different denominations. Alluding to a Broadway success of 1908, Charles Rann Kennedy's *The Servant in the House,* he told of Robert, drainman and sewer cleaner, and the new Indian butler, Manson Servant. Robert described the new religion, socialism, concluding, "Funny, ain't it?" Manson Servant replied, "I don't think so. For it's my religion too."

This was Holmes' religion too, as now, only two years after his arrival, he assumed full direction of the church although still listed as Junior Minister. Collyer had been Minister Emeritus since 1903 and, despite the one-year return to the pulpit, was in semiretirement. Holmes' was the guiding hand. In the 1909 *Year Book of the Church of the Messiah,* fifteen reports of different organizations in the church were prepared and signed by Holmes

—not only "The Report of the Junior Minister" and "The Messiah Pulpit," but also "The Committee on Charities," "The Good Citizenship Class," "The Messiah Study Class," "The Messiah Lending Library," "The Friendly Aid Society," "The Messiah Home for Children," etc.

This parish work was only part of his ministry, for he had a public ministry too. During the church year of 1908–1909, Holmes prepared an address in response to an invitation from Stephen Wise, as one of eight Wise presented at the Free Synagogue on the third Sunday morning of each month from November to May. The subject of the lecture course, "Some Phases of Modern Unrest," was suggested by a popular series of articles by Ray Stannard Baker in the *American* on "The Spiritual Unrest." Baker had pointed to the great gap between the churches and large segments of the American population because religious institutions had failed to grasp their opportunities.

In his talk, Holmes listed the various kinds of discontent characteristic of the day, in particular the moral unrest. Here was an ethical and spiritual phenomenon which reflected "the great cry of our age . . . not for increased efficiency or greater happiness or enlarged prosperity, but for simple justice—a cry not for the flesh pots of Egypt but for the birthright, a moral protest against the well-nigh universal injustice of the existing social order."

He contrasted the nineteenth century's material progress with the twentieth century's lack of moral progress: "Our ethical achievements have been practically nothing and morally the race has stood still, while materially it has advanced beyond the wildest dream of its progenitors. We are today, in all things moral and spiritual, exactly where our fathers were a hundred years ago, while in all things material we have virtually transformed the world." He ranged far in his denunciation of the wrongs in modern society.

In advocating the ethic of love, he excluded an individual ethic which forgot social responsibilities, for that love is meaningless which does not embrace everybody; and consecration is a mockery which is confined to a few within a family circle.

Bitterly, he charged: "Pirates and thieves and even murderers, as they are in their public activities, still seem to feel that there

is one place in the world, namely the home, where such things
cannot be and this place they keep inviolate at any cost. Here
we have the employer of child labor who is a devoted father,
the politician who collects his tribute from prostitutes and is a
tender husband, the corporation magnate who ruins his competi-
tors and plunders the public, and is still a generous and unselfish
friend."

Following this arraignment he proposed: "What is necessary
is to teach a man of this kind the impossibility of thus dividing
life and thus living doubly. He must be induced to widen the
bounds of the home until it shall reach the horizons of the universe, to extend the circle of friendship until it embraces all
mankind. He must be made to see that a man's one true home
is the world; his one true family, humanity; his public relationships as intimate and real and sacred as those which he has been
taught to regard as domestic and personal. . . . He must be made
to know that 'God is no respecter of persons' and that the poorest
and meanest and most wretched, equally with the noblest and
proudest and most happy, are still his children, still brothers
one of another, and still worthy therefore of all kindness, gentle-
ness and love."

Here was the "Social Gospel" in its most compelling form. If
men were shown their evil ways, they would mend themselves
and their habits. Appeal to a man's better nature, and society
would change. Make idealism intense and fervid enough, and
ideal ends would be achieved. Rely on moral suasion, and society
would be molded anew. The "unrest" was a precursor to the
change that would come as the dawn follows darkness. At the
heart of nature and society lay the evolutionary process which
brought about the change. On this one could rely.

Stephen Wise wanted Holmes to draw such inferences from
Baker's articles and carry them into the realm of religion and
society, raising another girder in the bridge across the canyon
separating churches and the people; thus they were fulfilling
Emil Hirsch's assertion that all synagogues and churches could
be worthy of successorship to Israel's prophets, if they refused
to "pact with the new dogmatism of wealth."

It was this same Emil Hirsch who influenced not only Wise

but also a young rabbi named Sidney Goldstein. A student of the archeologist James Breasted, and of the young philosopher John Dewey, at the University of Chicago, Goldstein graduated from the Hebrew Union College in Cincinnati in 1905 and soon published an article in the magazine *Charities and Commons* which highlighted the social problems of hospital patients for whom little was done to supplement medical care. Wise, still in Portland, read the article and asked Goldstein to meet him on his next visit to New York. Wise then described the new synagogue he planned to form, noting that it was to be not only for preaching and teaching but also for practicing religion. Would he, Goldstein, direct the Social Service Division? Goldstein accepted eagerly, and, by the autumn of 1907, began his work; within two years, he asked for the sum of ten thousand dollars to run the Division; this was almost as much as Holmes' congregation raised for its entire parish and pulpit program.

Wise believed in and warmly supported the Free Synagogue's religious center for community service and social pioneering. At each service he had a special collection for the project and Goldstein explained the work. Units were founded at West 81st Street and at Clinton Hall. Goldstein lectured to the congregation and its groups frequently, but gave most of his attention to the ward work in the Bellevue Hospital and the problems of the Jewish patients. He ran a training course for volunteer social workers. He gathered gifts of clothing for poor people and began co-operation with the parole and probation officers of the Elmira Reformatory, the Night Courts, the Court of General and Special Sessions, and Sing Sing Prison, working closely with the United Hebrew Charities and its director, Morris Waldman. He began a program of emergency assistance to people in need and the counseling of troubled persons, and started a series of lectures and book reviews to inform the congregation of this program and the ever-widening needs of his Social Service Division. Here were concrete examples of "doing justly and loving mercy."

The popular *Harper's Weekly* commented at the turn of the year 1908–1909: "The Free Synagogue has made a beginning so notable, so effective, that the merest sketch of it challenges the interest of all who would benefit their fellow men. This allusion to a few of the activities at the Free Synagogue will give a hint of the large and catholic program which the institution has planned. The people of the Free Synagogue do charity, but they do not talk charity. With them every means by which man can be helped is known as Social Services. Their work is constructive, re-creative."

In co-operation with Goldstein, Wise launched his own program of education, quite apart from the work of the Social Service Division, and enabled the congregation to hear many different speakers whether at Sunday morning services or in weekday meetings: Miss Maude Miner, probation officer of the Night Court, Edward A. Ross, professor of sociology at the University of Wisconsin and author of *Sin and Society,* John Dewey, then of Columbia University, and John Lovejoy Elliott of the Hudson Neighborhood Guild.

At the Student-Faculty Forum at Union Theological Seminary, Wise was asked by a student one day, "Why don't the Jews accept Jesus Christ?" In the tense silence, Wise responded, "We Jews take Jesus Christ seriously. Do you Christians?" The only response was an embarrassed titter in the rear of the hall.

He pointed out that he was speaking of Christianity in his criticism, not of the religion of Jesus: "The religion of Jesus is not Christianity. Christianity is a substitute for the religion of Christ. I am not an anti-Christian, I am an ante-Christian."

9. I, the Lord, Love Justice

The conscious recognition of grave national abuses casts a deep shadow across the traditional American patriotic vision.

—HERBERT CROLY, 1909

FEBRUARY 12, 1909, WAS A BUSY DAY for both Stephen Wise and John Haynes Holmes.

In the morning, Wise appeared in Albany before the legislative hearings on direct nominations for the State Legislature and returned to New York in the early afternoon to meet as a mediator with the principals in strikes at the Butterick Company and Fleischman's Bakery. He then sandwiched in a wedding and met with Maurice Wertheim and Alma Morgenthau to plan their marriage ceremony for April 15. In the evening, he spoke, together with Governor Charles Evans Hughes, at the Academy of Music in Brooklyn on the hearing in Albany. He could not therefore attend an important meeting that evening called by Oswald Garrison Villard, William English Walling, and Charles Edward Russell.

Holmes spent much of the day preparing for the printer the manuscript of the sermon he had given the previous Sunday on "Religion and Evolution" in commemoration of Charles Darwin's one hundredth birthday. In the afternoon, he spoke on Abraham Lincoln's centenary before the Women's Alliance of the Church of the Messiah. As was his custom many nights of the week, he did not return to his Brooklyn home for dinner. He was able, as Wise was not, to attend the meeting that evening. Its purpose was to describe injustices under which the Negro

suffered and, on the birthday of the Great Emancipator, com-
pose a proclamation, "The Call," for a nation-wide conference
later in the year in New York. Holmes and Jane Addams helped
to prepare the program. Villard composed "The Call" of which
Wise was a co-signer, along with John Dewey, Lincoln Steffens,
and Holmes. The call for the two-day meeting on May 31 and
June 1 listed wrongs Lincoln would have found had he been able
to revisit the United States in his one hundredth year: disfran-
chisement at the polls; widespread discrimination in employment, transportation, and education; denial of justice in the
courts; and lynch rule by mobs throughout the country—at the
rate of two per week.

This new movement of 1909 was incorporated a year later
under the laws of the State of New York as the National Association for the Advancement of Colored People. Holmes was one
of the five incorporators.

William E. Burghardt DuBois was called from Atlanta to become Director of Publications and Research and, in the fall of
1910, initiated a monthly magazine, *The Crisis*. One of its features, "Following the Colour Line," was named after a series of
articles—published by Ray Stannard Baker in the *American*
magazine during 1907—which gave documentary evidence of
discrimination all over America.

The National Association for the Advancement of Colored
People now began to combat the "Grandfather Clauses" which
destroyed the Negro vote; to seek enactment of municipal ordi-
nances for residential desegregation; to oppose discriminatory
policies in the majority of labor unions; to highlight the neglect
of Negro education; to protest the railroads' Jim Crow transportation in the South; to fight the exclusion of Negro patients,
physicians, and nurses from public and private hospitals; and to
resist racial segregation and discrimination in the military forces
of the United States. The NAACP wanted to go beyond the
teachings of Booker T. Washington as well as the tolerance of
segregation which still prevailed among so many Negroes. The
Negro was now asked to do more than educate himself along
technical lines; he was urged to help himself and join with white
people in aiding other Negroes.

The desire of the NAACP to rid the land of such barriers to
equality and justice was shared by Holmes, Wise, and many
others, such as Jacob Schiff, the philanthropist and banker. Wise's
wholehearted approval of the movement from its inception, his
quick acceptance of the invitation to join in "The Call," and
the many messages he sent to the NAACP meetings through the
years indicate that he always thought of himself as a founder.
Holmes remained close to the movement from that first meeting;
after 1910, he served as a vice president of the organization and
attended board meetings regularly.

In the winter of 1909, especially during the month of Lincoln's
birthday centenary, Wise spoke on this subject to the Free
Synagogue both uptown and downtown, the Episcopal Church
in Matteawan, New York, the Union League Club in Brooklyn,
the Lincoln Association of Jersey City, the Y.M.C.A. on West
57th Street, the Central Congregational Church of Brooklyn, and
Protestant churches in Norwich, Connecticut, and Worcester,
Massachusetts. He never lost an opportunity to remind Christians
that Lincoln did not formally belong to any Christian church
and, while attending several, had never joined because none
asked for simple assent, in Lincoln's words, "to the Savior's
statement of the substance of the Law—'Thou shalt love the
Lord thy God with all thy heart and with all thy soul and with
all thy mind, and thy neighbor as thyself.'" Lincoln's sustained
concern for the rights and security of workingmen served too as
a good reference from which to deduce the need for greater
justice to the working classes irrespective of race and for bridg-
ing the gap between the workingman and institutional religion.

Neither Wise nor Holmes was deterred by the complexity of
issues or the intransigence of evils they attacked. Had the society
been less complex and more just, they would doubtless have
been frustrated. Instead they exulted in their crusades. When
accused of preaching politics, Wise and Holmes would answer,
"It is our duty to take into the pulpit for consideration every
problem of public life that involves a moral question."

Their message was made explicit in a series of talks given at
the Downtown Branch of the Free Synagogue at Clinton Hall
on "The Ethics of Life's Callings" by authorities on the ethics

of journalism, Norman Hapgood of *Collier's* magazine and
Oswald Garrison Villard of the New York *Evening Post;* on the
ethics of politics, by Seth Low, Mayor of New York; I. N. Seligman, on the ethics of business; S. Parkes Cadman and Rabbi
Henry Berkowitz, on the ethics of the ministry. Aided by Eugene
H. Lehman in the religious school and Sidney Goldstein in the
growing Division of Social Service, Wise made his entire program in this, the third year of the organization, more and more
attractive to his fellow Jews.

Occasionally some skeptical souls would express doubt about
the "spirituality" of a religious institution encompassing so many
issues and activities. To allay their fears and reassure these people, Wise would quote from a letter written to the *Jewish
Chronicle* of London by a young English Jew after he had attended a service at the Free Synagogue:

> The services are held in a hall packed with about 700 men and
> women, far more men than women and mostly young men and
> women, who hang on the words of the preacher with an earnest-
> ness I have never witnessed in a synagogue before, and who
> join in the prayers of that service, every word of which they
> comprehend, with a fervour unusual in congregations in Great
> Britain, or London, whether the prayers are said in the East or
> in the West. And if you tell me that such a service is a "menace
> to Judaism," then I say, with as much energy as I can convey in
> writing, that I believe such services will tend to the salvation of
> Judaism rather than to its "menace."

To Wise there were impetus and incentive enough for religious living in the Hebrew tradition. This view he explained
fully in a sermon, "Two Views of Life: Hebraic and Hellenic."
He maintained that emotional elements, the protestations of the
heart on behalf of justice and equity, must inevitably prevail
over rational precepts, such as the Greek emphasis on the head
over the heart.

In 1910, shortly before Wise left on a speaking tour of the
British Isles, he arranged a dinner at the Hotel Astor to observe
the third anniversary of the Free Synagogue. Not satisfied with
having as speakers such distinguished men as his own supporters

Henry Morgenthau and Jacob H. Schiff, he brought in George
E. Chamberlain, United States Senator from Oregon, Nicholas
Murray Butler, president of Columbia University, and Governor
Charles Evans Hughes. All congratulated Wise in particular and
the congregation in general on three years of unusual progress.

Governor Hughes sounded the high note. Everyone realized
the nation's indebtedness to "the strong and virile ministry of
your leader." He pleaded for more such men in New York: "We
need their message, their fire, their capacity to communicate
enthusiasm, their ability to generate moral resolution, their devotion to good work and their sincere desire to be a real benefit
to their fellow citizens."

During Wise's absence in Great Britain in midspring, the congregation prepared a surprise for his return to New York. While
he spoke to large, appreciative audiences on his tour under the
auspices of the Jewish Religious Union of London, a special committee found an auditorium they thought worthy of him. Carnegie
Hall was available, for Felix Adler's Ethical Culture Society
no longer had any need of it, having erected a building of their
own. Wise returned to learn the good news and laid plans for a
wider audience and an even more representative list of speakers
to supplement his sermons in the fall.

He now had an auditorium seating 2,500 people. Beginning
with his first service of the High Holy Days, he filled it to capacity virtually every Sunday morning. Just as in early 1909 Wise
had given scores of varied interpretations of his basic theme of
Lincoln, so now on his return from Britain in May, 1910, he gave
an untold number of addresses on "Theodore Parker, Preacher-
Prophet" to mark the centenary of Parker's birth. Holmes, unable
to appear at Wise's third anniversary celebration in February
because of commitments in the Midwest, exchanged pulpits with
him in the late spring; each interpreted to the other's congregation Parker, who had inspired both of them.

In his sermon Holmes recalled that the greatly loved minister
of Boston had predicted fifty years earlier: "The religion I preach
will be the religion of enlightened men for the next thousand
years"; but Parker had erred. "He had been modest in this statement," said Holmes, "for the religion he preached, in its funda-

mentals, is destined to be the enduring religion of all future times."

To both Wise and Holmes, these days provided many opportunities to speak on their favorite themes. Holmes continued to plead for an interpretation of Jesus as "the servant of a new humanity . . . not only a prophet of religious truth, but an instigator of social reform, concerned not only with the sins of individuals but also with the evils of institutions." This might mean social revolution, but it could be accomplished in the spirit and name of Jesus.

He paid tribute to the fathers of the "Social Gospel," Josiah Strong, Richard Ely, and Washington Gladden. "These three prophets are with us, fortunately, and how their hearts must glow as they see the change which has now come over the face of Christendom and to the accomplishments of which they themselves, through all these twenty-five years, have been contributing so much. The battle is not yet won by any means, but—!"

In Holmes' eyes, the goal was in sight. Society could be transformed. In that vein he continued to write hymns. None had as yet become famous or widely sung; yet they retained his high idealism and unrestrained optimism and in later years several were included in most Protestant hymnals.

Toward these ends the church was merely a means, for Holmes was constantly critical of organized religion. Often he quoted from the well-publicized President's Address by Charles William Eliot at the 1909 Summer School of Theology at Harvard, "The Religion of the Future," and like Eliot, claimed there was more religion in a trade union than in the churches of New York, more idealism in the Socialist Party than in organized Christianity, a truer ministry in the work of a physician than in the ministrations of a priest. He interpreted Eliot's thought as calling for a "New Religion," defined as truth, not tradition; liberty, not authority; justice, not charity. Now men could cast aside fetters forged with the dogmas of centuries and regain the freedom originally granted by Christ.

He hoped for the widespread acceptance of such ideas and took heart: "Like a great wave sweeping down from the lofty reservoir of knowledge, President Eliot's utterances swept the

whole fabric of the church's theology to destruction. The whole
theological conception of the history of the world and the nature
of man, upon which the idea of salvation was founded, has been
overthrown for good and all by the wonderful advances achieved
during the space of the last fifty or sixty years."

In his mind, as in Stephen Wise's, justice was on the way.
Religion was to use the church whenever and wherever possible,
but look upon it as, at best, an inadequate mechanism in the
struggle. Far more important than clerical collars and church
budgets were the zeal and the zest of the reformer, whether in
welcoming the Muckrakers' exposés of injustice in the social
order or aiding Margaret Sanger in her crusade for birth control.

10. To Publish Good Tidings

The advance of liberalism, so-called, in Christianity, during the past fifty years, may fairly be called a victory of healthy-mindedness within the church over the morbidness with which the old hell-fire theology was more harmoniously related.   —WILLIAM JAMES, 1902

TO HOLMES THE GOOD TIDINGS of the Old and New testaments were a gospel of social salvation. Men needed to be saved from their sins, but their sins were primarily of the social order. Crusades must therefore be waged against the ills of poverty and disease, ignorance and injustice. As in his speaking, so in his writing, Holmes' religious imperative was fused with a socializing impulse.

Among his Unitarian friends he pressed for action on the social front. He asked them to read, to think, and to move toward the objectives of a better world based on justice for all. He sent his sermons for publication to the *Christian Register* at Unitarian headquarters in Boston, wrote articles for the *Pacific Unitarian* on the West Coast and *Unity,* house organ of the Western Conference; he mailed duplicate material to *The Unitarian Advance* of the Unitarian Conference of the Middle States and Canada. Jenkin Lloyd Jones, editing *Unity* in his office at the Abraham Lincoln Center in Chicago, found in Holmes a kindred spirit and made him an associate editor. George Badger of *The Unitarian Advance* may have disagreed with him often but for that reason appointed him a contributing editor and later associate

108

editor; and in these pages, in January, 1910, Holmes began a new department, "The Modern Church." Each month he contributed long, fervent articles on the church's social mission. He suggested books by Taussig and Commons, the Webbs and Spargo, Gladden and Rauschenbusch, only a part of "the veritable flood which has been pouring from the printing presses reflecting the consummate public interest in the social question and the determination of intelligent people to know the facts of 'things as they are' and to find the way of things as they ought to be." He urged his friends to support the recently founded Unitarian Fellowship for Social Justice.

His readers were not always of one mind and some soon began to object. From Wilmington, Delaware, one subscriber expressed his "profound weariness with the berating" and deemed it "absolutely valueless for the best class of minds." He wanted a vision, not a spanking.

In the same vein later that winter, another objection came from Montreal: "I wonder how in God's name Mr. Holmes thinks the Modern Church is going to reconstitute Society, if it is going to have nothing to do with the building of character. I never read the articles by the gentleman, without a queer little feeling in the bottom of my heart that I know more about the social question than he does, though I never read a book on socialism in my life. It seems to me a great pity to waste so much good ammunition."

Holmes hewed to his line, however, publishing thousands of words each month from lectures and sermons, and explained that the "Social Gospel" stemmed from at least a half dozen different developments in the nineteenth century, each distinct in itself but often interacting with the others: (1) the decline of individualism in orthodox Protestantism; (2) the rise of historical criticism of the Bible; (3) the growth of the democratic ethos; (4) the spread of humanitarianism; (5) the surge of socialist trends; and (6) the expansion of the labor movement. All of Protestantism now felt its conscience quickened. The prophets and their teachings were seen in a new light. Jesus' concept of the Kingdom of God was freshly relevant for the here and now.

Impelled by such convictions, Holmes joined Wise and Frank Oliver Hall of the Church of the Divine Paternity (Universalist) in the fall of 1910 to sponsor nonsectarian union services each Sunday evening on "Religion and the Social Problem." The crowds were so large that hundreds were turned away from the first meeting at the Universalist Church when Judge Ben Lindsey, Juvenile Court Judge of Denver, gave the opening address, "The Battle with the Beast." Through the winter and into the spring the services continued with a second series at the Church of the Messiah, and then a third series at the Free Synagogue's place of origin, the Hudson Theatre.

In the 1910–1911 and 1911–1912 series, leading authorities spoke on "The Application of Religious Principles to the Social Life." In the second series, centering on "Social Justice" for six successive Sunday evenings, men specially qualified by their professions discussed their particular fields—John Mitchell of the United Mine Workers and ex-Mayor Seth Low upheld the rights of the individual workingman; Washington Gladden outlined the evolution of social justice; Dean George W. Kirchwey of Columbia University and A. Leo Weil, a Pittsburgh lawyer, emphasized the legal aspects; Gifford Pinchot, the conservation advocate, Oswald Garrison Villard of the New York *Evening Post,* and Paul U. Kellogg of *Survey* pointed out the relation of democracy to its political aspects; and Bishop Charles D. Williams of Detroit explained how the church might co-ordinate its actions with religious principles.

Many Jews, however, looked with horror at such interfaith gatherings and hurled bitter denunciations at Stephen Wise. A Yiddish paper on the East Side even threatened violence against him. One of Wise's chief supporters, Jacob H. Schiff, also differed with the rabbi. He told a public meeting of the Young Men's Hebrew Association that a union of this kind was impossible as long as the Christian world attacked the Jews: "Christians are still persecuting Jews with atrocious cruelty in Russia. Why then is it seemly for Jews to meet with Christians in common worship in New York? First the atrocities must cease."

The three sponsoring clergymen—Holmes, Hall, and Wise—tried to reason with Schiff in letters and personal interviews that it was not the Christians of New York who persecuted Jews in Russia, and that the two Christian churches involved in the experiment were of that segment of Christianity which fostered religious liberalism and countered such persecutions; but Schiff was not persuaded. He withdrew support from the Free Synagogue, reserving his contributions solely for the Social Service Division. Wise returned his subscription.

The sharpest criticism came from Samuel Schulman of Temple Beth-El: "If Jews can meet in common worship with the Christians one night in the week, why not every night? If one service can be shared with the Christians, why not all? And then what becomes of historic Judaism?"

Wise, Hall, and Holmes had planned to rotate their pulpits and serve as guest preachers on the first Sunday in December of 1910; but with such attacks to answer, each man remained in his own pulpit.

Holmes, too, met with opposition, not in his church but among his fellow ministers. As they called for a return to the Gospel of Jesus Christ and an emphasis on the individual rather than on society, Holmes pleaded instead for the New Gospel of Socialization. He wanted a merger of the secular with the sacred:

> The church will care not so much for rites of baptism as for public baths and playgrounds; not so much for the service of Communion at the altar, as for that wider communion at every hearthstone which shall give bread to all who hunger and drink to all who thirst; not so much for clerical robes and choir vestments, as for clothing for all who are naked; not so much for splendid churches and towering cathedrals, as for decent and comfortable homes for all men, women, and children; not so much for an atmosphere of prayer and worship in the church edifice, as for fresh air to breathe in the tenements and slums; not so much for teaching men to believe, as for giving them means wherewith to live; not so much for keeping Sunday inviolate from open theatres and concert-halls and sports, as for keeping every day inviolate from dishonest stock-transactions, piratical business deals, child labor, starvation wages, preventable diseases, selfish wealth and grinding poverty; not so much for saving the heathen overseas, as for saving the Christians who are perishing at our very doors; not so much for emancipating men from what we call sin, as for emancipating them from the conditions of life and labour which make sin inevitable; not so

much for saving souls, as for saving the society which moulds the soul for eternal good or ill.

In the early winter of 1911, Holmes went to Pennsylvania for Convocation Week at the Meadville Theological School. He was in eminent company: Washington Gladden of Columbus, President W. H. Faunce of Brown University, and Richard C. Cabot, a young physician from Boston, who supported the Emanuel Movement of Religion and Mental Health. Gladden outlined his more restrained approach to the Christian impact on society, Faunce spoke on religion and education, and Cabot discussed "The Consecration of Affection," a tactful approach to sexual problems. Holmes gave two lectures: on "The Moral Unrest of Our Time—Its Cause and Cure," and another, new to his audiences and the basis of a book he was writing, on "The Revolutionary Function of the Modern Church."

The discussions in the meetings, in the corridors later, and in the guest rooms until after midnight, centered mainly on Holmes' blunt rebuke of the church. The revolutionary function of the modern church, said he, was to engage in a New Reformation and thus create a new church. The next step would be creation of a new society. Give up individualism and adopt socialism. Forsake absurd and antiquated denominationalism. Replace dogma with brotherly love. The church should cease serving as an institution of the privileged classes and become a forum for all the people, changing itself into a defender and servant of humanity at large: "If the church of the 'forties' had been doing its full duty by society, there would have been no Anti-Slavery Society. The church in all its manifold branches would itself have served as the Anti-Slavery Society which was needed."

Looking to the present, he said: "In the same way, if the church today were doing its full duty by society—serving the world as Christ would have it served—there would be no Child Labor Committees, no Peace Societies, no Consumers' Leagues, no labor unions, no Socialist Party. The church would itself be all of these —and exclusively these—until the Kingdom of God would come upon earth and make all these redemptive organizations unnecessary."

On Chestnut Hill, covered with snow in the sub-zero weather, some of the audience contended that the church was not meant to accomplish these ends and must have a greater concern for the individual. Holmes insisted all the more energetically that the church must go into fields of industry, force labor and capital to cease warring and unite on a platform of mutual co-operation, enter the realm of business too, and serve God in the market place as well as in the sanctuary, and do His will in commercial transactions as in ecclesiastical performances. The complexity of contemporary capitalism fazed Holmes not a whit, no more than did the tumble and turmoil of politics where the church had the duty to purify the Augean stable of its rottenness and render the city hall, state capitol, and state court house as sacred a shrine as a cathedral. A public servant of the state would be as truly a minister of religion as a priest praying before an altar.

A minister from the Midwest asked him about the work done in the previous year by Charles Stelzle in the revival of a moribund Presbyterian church in New York and its transformation into a "Labor Temple." Holmes answered that while he admired Stelzle and approved of the Labor Temple as a fresh beginning, perhaps even a new departure in social Christianity, the creation of such an institution resulted in only a new class church, geared solely for the workingman. He wanted no Labor Temple with its particular stratum of the social order but rather a church with no restrictions or boundaries, a church preaching a gospel without barriers or fences. There were, he admitted, many obstacles in the way of achieving such a socialized church: the philosophy of individualism in American life, the inexcusable scandal of denominationalism, the lure of otherworldliness, the freight of dogma, false distinctions between sacred and secular in society, and the inescapable fact of class consciousness. All these could be wiped out, however, driven out of the church, he optimistically said, just as "Christ drove the money changers out of the temple."

The following Sunday evening Holmes met Wise at the union services and told him of the Meadville meeting. Wise in turn told Holmes of that morning's Carnegie Hall services commemorating Lincoln's 102nd birthday. The program included a prize poem by the nine-year-old James Waterman Wise. Senator Wil-

liam Borah of Idaho, the scheduled speaker, had become ill earlier in the week and was compelled to cancel his address. Wise
had frantically telephoned every famous man he knew in New
York and finally reached Robert Collyer. His daughter took the
message; and to her and Wise's surprise, Collyer, then eighty-
seven, accepted and spoke with charm and power.

A few weeks later, as spring came to New York City, the tragic
Triangle Shirtwaist Company fire occurred in Washington Place,
resulting in the death of 147 persons. On the following day,
Sunday, March 26, 1911, Stephen Wise spoke to a meeting of
twenty philanthropic organizations at the headquarters of the
Women's Trade Union League and said he was willing to take
no man's word, especially no city official's word, about purported
facts of the fire.

"We have seen the terrible evidences of what officials can do
in the way of avoiding the search for facts in the case of the
recent legislative investigating committee which passed so skill-
fully all opportunities really to find out the scandals of race track
gambling. . . . I want the citizens of New York to find out for
themselves, through the medium of a committee named at a
general mass assembly. If this thing was avoidable, I want to see
those responsible punished. If it was due to some corrupt failure
to enforce the law, I want to see that determined. And I do not
trust public officials to determine it for us; it is our own task
to do that for ourselves."

That evening, Wise spoke in Holy Trinity Church in Brooklyn
at the invitation of its rector, John Howard Melish, and observed
that funds would doubtless be speedily gathered for relief of the
victims of the fire, a right and just move, but such an action
could not undo the wrong committed. "This disaster calls for
charity, but more loudly it demands that justice be done to the
workers of the nation. The pleasures of the idle rich, however
hazardous, are rendered comparatively secure, but the work of
the unceasing toilers is surrounded with manifold dangers and
endless peril."

His sympathy and pity were welded to a denunciation of the
wrong: "It is not enough to bewail the fate of those who are lost
nor to wring our hands in horror. We stand not before an in-

scrutable decree of Divine Providence but before the outcome of an unscrupulous degree of human improvidence and human greed." He had a solution: "Instead of having safety appliances in a museum, however laudable its purpose, we ought to put in a museum any man who is unwilling to utilize every possible industrial appliance for the safety and security of the toilers."

By the next Sunday afternoon, he had made up his mind to insist on a permanent citizens' committee on fire protection and made such a demand at a mass meeting in the Metropolitan Opera House.

Wise made the meeting memorable by objecting to the audience reaction to the previous speakers. Considerable applause greeted the announcement by Jacob Schiff, chairman of the meeting and of the Relief Fund, that the $75,000 already gathered must be regarded as "conscience money." When Bishop David H. Greer of the Protestant Episcopal Diocese characterized the fire as the responsibility of all—"The sin, and sin there is, is at our own door"—there was tumultuous applause. Wise became angry at such an unseemly display at a gathering in memory of the dead and from his place on the platform strode to the front of the stage, holding up his hands as a signal that the applause must stop.

"Not that, not that!" he shouted, as soon as he could make himself heard above the clapping hands. "This is not our day for applauding. It is our fast day, our day of guilt and humiliation. Let it not become a day of unavailing regret, but let it be a day of availing contriteness and redeeming penitence."

As the audience lapsed into sheepish silence, Wise made this the occasion for his own speech and continued, "It is not the action of God, but the inaction of men that is responsible. The disaster was not the deed of God, but the greed of man. This was no inevitable disaster which men could neither foresee nor control. Some of us did foresee it, and others might have foreseen it, but they chose not to do so. We would not yield here to unbridled wrath, but let this meeting find voice in such noble anger as shall translate itself into high and resolute and ceaseless determination to safeguard the toilers of the nation."

The applause which the rabbi had deplored now burst forth

from orchestra and galleries alike in spite of his efforts to restrain it.

"We have laws," he then continued, "that in a crisis we find
are no laws and we have enforcement that when the hour of
trial comes, we find is no enforcement. Let us lift up the industrial
standards until they will bear inspection. And when we go before
the Legislature, let us not allow them to put us off forever with
the old answer, 'we have no money.' True, we have no money for
the necessary things of enforcement of the laws which safeguard
the lives of the workers, but it is because so much of our money
is wasted and squandered and stolen."

He pointed out to the hushed assemblage that "this meeting
was not summoned to appeal for charity. What we need is the
redress of justice and the remedy of prevention. The summons
to action comes indeed from the courts, for the recent decision
of the Court of Appeals invokes, as it were, a referendum to the
people on the question of employers' liability and compensation
in industry. We know we cannot and should not take away property without due process of law, but neither may we take away
life without due process of law."

He drew the inference of what he was saying by calling for a
democratic imperative: "It behooves us to remember that ours
must not be a government of the people and by the people
but a government for all the people—for children first, for
women next, and for the men, who are the makers of the
law, last of all. The lesson of the hour is that while property is
good, life is better; that while possessions are valuable, life is
without price. Because life is sacred, we realize today the indivisible oneness of human welfare. These women and these men
will have died in vain unless we today highly resolve that my
brother's wrong is my wrong. I am not merely the keeper of my
brother and my sister, but the justice-dealing brother to all men
and women in God's world."

When he turned from the audience and walked back to his
chair, no one could stop the applause. The result of the meeting
was the formation on a permanent basis of the committee for
which he called and swift action in Albany, sponsored by such
young liberals as Alfred E. Smith and Frances Perkins, which

ultimately brought about "the redress of justice and the remedy of prevention." The records of those days reflect the close collaboration of both Wise and Holmes in the campaign of protest and the effort to prevent the recurrence of such a tragedy.

One of the most trying times the two clergymen experienced took place in the winter of 1911–1912. Over the Thanksgiving weekend, the news came from Los Angeles that the McNamara boys had confessed. Until then, the McNamaras had not wavered in their profession of innocence in the bombing a year before of the Los Angeles *Times* building during labor strife on the West Coast. The bombing resulted in great loss of life and scores of injuries. An investigation pointed to John J. McNamara and James B. McNamara as the men responsible for the act. Both the American Federation of Labor and the Socialists supported the McNamaras and discounted the investigation of William J. Burns, the detective hired by Mayor Alexander to find the *Times* dynamiters. The sympathy of the labor movement and liberals was with the McNamaras and against General Harrison Gray Otis, owner of the *Times*. Clarence Darrow accepted the case as defense attorney.

When the men confessed, the labor forces were more than embarrassed. Samuel Gompers, president of the A.F.L., wept; Eugene V. Debs, editor of the Socialists' *Appeal to Reason*, tried to trace the crime to the fact that the men were Democrats; and Darrow was on the verge of a breakdown.

Wise did not justify or defend the men but argued: "As long as labor organizations are denied a hearing save just before election seasons; as long as they are treated with scorn and contumely; as long as they are cast out and denied, it is not to be wondered at that the leaders, finding themselves and their organizations outlawed, should in turn be guilty of outlawry; that being cast out, they should resort to the weapon of the outcast; that being denied a hearing after the manner of orderly and reasoning friends, they should make themselves heard after the manner of destructive and unreasoning foes."

Holmes was in complete accord; but he sought to explain that such acts often go beyond excuses or justification and have an ultimate explanation: "When John Brown captured Harper's

Ferry and instigated armed rebellion against the United States, I remember that Theodore Parker applauded the exploit and comforted the old hero of Osawatomie with the declaration that the road to heaven was as short from the gallows as from the altar and throne. When the Nihilists of Russia began that awful series of outrages in Russia, in the early 70's, which culminated in the assassination of Czar Alexander II, I remember that Wendell Phillips approved these acts of violence, on the ground that there was no other way of fighting against the despotism of the empire and that if he were in Russia the bomb would be his weapon. I would not justify the McNamaras; 1911 is not yet 1859, and America is not yet Russia, even in the steel industry."

Holmes arraigned the steel industry, tacitly supported the Mc-Namaras by identifying himself with them, and then began a new, easily misunderstood train of thought: "This I would say! The McNamaras, not criminals in the ordinary acceptance of that word, committed their offenses in no spirit of selfishness or lust, destroyed property and life with no thought of personal gain, rightly or wrongly regarded themselves as soldiers in the cause and thought they were serving a 'principle,' as one of the brothers has said. When I see a steel corporation, on the one hand, fostered by an exorbitant protective tariff, manning its works with the cheapest pauper labor of Europe, getting its raw material out of mother earth, which belongs of right to no private individual or aggregation of individuals, using its stupendous power to destroy all organizations of labor, working many of its helpless and cowed laborers seven days a week, twelve hours a day, and paying them the most wretched starvation wages—when I see this corporation, I say, on the one side, with its manifold social crimes—and then see, on the other side, these foolish McNamaras, with their bombs and torches—I say to you this, that I believe there is infinitely more peril to America in the criminal corporation than in the criminal laborer. And I say to you this also—that if I had to make my choice between being a respectable and honored leader of this corporation and being the bloodstained criminal in the dungeons of San Quentin, I would gladly choose to be the latter."

There was no doubt where both men stood. In fact, Holmes

realized his sermon might be misinterpreted and misquoted; but he had to speak bluntly: "I want you as my people to know, beyond all doubt, just where I, as your minister, stand on this burning question. I want you to know that, in this present fight, I am on the side of labor. I excuse none of its crimes, I pardon none of its criminals, but no crime and no criminal can ever shake my faith in the justice of its cause."

The next month, *American Industries* featured an editorial entitled "McNamaras of the Pulpit" and said, "It must be a strange obsession which would permit a minister of the Gospel to condone violence and assassination." The church had every right to denounce the so-called evils of capitalism or infraction of the law by employers of labor, "but when members of the church knowingly and with emphasis undertake to defend or apologize for such dastardly acts as those committed by the McNamaras, a halt should be called to their activities. We have had two particularly vicious examples of ministerial radicalism run mad during this past month."

Quoting both Holmes and Wise extensively, the magazine turned the attack specifically against Wise. The editors refuted his contention that labor had been denied a hearing and argued that "if the rabbi knew more of the subject, he would feel as other citizens do, that organized labor is the Big Noise of the country. When labor leaders are not clamoring for more pay and less work, they are clamoring for less work and more pay."

When Wise read the editorial, he saw little else than the diatribe against himself and Holmes. He telephoned Holmes and asked him to unite in a joint libel action. Holmes, not sure of the law, was hesitant about going to court. He was both dubious about the seriousness of the attack and wary of the inroads on time and money such a suit would entail. Perhaps Wise would understand Holmes' diffidence if he knew a little more of the state of Holmes' finances. Holmes wrote to Wise:

> I have never told you anything of my private affairs, but the fact is that I have not a cent in the world other than what I earn from month to month, and this, as you may imagine, is spent each month down to the last dollar. I, therefore, have not a single cent to fall back upon for the sinews of war in such a case as this,

and I fear, therefore, that this handicap is too great for me to overcome.

Yet he had confidence in Wise's judgment and would abide by any decision he made:

> If you have talked this matter over, however, with any competent lawyer, I shall be grateful to you if you will let me share in his counsel. If, knowing all the facts in my case, he advises me to enter upon such a suit as this, I should not hesitate to follow, as I believe in being obedient to expert opinion.

Within a fortnight Wise reported to Holmes that expert opinion was against legal action. Benjamin Cardozo, one of the most brilliant men at the bar and later a Supreme Court Justice, had so advised him. While the heading of the article, "McNamaras of the Pulpit," was a libel, and the assertion that Wise had condoned and defended violence or assassination was equally libelous, Cardozo counseled caution. A libel suit, he pointed out, would be feasible only where "resort to the law becomes a real duty in order to vindicate a deep and not merely nominal injury to one's character and reputation." He agreed that the two men had been subjected to "an unjust—a cruel and unjust—interpretation of the meaning of your words"; but he would not advise them to sue.

Not long after, Holmes sent Wise a copy of his new book, an expansion of the Meadville lecture, *The Revolutionary Function of the Modern Church.* Holmes' publisher, G. P. Putnam's Sons, had doubted the book's prospects, for its title was incendiary and the author comparatively unknown. Holmes was persuaded to provide funds for printing while Putnam undertook advertising and marketing. To enable John to subsidize the book, Madeleine, always the thrifty housewife, trimmed the household budget. All clothes were mended and every meal consisted of plain food; meanwhile seven-year-old Roger and four-year-old Frances watched Father carefully read the long pages of printer's proof.

Audacious in subject matter and name, *The Revolutionary Function of the Modern Church* was Holmes' first major book and made an impact on its readers. Dedicated "to the glorious memory of Theodore Parker," it reflected on every page Parker's emphasis on "the supremacy of religion and its commanding power in every relation of life, both the life of the individual and the life of the state." The New York *Times* judged it "an earnest, rational, and illuminating presentation of practical conclusions as of the social duty of the church," and the Boston *Transcript* considered it "both historical and prophetic, a vigorous statement." The book took hold immediately and sold well.

Wise, too, had a book in mind. Up to now he had published only occasional articles, his sermons, the *Beth Israel Pulpit* and *The Free Synagogue Pulpit,* and his doctoral dissertation on Solomon ibn-Gabirol. This book would be based on his eventful two decades as a rabbi. Wise was up at five every morning, sometimes earlier, and began to outline some of the adventurous chapters of New York in the nineties, Portland's six happy—and, now in retrospect, idyllic—years, and these last five crowded years in New York. This book he must write. Perhaps next summer at Lake Placid on Buck Island in the quiet of Camp Willamette.

Other things came first, however. In late April of 1911, Wise and Henry Morgenthau had visited Governor Woodrow Wilson of New Jersey at the Hotel Plaza in New York and asked him to speak at the fourth anniversary dinner at the Hotel Astor. Wilson delighted Wise by his knowledge of the Free Synagogue's program and his willingness to attend the banquet. As the men thanked him and then prepared to leave, Wilson introduced his wife, Ellen Axson Wilson, who told Wise she read everything of his she saw in print and added, "I thank you for what you have been saying about Mr. Wilson."

Two and a half months later, Henry Morgenthau, as presiding officer, introduced the speakers at the Astor dinner. In an entry in his journal, kept faithfully during those years of 1911 and 1912, Wise expressed disappointment that Senator William Borah's talk was "a blank cartridge." As for Holmes, Wise reported "a seven minute speech that was brilliant. It was such a generous, warmhearted, and loving utterance with regard to me, and so full of the magnanimity which he always shows and feels toward me that he just won the hearts of all, who gave him a stirring welcome and a magnificent storm of applause at the close."

Wilson's talk was, however, the most remarkable: "I don't know that I have heard a public address which made upon all uniformly the deep and convincing impression which his address did. He was simple, quiet, and precise in his mode of utterance, but the man, real, genuine, singleminded, shines through every luminous word. It was a wonderful climax to the whole evening, and withal he is so modest and simple."

Wise had been a Republican; but with this "philosopher-king" in prospect, he would forsake the Republican Party. Wise had no respect, let alone love, for the Democrats, especially after having lived most of his life amid the stench and chicanery of Tammany. Had the Republicans intended to choose Charles Evans Hughes, then Associate Justice of the Supreme Court, Wise would have been inclined to vote for him. For Taft he had great affection but little regard; and as for Theodore Roosevelt, he thought him an exceedingly able man but not to be compared with Woodrow Wilson.

Wise discovered that George Foster Peabody, the philanthropist and humanitarian, agreed with him about Wilson. In the late winter of 1912, Wise traveled to Glens Falls in upstate New York to speak on "Religion and Industrial Justice" before a large audience in the First Baptist Church. Afterward, Peabody took him by trolley to Lake George where a horse-drawn sleigh awaited them for the ride to Peabody's lakeside home, deep amid the snow-laden pines. Before a roaring fire in the living room the two men talked until one in the morning, and then again after breakfast during a sleigh ride across the hills. Both felt Wilson was the only hope for liberals; without him, another party would have to be started.

Adolph Ochs, publisher of the New York *Times*, was certain that William Howard Taft would be nominated and that Theodore Roosevelt in his bid for the Republican nomination would be badly beaten. The Democrats, he predicted, had little chance even with such a forlorn hope as Wilson. Wise was furious at this and told Ochs, "The *Times* and all other journals in this country have done us a great wrong in refusing to allow the public to form a fair judgment of a great man like Wilson."

Ochs retorted, "Why didn't Wilson make the right impression on uncontrolled journals, such as the *Times?*"

Wise fumed, and then resorted to the solution he found increasingly satisfying. He confided to his journal: "Ochs is a very little man in a very big place."

By mid-June, the Wise family was settled again at Lake Placid, and the rabbi started work on the book *My Twenty Years' Battle in the Ministry;* but interruptions were legion. Letters and telegrams, centering mostly on presidential prospects, intruded almost hourly.

The Republican Convention seemed deadlocked between Taft and Roosevelt; Charles Evans Hughes loomed as a compromise candidate. When the New York leaders sent Judge William H. Wadhams to ask Hughes for permission to nominate him, the Justice refused. In his Lake Placid home, Camp Abenski, Hughes talked over the matter with his neighbor, Stephen Wise, and prepared a statement outlining his reasons for declining any nomination even before it could be made. A man cannot step from the Supreme Court bench to elective office, Hughes asserted, for then Supreme Court decisions might be prepared for their political effect and be criticized for partisanship. Nothing would more swiftly weaken the nation's confidence in its courts. In no other way could the judiciary steadfastly remain independent.

Wise asked him, "But Mr. Justice, if there were an extraordinary crisis in the land, would that not make it your duty to accept the nomination?"

Hughes, who would change his mind four years later, answered without hesitation, "No man is as essential to his country's well-being as is the unstained integrity of the courts." Wise then accepted Hughes' invitation to announce the decision to the press.

On the second of July, Wise was in the town of Lake Placid and walked by the Western Union office just two minutes after the operator had received word that the Democrats in their Baltimore Convention had nominated Woodrow Wilson for the Presidency. The Western Union man called the news to Wise, who shouted aloud in joy.

Wise's views on Woodrow Wilson's nomination were those of Henry Morgenthau's telegram to him: "Too good to be true—the greatest moral victory of the century."

Wise now laid the planned book aside and devoted himself to the campaign. A few days later, he wrote a number of lifelong Republicans and asked them to join in presenting Wilson with a program to supplement the Democratic platform. Nothing ever developed from the proposal, and, by the fall, Wise had been swept into the vortex of the campaign by the Democratic Party.

The Progressives nominated Theodore Roosevelt as the "Bull Moose" candidate; to him Holmes gave support, but not without uncertainty, for Wise, ruminating about the campaign, wrote one summer night in his journal:

> Dear Holmes wrote me a characteristically beautiful letter in which I can see that he is all at sea. He does not know what to do, seeming to hesitate between Roosevelt, whom he only half trusts, and the Socialist [Eugene V. Debs] from whom he instinctively shrinks, as do I.

Wise regretted, however, that the Democratic Party platform was so mild:

> If the Democratic party platform were that of the Progressives, it would be much easier for me. But I cannot help sharing to a very small extent the fear of Holmes and the rest that Wilson may not be strong enough, because no man would be big enough to avoid being influenced, if not dominated, in some degree by the rotten and terribly corrupt bosses of the Democratic Party.

Wise was apprehensive about Wilson's chances:

> There are too many conservative people in his entourage and he has not met the issues now before the people with the same simplicity and directness which we have come to associate with his public utterances. Personally, I do not feel that I need any reassurance of his own progressive principles and devotion to social reform, but unless he begins to strike, and strike hard, he will lose the Progressive votes, which may go to Roosevelt and even possibly elect him, although the latter is hardly likely.

Announcing himself as a Republican in support of Wilson,

Wise then prepared a statement for publication and distribution among the voters of Maine and Vermont.

A week before the election, Wise was in Philadelphia on the same platform with Wilson, who spoke for an hour in the same simple, earnest fashion. Wise noted: "He had a fine reception, although one missed the roar which one is accustomed to hear at the Roosevelt meetings. He may not command the frenzy of the zealous, but he does command the respect of the thoughtful, which to me is better."

Holmes' support of Theodore Roosevelt put him in an embarrassing situation on the Sunday before election when there occurred an incident of which there are varying accounts. Holmes remembers that, shortly before the Sunday morning service, his head usher received a phone call from the Secret Service informing him that President William Howard Taft, prominent in the Unitarian Church, was in New York that day and would attend the Church of the Messiah. Holmes made no change in the service and preached the sermon he had prepared. That was all.

Wise's version was different. He recalled on many occasions, as in this version related twenty-six years later, that Justine, then nine, answered the telephone and heard Holmes say: "Justine, I must speak to your father at once. It is very important. Hurry!"

Wise then picked up the telephone. "Yes, Holmes, what is it?"

"Wise, I just heard that President Taft is coming to church this morning."

"That's splendid, Holmes, just splendid. When I saw him in Washington some weeks ago, I told him he should do just that, for his old friend Collyer had a successor he should hear. I'm delighted to hear it. If you can, give the President my warm regards."

"But, Wise, don't you understand? This is going to be difficult. I am preaching this morning on the subject, 'Why I Plan to Vote for the Progressive Party.' "

Wise answered: "There's nothing to do but stick to your guns and be as kind as you can be." Holmes did so; and as *The Unitarian* reported, deleted only one paragraph, an unimportant statement by Senator Albert Beveridge.

As Wise enjoyed telling it in after years, he saw Taft in the diner of a train one day and asked him how he had enjoyed Holmes. Taft chuckled and, his massive frame shaking with laughter, said, "Yes, Rabbi, I went to the Church of the Messiah and heard your young friend Holmes. I must say, the only thing he did *not* do for Teddy that morning was to take up a collection for the Bull Moose Party!"

Several days later, the eighty-nine-year-old Robert Collyer became ill, rallied briefly, and then sank swiftly. Wise called Holmes to ask if he might visit Collyer and, the next day, received a note:

> I spoke to the Collyers about your offer to call upon the Doctor, and they were greatly pleased by your thoughtfulness. Just at present, however, they feel that the Doctor ought not to see more than his two or three regular callers, and therefore they are going to ask you to wait for a little time and hope that he may improve sufficiently to see you. I shall be glad to give you the word when you can come.

The word never came because near midnight on Saturday, November 30, Robert Collyer died. Holmes' announcement in the church service the next day was the first news the congregation had. Holmes' voice suddenly broke as he told the congregation: "Like Enoch in the Bible, of whom Dr. Collyer preached so often, he was not, for God took him."

11. If I Forget Thee, O Jerusalem

> *If I were to sum up the Basel Congress in a
> single phrase—which I would not dare to make
> public—I would say: In Basel I created the
> Jewish State. Were I to say this aloud I would
> be greeted by universal laughter. But perhaps
> five years hence, in any case certainly fifty
> years hence, everyone will perceive it.*
>
> —THEODOR HERZL, 1897

ZIONISM, to which Stephen Wise gave so much time and effort
after 1897 and which remained a burning conviction in the following decades, was now to become an ever more important
part of his life.

With the Free Synagogue well established, the Wises decided
to visit Europe and Palestine in 1913. The entire family toured
part of the Continent; then the children were put in school in
Germany, while Stephen and Louise traveled to Palestine, at that
time regarded as unsafe for children.

Holmes, too, planned a trip abroad, but only to the British
Isles. He and Wise met briefly in London early that summer, for
he was on his way to Yorkshire. In the spring, the Collyer family
had asked Holmes to prepare a biography of his late associate;
Holmes began gathering a number of Robert Collyer's unpublished poems and addresses and preparing them for the publisher
under the title *Clear Grit*. Now he would travel through the
countryside from which Collyer had come.

Collyer's habitat impressed Holmes. He relived the history
of the region made famous by Cromwell and his Roundheads,

127

the Wars of the Roses, and the riots of the Chartists. He visited the scenes of Collyer's childhood and youth, the grubby factory at Blubberhouses where the boy had worked, and the little home where Collyer had lived more than three quarters of a century before. He walked the lonely moors, changing from green of springtime to late summer's purple, and often enveloped in mist. He photographed the birthplace, the old smithy, the schoolhouse and church, and scanned the registers of the parish chapel. He now understood why the old man, when asked about his origins, would jest, "We have no family tree, only this low bush."

After his stay in Yorkshire, and later in Scotland and Wales, Holmes boarded the S.S. *Laconia* for home. He was disturbed by an unfulfilled commitment: He had promised to write a hymn for the Young People's Religious Union and their early fall conference and as yet he had composed nothing. As the *Laconia* drew closer to New York, suddenly the inspiration came. It was one of those "explosions of the mind" to which he always ascribed a creative event in his intellectual life. He hurried inside, found a desk in the writing room, and began to write. He could scarcely put the words on paper fast enough, so swiftly did the lines come.

He copied it afresh and from the pier mailed it to the committee. A week later he attended the conference and heard the young people sing his words to the well-known melody of "Webb." His hymn, "The Voice of God Is Calling," was to become one of the most popular of the Social Gospel era and Holmes would hear it sung hundreds of times in later years, not only in its English version but in German, Spanish, and Japanese translations too:

> The voice of God is calling
>   Its summons unto men;
> As once he spake in Zion,
>   So now he speaks again;
> Whom shall I send to succor
>   My people in their need,
> Whom shall I send to loosen
>   The bonds of shame and greed?
>
> I hear my people crying
>   In cot and mine and slum;

No field or mart is silent,
No city street is dumb.
I see my people falling
In darkness and despair.
Whom shall I send to shatter
The fetters which they bear?

We heed, O Lord, thy summons,
And answer: Here are we!
Send us upon thine errand!
Let us thy servants be!
Our strength is dust and ashes,
Our years a passing hour!
But thou canst use our weakness
To magnify thy power.

From ease and plenty save us;
From pride of place absolve;
Purge us of low desire;
Lift us to high resolve.
Take us and make us holy;
Teach us thy will and way.
Speak, and, behold! we answer;
Command, and we obey!

Meanwhile Stephen and Louise Wise journeyed to the Holy Land. Their entrance was not propitious, for they were angered and humiliated by the Turkish requirement that they sign a document promising to leave Palestine within four weeks. But once within the country, they were stimulated and inspirited by their observation of new Jewish life in ancient communities.

After two days on the coast, they made the journey "up to Jerusalem." Here Wise's first act was to visit his grandmother's grave which he found in a place of honor among the burial sites of famed rabbinical scholars. She had not been forgotten, for many recalled to Stephen, even after twenty years, the charity she had dispensed by living on little and giving much to the poor.

The Wises were moved by the aspiration, the hardships, and the endurance of the Jews. The comparatively small Jewish population in Jerusalem and the fewer than one hundred thousand

Jews in all of Palestine possessed a certain dignity. They gave the land a unique quality by founding communal settlements, the *Kvutzot,* reviving the ancient Hebrew language, and beginning a new Hebraic art and culture. Wise never forgot the stubborn pioneers at Dagania and Hadera who doggedly irrigated arid land, drained malarial swamps, and afforested barren hillsides, despite a Turkish tax on each new tree. An innovation in Palestine was the medical assistance of an American women's organization, founded in New York by Henrietta Szold only the year before and called Hadassah, "the healing of the daughter of my people."

Yet all this was a far cry from the Jewish State envisaged by Zionists the world over. While in Palestine, Wise was impatient with delays, angered by the deceptions and lies of Turkish officials, nauseated by filth and odors, oppressed by poverty and ignorance everywhere, and debilitated by the heat, even in those midspring days. He wondered if there would ever be a Jewish State.

As their ship started its voyage across the Mediterranean to Europe, he could see in the distance the few houses of a new city rising on the sand dunes, hopefully bearing the name Tel Aviv, "Hill of Springtime"; its optimistic and enterprising mayor, Meir Dizengoff, had told him it would perhaps someday grow to have a population of as many as a hundred thousand Jews.

In the first months of 1914, Stephen Wise began working with a group of his closest associates in American Jewry to gather funds and send a Commission of Investigation to Palestine; among the supporters were Jacob H. Schiff, Henry Morgenthau, Louis D. Brandeis, and Nathan Straus. Wise persuaded each to contribute a large sum toward the project.

Soon he heard disquieting reports about Schiff's flagging interest in things Palestinian and he feared "the Haifa Affair" might be the cause. Palestinian Jews were insisting that Hebrew, not German, become the language to be used at the Technical Institute in Haifa. To this move, overseas founders of the Haifa Technion took exception; American Jews of German extraction, among them Schiff, lodged especially strong objections. Schiff told Wise that, in his opinion, Palestinian Jewry was largely controlled by Jewish nationalists who had little interest in or attachment to Judaism itself; as for himself, he intended to withdraw from the project. The loss of Schiff's sponsorship in both name and funds was no small matter. Yet, though Schiff's place was filled by no other, his unfulfilled commitment was absorbed by the remaining members of the planning committee.

The Commission was chosen to make a social survey of the conditions in the Jewish community in Palestine and was sent amid considerable publicity. When it appeared that the name of Henry Morgenthau as a backer of the Commission might prejudice its success because he was ambassador to the nation controlling Palestine, Wise's quick trip to Washington cleared that problem; and he was able to announce Morgenthau's withdrawal.

When war broke out in Europe that summer, it was apparent to Wise that organizations in the Jewish community would have to band together on a more democratic basis. Only thus could American Jewry provide the kind of leadership which, in his mind, had not been coming from Jacob Schiff and Louis Marshall who guided the affairs of the American Jewish Committee. Wise became involved in many meetings preliminary to the formation, many months later, of an American Jewish Congress.

His time and energies were drained. Wise was lonely and weary while waiting in Washington to meet Secretary of the Navy Josephus Daniels in order to arrange for the shipment of produce for Palestinian Jews aboard an American cruiser. He wrote to Louise that he was about to attend an American Jewish Congress meeting "that will probably last hours. It is hard and wearing, but I should feel that I were perfidious as a Jew and disloyal as an American not to have my part, such as it is, in guiding the superbly democratic passions of the representative body of Israel in America."

At the end of August, 1914, Wise helped to establish the Provisional Executive Committee for General Zionist Affairs. Its chairman, Louis D. Brandeis, well known as a recently convinced Zionist and famous as "the people's lawyer," gave leadership second to none in the Jewish community. To Wise, Brandeis was an embodiment of Lincoln and Isaiah; Lincoln because he looked like his fellow Kentuckian and was moved by the same compassion, Isaiah because he was of peerless moral stature.

In addition to his Zionist activities, Wise was at this time busy from daybreak, when he arose to read and write and then have breakfast with the children, until after midnight meetings had come to an end. It was something of a minor miracle for him to find the time to take Louise to the farewell performance of the great English actor, Sir Johnston Forbes-Robertson, in G. B. Shaw's *Caesar and Cleopatra*. Such moments of relaxation were rare, for if synagogue and Jewish matters did not claim him, social problems did. He gave careful attention to the co-operation between the Social Service Division of the Free Synagogue and the Church of the Messiah, and secured large gifts of money and clothing for the ever-growing numbers of unemployed in those years. He often referred to Holmes' statement in the Messiah pulpit in 1914: "I want to smash this social system and replace it with such an order of economic justice as would at least lift the thousand ills of poverty now weighing upon us like a millstone around the neck," and recorded himself as in agreement.

Holmes was more restrained in his statement than in 1911 when he seemed to give a blanket approval to the action of organized labor and its representatives in the struggle against management and capital; as an adherent of socialist views, he now laid the blame more on the "system" than upon the key men who ran the system. His unsympathetic attitude toward the social order but a more sympathetic, understanding critique of the ruling groups were reflected in a letter of May 6, 1914, to Upton Sinclair. Sinclair was a leader in the protest demonstrations against John D. Rockefeller, Jr., in particular and the Colorado Fuel and Iron Company in general. He invited Holmes to take part in the picketing of the Rockefeller offices at 26 Broadway and thus lodge a tangible objection to the policies which had resulted in the "Ludlow massacre" of late April, 1914.

Holmes readily recalled the gunfire between the militia men on one hill and the tent colony of the striking miners and their families on an opposite hill, the militia's burning of the miners' camp, the loss of life among the strikers on the firing line of battle, and the discovery the following morning of eleven children and two women who had suffocated at the bottom of a cave in seeking refuge from the cross fire. He assured Sinclair that he felt "as strongly as you do—indeed as strongly as any man can —about the Colorado situation," for, he said with understandable overstatement, "a more terrible and inexcusable horror has never been perpetrated, I believe, in the history of our nation."

Yet Holmes wanted Sinclair to know that "in regard to the agitation which you are now conducting at 26 Broadway . . . I cannot agree at all." He had no question as to Sinclair's "sincerity," and he had "the closest sympathy . . . with your feelings, but I cannot for the life of me see that you are accomplishing anything by this funeral parade business." Not only did Holmes question "the character of the movement which you have set on foot against Mr. Rockefeller," but added: "Nay, I go further, and say that I cannot see wherein such an agitation as this fits in with our socialistic philosophy at all."

Holmes wanted to remind Sinclair of the basic beliefs which had undergirded their thought and action in previous years and made specific his disagreement:

> I believe, as I thought you believed, that we are up against *not* cruel individuals, but unjust social conditions. Rockefeller is no Nero, that he should be prosecuted in this fashion. . . . My supply of ammunition in this battle is limited, as is that of every individual. I have just so much time and so much strength and so much money that I can give to the cause. This being the case, I propose to fire not one single ounce of this ammunition at any individual, however atrocious his attitude may seem to be, but level my whole battery at the social system itself.

The gradual realization on the part of John D. Rockefeller, Jr., that he had been badly briefed by his executives in both New York and Colorado and his enlightenment after a visit to the Colorado mines resulted in a statesmanlike labor-management policy that became known as the "Colorado Plan." His change of mind was anticipated in part by Holmes' insistence to Upton Sinclair in the spring of 1914 that Rockefeller was "simply a poor, ignorant chap whose ideas have been wholly perverted by the environment in which he has been reared and by the counsellors by whom he has been surrounded, and who, in his weak, pietistic way, is just as sincere in his desire to do good as you are." While Holmes and John D. Rockefeller, Jr., never met and at no time had views entirely in common, the attitudes of each, insofar as social consciousness and awakened consciences were concerned, slowly came nearer each other in subsequent years.

Wise had the opportunity to utter similar views when in 1915 the Central Conference of American Rabbis appointed him chairman of the Commission on Social Justice. Here was his chance to urge Reform Judaism to found a Social Justice Commission as had the Methodists, Congregationalists, and Unitarians.

Holmes, himself busy beyond belief, looked at Wise and marveled at the man's stamina and resilience. When B. W. Huebsch asked Wise to do a book on *The Art of Living*, there was a certain irony, for while Wise exulted in "the strenuous life," he was the first to admit there was little time for art in such a crowded schedule.

By 1916 Wise was able to carry on his activities, encourage the Free Synagogue in its ninth year of existence, and, at the same time, aid his wife in the founding of a Child Adoption Committee. Louise's committee changed the program of Jewish child care in New York City, for in those days unwanted children were assigned to orphan asylums or boarded out in foster homes. She felt that children deprived of a home and the love of parents could not grow to normal adulthood. Aided by Sidney Goldstein and his staff, she started a plan of placing "homeless children in childless homes" and soon had a long list of applications.

Children who had formerly been left in orphan asylums were now moving out into homes across the country. Before each trip that he took Louise would give her husband the names and addresses of families so that he could, whenever possible, call or see them. On one such trip he wrote from Iowa:

> I saw today how good and blessed is your work. I told the D——'s, with whom I stayed, of your Child Adoption labors and they said at once that I must see the little N—— girl. At night, at the Temple, I saw the parents and visited them this morning. We do not, cannot love our children any more than

these people love their little girl, whom I dimly remember. I
want to write a report of the home.

A few months later, he wrote from Philadelphia:

> . . . A moment ago I was touched by something that I prize
> more than a French decoration—a poor Jewish newsboy came to
> me saying, "I know who you are and what you have done for the
> Jews. God keep you alive for the sake of our people." More than
> I deserved but exactly what I most coveted. Well, dearest, we
> have some form of immortality before us—for you the blessings
> of the babes, though they know it not, and as for myself a day's
> remembrance by my people. A day is a long time for a little.

Wise concentrated now on the American Jewish Congress. In
March, 1916, he gave a keynote address that asked for open
deliberations and no secret negotiations: "Secrecy, always futile
as a curative method, has proven disastrous in prolonging and
intensifying Jewish woes." He repudiated the idea of relief to
Jews as the sole policy of the Congress; he sought for his fellow
Jews "not relief but redress, not palliation but prevention; not
charity but justice—the only program worthy of a great and proud
people."

Once again Wise tried to help his fellow Jews understand the
greatness of their history. Sufferance was their badge but with
strength they might achieve another fate. He scorned the as-
similationists who tried to wipe out distinguishing characteristics
and allow themselves to be absorbed in Gentile society. While
he did not believe in segregation of the Jew, he also did not
believe in an integration that would lose Jewish distinctiveness.
Toward these ends—an awareness of the peoplehood of the Jews,
a realization and fulfillment of their ethnic consciousness in
Zionism, a broad democratic representation of the American Jewish community, and the achievement of equal rights and full
justice for all creeds and races—the American Jewish Congress,
he felt, was to press steadily and surely.

It was disconcerting for him to have to counter the assertions
of his friend and supporter, Henry Morgenthau, who, in an address in Cincinnati on "Palestine and Zionism," excoriated Zionism as un-American and contended that Palestine was cursed

with economic conditions which made Zionism only an illusion. Wise's opposition to Morgenthau's anti-Zionism was expressed in a sermon at Carnegie Hall, but was made more difficult and complicated by an incident the following spring. Wise asked Morgenthau, as Chairman of the Board of Trustees of the Free Synagogue, to preside at a Sunday morning service while he was absent in Washington, but he did not disclose to Morgenthau the purpose of his trip to the capital. The former ambassador was at first astonished, and then angered, to read in the Monday New York *Times* a Washington dispatch concerning a conference at the White House the previous day between Woodrow Wilson and a group of Jewish leaders, who sought presidential approval for a declaration by the British on behalf of a Jewish National Home in Palestine.

Morgenthau immediately telephoned Wise and said it was incongruous for him to have replaced Wise at the time the rabbi was seeking presidential sanction for a project to which he, Morgenthau, was and always would be unalterably opposed. He was therefore resigning as president of the Synagogue. When Wise returned from Washington, he went immediately to Morgenthau's home; but his friend refused to rescind the resignation. Morgenthau pointed out that he was not relinquishing lay leadership of the congregation, but resigning only from the presidency. He was, furthermore, not questioning Wise's freedom or his own freedom "regarding Zionism." He hoped "the friendly and cordial relations which have long obtained between Dr. Wise and myself will be unaffected by this decision," but he had to forgo "the happy and inspiring association with Dr. Wise because our views of Zionism . . . are so diverse and apparently irreconcilable."

That whole year of 1917, up to the time of the announcement of the Balfour Declaration by Great Britain, was one of the most hectic Wise had ever known. Early in January of 1917, he noted in his engagement book: "Celebrate early in month the Hudson Theatre Addresses"; but he had no further chance to plan an observance in the following weeks. Occasionally, on his trips in and out of town, mostly to Washington, he was able to reflect on the many objectives achieved since 1907. At the end of January he did help Holmes celebrate his own tenth anniversary in New York; but by April, when the tenth anniversary of the formal organization of the Free Synagogue could have been observed, events came so swiftly that he had little time even to take note of the day. America's entry into the World War was imminent; and not until late in April could he ask the rhetorical question at a celebration, "Is the Free Synagogue Worthwhile?"

There was no doubt in his mind as to the answer. He had a base of operations from which he could write and speak at will, but also a source of spiritual vitality with which to seek a better world. Most significant of all was the opportunity this post afforded him to participate in the formulation of the Balfour Declaration, which, when issued on November 2, 1917, stated that His Majesty's Government looked with favor upon the establishment in Palestine of a National Home for the Jewish people. Here he played a key role, first in securing official approval from the White House, then in working on its specific phrasing. The rest of his life was devoted to securing its implementation.

12. Why Do the Nations Rage?

> *Break Thou the spell of enchantments that*
> *make the nations drunk with the lust of battle*
> *and draw them on as willing tools of death.*
> *Grant us a quiet and steadfast mind when our*
> *own nation clamors for vengeance and aggres-*
> *sion. O Thou strong Father of all nations, draw*
> *all Thy great family together with an increas-*
> *ing sense of our common blood and destiny,*
> *that peace may come on earth at last, and Thy*
> *sun may shed its light rejoicing on a holy*
> *brotherhood of peoples.*
>
> —WALTER RAUSCHENBUSCH

IN EARLY AUGUST, 1914, when the Great War broke out in Europe, John Haynes Holmes immediately laid plans for a Peace Meeting at the Church of the Messiah. He invited his colleagues of the nonsectarian services of two and three years earlier, Frank Oliver Hall and Stephen Wise, to reaffirm with him their hope for a warless world. His outlook, reflected in magazine articles, was one of optimism: "Peace is at hand after all, for we see, in this final agony of blood and iron, the terrible spectacle of the devil of militarism rending its way out of the stricken body of humanity."

Yet from optimistic heights Holmes soon plunged to depths of despondency as the carnage and destruction increased and spread. In "A Minister's Letter to His People," he wrote: "The dance of death begins anew. Civilization is gone in one fell instant; and in its place is barbarism, with all its train of robbing, ravishing, and killing. What is civilization that it avails nothing at this hour? What is religion that it is impotent to still the devouring passions now raging through the world? We have talked much in days gone by of progress, brotherhood, and peace. What now, in the lurid light of present events, do these things mean?"

There seemed but one answer: these things meant that "all must become as crusaders battling for a holy sepulchre . . . fight war and the ideas of war with singleness of purpose, unyielding tenacity of war, consuming fires of passion, and all the unsparing and uncompromising fanaticisms of zeal."

In that crusading spirit, Holmes could willingly take part in Woodrow Wilson's Peace Day in October, 1914. The President's call, sent out to 130,000 churches by the Federal Council of Churches of Christ in America and by the Church Peace Union, included prayers by Bishop David H. Greer and the Rev. William T. Manning, and a hymn by Holmes.

In the late winter of 1915, at the eighth anniversary celebration of the Free Synagogue, Holmes' appeal for "Cessation of War" not only condemned war but also deplored militarism and refuted the claim that war was necessary to save civilization from extinction:

> There are some—yea, there are many!—who are ready to assert that this foul business is sometimes and somewheres justifiable. This I deny without qualification or evasion of any kind. War is never justifiable at any time or under any circumstances. No man is wise enough, no nation is important enough, no human interest is precious enough, to justify the wholesale destruction and murder which constitute the essence of war. Human life is alone sacred. The interests of human life are alone sovereign. War, as we have now seen, is the enemy of life and all its interests. Therefore in the name of life and for the sake of life, do I declare to you, that war must be condemned universally and unconditionally.

He used Walt Whitman's language, "as forceful as it is inelegant," to remind them, as Whitman had his generation: "O God! This whole war business! I say, 'God damn the wars—all wars: God damn every war! God damn 'em! God damn 'em!' "

When the S.S. *Lusitania* was sunk by a German submarine in

May, 1915, Holmes was asked whether retaliation was now justified. He responded: "This is an hour for lamentation but not for
anger, an hour for grief, not for madness. There is no more reason
why we should go to war with Germany today than there was
yesterday. In the face of this monstrous horror, we should reaffirm our love of peace and our faith in reason and good will.
The President, guided by divine wisdom, will find the right path
and must be supported as he strives to lead us therein."

The President's "wisdom," whether divinely inspired or
humanly impelled, led him, however, to talk of preparedness;
and toward this end, Wilson appealed for public support. But
Holmes had only scorn for the men running about the country
and calling for preparedness. He distilled this disdain in a letter
to Henry Wise Wood, chairman of the Conference Committee
on National Preparedness, who had asked him, along with tens
of thousands of other ministers, to urge preparedness:

> I regard your letter as very like an insult to the profession of
> which I am a member and to the church which I have the honor
> to serve. I regard your movement as a betrayal of the Chris-
> tianity I serve. I look upon it as a menace to the America
> I love. . . . There may be ministers of Christ who are ready to
> give aid and comfort to the business which your Committee has
> in hand, but I am not one of them. On the contrary, I am pledged
> to the gospel of love, to the task of brotherhood, to the ministry
> of reconciliation.

Such a ministry was the basis on which pacifists banded together in the autumn of 1915 when Holmes and his peace-
minded friends formally founded the American branch of the
International Fellowship of Reconciliation. Earlier that year, John
R. Mott of the World's Y.M.C.A. had brought to America the
English Quaker, Henry Hodgkin, who had organized the Fellowship of Reconciliation in Great Britain in 1914. The F.O.R. was a
group of religiously impelled pacifists who refused to take part
in war and articulately mounted an attack on the evils of warfare.
As militant pacifists, they considered pacifism a vocation, a duty,
a religious imperative.

Under the auspices of the Fellowship of Reconciliation in the
winter of 1915–1916, a member of the British Parliament, Francis

Nielson, came to America and spoke at Holmes' church on the causes and cures of war, and, at the Free Synagogue, on "National Armaments and International Hatreds." For both Holmes and Wise, especially for Holmes, Nielson's trip to America began a warm friendship and professional relationship which lasted over the next four decades. Nielson soon became an American citizen and brought new insights and fresh impetus to the peace movement in the United States.

Holmes' pacifist views now took the form of a book, *New Wars for Old* (1916). In its pages, he dealt exhaustively with arguments about force versus nonforce and developed fully his pacifist position in relation to the Great War raging in Europe. He argued for a new technique: nonresistance. Force is not the only way to settle conflict, he maintained, for the pen is mightier than the sword.

Holmes ranged widely in this exposition of radical pacifism and referred not only to the usual authorities—Emerson in his *Lecture on War* and John Fiske in the essay on *The Destiny of Man*—but quoted as well from *Christianity and International Peace* by Charles E. Jefferson of the Broadway Tabernacle, *Non-Resistance* by Clarence Darrow, and *The War God* by the novelist and poet, Israel Zangwill, a friend of Stephen Wise's.

Wise, though pacifist-minded, was not so certain as Holmes about the efficacy and validity of absolute pacifism. He saw that issues of war and peace were not always clearly discerned in blacks and whites but included many shades of gray. From 1914 to 1916, he still maintained, however, an antiwar stand; and although he supported Woodrow Wilson for a second term in 1916, he made known to the President his disagreement with the preparedness policy.

Wise took an active part in two different peace organizations. One was the American Union Against Militarism, of which he, like Holmes, was a charter member. Under its auspices, Wise delivered many addresses in opposition to the National Security League, composed mostly of Republicans and intent on a larger army and navy.

The other organization was the League to Enforce Peace, founded and inspired by former President William Howard Taft.

Here both preparedness advocates and pacifists found themselves welcome; among them were Adolph A. Berle, Sr., a Congregational clergyman and author of *The World Significance of a Jewish State,* and Amos Pinchot, brother of the conservationist Gifford. They, and Wise, disagreed with Holmes' indictment of the League to Enforce Peace as just another means to promote militarism in America. In fact, under its aegis the three men traveled through the Middle West, condemning militarism, urging arbitration as the solution for international conflicts, and countenancing war only as a last resort to enforce peace.

From Detroit, Wise wrote to his wife with both exultation and concern: "The town is full of the meeting and we are truly helped. Pinchot is so fine and Berle hearty and real. The papers are full of war talk and preparedness, and the militarists are 'trailing' us with meetings. The fight must be made. Thank God, there is an anti-war feeling in the country; and we're going to make it stronger. I wish I had ten times the strength."

By the winter of 1916–1917, he had begun to move toward a less pacific view; he wrote from Chicago: "I should like to start a movement to say to Germany: either peace terms now and reparation and security, or else war with us." Some weeks later, enroute to the Midwest: "Alas for another German victory on the sea!"

When Louise confessed her relief that their son, then sixteen, was under age for military service, Wise wrote: "I cannot share your joy in Jim's youth. I wish he were old enough to serve and I young enough."

On the train to Omaha some days later, he reported, "As I go along and talk to folk, I notice that Wilson and the rest of us so thoroughly indoctrinated the country with anti-bellicism that now it has become difficult for them suddenly to turn the corner."

After zeppelins bombed England: "What a noble deed the Germans yesterday wrought in London! Why are they bent upon plumbing the utter deeps of infamy? For centuries German will be synonymous with Hun, and worst of all the armor of their self-approval is impenetrable."

Wise no longer felt comfortable in the meetings of the American Union Against Militarism. Reading aloud the draft of a future sermon which dealt with a peace advocate's outlook on the European War, he cited the heroic example of the Abolitionist William Lloyd Garrison. In the discussion that followed, he was attacked by Oswald Garrison Villard, who was angered that his grandfather's name should be invoked to sanction Wise's equivocal views; Villard took strong exception. If Wise were to preach such a sermon, Villard would not want to speak to him again.

It was an awkward hour for Wise. Perspiration poured down his face, and he intimated he might not deliver the sermon. Yet, shortly thereafter, he did preach it, for his mind moved inexorably toward a position of approving America's entry into the war; and relations between him and Villard were thereafter anything but cordial.

In February, 1917, he suggested a peace plan, an appeal to German-Americans to unite in influencing Germans for the overthrow of Hohenzollern Prussianism. He was critical of Wilson's diplomacy and unreservedly condemned universal military training "as an attempt to Prussianize the United States; and though we have technically every excuse for going to war . . . least of all, we shall not be driven into war by the governmental action of a people, temporarily drunk with bloodlust and obsessed by a mania for self-glorification."

By this time Wise felt it necessary to retreat from his pacifist stand. Consequently he resigned from the American Union Against Militarism. The members of the Union remembered the occasion sadly, for he sweepingly denounced most of his old comrades as pro-German, a startling contrast to the stand he had taken not many months earlier at a large Carnegie Hall meeting. During that gathering, early in 1916, he told the overflow audience he had brought his son to hear him say that no matter who else supported the war, he never would. The principals of the peace organizations of World War I recall that for his contradictory action Wise was not held in great respect in pacifist and near-pacifist circles in the New York area. They felt he had a right to change his mind about the war but not to indulge in what they interpreted as abuse, and that he might have credited others with the sincerity which he correctly attributed to Holmes.

Holmes' pilgrimage was even more arduous, for it went along the straight path of absolute pacifism. To him, war was evil, irrefutably against the will of God. If "sin" was defined as rebellion against the will of God, then this was one time Holmes would invoke the word, no matter how unfashionable "sin" had become in the lexicon of the religious liberal. He had said this for years; and he would say it over and over again.

On the first weekend of February, 1917, he stood virtually alone in New York in refusing to sound the war cry. William Howard Taft addressed a meeting of the League to Enforce Peace in Brooklyn and called for conscription. In Manhattan, Nicholas Murray Butler assured newsmen that Columbia University was preparing for war "at this gravely serious moment." On Wall Street, the Rector of Trinity Church, William T. Manning, announced his support of President Wilson's position against "open and brutal lawlessness and unprovoked aggression"; and on Morningside Heights at St. Luke's Church, G. Ashton Oldham followed the choir into the sanctuary behind a large American flag and told the congregation: "I for one am ready to lay down my life, if my country needs it, for the rights of humanity and what I believe to be the cause of God."

By late March, Holmes felt that the country was about to plunge into the war and announced that the following Sunday, April 1, he would give "A Statement to My People on the Eve of War." He then left the city and went to Boston for a week's stay with his father and mother in Cambridge. In their house near the Harvard campus, Holmes remained in seclusion and again thought through his views on war. He paced the floor. He muttered to himself. He rehearsed sentences or lapsed into complete silence. His mother respected the need for quiet; normally a talkative person at the dinner table, she said little, asked less.

By the end of his week in Cambridge Holmes had cleared his mind and calmed his spirit. He returned to New York and, on Sunday morning, arrived at a church crowded as never before. The throng occupied every available seat and latecomers sat on the balcony stairs, the platform below the pulpit, even in the aisles. The worship service was reverent, as it always was under his leadership. He showed not the slightest anxiety as he moved not into the pulpit but to the center of the lower platform, and, in a procedure unusual for him, read from a carefully prepared written statement.

In tempo much slower than his usual swiftness of speech, he reviewed his statements on war over the years. Once more he shared his conviction, as well as "the judgment of ethics and religion, that war is wrong . . . an open and utter violation of Christianity." He was speaking as a Christian: "If war is right, then Christianity is wrong, false, a lie. If Christianity is right, then war is wrong, false, a lie." In his mind the contending forces were both at fault: "Why is war directed only against Germany, and not against England, which is an equal, although far less terrible, violator of covenants between nations?"

If any member of his church answered the call to arms, he would not only not attempt to restrain him, but would bless him as he went to perform what he considered to be his full duty as a man. As for himself, he would not heed a call for volunteers and would refuse to register in an enrollment of citizens for military purposes. If conscription were adopted, he would refuse to serve: "If this means a fine, I will pay my fine. If this means imprisonment, I will serve my term. If this means persecution, I will carry my cross. No order of president or governor, no law of nation or state, no loss of reputation, freedom, or life, will persuade or force me into this business of killing. On this issue, for me at least, there is no compromise."

As for the pulpit becoming a recruiting station and the church an outpost for the military forces: "So long as I am your minister, this pulpit will answer no military summons. Other pulpits may preach recruiting sermons; mine will not. Other parish houses may be turned into drill halls and rifle ranges; ours will not. Other clergymen may pray to God for victory for our arms; I will not."

To him human brotherhood was paramount: "In this church, if nowhere else in all America, the Germans will still be included in the family of God's children. No word of hatred shall be spoken against them—no evil fate shall be desired upon them. So long as I am priest, this altar shall be consecrated to human brotherhood; and before it shall be offered worship only to that one God and Father of us all 'who made of one blood all nations of men to dwell together on the face of the earth!' "

At the close of the service, as people began to leave the sanctuary, many remained to express agreement. Nine persons signed the Covenant of Membership that day, three more during the next week. The following Sunday, 31 joined; in the next two months, 42 and, during the summer months, an additional 13— or a total of 98.

It became fashionable, though erroneous, to say that at the time of America's entry into the Great War, Holmes preached his church empty and then preached it full again; even Holmes was accustomed to say that the church had lost more than one third of its membership. Quite the contrary was true. Only 15 members resigned. The church had a net gain of 83 new members during those crucial weeks; and over the entire church year of October to June of 1916–1917, 208 persons joined, a gain two and a half times as large as any previous growth in a similar period of time.

The trustees sensed that Holmes' avowal of pacifism in a time of war could be construed by some as tantamount to an implicit offer of resignation, if his stand were not sanctioned by the church. The next afternoon, at a predinner hour, they met briefly. Holmes waited in the anteroom with reporters sent by the metropolitan dailies. A spokesman soon emerged to announce that, although the trustees were almost to a man opposed to his viewpoint, the minister's right to speak freely had been affirmed, no matter how they or the congregation might dissent.

There was no need now for Holmes to resign, as he thought he might be asked to do. He had not been wrong in his estimate of the strength of this free church. As their minister, he was free to utter the truth as he saw it, free to oppose the national policy if he felt he must, free to preach a radical religion that tried to probe to the root of society's evils.

The following Sunday, April 8, Stephen Wise preached to his congregation in Carnegie Hall on "The World War for Humanity." The Congress of the United States had declared war on Germany on Friday, the sixth; and Wise now called for unity under Wilson's leadership. He praised the President's War Message as "the world's Magna Charta, spoken for peoples of every race and faith and tongue"; Wilson had served notice on the German people that they "must choose between Hohenzollernism and Despotism on the one hand and liberty and world peace on the other . . . make the fateful choice and . . . cleanse their name from the defiling shame of a pitiless Caesarism."

He repeated his abhorrence of war, his resistance to militarism, and his belief that war was perhaps the most terrible of earth's sorrows. Now, however, humanity was to be liberated; and war was a necessity, regrettable and tragic and terrible, yet a necessity.

In the midst of this plea for national unity, "a united and indivisible people fused together by a high and irresistible purpose . . . to liberate humanity everywhere and establish democracy as the norm of the nations of earth great and small," Wise broke in to salute a dissident:

I would refer today to my pride, yea more than pride, in the word and action of a friend, honored and cherished, the minister of the Unitarian Church of the Messiah of this city, one of the bravest and noblest preachers of our time. We are not of one mind touching this war, though for years we have been anti-militarist fellow-workers. He has taken the perhaps more uncompromising position that war is never justified and that non-resistance must be the rule of life for individuals and nations from which there can be no departure without compromise and without sin. Nothing could be more splendid than his courage, unless it be the fine determination of the people of his church, even though they are not at one with him, not to suffer any denial of his freedom of utterance within their pulpit. Prussianism is become the shame and confusion of the great German people because of its insistence that all men shall think alike and speak alike, because of its insistence upon the regimentation of the intellectual and spiritual life of the people. I thank God for the consequence-scorning nobleness of a minister of religion, ready to lay down his office and to brave the frowns of the world rather than compromise with the truth as God gives it to him to see the truth. But the congregation of the Church of the Messiah matches the nobleness of its leader, for, though it does not stand with him any more than I do in non-resistant neutrality toward this war, it sets a new standard for the liberty of the pulpit to which it is the abiding distinction of John Haynes Holmes to have given a new honor and a new glory.

Holmes' struggle had only just begun, however, as he learned the next month. In late May, he went to Boston for the annual meetings of the American Unitarian Association. He had been chosen as the chairman of the General Council of Unitarian Churches, scheduled to meet in September in Montreal as part of the Twenty-Seventh Conference. When he read the call to the Montreal Conference and saw the direction of resolutions, he realized that the tide would probably run against him. He heard Samuel A. Eliot, president of the A.U.A., declare: "We are in honor bound to resist the aggressive hypocrisy that tears up treaties as mere scraps of paper to trample in the dust, that casts the helpless into bondage." Then he listened to Carl August Voss of Pittsburgh, who, *The Unitarian Advance* reported, "with the flags of the Allies draped above the platform, pledged in stirring words the allegiance of the 'German-American' to the Allied effort."

The Unitarians, it was obvious to Holmes, were not pacifist-minded. Dissent from his pacifist views seemed in store for him at the Montreal Conference.

In his "Report of the Minister" for the 1917 *Year Book of the Church of the Messiah* on which he was working in the last days of May, he observed: "As I look at the problems of our church life from the standpoint of my own personal experience, I discover that the year 1916–17 was by all odds the busiest, most fruitful, and most exciting that I have ever passed in New York. At the same time has it been the easiest in terms of exertion and nervous tension, and the happiest in terms of inward satisfaction."

In June, he withdrew from the confusion of the city to the quiet of the Connecticut hills. The Holmes' next-door neighbor on Sidney Place in Brooklyn Heights, Ruth Standish Baldwin (aunt of Roger Baldwin, the new director of the National Civil Liberties Bureau of the American Union Against Militarism), offered Holmes the use of her home in Washington, Connecticut, where he would have the solitude to finish his long-planned biography of Robert Collyer. In early June, he transported to this rustic retreat the huge boxes of documents over which he had pored and with which he had been able to do so little in the previous four years.

He then swiftly wove the letters, sermons, poems, and lectures of Robert Collyer into a stirring narrative. He could not but identify himself with Collyer, and the old man lived again for him during those peaceful, uninterrupted days. The two men had much in common: humble origins, happiness in marriage, a passion for books, the gift of speech, public careers, devoted congregations at the Church of the Messiah, lecture audiences across the land, a zest for travel, and an army of famous friends.

By summer's end, Holmes finished the manuscript, which became two loving volumes of the *Life and Letters of Robert Collyer*. As he gathered his myriad notes before leaving for a brief vacation in Maine, he completed his work by drafting the preface: "If I have brought little to this book, it has brought much to me. It has disciplined me to the doing of arduous work. It has lifted me to the dignity of a noble purpose. It has restored to me the companionship of a rare and radiant spirit. It has given me friends whom I would otherwise not have known. And amid the agony and terror of an age of war, it has offered a quiet shrine, for I have held converse with things good and beautiful and thus restored my soul."

He had need of such dignity and serenity a few weeks later in the Unitarian meetings at Montreal when William Howard Taft, chairman of the conference, called for the churches' complete support of the President in prosecution of the war.

John Haynes Holmes offered three policies of action: first, to say nothing about the war since the issue was disputed, but that would be ignoble; second, to give a statement of views held by the majority of the council, but that would be partisan; and third, to acknowledge the great concern of all but allow expression of every different viewpoint. He emphasized the continuing need "for a ministry of reconciliation, the preparation of peace, the establishment of social justice, the proclamation of God's law."

Then the storm broke. Taft asked the secretary to replace him in the chair. Walking slowly toward the front of the platform, the huge man asked for a suspension of rules that he might make a motion. The request granted, he proceeded to denounce Holmes' report. Taft demanded outright approval for all the war measures of President Wilson and the Congress and adoption of a resolution that "the war must be carried to a successful conclusion to stamp out militarism in the world."

Taft was blazing with wrath in sharp contrast to his usual genial good humor. He castigated Holmes without mercy. The atmosphere of the meeting hall in this major city of the British Empire, involved in the war for three years, did not ease the situation. The audience was overwhelmingly with Taft; and Samuel A. Eliot, executive officer of the A.U.A., supported the Chairman. The motion was put, and the Taft resolution carried: 236 to 9.

Outwardly calm, Holmes boarded the train that night for New York. He slept restlessly but traced that to the tension of three days of meetings. He arrived at Grand Central Station fatigued but went directly to his office. All day he worked steadily, yet with discomfort. That evening at home he could eat no dinner and soon became violently ill.

Once more Stephen Wise saluted Holmes' courage at the next meeting of the Liberal Ministers' Club. Wise and Holmes now found themselves in different camps, but with their relationship unbroken. They discovered one means of surmounting variant opinions by planning for the Free Synagogue and the Church of the Messiah to unite in a Union Thanksgiving Service. Thus, on Thanksgiving Day of 1917, the two congregations, whose ministers differed on war, united in thanks to the God and Father of them all.

13. A House of Prayer for All People

*I believe in the Church Universal, the deposit
of all ancient wisdom and the receptacle of
modern science, which recognizes in all prophets and saints a harmony, in all scriptures a
unity, and through all dispensations a conti-
nuity, which abjures all that separates and
divides and always magnifies unity and peace,
which harmonizes reason and faith, yoga and
bhakti, asceticism and social duty . . . and
which shall make all nations and sects one
kingdom and one family in the fullness of time.*
—KESHAB CHANDRA SEN

FOR HOLMES AND WISE, 1918 and the first half of 1919 were as
filled with activity as any eighteen months they had ever experienced. For Holmes, developments in the Church of the
Messiah were central during this period. For Wise, the major
part of his time, apart from duties at the Free Synagogue, was
devoted to two objectives: support of America's role in the Great
War and the interests of the world-wide Jewish community.

Holmes now took on new literary responsibilities. In addition
to his frequent articles for Herbert Croly's *New Republic* and
Oswald Garrison Villard's *Nation,* he wrote guest editorials,
articles, and book reviews for a number of other magazines. His
congregation was proud of its part in the preparation of *Readings
from Great Authors,* a collection of supplementary scripture readings chosen by the members and Holmes from the religious and
secular literature of ancient and modern times: Lao-Tse, Buddha,

151

and Seneca, as well as H. G. Wells, Woodrow Wilson, and Romain Rolland. Holmes was assembling an anthology of readings about immortality (*The Grail of Life*) he planned to publish by the beginning of Lent. He helped launch the Fellowship of Reconciliation's unofficial publication, the *New World*, edited by Norman Thomas. To this magazine, its name soon changed to *The World Tomorrow* ("A Journal Looking toward a Christian World"), he agreed to send an article every few weeks. In March, 1919, he became editor of *Unity*, the liberal religious weekly founded forty years earlier by Jenkin Lloyd Jones, and selected Francis Nielson as coeditor. Each week Holmes sent articles by himself and friends, plus his own editorials and brief sentences, "Jottings," to the Abraham Lincoln Centre in Chicago where the editorial offices were located.

He now took less and less part in Unitarian activities. *The Unitarian Advance,* for which he had written regularly, had expired; and he chose no longer to write for the pro-war journal of the American Unitarian Association, the *Christian Register.* He had resigned his vice-presidency of the Middle States Association in early 1918 and served notice he was relinquishing his life membership in the A.U.A. By autumn, he withdrew his affiliation with the Unitarian General Conference. In writing and speaking to the congregation, he went beyond the Unitarianism of the past and dwelt on "The New Religion," as interpreted by Charles W. Eliot ten years earlier, and encouraged the members of his church to rethink the purpose and place of the Church of the Messiah in a changing world.

Holmes had now gone far beyond his Unitarian forebears, even further than the pioneering William Ellery Channing, whose words of a century earlier he often quoted in these days:

> I take cheerfully the name of Unitarian, not because I wish to regard myself as belonging to any sect, but to the community of free minds, of lovers of truth, both in earth and in heaven. I desire to escape the narrow walls of a particular church and to live under the open sky, in the broad light, looking far and wide, seeing with my own eyes, hearing with my own ears, and following truth meekly but resolutely, however arduous or solitary be the path in which she leads. I am a Unitarian, then, but as such I am no organ of a sect, but speak for myself alone.

The last phrase foreshadowed the title of his autobiography forty years later, *I Speak for Myself* (1958).

During these autumn months, the war was uppermost in everyone's mind. In the spring and summer of 1918, the German armies drove toward Paris in furious attacks but were repelled by the weary forces of the French and British, now mightily reinforced by newly arrived, freshly trained American troops. Daily the long casualty lists appeared in the newspapers and America began to feel the force of the struggle.

Holmes could not pretend to be happy about the publicity given to Stephen Wise's activities that summer. Wise and his son were being exploited, he felt. Jim, sixteen and ready for Princeton, had not been able to enlist because of his youth and joined his father in working at a shipyard in Stamford, Connecticut. Each morning father and son pedaled their bicycles from their vacation cottage on the Sound to the trolley terminal and boarded a streetcar for the Luders Marine Construction Company. Quietly they worked at their jobs, unknown to the laborers. Their identity was not discovered until Wise was asked to address a meeting in Washington and accepted on the condition that he be released by the foreman of the yard gang for the necessary two days. Word leaked out, and newspapers all over America broke the story of the rabbi who worked in a shipyard to help win the war. To those skeptical of Wise's motives, his work was a publicity stunt; Oswald Garrison Villard commented cynically about the rabbi's ability to secure publicity so accidentally. Holmes did not distrust Wise; he only regretted the notoriety his friend had received.

In New York, Holmes had a full summer and a busy autumn made more distracting by building activity around the church. The old porch and vestibule of the Church of the Messiah had been demolished and a more handsome and useful entrance built. But the construction was delayed; not until midwinter were the temporary entranceways removed and the scaffolding dismantled.

Then came a scourge: the Spanish influenza. Reminiscent of a pestilence in the Middle Ages, it swept through cities and towns, the simplest homes and most remote army camps, taking a toll comparable to that of the battlefields in Europe. Only after terrifying months did life become normal.

In the early autumn of 1918 Jenkin Lloyd Jones died; and tributes to the doughty liberal came from all over America to Chicago. In mid-November Holmes gave a moving address at a memorial meeting in the Abraham Lincoln Centre. It was almost inevitable that he should be asked to succeed Jones as Director of the Centre.

Now he found himself in conflict. His congregation at the Church of the Messiah loved him and he in turn was devoted to them. His pulpit was free and his pacifism, central to his thought, wholly acceptable and respected. The Holmes house in Brooklyn was comfortable. Holmes' church staff was what he had hoped it might be, for he had a more than adequate associate minister in Harvey Dee Brown and a committee was looking for a third minister. In New York he had a host of friends and was active in a score of organizations. Never had he been so happy in his work and though the schedule was heavier than he had ever undertaken, his health was excellent.

In Chicago lay all he had ever dreamed of in a church and he felt the pull of the great liberating tradition of Jenkin Lloyd Jones, an inspiration to him as to his Grandfather Haynes a generation earlier. The Centre was enough to attract any man, regardless of his desire to maintain the Jones heritage.

Holmes' summer neighbor at Kennebunk Beach, Salmon O. Levinson, was a member of the Centre's Board of Trustees. He urged Holmes to accept the offer. Holmes liked Levinson as a stimulating and provocative person, an ardent devotee of the social good. Here was a man to work with and depend upon for support.

Holmes asked himself why he should stay in the maelstrom of Manhattan. Its pace was exhausting, its demands merciless; in some ways, the place was artificial and not central to America's social and political life. At best only a hothouse of liberalism and radicalism, New York was far from the American heartland whence had come the impulse for such indigenous movements as Populism and Progressivism and the followings of John Peter Altgeld of Illinois and Robert La Follette of Wisconsin. Perhaps he had made his contribution and a new man might give fresh stimulus to the Church of the Messiah. The past twelve years had been creative and exciting. In this, his fortieth year, it might be wise to start anew in surroundings even more favorable for his work and equally hospitable to his views.

On the other hand, in New York he had many friends active in liberal and radical circles—Norman Thomas, already a leader in the Socialist Party; Roger Baldwin of the National Civil Liberties Bureau (sentenced that November to a year in prison for his refusal to have a physical examination when called up by the draft); Oswald Garrison Villard of the *Nation;* Paul Kellogg of *Survey;* and John Nevin Sayre, who was soon to leave his parish to work with the Fellowship of Reconciliation. His friends in the ministry could be matched nowhere else in America: Stephen Wise and Frank Oliver Hall, Judah L. Magnes and John Howard Melish, Percy Stickney Grant and John Lovejoy Elliott.

When two members of the Chicago church-settlement came to New York to convey the Centre's call during Thanksgiving week, only a fortnight after the joyous response of the nation to the end of the war, Holmes asked for time—at least until the end of the year—before he made his decision.

On Monday evening, December 30, Holmes faced an overflow congregational meeting composed of many hundreds of the almost one thousand members. Having learned they might soon lose their minister, they came to hear his plans for them and for himself. Since the parish hall was too small, they voted to move the session to the sanctuary.

Holmes then described the Chicago situation, weighed the reasons for and against his move, but said he would feel constrained to stay if the congregation acted favorably on five major matters. Standing again in the center of the platform where he had officiated as minister hundreds of times since 1907, Holmes listed for them his five requests:

1. To understand the motives which impelled his various resignations from Unitarian affiliations and the official roll of Unitarian clergymen to become "an Independent, at one with all men everywhere, at home with the family of mankind";

2. To make their institution undenominational, an authentic community church, enabling the members to clear themselves "of ancient entanglements to such degree that we may invite

people openly and honestly to come into our portals, not because they want to profess themselves Unitarian but because they want to confess themselves lovers and servants of mankind";

3. To choose a new name for the church, ridding it of the word "Messiah," and decide on something more appropriate . . . something relevant to current needs so that his church might "baptize itself afresh in the language of our own time and in the spirit of our own life";

4. To abolish pew rentals, "an abomination already abolished in countless churches more orthodox than our own and a scandal in any church claiming to be liberal or democratic";

5. To adopt a noncovenanted basis for membership.

If the members were to do this, he would consider remaining in New York and might possibly announce a favorable decision on Sunday; but if there were no such possibility and change were not in the offing, he would accept the Chicago invitation. They must decide. He left the meeting and returned to his home in Brooklyn. For two hours the members debated the points. Then, on New Year's Day of 1919, he was assured by friends that a majority approved his five points. Still Holmes turned over in his mind the possibilities and the problems of the Chicago situation to which he felt so strongly drawn.

On Thursday, January 2, he sent his decision to the Chicago committee. He asked them not to disclose it until Sunday morning so that he could first inform his own congregation.

On Sunday, January 5, the audience came early. Long before the organ prelude began, the doors were closed, for people thronged the church and many were turned away. In the sermon Holmes quickly reviewed his presentation the previous Monday, emphasizing his belief in a ministry of social concern and universal range. He alluded only briefly to the considerations which made him take the Chicago opportunity seriously.

He intimated that support would be forthcoming for his program in New York and that he was certain the congregation wanted him to stay: "In my own soul, which must be the last court of decision after all, I have become convinced that I am confronted here by a situation which I can neither ignore nor evade. My challenge to you has been answered by a challenge to myself. To refuse this challenge is impossible. To leave this fruitage of my twelve years of plowing and planting unharvested, and thus to wither and to be scattered, would be a crime." Then, pausing for an instant, he announced, "I have therefore declined the call to Chicago—and will remain here as your minister." The organist, Clifford Demarest, either in exuberance or gratitude and relief, began the doxology. The congregation rose and sang "Praise God from Whom All Blessings Flow." To Holmes the spontaneous reaction of the congregation and its organist was unexpected: yet he savored the moment. In later years, he laughed at the Messianic quality of it all.

But this assignment was also a responsibility. He did have to lead them. A week and a day later—on Monday, January 13— the members met again and granted all five requests. They approved Holmes' status as an "Independent," made the church undenominational, changed the name to The Community Church of New York, declared all pews free (with special consideration for those who did not want to make the change at the present moment), and made their membership requirements uncovenanted.

When he reviewed this list of changes the following Sunday, Holmes interpreted a community church as "democracy in the field of religion, a spiritual expression of the contemporary movement of democracy, the achievement at last of what was begun but not completed, promised but not fulfilled, in Protestantism. The Community Church is the logical completion and perfection of the liberal movement in modern religion. It accomplishes boldly what Liberalism has been attempting timidly, in that it finally (1) shifts the basis of religion from God to man; (2) moves from the individual to the social group as the center of religious life; and (3) accepts the community in place of the denomination as the unit of spiritual integration."

At the close of the service, 137 persons walked up the aisle, in response to his invitation, to sign the membership book. Now the church had attained—and exceeded—the long-sought goal of 1,000 members. For the first time there was a sizable surplus in a usually depleted treasury.

As new members joined in such large numbers—280 from

October, 1918, until June, 1919—Holmes made a special effort
to interpret the Community Church. He tried to have individual
conferences with each new member, an almost hopeless task, for
there were so many. Quite apart from trying to make schedules
coincide, the sheer expenditure of time was enormous; but he
met almost every new member in a personal way and was able
to point out that the Community Church was setting a standard for community churches throughout the country. Although
few churches wanted to be more than interdenominational in
make-up, some would have the courage to become, like their
own, intercreedal and interracial. The Community Church in
New York would now become, he predicted, the mecca for men
and women of many backgrounds, a church where barriers of
sect and class, nation and color were of no consequence.

The Community Church, he explained, was not a Union
Church, trying to bring together different denominations in Protestantism; not a Federated Church, uniting several different
groups within one fold; not a People's Church, based upon
rationalism; nor even an "institutional" church, trying to meet
the social responsibilities of a community. It was instead an
all-inclusive church, combining all these features in one way or
another but emphasizing its freedom from the domination of
dogma, money, and sectarianism. In place of these, it offered
intelligence and character and brotherhood. Primarily, the Community Church was a "splendid first step away from Protestantism, toward the new democratic religion of the future."

Holmes considered Protestantism to be a dead religion, dead
in all its forms, both orthodox and liberal, and therefore a subversive social influence, no less so than the medieval Catholicism
of four and five centuries earlier. Churches were weak. Their
status in American life was reflected by the many abandoned
churches found throughout America which were as depressing
as abandoned farms and homesteads. The Protestantism that had
flourished sixty or seventy years earlier had vanished; and nothing was ready to take its place except the Community Church
movement. Never before had the churches been so feeble and
the tide of America's spiritual life at so low an ebb; but now,
through community churches, organized religion would take a

new turn: "He who imagines that religion is to be found in the churches, save as it appears in the lives of devoted individuals who may belong to them, confuses 'Christianity' and ecclesiasticism and theology with the high things of the spirit."

The Community Church was launched with his hope and prayer for "a universal, humanistic religion which knows no bounds of any kind, not even Christianity . . . eliminating every last vestige of theology, thus relegating all matters of belief to private individual opinion, and putting membership and institution on an out-and-out citizenship basis, welcoming to our church any person who is part of our great American community, be he rich or poor, black or white, Christian, Jew, Hindu, or Parsee."

To many, Holmes seemed utopian, as indeed he was, for no unit of organized religion was capable of accomplishing what he had set out to do. But the Community Church, as an individual unit and as a nationwide movement, was to become for many a school of idealism and a fount of good works, devoid of denominationalism with its waste, inefficiency, and unbrotherliness.

During the winter of 1918–1919, Holmes' correspondence mounted in volume; in his *Annual Report* he said that he was writing between seven and eight thousand letters a year. Vast and far-reaching was his ministry of the mails. Most important in his eyes were the letters he was exchanging with a prisoner in the Atlanta Penitentiary: the Socialist leader, Eugene V. Debs, imprisoned for resisting the restriction of what he felt to be constitutional rights of free speech and free press for opponents of the draft law. Debs wrote on the backs of envelopes and on scraps of paper, for no stationery was allowed him, and thanked Holmes for the pacifist sermons friends had sent.

Though a pacifist, Holmes always admired John Brown and his direct action. Never critical of Theodore Parker's part as a collector of funds and sender of arms for the Harper's Ferry raid, Holmes cherished in his autograph collection a cloak-and-dagger letter by Brown and kept a lock of Brown's hair among his mementos. He avidly read the biographies of Robert E. Lee, Ulysses S. Grant, Stonewall Jackson, and other Civil War generals, and enjoyed replanning campaigns in the Civil War. He was considered an authority on Civil War history especially, and paradoxically, on military operations.

A pacifist, he yet accepted the gains of a civilization that had been won by clash of arms. He did not question the use of police power whether in the order imposed in the city or on a national scale to keep society from falling into chaos. The violence and conflict of an economic order, especially such an order as the mercantile society of a capitalist world, were taken for granted by him. His protestations of having nothing to do with violence seemed hollow to his critics.

None of these criticisms disturbed Holmes or his friends in the pacifist movement. They found an ever-increasing group of men and women, especially people in academic life, ready for their word. There were few uneasy moments even when the New York *Times* reported to Holmes that his sermon, "A Statement to My People on the Eve of War," had been dropped by German planes behind the British lines.

Holmes had no patience with Woodrow Wilson's unbending Calvinist conscience and its stern disapproval of Debs and the adamant refusal to release the Socialist from prison. Between the two men, Holmes and Wilson, there was no understanding on matters of war and peace. The cruel treatment of conscientious objectors in American prisons made him bitter about the obstinacy of Wilson and the silence of the Protestant churches, particularly the Federal Council of Churches.

At this time, Upton Sinclair published *The Profits of Religion,* which dealt in scathing fashion with organized religion, "a shield to privilege," and referred with less than pleasure to the church being built by Sinclair's own Episcopalians, the Cathedral of St. John the Divine. Sinclair inveighed against his denomination for pretending to build "a house of prayer for all people." He deplored the moral and spiritual bankruptcy of the churches.

Holmes wrote to Sinclair that he found the book to be "a powerful and on the whole justifiable indictment of the organized Christianity of our day." He confessed that *The Profits of Religion* had made him writhe, not because the statements were "untrue or unfair, but, on the contrary, because I know them to be the real facts." He told Sinclair: "You have done us all a service in the writing of this book." Yet the book was painful to read, for "I love the church as I love my home, and therefore it is no pleasant experience to be made to face such a story as this which you have told. It had to be done, however, and I am glad you have done it, for my interest in the church, after all, is more or less incidental, whereas my interest in religion is a fundamental thing."

Holmes objected, however, because Sinclair had not emphasized the real prophets of religion produced by the church in all ages, among whom were many who had worked inside the church with the support and approval of their church members. He told Sinclair that the "book would have been better balanced if this side of things had not been passed by so lightly." He regretted Sinclair's failure to name such men of his own day as Washington Gladden, Walter Rauschenbusch, John Howard Melish, and William E. Orchard. Holmes conceded that "of course the church has cast out many of its noblest leaders, but others it has cherished, sometimes through accident or fear, but sometimes also through a real revival, under undaunted personal leadership, of the true spirit of religion."

Upton Sinclair was certain of one thing: John Haynes Holmes incorporated in his life and work that "true spirit of religion." In his numerous writings and speeches Sinclair pointed out that, in his eyes, Holmes had indeed made the Community Church of New York a house of prayer for all people.

14. As of Right and Not on Sufferance

*Those who go with me will all become histori-
cally famous persons.* —THEODOR HERZL, 1896

WHEN STEPHEN WISE ASKED IN 1917, "Can We Win the War
Without Losing America?" he did more than reflect considerable
anxiety in the minds of the American people. He expressed his
own desire that America might measure up to "the nobleness of
our part in the strife, not for profit to ourselves nor yet for
punishment of others, but for the liberation of all people, including above all the people of the German Empire, from
Caesarism." Convinced of "the greatness and the nobleness of
our quest, the making secure forever of the sanctity of international covenants and the rights of smaller nations, of democracy
for all the world," Wise cried: "Wake up, America, and win the
war for the world, but hold and keep holy America's soul!"

His expression of such aims was neither bombast nor jingoism,
but rather the genuine core of his thought and action. His objectives included freedom and liberty for everyone, including
the Irish and Armenians on whose behalf he made personal pleas
to Woodrow Wilson. No sooner had America entered the war
in April, 1917, than he asked the President whether it might not
be possible to appeal to the British Government for home rule
for the Irish people, a plea Wilson acknowledged graciously
but about which he did little.

In August, 1918, he heard from two Zionist leaders, Judge
Julian Mack and Jacob de Haas, that it would be prudent for
him to see the President once more in order to clarify matters

regarding the Palestine question. Wise also intended to share with Wilson his impressions of the minds of the men working with him in Stamford. Accordingly, he requested an appointment at the White House and arranged for a few days off from his job at the shipyard. From this conference in Washington came the promise that Wilson would send a letter reassuring him of continuing support of the Balfour Declaration, a statement that would help the Zionists in view of the growing resistance of a small but articulate group of anti-Zionists in the American Jewish Community—Henry Morgenthau, David Philipson, and Wise's long-time opponent, Samuel Schulman, who were gathering other Jewish laymen and rabbis to lodge a protest against Zionism as not reflecting the true religious spirit of Judaism.

Four days later, the President wrote Wise, the recently elected president of the Zionist Organization of America, that he welcomed "the progress made by the Zionist Movement in the United States and in the Allied countries since the Declaration by Mr. Balfour on behalf of the British Government, of Great Britain's approval of the establishment in Palestine of the national home for the Jewish people." This letter prompted a brief but grateful note from Felix Frankfurter in early September, 1918: "Dear Dr. Wise: And the nations of the World, no less than the people of Israel, will arise and call you blessed."

Beside the Z.O.A. and his pulpit and pastoral duties at the Free Synagogue, Wise had another major responsibility, the American Jewish Congress. The Congress was to meet in mid-December, and constant consultations went on with such leaders as Louis D. Brandeis, then an Associate Justice of the U.S. Supreme Court, and Bernard G. Richards, the executive secretary. When, on November 11, the war ended, Wise had to choose between attending the American Jewish Congress meetings scheduled for Philadelphia in a few weeks and representing Zionist interests abroad, prior to the convening of the Peace Conference in Paris. He chose to go to Europe; and in early December, he and Louise left for England aboard the S.S. *Aquitania,* which he promptly dubbed, in a letter to the children, "a vulgar, floating cafeteria."

In his first letter home he wrote his son: "I wish you might know, you blessed rogue, how we hunger for the sight of your cuneiform script—even worse than my own. Poor, dear Mummie is just hungering for your and Pussy's first letter. May it soon be at hand!"

London, he observed, was an attractive as ever, ablaze with color and military stir, yet saddening, because of the wounded men: "What glorious men they seem, unheroic in their own sight alone." He reported that the London papers wrote of little else than Paris' rousing reception of Wilson. To the American President—as to no one else—Europe looked for deliverance from militarism.

There began a round of conferences, receptions, meetings, and social events which kept him and Louise busy for more than a month. Wise was hard-pressed to keep all the engagements made for him and at the same time maintain his equilibrium amid demands on many sides. Again he reverted to the expedient of making brief notes at a midnight hour or, after his usual few hours sleep, in early morning wakefulness.

As the President of the Z.O.A., he had to keep his American colleagues informed. Thus many pages of his private journal were marked "cable for de Haas," "cable to Brandeis."

Immediately after arriving in London, he requested an interview at the Foreign Office; and a hand-written acknowledgement came by messenger. Wise's session with Balfour was important, for it was his responsibility to give the Foreign Secretary the resolution of the American Jewish Congress urging the British Government to act as trustee for the Jewish Commonwealth of Palestine.

Balfour responded gravely: "Rabbi, American Jews have honored my country and its government by this request." When Wise asked him to interpret the phrase in the Declaration calling for "a National Home for the Jewish people," Balfour's reply was: "This means that Jews who either wish or require, now or in the future, to go to Palestine shall have the right to do so."

Wise's notes for Friday, December 20, read:

Breakfast Conference
P.M. [Lloyd George] & Herbert Samuel
Summary of British Commitments
        and desiderata
        including Palestine

"Palestine part of Arabic Confed.
    reasonable facilities for
    Jewish immigration
    opport. for bring. 4 million Jews
                in generation.
        Arabs don't want Palestine
        Would set up a Jewish
    Palestine, if America support
        gave him proposals."
            Get Palestine "as far as Litany [Litani]
                                        River
    & down to El Arisch
        Sykes-Picot agreement East to Hedjas [Hedjaz] rail-
        way to be torn up."

Lord Lionel Rothschild, the recipient of the letter containing
the Balfour Declaration on November 2, 1917, invited a group of
celebrities for dinner at the Ritz in honor of the Emir Feisal of
the Hedjaz. For this signal occasion, Wise made a longer entry
than was his habit:

Rothschild painful Speaker
    Samuel first—dignified and
    stately. I next rotten,
    nervous, commonplace, incoherent.
    Then Feisal, young, handsome, striking.
    Wonderful youth of about 30.
    He spoke for 15', see his typewritten
    speech and letter to Chief [Chaim Weizmann]. Frank, droll,
    delightful Lawrence, a young British
    Col. translated—
    Upshot—We can live as good neighbors.
    Fine word by Lord Robert Cecil next to whom
    I sat. To him Govt. refers piloting the League
    of Nations thru Peace Conference.
    Weitzman [sic] made "audacious" speech,
    purporting to be "irresponsible,"—
    & implying Sykes-Picot treaties must go.
    Robert Cecil rather rebuked him
    urging "England keeps all engagements,
    advantageous or not."
    Milner spoke few words.
    Walked home with Col. Lawrence,

—who urged me to bring Emir to Pres.
here, & not in France, to be free of
French influence—
I can see that his position insecure
& Feisal far from certain of British
guarantee. Will try at American
                    Embassy

Wise told his children that Chaim Weizmann, the key figure
in Zionism, was "forceful, terribly clever, but no Brandeis—lacking the latter's austerity and exaltation." Weizmann said to him,
"What do I care for mandates from the Zionist Movement? I
have done more for Zionism in three months than Herzl in his
whole life." Wise added that Weizmann was "a great personality.
He is a splendid fellow if he does not prove too big for his boots.
He is not a democrat, but a hopeless autocrat. Zionism is a
supremely democratic movement, but Weizmann is no democrat." After an all-day conference with Weizmann, Wise summed
it up for his children: "He is a really big man—and I have come
to have great respect for him. I don't know whether we shall love
him . . . one cannot help admiring his mind and power." Wise
could now understand why Henri Bergson, the French philosopher, had said to him, "Wise, I am a non-Zionist; but get rid of
Weizmann, and we'll be with you."

Wise realized how important it was to bring about a meeting
of the Russian-British scientist with the American President. He
suggested to Colonel Edward House, during the December days
in London, that an appointment to introduce Weizmann be
arranged. Three weeks later in Paris, he importuned House once
more; and on the morning of Tuesday, January 14, a telephone
call instructed him to be at the President's suite at five-thirty
that afternoon. To Wise's disappointment, Weizmann insisted
that he be closeted alone with the President. Reluctantly, Wise
consented. Weizmann, aware of his own talent as an advocate,
especially in private conversation, wanted no competing personality.

In the few minutes Stephen Wise had with Woodrow Wilson,
he discovered that the President was for the first time worried
about the Palestine problem, not, as Wise had at first surmised,

by protests from anti-Zionists in the Jewish community of America—"few in number and negligible in quality," Wilson reassured
him—but rather about the Arabs. "I can see that his mind has
been poisoned," Wise wrote home. "Somebody has been getting
at him."

Weizmann was his usual persuasive self. At ten minutes past
six, the two men, Weizmann and Wilson, emerged from the
President's improvised study-reception room and it was apparent
that the mood was mellow, the two men in accord.

As the scientist and the rabbi left the American President and
walked down the rue de Crillon in the wintry evening, Weizmann turned to Wise with delight and said, "Your super goy is
all right!"

Wilson had to be all right, for he had many pressures to resist: from a few but influential anti-Zionist Jews in the United
States, from Christian missionaries anxious not to anger the Arab
world with a Jewish State, from State Department officials irked
by Israel Zangwill's suggestion that the Arab population of
Palestine be moved. ("It's high time," Zangwill had said, "they
trekked, like the Boers from Cape Colony.")

Woodrow Wilson was not swayed by these influences; and six
weeks later, Wise, accompanied by Judge Julian Mack, Louis
Marshall, and Bernard G. Richards, met in Washington with the
President and found him no less cordial. As a delegation from the
American Jewish Congress, they came to discuss the minority
treaties under consideration at the Peace Conference and to receive any advice the President might offer on the Palestine
question.

Marshall's presence was of special importance. Not only did he
represent the American Jewish Committee, a select group of
wealthy Jews of German background—like Jacob H. Schiff and
Felix Warburg—but he also had ability and integrity. He and
his friends in the American Jewish Committee called themselves
"non-Zionist," an important distinction in contrast to "anti-Zionist." In Wise's eyes, their lack of enthusiasm stamped them as
being virtually anti-Zionist. Yet in these days of decision, he was
grateful for their co-operation, as he wrote to Nathan Straus:
"Nothing could be finer than the way in which Marshall is work-

ing with us. His support of and participation in the Congress is beyond praise. It is of enormous value to us—of greater value than he himself knows."

The four men found Wilson toughened by his experience in Paris with Lloyd George, Clemenceau, and Orlando, and even more familiar with details about Palestine and minority treaties than before. Wilson understood the problems in such a notoriously anti-Semitic country as Poland; when Judge Mack reminded him of complicating factors, the President answered: "Racial minorities must be taken care of everywhere, not only in Poland. There will be hell to pay if they are not. Excuse my strong language, gentlemen."

The President saw Wise scribbling memoranda on a pad of paper and said, with a twinkle, "You remember the lines of Burns, gentlemen: 'There's a chiel among ye takin' notes." Then he continued, "There is one matter over which I almost despair, arising out of the difficulties of the Italians with Yugoslavia. It is one thing to secure equality in law for racial minorities, but how are you going to prevent corporations from refusing to give work to certain racial groups of employees?"

Marshall agreed: "It is very difficult to deal with such a question—the question of discriminating in the choice of employees."

Wise then turned to his three colleagues and told them the President had informed him that, at the present time, little more could be said; but Judge Mack interposed: "Mr. President, we hear there will be no trouble in Palestine. M. Tardieu [the French Foreign Minister] gave an interview in Paris yesterday which was printed in Saturday night's New York *Globe*. He declared the question is settled."

Wilson replied wryly, "M. Tardieu has a great nose for the weather. He reminds me of an old salt, who, after spending his life at sea and having retired, would spend most of the day going out on his countryside porch and sniffing the weather."

Mack then asked, "Mr. President, we shall soon be going to Paris. Where do you think we ought to bring pressure?"

Wilson replied, "I have only one suggestion to offer you, gentlemen: do not seek out the counsel of any one particular group. Distribute your conversations and convince all the groups."

Woodrow Wilson, conscious of the growing opposition to his peace program in the United States Senate and sensitive to the effect of any statement he might make, dictated to Stephen Wise the following sentence which they might give the press on leaving the White House: "The delegation of the American Jewish Congress found the President, as always, sympathetic with the incontestable principle of the right of the Jewish people everywhere to equality of status."

As was his custom, Wise had prepared a paragraph on the Palestine question. When the President read it, he crossed out the word "anent" which Wise had used and substituted the word "regarding"; then looking at Wise with a smile, he said: "You see, rabbi, 'anent' ain't in my vocabulary."

Wilson deleted a phrase concerning a subject not yet settled: "that the League of Nations will through mandate confer upon Great Britain trusteeship over Palestine," and disposed of the matter by telling the men: "You may quote me as having said, 'As for your representation touching Palestine, I have before this expressed my personal approval of the Declaration of the British Government regarding the aspirations and historic claims of the Jewish people in regard to Palestine. I am, moreover, persuaded that the Allied Nations, with the fullest concurrence of our own government and people, are agreed that in Palestine shall be laid the foundations of a Jewish commonwealth.'"

The delegation thus received all they had come to seek, and a bit more too, for Wilson made a point about his Allies they never forgot: "The only game they do not know is the only game that I do know—the game of frankness."

When the delegation was ready to leave, Wilson made a famous remark which Wise relayed in his March letter to Nathan and Lena Straus, vacationing in Aiken, South Carolina: "The President seems to have no doubts that Palestine is to be ours." Yet Wise had his own doubts as to whether or not "the Jewish people will be equal to the opportunity, as I believe the opportunity will come to them."

To this end then his work among the Jewish people, made possible by the American Jewish Congress, was a cause to which Wise gave himself in the months ahead. He was nettled later that year by word that the Zionists were planning a testimonial reception for Louis Marshall, who was not even a member of the Zionist Organization. The planning committee, either by intention or neglect, did not invite Wise, despite the fact that, for the previous two years, he had served as president. Wise contemplated resigning from the Z.O.A., but he refrained.

It was important for him, he felt, to stay by the side of Brandeis, who had withdrawn from active work in the American Jewish Congress because of bitter attacks from Judah Magnes. Magnes had contended it was wrong for a Supreme Court judge to be in political life. Brandeis was still in the Zionist Organization, however, working on the sidelines and serving as an elder statesman. When Brandeis returned from his first trip to Palestine in 1919, he described its progress and assayed its needs before the Zionists' Executive Committee; he was, Wise told his family, "so rapt with hope for the future" that Wise could only marvel: "Such simplicity, such nobleness of utterance, and back of it all a deep Jewish spirit and a most passionate and mystic love for Palestine!"

Wise foresaw grave trouble ahead because Brandeis would not accept public leadership of the movement; everywhere he detected "a great deal of dissatisfaction and unrest." In his travels over America, as far-reaching as ever, Wise saw other problems, quite apart from the Zionist movement. He sensed that, in this last year of Wilson's administration, there was throughout the land an even greater "dissatisfaction and unrest," much of it centered in the labor movement. The upsurge of protest against long hours and low wages now absorbed his attention, especially in the latter half of 1919 and the first part of 1920.

15. The Laborer Is Worthy

*You can't let men live like pigs, and expect
them to be good citizens.*

—JACOB A. RIIS, 1900

IN EARLY SEPTEMBER, 1919, John Haynes Holmes spent three to
four hours each morning in the tiny study of his brown shingle
house at Kennebunk Beach and planned his work for the coming
year. Most important were the sermons. These must be kept
timely and provocative, for the large audiences every Sunday
would melt away if he did not maintain the same high level. One
of the first in the fall would be "Who's Who in Prison: A Plea
for Political Amnesty," a defense of Eugene V. Debs, Roger Baldwin, Rose Pastor Stokes (a ten-year term for the innocuous
statement, "I am for the people, and the government is for the
profiteers"), and the conscientious objectors. He made a note to
write both Debs and Baldwin before he, Madeleine, and the
children closed the house and returned to the city. He would also
write the National Civil Liberties Bureau for more information
about the Espionage Act of 1917, the Sedition Act of the previous
year, and the Deportation of Aliens Law; then his references
would be accurate.

In November, there should be a summation of gains and losses
in the year since the end of the war. Some time during the winter
or spring of 1920, he must give an appraisal of liberal movements
in America, now that the old "Bull Moose" Party was dead, the
Socialist Party of limited influence, the Muckrakers already out
of date. And then, in the spring, would come the centenary of
Herbert Spencer's birth, which could be commemorated by a
sermon.

The series of vesper services on "Immortality," given during Lent four years before, could now be repeated and with new emphases. Harvey Dee Brown wanted to deal with Sigmund Freud and Carl Jung as "The Psychoanalysts," and Holmes would treat the scientist Sir Oliver Lodge and the psychologist James H. Hyslop. If the congregation's committee was successful in securing John Herman Randall as a co-ordinate minister on the staff, then Randall could speak on immortality in the thought of Maurice Maeterlinck and William James. Holmes planned to announce the subject of the vesper services as "Is There Any New Light on the Old Problems of Immortality?" and to start making notes for the final talk: "What Is the Conclusion of the Whole Matter?"

The list was long, but Holmes had spent a good summer. Neither energy nor enterprise was low.

Shortly after dinner on the chill night of September 11, a member of his church telephoned from New York to Kennebunk Beach to tell him that a disastrous fire had occurred that afternoon. At three o'clock, as Harvey Dee Brown was beginning the funeral service for Walt Whitman's friend, Horace Traubel, in the Church House, flames sprang high in another part of the church, the sanctuary. The funeral was moved to the Rand School on East 15th Street and the firemen fought the blaze. By seven thirty, the fire was extinguished; but the church was in ruins.

When Holmes returned after a grim overnight ride on the State of Maine Express, he found the church a charred shell, the interior destroyed, and the cherished memorial stained-glass windows shattered. Fortunately, the Church House had been saved, though it was badly damaged by water and smoke. Only the office remained intact, furnishing quarters to transact the church's daily business and maintain contact with the parishioners.

Services were canceled until the end of the month. Insurance claims were sent in, the Church House replanned. The Randall appointment was postponed and offers from other churches to use their quarters considered carefully—and gratefully. Offers had come from William Pierson Merrill of the Brick Presbyterian Church and Percy Stickney Grant at the Church of the Ascension, from the Society of Friends on Stuyvesant Square, the Bahaists, the Rand School, the Ethical Culture Society, and Stephen Wise at the Free Synagogue. Wise really had no facilities to offer, for he was using Carnegie Hall in the mornings; and union services would be satisfactory for only a brief time.

Except for the initial service held on September 28 in All Souls' Unitarian Church, the New Amsterdam Theater was the Sunday morning church home for the entire year of 1919–1920.

Consoling editorials and encouraging letters came from all over the country. Plans for rebuilding moved slowly and funds in the uncertain economy of the time did not come quickly. Checks came from a rabbi in the Midwest, a religious liberal in London, a sympathetic minister in San Francisco; but these were not enough. The insurance was meager and woefully inadequate in an era of mounting costs.

More difficult was the problem of finding a place for the Community Forum. The Social Service League, supporting the Forum, had no money for rent; and Holmes turned to the several sympathetic churches which had offered facilities for the Sunday morning services. Would they allow Sunday evening meetings for the Forum? The invitations sent so generously were, for the most part, withdrawn. For a few weeks a public school building was used; but soon dissent in the School Board ended that arrangement for they questioned the wisdom of a "radical" forum meeting in a public building. Fortunately, the Ethical Culture Society offered its auditorium on West 64th Street for only a nominal maintenance fee.

Similarly, a meeting place for the Lenten Vesper services posed another housing problem. Once-hospitable Protestant churches became skittish and barred their doors, even for devotional services that had no controversial overtones. Finally, Charles E. Jefferson and the Board of Trustees of Broadway Tabernacle (Congregational) offered their church on West 56th Street.

The fire gave new purpose and life to the church. True, the improvised facilities were anything but ample, yet something significant had happened to the congregation; and the year proved to be one of the most creative in the history of the church: larger attendances, growing membership, firm financial standing, and a clear vision for the future.

On New Year's Eve, Holmes led the congregation in a Watch

Night Service amid the ruins of the church. To him and the people, it was meaningful to sing his words:

> We stand as those who driven far
> By waste of fire and sword,
> Find not in unfamiliar ways
> The presence of the Lord.

Over them hovered a Presence on that last day of 1919:

> We have Thee, Lord. Our house is dust,
> But Thou art living still
> Within the loved community
> Of souls that do Thy will.

In this hour of disaster, another community church began in Boston. Less than two weeks later, Holmes formally established a duplicate version of his own church, an independent congregation, the Community Church of Boston which met in Steinert Hall on Boylston Street. At a preliminary meeting the previous October at Wesleyan Hall in Boston, about thirty people had met with Holmes and Clarence R. Skinner to make plans. Skinner, a Universalist minister and Dean of the School of Religion at Tufts College, offered to serve as an unsalaried "leader" (preferring that title to "minister"), gathered prospective members, and launched the project.

The purpose was similar to that of New York's Community Church, but the atmosphere was more secular. The group, slowly growing, met each Sunday to hear an outstanding speaker on a topic of religious import and contemporary concern. With Holmes helping as an associate minister *in absentia* and Mrs. Gertrude Winslow serving as secretary, the Community Church of Boston grew large and strong in a brief time. Holmes came every fourth or fifth Sunday to preach again a sermon delivered at an earlier date in New York and to bring the stimulus of a parallel organization. Now that Holmes came to Boston on schedule and preached in university chapels and local churches all over the country, he was absent from his own pulpit half of the time; but in John Herman Randall he had now the co-minister he had long sought.

Two additional factors aided the Boston church: Holmes attracted to it a wide assortment of pacifists and social radicals and at the same time emphasized its nondenominational character; and the hard working, genial Skinner lent something distinctive. Loved not only by his students but by a larger group of older people, he had a mystic quality which gave the otherwise secularized church an unmistakably religious spirit.

In Philadelphia, the community church idea did not take hold. When Holmes, aided by Brown and Randall, responded to invitations from friends in Philadelphia, they met in the Garrick Theatre each Sunday and preached to large crowds; but an emphasis on any kind of ritualized service and the need for organization had little response. Within a short time, the venture failed and was never revived.

Throughout the country, however, community churches began to spring up; the New York and Boston experiments helped to further the community church movement. Despite the tension and conflict of the times, such churches maintained fellowship with each other. They reflected a hope that sometime, somewhere, there would be many others as foundation stones for the Universal Church. Yet such a Universal Church never developed into anything more than a hope and a dream. Community churches throughout the country varied. Some were federated, some interdenominational, some merely an expedient to save money in new real estate developments. Other cities did not wholly accept the high ideals and noble precepts of Holmes' new church. More cities resembled Philadelphia in its rejection of the idea, than Boston and New York in their acceptance of it.

During these days of upheaval, Stephen Wise was also busy with many plans—the Free Synagogue, the Zionist Organization, the education of young rabbis, the American Jewish Congress, and aid to the labor movement.

His son Jim, although an able student, had found university life neither satisfying nor rewarding and decided to remain at home for a year or two before going to Europe for further study. He planned to read under Wise's guidance. Wise, remembering his own studies a generation earlier under the care of such scholars as his own father, Alexander Kohut, and Gustav Gottheil, wrote in his journal: "Unspeakably happy over plan and his wish."

At the Free Synagogue, Wise met regularly with his rabbinical staff and lay leadership to gather a building fund; the war was over and long-postponed plans to build an adequate structure for the Free Synagogue could be completed. The congregation might now look forward to transferring the Sunday morning services from Carnegie Hall to a home of its own.

To Wise came many young rabbis, seeking to study under his direction and to take courses from the European scholars whom Wise brought to America on his Lewisohn Lecture Foundation. With Sidney Goldstein and Louis Newman, Oscar Straus and Joseph Levine, he planned a summer school which might eventually develop into a year-round school, a theological seminary to work in conjunction with Columbia University. His dream of twelve years earlier was about to become a reality.

The American Jewish Congress was still in existence but, according to agreement, was soon to be disbanded. Most of the men who had co-operated in the congress insisted on its dissolution as soon as its purposes, tied specifically to the Great War, had been achieved. Wise discerned and felt a rising tide of support for a move to revive the congress as a temporary organization immediately upon its adjournment and then move on to a permanent basis.

Foremost in his thoughts lay the problems of labor. When he learned that Samuel Gompers, the cautious, conservative president of the American Federation of Labor, finally had yielded to more enterprising men around him and planned to launch an organizing campaign, especially among the steelworkers, Wise offered his services. But when Wise heard that President Wilson had summoned an industrial conference, he canceled his offer to the A.F.L. Now that the federal government manifested both interest and concern, it seemed sensible to await the outcome of these sessions.

The Protestant churches had also become involved, as an item in the October 4 New York *Times* noted: "In a decision made at the National Industrial Conference of the Inter-Church World Movement, the Protestant churches of the United States, acting through their social service organizations, will investigate the Steel Strike." Bishop Francis J. McConnell of the Methodist Church would serve as chairman of the inquiry.

When Judge Elbert Gary, chairman of the board of directors of the United States Steel Corporation, testified before the United States Senate Committee, as Wise felt, in "immeasurable arrogance," it appeared to be time to speak out. Furthermore, William Z. Foster, author of a book on syndicalism, was leading the strike; and the cry of Bolshevism was now raised by the steel industry. Wise therefore announced that on Sunday, October 5, he would preach on the subject: "Bolshevists at Home—Who Are They?"

The prime target was Judge Elbert Gary, "a perfect representative of the eighteenth and early nineteenth centuries, a very interesting survival; and though Judge Gary may win, the eighteenth century is going to lose. In ten years or less we shall laugh at the Garys and the Gary autocracy will be as obsolete as the Hohenzollern autocracy." "Garyism," the unwillingness of the heads of industry to deal with organized working men, was also a target: "Garyism is today the most prolific breeder of revolutionary and Bolshevik sentiment in our land."

Wise contended that the employers had an organization of their own, a billion-dollar steel trust. It was axiomatic that employees must organize effectively to insure their safety, demand sanitary conditions, regulate hours, and adjust wages to fair and reasonable standards. Was it not unjust for employers to band together to prevent employees from belonging to labor organizations? The "open shop" meant that employees could not form unions for fear of dismissal.

Up to that time, the courts had held unconstitutional any legislation which forbade employers to discharge employees because of membership in labor organizations, a verdict that was, in Wise's mind, unfair and unjust. Labor, he maintained, should be encouraged to organize and not be compelled to resort to violence and "direct action"; but at the same time, he maintained, labor organizations should discipline their members, retain high standards of workmanship, and administer planned insurance so that their members need not become objects of pity or charity, either private or public. It was, he charged, the opposition of employers to such objectives of employees that caused the less praiseworthy tendencies of labor organizations to develop. If violence resulted, then employers were equally at fault.

Never for a moment, Wise maintained, had he come under the spell of Bolshevism, the lawless, disorderly, and anarchic overthrow of all the sanctions of government: "I deplore Bolshevism with all my soul because, more than anything else, it stands in the way of world peace. I am as unalterably opposed to Bolshevism as I was to Prussianism. To me Lenin and Trotsky are no less odious than Czar or Kaiser. The Lenin-Trotsky regime spells ruthless despotism; therefore to me it is loathsome and intolerable."

His assault was not against Russian Bolsheviks that early October Sunday in 1919; on the contrary, he was talking about certain men "who, in my judgment, are making straight, inevitably and irrevocably, for Bolshevism in America though they would laugh at my claims, though they would sneer at my word." The blame was on them in resorting to coercion and violence and falsely claiming that only a minority of workers were asking for organization. The International Workers of the World, the "Wobblies," had a growing number of adherents to their syndicalist viewpoint; direct action and resort to violence were "the logical issue of unwillingness of the heads of industry to deal with organized workingmen" by crushing the freedom of the workers, even for a brief while. This was the essence of Wise's attack on Gary and Garyism.

"The pulpit," said Samuel Schulman of Temple Beth-El, "has been turned into a soapbox and I, for one . . . protest against it in the name of a great rabbinical tradition."

Wise also began to receive resignations from the congregation, not many and not influential, but enough to disturb him. Wise answered every letter of resignation. He urged those who resigned to defer final decision until after the following Sunday when he would preach a still more powerful sermon.

The resignations were not, as Wise would recall in later decades, "in large numbers." There were only nine. Yet they were symptomatic of a greater loss to the Free Synagogue in the diminution of financial support and the threat posed to contributions from generous donors. Not without reason had he remarked to his wife the previous Sunday morning as they left for Carnegie Hall, "Today I am building a million dollar blaze."

The following Sunday, October 12, Wise defended himself against the charge that he had spoken disrespectfully of Judge Gary:

> I have not willed to speak disrespectfully. I will to speak truthfully of him. I believe that I have done this. In my judgment Judge Gary has been guilty of a deep and terrible wrong against the life of our democracy. I cannot bring myself to speak with any special show of respect touching a man, who has inflicted grave and perhaps irreparable injury upon the fabric of our common life. Why should Judge Gary be spoken of with special respect? Is it because he is the head of a mighty industrial corporation? Is our respect for a man to be proportioned to the measure of power that he wields without regard to the uses to which that power is applied? Is Judge Gary to be alluded to in terms of respect and of honor merely because he represents the most powerful and, as far as his leadership is concerned, the most absurdly reactionary aggregation of capital in the nation?

To the charge that he had hurt the Jewish position by his statement, Wise replied: "If I am to be silent on every great moral issue because I am a Jew, if my lips are to be sealed when truth and conscience bid me speak lest I hurt the Jewish name, then I wish to live in some place, small or large, near or remote, where a man can live without forfeiting his self-respect."

Then came his offer: "I offer my congregation the privilege of passing upon the question whether or not I ought to remain as their rabbi and continue to be free to speak as I have spoken. I shall not be offended by any action which my people may choose to take. If it seems best in their sight that I withdraw from their ministry, as God is my witness and as I believe that God will judge between me and them that assail me, I will withdraw with nothing but friendship and good-will and affectionately remember the congregation whether I continue to serve it or the hour has come for my withdrawal."

This was not an announcement of resignation. As they knew,

his resignation was always in their hands; so had it been from the hour in which he became their rabbi twelve years earlier.

He admitted that some of his executive committee "might wish . . . I were a little more amiable and gentle in manner, somewhat more irenic in speech," but this was not the problem. Here was not an issue of pulpit freedom but rather a practical matter, for some officers of the Synagogue had expressed alarm that if his views prevailed, great loss and hurt to them might result. Therefore his mind was made up: "If my kind of preaching be incompatible with the maintenance of an institution such as our own, then, as far as I'm concerned, the institution must go on—that is to say, it must go on without me. If it go on without me as it is free to choose to do, I will be heard without the Free Synagogue, as you my people, loved in the past and beloved by me for all times, have made it possible for me to be heard within the pulpit. Whether I am to be heard by this congregation without or within this pulpit is a question which must be left to your decision. My decision is made."

By the middle of the week, their decision was also made. The executive committee met. In a very short time, the verdict was rendered: Wise must stay. The Free Synagogue would remain free. The rabbi spoke not *for* the congregation but rather *to* the congregation.

Two hundred miles to the north, amid the beauty of a Saratoga autumn, George Foster Peabody read of the unanimous vote of confidence and sent congratulations: "The quite exceptional demonstration of the soundness of American public opinion will be heartening in many ways. I cannot refrain from saying that I believe it is probably true that no congregation but a congregation of Hebrews who have drunken for years and ages the spirit of the Prophets could have made so splendid a prompt response to an appeal such as yours, because you certainly went the limit as regards the personal equation in pillorying Judge Gary."

As winter came, disillusionment hung in the air over much of America. Wise sensed this when he planned to go to Pittsburgh, tour the near-by towns, and aid the strikers. The strike leaders wanted a leading figure, preferably a clergyman, to interpret their cause before the hostile community, and through Paul Kellogg, editor of *Survey*, invited Wise. Would he not bring a message to stiffen the morale of the strikers? Wise said yes; but he never went, for the strike was almost over and the cause well-nigh lost.

Bishop McConnell's Commission of Inquiry began to investigate and, in November and early December, tried to mediate, but with no success.

The disappointment of Wise and his fellow liberals was evident in the poor response to an invitation sent by John Haynes Holmes on behalf of the Joint Steel Strikers' Aid Committee to picket the U.S. Steel Company's offices at 71 Broadway during the noon hours on each business day beginning January 5. Holmes' letter to ministers and leading citizens claimed that "the strike is running strong despite every effort of the Steel Trust and their allies to kill it off." The game was up, however; and by January 10 Wise wrote to the editor of the *Brotherhood of Locomotive Firemen and Enginemen's Magazine* in Cleveland:

> I am deeply pained to think that the strike has failed. Everything considered, that failure was inevitable, but it is a thousand pities that it could not have been more wisely led. Had it been more wisely led and no excuse given for maintaining the strike with engineers in the interest of Bolshevism, I think it would have been won. Mr. [William Z.] Foster may be the best of men, but the moment he came under attack, he should have had the wisdom and generosity to have gotten out.

This hindsight was as rueful as that of Holmes in the summer of 1920 when the Inter-Church World Movement issued a *Report* highly critical of the steel industry, of the legal authorities in Western Pennsylvania, and of Pittsburgh's Protestants. In *Unity* he described the *Inter-Church World Movement Report on the Steel Strike* as "tardy as Grouchy at Waterloo . . . but complete, uncompromising, and courageous . . . undoubtedly the most remarkable document ever issued by a religious body in this or any other country."

The *Report's* two hundred and seventy-one pages had given damning evidence: factual information about working conditions, hours, wages, jobs, etc., in the steel industry. It deplored the

arbitrary control of the plants by the Steel Corporation and a
small group of financiers who had only a remote relation to the
producing forces in the plant and scarcely any information about
working and living conditions of the employees. The *Report*
regretted the limited influence of churches and press, educational
institutions, and judicial staffs to redress conditions. It termed
the cry of Bolshevism a fraud on the public and it scoffed at
baseless excitement over the subject. The solution it offered was a
suggestion for free and open conference between employers and
employees, a procedure successful in the bituminous and anthra-
cite coal industries. Otherwise, it warned, a renewal of the
conflict was inevitable.

In the fall of 1920, almost a year to the date of his sermon
about Gary, Wise asked, "Who Killed the Inter-Church World
Movement?" and quipped that a steel splinter had gotten into the
eye of this child of Protestantism. It had thus been done to death.
The movement had collapsed, in great measure owing to the
shrinkage of financial aid from Protestant denominations unwilling to support such social-service projects.

Meanwhile, there was work to do in dispelling the anti-Bol-
shevik hysteria prevalent in the land, in protesting the raids made
by Attorney General Mitchell Palmer on the homes of suspected
radicals, and the curtailment of freedom of speech in many
places. Court cases had to be fought to the highest court, the
suppression and censorship of newspapers opposed, the prosecution of speakers and raiding of meetings protested, and the
right to criticize the government upheld. The suppression of un-
orthodox and unconventional opinions, both economic and political, had to be fought, partly because the American tradition of
freedom of speech was endangered and partly because due
process of law had not been observed.

To achieve these ends, an independent organization, akin to
the National Civil Liberties Bureau of the American Union
Against Militarism, was needed. A tremendous amount of work
was now begun to combat the deportation of aliens for radical
beliefs, ordered by Attorney General Palmer, and to oppose attacks on the I.W.W., the anarchist labor organization. The right
of trade unions to hold meetings and organize had to be sup-

ported and efforts made to secure release from prison of the
hundreds sentenced during the war for expressing antiwar
opinions. Holmes now joined Harry F. Ward and Roger Baldwin
in organizing the American Civil Liberties Union, with Wise
once more by his side.

IV. Between Wilson and F. D. R.

(1921–1932)

Greatness once and forever has done with opinion. O friend, never strike sail to a fear! Come into port greatly or sail with God the seas.

—RALPH WALDO EMERSON, 1850

16. What Doth the Lord Require of Thee?

*Feel a little blue today on the eve of Harding.
He is so little fitted to cope with the problems
that press. He represents such a decline from
Wilson.* —STEPHEN S. WISE, 1921

STEPHEN WISE PRAYED with his people at the naming of an infant, at the confirmation service, at the marriage feast, and at the funeral service. The members of the Free Synagogue found that, amid myriad duties elsewhere in the land, Wise could counsel effectively and comfort constantly. He often amazed people with his memory of details concerning their problems and his careful attention to their needs.

On one occasion a family, not affiliated with the Free Synagogue, telephoned him after midnight to ask if he could come to the bedside of a dying mother. Other rabbis in the city to whom they had telephoned said they had retired but would try to come some time the next day. When Wise was asked, he instantly rose, dressed, and went. He offered prayers. He consoled the family. He remained for several hours until the aged mother died. Such kindnesses were legion and discomfited his critics who failed to understand that commitment to great causes never diminished his infinite love and concern for every human being.

His funeral services were sensitively rendered and brought solace to the bereaved. In his eulogy, Wise could be both incisive and perceptive; and as the procession moved slowly to the grave,

Wise, in the tradition of his people, would repeat the Twenty-third Psalm in his melodious voice.

Public speaking he enjoyed most of all. Once he visited a Quaker meeting house in eastern Pennsylvania and the clerk of the meeting invited him to speak if the Spirit moved him. Wise wrote home, "I assured him It would!"

The quotations of his lectures and addresses, as reported in newspapers, were not always accurate, for Wise was not an easy man to report. The address, when spoken, carried people to what lay behind the words, but often the sentences did not read well in cold print. Too often his style and mannerisms blurred the outline and the content. Yet he carried conviction to his audience. In discussion groups after a lecture, they delighted in his informality, his interest in other points of view, and in his humor which could be gay and rapier-like in turn. They saw the open-heartedness of the man who granted interviews freely, charmed newspaper reporters and, once met, was never forgotten. The cordial welcome of the Pullman porter, recognizing him and ushering him into the train, gave the local folks a glimpse into the nature of the man. He would talk to everyone who in any way knew him or recognized him. Friendship flowed from quick acquaintanceship. Letters and exchanges of gifts resulted, whether from a voyage on a transatlantic liner or on a streetcar in some distant city. Platform gestures were then forgotten and the orator's manner discarded.

In the midst of all this, he never forgot his family. Notes flowed constantly to Louise, often written on telegraph blanks and dining car menus. One told of his guilty feeling when, at a Zionist meeting, Justice Brandeis had said, "We must save and stint for Palestine." And Wise wrote to Louise: "He makes me ashamed of my tennis court, except that I built it that we might feel our children near us these years of our life." To the three of them—Louise, Justine, and Jim—Wise dedicated his book, *How To Face Life*; and he welcomed their advice and criticism when he prepared another book, *Child Versus Parent, Some Chapters on the Irrepressible Conflict in the Home*, which he adapted from a popular lecture.

In the late winter of 1921 an illness attacked Wise and the

doctors decided on surgery. Warned that an operation might be fatal, he wrote a letter which Jim and Justine discovered almost thirty years later, requesting, in the event of his death, a private funeral marked by simplicity. There was to be no eulogy and—this they must not forget—Holmes was to read the Ninetieth Psalm: "O Lord, Thou hast been our dwelling place in all generations . . ." Then he added, realistically, that if a larger place must be used for the funeral, Carnegie Hall would be suitable.

Wise recovered quickly, however, and seemed to gain new strength. At the Free Synagogue's fourteenth anniversary celebration at the Hotel Pennsylvania in April, 1921, where Albert Einstein was the guest of honor, Wise reported on growth that included a membership of more than one thousand families; five divisional synagogues—on the East Side, in the Bronx, in Washington Heights, in Flushing, and in Newark; more than a thousand children in the educational program; and a budget that had grown 1,000 per cent since 1907. Yet these were outward visible things, whereas he was concerned with the spiritual ideals which "affect the moral fortunes of a people."

In contrast to the Wises, the Holmes family adhered to the traditions of New England: less display of outward affection, more restraint of the emotions, and as little overlapping of private and public life as possible. Madeleine Holmes was not as much in the public eye and mind as Louise Wise; moreover, Madeleine was shy and retiring to such a degree that she literally suffered when it was necessary for her to appear in public. This characteristic was intensified when, in her thirties, she discovered that she had inherited the deafness that plagued each generation in her family. Deafness was neither accepted nor helped then as it is today, and as the infirmity progressed, it made her withdraw even more into the background. As her husband became more famous, she finally asked him to promise that she would never again be forced to sit at a head table or become conspicuous in any way. He respected her request.

Madeleine Holmes was vitally interested in everything pertaining to the church and the many outside interests of her husband, and Holmes never wrestled with any problem or made any decision, large or small, without discussing it first with her.

In her quiet way, she gave considerable time to the church and its activities. It was a rare occasion when on Sunday morning she was not in her accustomed seat in one of the back rows where, although she could not hear the service, she could, without being noticed, see that all was going well. With the exception of a handful of people in the church, several girlhood friends, her many relatives in Brooklyn, and her immediate family, most people did not know her well; and thus her seeming aloofness was often misunderstood. She had a fine and active mind, a joyous sense of humor, and her thoughtfulness and generosity knew no bounds. Christmas was her golden moment, but there was not a time throughout the year when she was not planning some event or gift to make someone happy, a pastime which gave her as much pleasure as it did the recipient of her kindness. Her primary concern, however, was always her husband and his well-being and comfort. Even though John would remain in the city for meetings as many as five nights a week, Madeleine made sure it was in a well-run and quiet household that he spent the few hours the family had together.

In the early years, the children were with her most of the time, while Holmes was either in Manhattan or traveling about the country. The penalty of a house in Brooklyn Heights, lovely and gracious as that area was, lay in the frequent absences of the father and husband. No less attached to wife and children than Wise, Holmes was nonetheless more remote. He was much too busy and there was little time left for Madeleine and home, for Roger and Frances. Both she and the children paid a heavy price for Holmes' public life, yet they seemed to understand.

The readers of his magazine *Unity*, scarcely exceeding two thousand, included many influential American citizens, as well as many equally prominent men and women in Europe. He wrote editorials, book reviews, and interpretative material at the rate of five thousand words per week. Apart from his sermons to the Community Churches of New York and Boston and addresses on at least two hundred platforms per year throughout the country, he prepared an entirely new, unpreached sermon for publication each Saturday evening in the New York *Herald*. His correspondence was still as large as ever and sometimes reached a total of ninety to a hundred letters per day.

To Stefan Zweig, Romain Rolland, and H. G. Wells across the sea had come word of the Community Church, a new and distinctive development in the life of organized religion in America. They wrote Holmes to congratulate him. He reported to them that his congregation was now rich in non-Nordics who came from all creeds, classes, races, and nations. Not a few were Jews and many were Negroes. A number were Orientals and South Europeans and quite a large group came from lower-income groups. All began to attain a new level of democratic thought and action, sensing something of the brotherhood which, they hoped, would some day be established throughout the earth.

This was Holmes' new language. No longer did he speak assuredly of the Kingdom of God coming on earth. Now more realistic, he did not expect this Kingdom to come swiftly. There was the hope, however, and it spurred them to new efforts.

Plans were made to gather funds and replace the burned edifice on the foundations of the old. This would not be the old-time religion in an old-fashioned church, for the institutions of religion were compelled to face a changing world: "In the light of what has transpired since the vast upheaval of the War and is now transpiring the world around, there would seem to be no institution more unstable than the state, save only the church; and both of these institutions are now in process of a radical transformation at the hands of a democratic spirit."

So he wrote in a new book, *New Churches for Old: A Plea for Community Religion.* The trouble with churches was their failure to rid themselves of ideas and practices in which modern man had no interest at all. He may have overestimated the desire of his generation to cast off the old and put on the new, but in his mind the issues were clear:

> To attend a religious service on Sunday morning is to witness a spectacle which demonstrates in vivid dramatic form the alienation of the modern mind from all that is the most real and precious to the church. . . . Here is a literature, offered as sacred, which contains no word written down later than two hundred years after the death of Jesus, and no idea later than the Neo-Platonic speculations of Alexandrian Judaism. Here are readings, prayers, instruction, exhortations, couched in language Pauline, Augustinian, Lutheran, Calvinistic, Wesleyan, and

therefore as unintelligible today as the jargon of alchemy or astrology. Here are ideas which embody science, history, psychology, philosophy, of a type which has disappeared long since from every hall of learning, and from all literature save that specifically labeled "religious." Here is an attitude toward the universe, toward life and its destiny, toward society and its problems, which is as strange to the modern man as that of a foreign country, a distant age, or even another planet. Above all, there is an atmosphere in this place which seems as remote from our every-day world as the atmosphere of a buried city; from it there seems to be excluded everything that breathes of life and joy.

It seemed incredible to him that men could have one foot firmly planted in the twentieth century and the other foot in a completely out-of-date world of another day:

By what imaginable reversion of attention can persons who have learned the lessons of Newton and Darwin, and are now sitting at the feet of Bergson and Einstein, be persuaded to hold interest in affirmations of the Trinity, the Atonement, the Resurrection, Redemption, Salvation, and the rest—much less to express their spiritual ideals in terms of these conceptions? We do not expect men today to light their houses by rush-light, to travel in stage-coaches or on horseback, to converse in Latin, to live in the thought-world of Plato, or Kant, or even Herbert Spencer. Why should we expect them to accept the ideas or even retain the phrases of the Nicene Creed or the Westminster Confession?

This was religious liberalism: to liberate men from the concept of a transcendent God who threatened eternal damnation for all. Had it not now become clear that God and man were one? Man must worship the immanent God, the divine within himself, the God with Whom he could become a co-worker.

John Haynes Holmes believed with Henri Bergson that God was struggling, failing, and then beginning again, falling and then rising again. As with God, so with man. The organic growth of God Himself in time drew men on and impelled them to express the divine within themselves. Similarly, society struggled. Slowly but surely, "with groaning and travailing together," freedom would develop into fellowship and thence into the community ideal.

The ideal society would result from the impulse of the idea of the Kingdom of God, an earthly concept, a this-worldly view which would transform the world. Mankind would ascend to the Kingdom by the almost automatic escalator of the evolutionary process: onward and upward to a far-off divine event toward which the whole Creation moved. The Kingdom, now thoroughly secularized and inevitably an earthly regime, would become the expression of true democracy. As for any obstacles along the road, they could be surmounted by appeals to reason and moral suasion. Abundant good will would mitigate the class struggle, persuade entrenched interests to relinquish their positions of privilege, and achieve reconciliation.

The ideal of love was uniquely illustrated by Jesus of Nazareth who was no longer "the Christ" and had little meaning as an empirical event. Jesus was not the Center of History who once and for all had revealed the ultimate meaning of life and reflected supremely the divine initiative; instead, Jesus was a "revolutionary" who brought mankind the potency of love in place of scepters that ruled and swords that killed. From his day on, Jesus had been the disturbing, upsetting factor in the world; and there could be no peace until his spirit entered the souls of men, condemning the world as it was and pointing to a new, better world to be established in its place. Love, not force, brought and held men fast together. Force, not love, would be destroyed.

Sin, in the eyes of Holmes and his contemporaries, was an ancient, outmoded concept. In reality, sin was only ignorance, and salvation from this cultural lag was achieved by education. What better means could one adopt to bring salvation to men than to have a John Dewey and a Harry Overstreet, a James Harvey Robinson and a Harry F. Ward, speak in the Forum at the Community Church and turn a blazing light of intelligence on breeding areas of prejudice and hate?

To Holmes, H. G. Wells was a prophet and seer who had coined a piquant phrase, "the race between education and catastrophe," which discerned the future accurately. In 1916 he had described Wells as prophetic because he spoke to the needs of the time and he so described Wells in an article in *The Bookman*. When, in 1921, he read the two volumes of *Outline of History*, he mentioned the book repeatedly in sermons and lectures and recommended it to his hearers as an example of a fresh, provocative mind at work creating religious imperatives for the future.

Holmes' religious liberalism sought to transmute religion from a system of theology to a program of social life. He had confidence in man; thus his liberalism was a friend of science and art, the champion of all cultural and humanitarian movements of reform. In place of the ecclesiastical and the theological he would offer the ethical point of view, the moral beauty which was the sign of healthy human nature. Human nature, because of its capacity of virtue, was divine. He was therefore saying once more what Jenkin Lloyd Jones had said a generation earlier: "Our shift of spiritual viewpoint from God to man has carried us straight from theology, through ethics, to sociology, for man delivered from theologizing is as truly made for love as the stars for shining." Now the Community Church said it anew.

He rewrote statements of purpose of the Community Church and circulated them throughout the country, for the New York church was now a pilot plant of the Community Church Movement. He made no claim then or at any later date that he had originated the Community Church trend in American life. Instead, he pointed to Carl Stoll of Buffalo as the father of the Community Church idea and founder of the National Conference of Community Churches.

To Josiah Royce, his teacher at Harvard and originator of the phrase, "The Beloved Community," and to John Fiske, the historian and philosopher of evolution, he traced the seminal sources of this innovation in organized religion. He had no apology for making democracy the religion of his place and time, for democracy helped to identify religion with the larger human interest of emancipation. What was democracy, he asked, but the attempt to liberate the soul? Could democracy do anything other on all of its levels—political, social, and economic—than transform the human into the divine? This, in simplest terms, was the spirit of Jesus at work. Thus could religion fully express personality and assure the sanctity of the human soul.

These certainties did not leave him without conflicts inside himself. Of those he had the normal quota, but he had certitude.

In the eyes of his critics, he had too much certitude, as they would readily have affirmed, had they seen the letter he wrote to Zona Gale, the novelist, in the summer of 1920. While he was recovering from a hernia operation, Holmes reflected on the coming presidential election:

> Well—the political conventions have been held, and the proceedings have run true to form. Harding and Cox!! Ye gods, what has happened to the political life of this country that, like the mountain, it labors and brings forth such mice? But what a question! For we know well enough what is the matter. Now if we could only get the public to know, and act upon that knowledge, the promised third party might have some chance of victory this fall. I am praying that a firm and true amalgamation of all the various parties and groups of liberals may be effected in Chicago this week. I wish in my own heart that Debs might be the nominee—but La Follette will do!

Holmes' hopes were too high. The third party did not develop; Debs, chosen by the Socialist Party and waging his campaign from a prison cell, was Holmes' choice, but he had no chance. Warren Harding was out of the question. As for Cox and his running mate, Franklin Delano Roosevelt, he thought the former too conservative a candidate and the latter a young aristocrat, arrogant and untried, representing the Groton and Harvard cliques for which Holmes had had only contempt in Cambridge twenty years earlier.

Life, then, for Holmes was mainly work. His hobbies were few: he collected autographs; he would go to baseball games at the Polo Grounds, root for the Giants, and even memorize batting averages, though sports were not a major interest; a game of cribbage with his wife late at night was another way to relax; and playing Mozart, Handel, and Beethoven on the piano, whether at home, in the church, or as on one signal occasion at the Ford Hall Forum, was a joy. But reading and letter writing were his favorite means of using spare time, traveling and lecturing his main activities outside the church. Always available for counseling, he still found time to be by himself, usually on a train or in a hotel room. He had a seemingly inexhaustible store of nervous energy that flowed at full tide to match his physical endurance.

In the summer months, however, it was quite a different story for the Holmes family. Beginning in 1908, they went each year to Kennebunk Beach in Maine and for three months had a relaxed, rewarding vacation together. With the exception of the mornings spent in his study and the time allotted each day to mowing the lawns and clipping the rose bushes with meticulous care, he joined his family in many of their activities at the Beach. The most memorable hours were those when the family gathered for meals; there was sparkling conversation on subjects of interest to the children as well as the adults, and much laughter and joking. There was swimming in the late morning, long walks in the afternoon, and a family game of anagrams or hearts each evening. They owned a small boat and would row up the river or venture forth on the ocean when it was calm. This was a happy time for John and Madeleine and the children; and it served a double purpose: it not only gave Holmes much needed rest and relaxation and thus renewal of mind, body, and spirit for the rigors of the coming year, but it also gave the family the opportunity to be together in a normal relationship. These summer months at Kennebunk Beach year after year provided the happiest of memories for all four of them.

For strangers he was not an easy person to know. There was too much to do. As for fools and bores who spring up everywhere, he found it hard to suffer them gladly. He did not, like Stephen Wise, enter the diner or club car of a train and hold court among friends. Wise seemed to draw strength from each person with whom he talked; Holmes sometimes found people to be a drain on his strength. Furthermore, Holmes considered the diner too expensive and Madeleine would pack a lunch for him; and he avoided the club car, for he wanted privacy to work. From the vendor going through the day coach he would buy milk, not coffee or tea, for he never took stimulants. Work was stimulus enough. Not to be disturbed in the writing that never ceased, he would throw back the adjacent seat when the day coach was not crowded and spread out manuscripts, correspondence, magazines, and books as a moat against an invading public. After a lecture he would hurry back to his hotel room and write the weekly stint of articles and editorials for *Unity*. Singleminded and undismayed, he pressed on in his "high calling" toward a better society and a juster world.

Only forty-one in 1920 and still seeking new worlds, Holmes designed a book plate to symbolize his search for a golden fleece. In conventional fashion it read: "John Haynes Holmes: *Ex Libris*," but it had a pen-and-ink drawing of a bark tossing on a tempestuous sea beneath troubled skies. Below the sketch he inscribed the last line of Tennyson's *Ulysses*: "To strive, to seek, to find, and not to yield!"

17. Who Is the Greatest Man
in the World?

> He [Mahatma Gandhi] is a dangerous and
> uncomfortable enemy, but his body, which
> you can always conquer, gives you so little
> purchase upon his soul.
>
> —GILBERT MURRAY, 1918

IN 1921, JOHN HAYNES HOLMES stated without apology: "When I think of Mahatma Gandhi, I think of Jesus Christ."

The parallel with Jesus constantly presented itself: "The Nazarene, or divine personality, taught the law of love and laid down a program of soul force for its fulfillment; He sought to establish the Kingdom of Heaven on earth, so also with Gandhi. This Indian is a saint in personal life; he teaches the law of love and soul force as its practice; and he seeks the establishment of a new social order, which shall be a Kingdom of the Spirit."

Three years earlier, Holmes had chanced upon an article in the *Hibbert Journal* by the Oxford classicist Gilbert Murray. Murray had written about the concept of the soul among the ancient Greeks and Romans, and among such contemporaries as Henri Bergson, Stephen Hobhouse (the English Quaker, confined to hard labor in a British prison as a conscientious objector), and Gandhi. In deploring the penalties inflicted upon Hobhouse, Murray did not know that his words would some day apply to Britain's treatment of Gandhi. He warned Great Britain that a government which sets out to prosecute its saints is not a wise

or a generous government, a nation which cannot live in peace
with its saints is not a very healthy or high-minded nation.

Holmes tried to find out more about Gandhi but discovered
that few knew anything about him. Not long afterward, he received from India a pamphlet, torn in the mail and without a
return address, that told about the Mahatma. In later years, he
said many times that on this day he knew how John Keats felt
when first he read Chapman's translation of Homer.

Holmes then reread the Murray article and chose as a title
for his sermon, "Who Is the Greatest Man in the World Today?"
In the Lyric Theatre on April 10, he preached about Gandhi to
an overflow congregation which expected to hear about Woodrow
Wilson or Sun Yat-sen, Lloyd George or Lenin. Holmes gave an
account of the man whose soul force was already greater than
any other in the world. He recounted the years of Gandhi's childhood and adolescence in India as the son of a high-caste Hindu
family and the carefree student days in London. He told of the
marriage, arranged and solemnized in the bride's childhood but
not consummated until later. He described Gandhi's fateful journey to South Africa as a young, ambitious barrister. He related
the shattering experience in the chill, barren depot near Pieter-
maritzburg where the dark-skinned man had been expelled from
the train and from that hour forever after identified with the dis-
inherited and dispossessed. He spoke of Gandhi's dramatic battle
over a twenty-year period for the civil and religious rights of his
fellow Indians in the Union of South Africa and the evolvement
of a resolute civil-disobedience based upon passive resistance; of
the return to India in 1913; of the Mahatma's support of Britain
in the 1914–1918 war; and of the subsequent slow, steady mounting of the Indian people's nonviolent rebellion against British
rule.

Here was a rebel against British imperialism and Western
industrialism but not an advocate of violence; a politician who
for years had been an ascetic and to millions seemed a saint; a
statesman who resorted to prayer and devoted a silent day each
week to meditation. In Gandhi, Holmes saw a unique strength,
a power stronger than steel, more potent than fire. When Gandhi
went from village to village in India, with crowds of fifty thousand

gathering to hear him, vast throngs approached him as to a holy shrine. In this mystic, clad only in a loincloth, Holmes saw "as stern a realist as Lenin in his political endeavors, at the same time an idealist, living ever in the pure radiance of the spirit." Like Jesus, Gandhi bade his disciples heed the counsel: "If any man would be first among you, let him be servant of all."

The sermon, widely read in America, was also republished in India many times. Now Holmes had a procession of friends of Indian independence coming to his study, men like Taraknath Das and Synd Hossain. He became known as a foremost American interpreter of Gandhi's views. Soon Holmes could refer inquirers to Romain Rolland who wrote of Gandhi with quiet eloquence.

Holmes hoped some day to meet Gandhi, but that day would not come for some years. He wished he could have gone on to India in 1922, when he spoke to the Women's International League for Peace and Freedom in Italy at Varese and addressed the European Conference of the International Fellowship of Reconciliation at Sonntagsburg, Germany; but in those days travel consumed too much time.

In Germany, he was moved by meeting Adolf Harnack, the eminent church historian, whose bowed frame and sweet smile conveyed more than did the halting exchange of his own broken English and Holmes' few German phrases. Again, he thought, why could not nations adopt Gandhian methods, wipe out warfare, and make impossible the privations Harnack had endured?

He went on to Russia, which, in his eyes, was on the verge of a new tyranny. Constantly he was shadowed by the secret police. Everywhere there was an atmosphere of fear. In the notes he dashed off for articles to *Unity* and for sermons and addresses in the coming months, he warned of tragic abuses of the freedom wrested from the czar and the inability of unguarded liberty to control the social order: "It simply cannot be trusted alone to work out the great ideals of democracy, by the best of men as well as by the worst, by the educated as well as by the ignorant. Liberty is always subject to abuse, and therefore becomes the means of destroying the very thing for the sake of which it was inaugurated."

On his return to America, Holmes continued his exposition of Gandhi. In December, 1924, *The World Tomorrow* devoted an entire issue to Gandhi. Holmes wrote the leading article and introduced interpretations by C. F. Andrews and E. Stanley Jones, missionaries in India, and by A. Fenner Brockway of the British Labor Party. In 1927, Gandhi became correspondent from India for Holmes' *Unity*, which began to publish in serial form Gandhi's autobiography, *The Story of My Experiments with Truth*.

When Holmes, accompanied by his wife and son, Roger, went to the Middle East in 1929, he again was unable to extend the journey to India. His long-cherished desire to meet Gandhi was not fulfilled until September, 1931, ten years after his famous sermon, when Gandhi came to Europe.

In that year Holmes was again bound for the Soviet Union. The 1931 trip to Russia was different from that of 1922, for now he had Sherwood Eddy's dynamic direction and genial traveling companionship. There was adequate food for travelers and the Russians welcomed tourists. Although Soviet restrictions on liberty and the limitations on democracy still lay heavily on Holmes' heart, Lenin's tomb gave him another, more sympathetic view of Russia.

In a sermon that fall at Community Church, then meeting each Sunday in Town Hall, he described the giant structure of red marble in spacious Red Square with the Kremlin wall bulking large on one side and at its base the graves of those killed in the October, 1917, street fighting. Among those graves had been scattered, at a later date, the ashes of Americans he knew: John Reed, Bill Haywood, Paxton Hibben. He depicted the long line of patient thousands reaching across the Square; the American's special privilege of admittance at the head of the line; his descent down a long marble stairway in complete silence; the awesome sight of the embalmed body lying as though asleep upon a bed.

In conclusion, he asked his congregation:

Shall I tell you what was one of the great religious experiences of my life? It was the last evening of my stay in Moscow. I had wandered into the Red Square, a few minutes before midnight, to hear the chimes within the Kremlin bell tower. Before me loomed the dark mass of Lenin's tomb. Behind the tomb was

the Kremlin wall, looking down upon an area which it had
guarded for ten bloody centuries. Behind the wall were golden
domes and lofty towers shining like silver in the flood of moon-
light which poured down upon the scene. Silently, one by one
upon the ramparts of the wall, there passed the sentinels, their
bayonets gleaming in the molten light. I waited for the hour
to strike, watching the motionless guard before the portal of the
tomb, or the domes upon Ivan's grotesque cathedral, or the
great clock as clear as day upon the tower. Suddenly above the
shuffle of passing feet and the distant roar of the city, there
sounded the twelve strokes of midnight. As the last tone died
away, it seemed as though for the first time a hush fell upon
the square. Then quickly after a long interval of silence, there
came sounding through the night the music of the chiming bells
as they rang the anthem of the "Internationale":

Arise, ye prisoners of starvation . . .

In cascades of pealing sound, like music pouring from the
heavens, the great hymn went flooding the vast spaces of the
city. As I listened, I thought I heard the voices not of angels
but of all the tired toilers of all the ages gone, now at last made
glad and free in the release of their brethren upon earth. Suddenly, as I looked at Lenin's tomb, it seemed as though out of
darkness there sprang a flame to consume injustice and light the
paths of men. And it *was* a flame, or very like a flame, for there,
high up above the mausoleum, there floated, in one clear shaft
of light, the Red flag.

The chimes were silent. I seemed to hear again the clamor
of the city. The moon disappeared behind a looming dome, and
Lenin's tomb was swallowed in great darkness. I turned back to
the Square of the Revolution and my hotel, and as I saw the
night slowly passing to the early dawn of the new day, I said
to my comrade at my side, "This is religion and its prophet
is Lenin."

Like many intellectuals all over the world, he wished to find
hope and promise of a better world in the Russian Revolution.
He lived to be disillusioned.

Now Holmes, having come from the Soviet Union where liberty
was dormant and democracy no more than a myth, returned
through Europe and traveled to the British Isles to meet the most
potent advocate of liberty and democracy in India, Mohandas
K. Gandhi.

During the spring of 1931, Holmes had heard from Gandhi of a possible journey from India to England; if he were to come to London, he looked forward to seeing his American friend. When the Viceroy and Gandhi failed to agree on an agenda, Gandhi announced he would not attend the Round Table Conference on Indian Affairs. Holmes then gave up hope of meeting him. The Viceroy and Gandhi soon settled their differences and announced a date for the meeting.

Holmes and Gandhi had exchanged letters, brief but cordial, affectionate and understanding. Friends had carried personal messages. If Holmes thought he would go to London to wait upon the Mahatma until the door opened to let him in, he underestimated Gandhi's feelings for him. He need not have been surprised when C. F. Andrews asked him to come down to Folkestone and greet Gandhi at the pier.

That Saturday, September 12, was foggy and cold. Heavy rains fell periodically. The Channel was rough and windy. Holmes, chilled and impatient, walked back and forth along the pier. Holmes recalled the day in his later years and recaptured the moments in an oft-told narrative:

> Suddenly I found myself talking with a young policeman, posted as a guard for the Mahatma. He was an intelligent man, a college graduate, who recognized me quickly as an American.
>
> "You're at an interesting point on the English coast," he said. "Do you see that projection of land over there, just to the north? That's where Caesar landed when he brought his legions to conquer England." He paused, as though to let me ponder this striking episode of history. Then, pointing in the opposite direction, to the south, he continued, "And through that fog there, not so far away, is Pevensey, where landed a second conqueror, the great William of Normandy." Then suddenly, as I gazed upon the sea, there came a moment of inspiration. "Here is a third conqueror," I cried within my heart, in expectation of Gandhi's arrival. A very different kind of conqueror, to be sure! He had no armor on his back, no sword at his side. He was accompanied not by a Roman legion or a Norman army, but only by a few scattered secretaries and friends.

Then presently the tiny white steamer appeared ghostlike out of the fog and slowly edged to the wharf. The British representative went aboard to arrange clearance while Holmes and his friends waited. Not long after, the group went below to Gandhi's stateroom.

Then the door of Gandhi's cabin opened and Holmes saw him for the first time, sitting in cross-legged fashion on his berth, clad only in his usual garb of loincloth and light shawl. When it was Holmes' turn for an interview, Gandhi rose quickly and came to him, welcoming him warmly. Holmes was captivated by Gandhi's charm and grace, by his childlike spontaneity and complete lack of pride. Gandhi's winsome conversation and natural humor put Holmes at ease.

In London, during the following days, Holmes was in the center of the many events in Gandhi's schedule and knew the inordinate demands made upon him. He marveled at the man's equanimity. Gandhi remained untroubled by attacks from the newspapers and the prospect of the Round Table's failure. The Mahatma was moved by the affection little children had for him but unmoved by the adulation of the crowds. He was unperturbed amid the noise of the city and rigorous in his devotion to a regimen of prayer and meditation. Holmes saw Gandhi parry with ease Laborite members of Parliament when for two hours they questioned him.

Gandhi asked Holmes to help him make up his mind about a suggested visit to America, urged upon him by many influential people. Holmes knew how complicated such a visit by Gandhi might be, how likely the public would be to ridicule him, how ill prepared America was for his message. Consequently, he dissuaded Gandhi.

Holmes grasped the chance of these meetings with Gandhi to discuss with him two matters which were of great importance both to Stephen Wise and to himself. The first was Holmes' suggestion that the Indian people, through Gandhi, send some of their leading men and women to America as "ambassadors." Recalling how effective Free Eire's representatives in Washington and other major cities had been in presenting Irish claims for independence and remembering how successful the Jewish Agency for Palestine had become in a few brief years in representing Zionism in several national capitals, Holmes recom-

mended a similar project for Gandhi's cause. Gandhi replied that
he would consider the proposal, but sounded skeptical. Nothing
ever came of the suggestion.

The other matter was a defense of the rights of the Jewish
people to Palestine and their movement for self-determination
and nationhood. Holmes, with memories fresh from his journey
to Palestine in early 1929, discussed Zionism with Gandhi but
found him unreceptive. Gandhi's struggle with the British
Empire was not only on behalf of his own people but in pursuit
of justice in general. Zionism was too particularistic. To Gandhi,
the Jews of Palestine were an artificial injection in the blood-
stream of the Middle East and he tended to support the cause
of the Arab peoples.

If illiteracy and poverty abounded among the Arabs, four
hundred million Indians experienced the same blight. Arabs
were indigenous to the region and would have to build their
own cultures and national structures on the mores of centuries
past. That the Jews in Palestine brought Western culture, technical skills, and scientific methods to the benighted backwaters
of the Middle East impressed Gandhi not at all. He was not
anti-Jewish nor was he specifically anti-Zionist; but he could see
no legitimacy in the Jewish cause. Similarly, he was never convinced that Jew and Arab could live and work together in
co-operative fashion in Palestine and the near-by lands.

When The Friends of Gandhi, of which Holmes was a founder
and the president for over twenty years, held a dinner in honor
of Gandhi's sixty-second birthday in New York City in the fall
of 1931, Stephen Wise accepted an invitation to speak. He used
the occasion to remind Gandhi in far-off India, this man so hospitable to truth, that there were almost no British bayonets in
Palestine until the Arabs began the massacres of August and
September of 1929. The Jewish settlers in Palestine, Wise argued,
could not rightly be accused of resting their case on force. They
had returned to Palestine not to hurt and not to wound, but to
serve, to enrich, to bless the land and all its people. This they had
done from every point of view: economically, culturally, morally,
and spiritually. Wise compared the status of the Jews in the
world with that of the people of India; if Gandhi's people were

denied their rights, so also were Jews. He shared Gandhi's hope for India's freedom, a hope that had the good will of all men who wanted peace and freedom for everyone in the world; but he urged Gandhi to travel the short distance from India to Palestine and see for himself what had been accomplished, to discover how parallel to India's interests were the aims of the Jews in Palestine.

Wise was also instrumental in having a special award given to Gandhi in the following spring. Holmes had inaugurated a special Community Church medal for an outstanding citizen of the world and turned to Wise for a suggestion. Wise nominated Gandhi. At the service, Wise spoke of Gandhi's prime attribute, his religious power, and likened him standing before the Viceroy to a "Nathan speaking with all the terrible power of unafraid truth to the King." Gandhi, he said, was the "outstanding spiritual figure of our time," who impelled people "to trust him, follow him, and love him because of the divine simplicity of his spirit, which moves him to stand before the leaders of the mightiest Commonwealth of Nations and demand that his people be set free."

Wise, never a thoroughgoing pacifist or devotee of nonviolent resistance, nevertheless realized the power of Gandhi's restraining influence: "He could, if he would, so move India to rise that its rivers would run red with blood, but . . . with malice toward none of the rulers of his people and with charity for all its millions, he seeks the equal good of all and shall yet achieve it, for he relies on the resistless weapons of love and truth without resorting to the arbitrament of arms and war."

Indulging his fondness for inverted phrases, Wise said Gandhi "relies upon the force of truth and denies the truth of force"; and he approved of the reliance on the "exposition and incarnation of *Satyagraha* or truth force or soul force." Not only was Gandhi what Holmes had called him ten years earlier, "the greatest man in the world," but more: "the loftiest spiritual figure of generations."

Whenever the subject came up, Wise argued with Holmes that Gandhi had neither clearly seen nor effectively dealt with the power and malicious designs of two empires, the British Empire and the Moslem Empire; the former denied to subject peoples the self-determination and independent status which it gave to its own peoples in self-governed lands, and the latter, by its Pan-Islamic dreams, meant only harm to those who wanted to live in freedom and dignity. This thesis he hammered home with all the power of rhetoric he could summon.

Wise could not go as far as Holmes did in making Gandhi a pattern for his personal life. Holmes, in a sermon on "The Dilemma of the Moral Life," spoke of the obedience of St. Francis of Assisi to the example of Jesus Christ:

> It is not the least among the services of the Christian church that it has kept alive through all these centuries the personality of the Nazarene, and thus enabled millions of men and women in the pious spirit of St. Francis to solve their moral problems by putting Jesus in their place. I have myself found incalculable help and guidance in recent years in taking Gandhi for my example. If I have been tempted to write an angry letter, I have asked myself, "Would Gandhi write such a letter?" If I have been irritated by some selfish boor who has stolen my time to serve his own designs and purposes, I have said to myself, "How would Gandhi treat this person?" If I have found myself perplexed as to what to do in this instance or that, I have again and again inquired within my heart, "What would Gandhi tell me to do if I should ask him?"

Wise, on the other hand, believed more in the individual's autonomous judgment and less in reliance on an authority, no matter how saintly that authority might be. To him, the problems of life were too complex to be solved by looking to a holy man of India.

Holmes in turn was sure of Gandhi's guidance and was never troubled by the Mahatma's seeming inconsistencies. Gandhi might oppose the machine and use the spinning wheel day in and day out, year in and year out to prepare the thread for *khaddar*, the Indian's substitute for foreign-made cloth; but this action was a legitimate protest, said Holmes, against the machine age and its deadening, stifling influence. Gandhi might revert to the loincloth and seem ridiculous to many in the world; but to Holmes this act was the method by which the Indian leader could identify himself with millions of his fellow Indians who had insufficient clothing for their naked backs. Gandhi might talk about soul force and nonviolent disobedience, while his boycott of British-made goods caused thousands to suffer and barely exist on a dole; but Holmes considered this counsel justified and in no way violent. Gandhi, though a devout Hindu, could yet see value in all faiths and bluntly tell Christians, even his devoted friend, C. F. Andrews, that Christianity had no uniqueness for him and Christian missionaries could justify their existence only by urging their own nations to be Christians; but Holmes felt these statements to be quite consistent. Gandhi could show great respect for all forms of human life and insist upon sanitation in villages where filth prevailed but oppose any kind of birth control in his land where the population was only somewhat held in check by the high incidence of disease and widespread poverty; yet to Holmes these views were in no way incongruous or contradictory.

Concerning the personality and performance of Mohandas Gandhi, Holmes and Wise held widely varying views and still retained respect for each other's opinions. Both men were aware of Gandhi's spiritual contribution to the time and felt that he had certainly made a more lasting contribution to the world's spiritual treasures than had Lenin. In their eyes he was indeed the greatest man in the world at that time. This remained true for Holmes, though not for Wise in later years.

18. He Hath Holpen
His People Israel

Let no American imagine that Zionism is inconsistent with patriotism. Multiple loyalties are objectionable only if they are inconsistent. . . . Every Irish American who contributed toward advancing home rule was a better man and a better American for the sacrifice he made. Every American Jew who aids in advancing the Jewish settlement in Palestine, though he feels that neither he nor his descendants will ever live there, will likewise be a better man and a better American for doing so. —LOUIS D. BRANDEIS, 1915

IN THE EARLY NINETEEN TWENTIES, among many activities, Stephen Wise, now in his late forties, centered his efforts on the establishment of a training school for rabbis. He planned a Jewish Institute of Religion, a school not to train theologues of Reform Judaism alone but designed to include Conservative and Orthodox students as well; but there were forces implacably opposed to his plan to found another theological seminary in New York City.

In a preliminary move in 1915, he had arranged for Louis I. Newman of San Francisco to work with him in the Free Synagogue and undertake graduate studies leading to ordination. Summer schools had been arranged and other young men had been added to the staff of the Free Synagogue. These expedients were no solution and Wise saw the necessity of a more formal school. The German-speaking Jewish population of Austria and Germany, numbering less than a million, had four theological seminaries—in Berlin, Breslau, Vienna, and Budapest—to ordain rabbis; but in 1921 the Jewish population of America, totaling more than three and a half million, had only five seminaries—the Hebrew Union College of Cincinnati, the Jewish Theological Seminary, and Yeshiva College's Rabbi Isaac Elchanan Theological Seminary in New York City, and two institutions in Brooklyn: the Rabbi Chaim Berlin Rabbinical Academy and the Mesivta Torah Vodaath. Wise began to gather members for an organizing committee and funds to launch the project. Soon he received the offer of a loan of temporary quarters, suggestions of possible permanent sites, and bids of men to teach.

Wise proposed that the Jewish Institute of Religion become an activity of the Union of American Hebrew Congregations coordinate with the Hebrew Union College of Cincinnati but remaining independent and autonomous. His institute would exchange professors, students, and academic credits, and, cooperating with the Hebrew Union College and the Union of American Hebrew Congregations in fund raising, would receive a minimum sum of forty-five thousand dollars per year for the first three years of the agreement. His proposals were rejected.

He set out to raise funds and gather the faculty on his own. On his way through the Midwest he offered the presidency to Emil Hirsch of the Sinai Congregation in Chicago and when Hirsch declined, offered him the honorary presidency.

By early summer of 1922 Wise was almost ready for the opening in the autumn: there were leading laymen on his organizing committee, a number of local scholars to begin the courses, and a strong, representative group of students for the first class. He had been fortunate to secure Samuel McChord Crothers and Holmes to lecture on "Aspects of Christian Worship and Preaching." He was not satisfied with the faculty and decided that, on his trip to Palestine that summer, he would stop in England and Europe to gather visiting professors for the following years.

In England, Wise met a more subtle opposition than the bitterness he had encountered in the Midwest and West. British Jewry's

Liberal leaders took their cue from the Cincinnati institution; and when he arrived in England, he found indifference and wariness. Conferences with such scholars as Israel Abrahams of Cambridge, Claude Montefiore of the Liberal Jewish Synagogue, and Travers Herford of Oxford reflected the hostile versions they had received from friends at the Hebrew Union College. Israel Abrahams was soon won over and promised to come to America for a course of lectures at the J.I.R.; Wise offered to make Abrahams available to the Hebrew Union College, a pacific gesture which impressed the Englishmen. Travers Herford, a distinguished Christian scholar and specialist on the Pharisees, finally consented to come. All the men gave Wise directions as to where to look on the Continent for permanent professors and visiting lecturers. His destinations were now Berlin, Breslau, and Vienna. Chief among his advisers on the Continent was Ismar Elbogen whom he went to see in Berlin.

The imminent problems of prospective faculty as well as students, courses, financial outlay, and headquarters for J.I.R. could have marred Wise's visit to Palestine, but the visit was rewarding for him and the whole family. Wise saw with pleasure how conditions had been improved since his last visit in 1913; and while the British caretaker government favored the Arabs, there was a stirring growth in Hebrew communities. The return journey through the Mediterranean gave the family time to rest and reflect on the Palestine stay; and the remainder of the trip in Europe enabled Wise to build even more solidly for the opening in the fall.

When the Jewish Institute of Religion opened its doors in September, 1922, it had an exceptional group of students, enough money in the treasury, and an excellent faculty. Only a permanent building was lacking. The first sessions were held in Temple Israel on West 91st Street; within a few months the new building on West 68th Street, next to the Free Synagogue and provided by its executive committee, was ready. Israel Abrahams came in January and, though he had been skeptical, wrote in his "Newsletter" to the *Jewish Guardian* of London: "Dr. Stephen Wise has done wonderfully well with his Institute in so brief a space of time."

Wise had already established the pattern which he was to follow for the next twenty-seven years. Each morning he walked along the paths of Central Park which lay parallel to Central Park West and arrived at his office in the Free Synagogue before eight. If any students were around, he invited them to his office while he slit open the envelopes addressed to him. As he scanned each letter, he read parts of it aloud and told the group of students gathered about him who had written the letter, what the man did in public life, and some incidents in relation to him. At eight fifty, they would leave the study with its bare stone walls and the large table in the middle, its tall chairs, plain wooden benches, and surrounding bookcases, to go to the small chapel. Here, too, the walls were of simple stone; and in this austere setting he would lead the students in their morning prayers with simplicity and sincerity. He then returned to his office.

On Thursday mornings at eleven, he met his students for the course on "Problems of the Ministry," nicknamed by the students "Schmoos Session of the Chief." The students were given a grasp of world Jewish problems by a man who consorted with presidents, prime ministers, and cabinet officials. To this informal seminar Wise invited outstanding men and women from New York City to tell the class of their work—in child guidance, psychiatry, organizing labor, administering a community organization, guiding a parish. To him and his students, New York was a social laboratory. He included labor leaders like Philip Murray and William Green, Sidney Hillman and Jacob Potofsky. For lectures and practical discussions he turned to social workers like Mary Simhkovitch, Lillian Wald, and John Lovejoy Elliott. In the early days, Morris Hillquit, the Socialist leader, and Edward Devine of *Survey* came to talk; in later years, the social reform leaders Paul Blanshard and Norman Thomas, Father John A. Ryan of the National Catholic Welfare Conference and Henry A. Atkinson of the Church Peace Union, Henry F. Ward of Union Theological Seminary and Hubert Herring of the Congregational Social Service Commission, Chaim Weizmann and Vladimir Jabotinsky, the gifted leader of the Zionist Revisionists. In this way, the students learned something about liberal and radical movements, about changing populations, about community chests. On each occasion, they felt the personal affection the visitors had for Wise. In turn, they would hear from him of the problems he had faced in New York in the 1890s; in Portland, at the beginning of the century; and, in more recent years, at the Free Synagogue.

In Bible class, half of his students sat bare-headed, while the other half would not read the Scripture or take part in the class without first covering their heads. In Talmud class, the Conservative men rushed to the assistance of their Reform colleagues who had insufficient background to handle this difficult subject; in the sermon preaching class, Ivy League-educated students helped the more provincial college students find the more polished phrase.

On Friday morning at eleven o'clock, he held the homiletics class. One student said in after years: "He was so quick to detect sham; so quick to remind us that there was no substitute for thoughtful content in our sermon."

In later life, students discovered that preaching before a crowded temple of two thousand worshipers during the High Holy Days was less nerve-wracking than their trial sermons before thirty fellow students, the professor of speech, and Wise. The professor would lead the first onslaught and by the time he had finished his criticisms about the boy's pronunciation, enunciation, aspiration, posture, grammar, and imagery, the student was ready to leave the rabbinate and become a carpenter. This was just a foretaste. Wise would then take the stand and begin to point out that there was only one way to speak correctly and "that is, first of all, to speak English—not some queer dialect from the South or New England or Brooklyn."

"English," he would shout, "English, boys, requires proper grammar and clear phrases. Not the use of long and learned words which no one understands, usually not even yourself. Speak so the people will know what you mean, not so that you sound like a walking dictionary."

With that warm-up, the man with one of the greatest voices in America thundered at the student preachers: "Don't become so infatuated with the sound of your own voice that you're

carried away by your own oratory. Don't become hypnotized by
the mellowness of your vocal vibrations and above all don't try
to imitate me!"

If the luckless student happened to have a rich voice, Wise
would tell him a fine voice could become a curse, because it
might cause the man to become foppish, more concerned with
the exterior form of his sermon than with internal content:
"A melodious voice is a very poor substitute for lack of brain
power."

Wise's oratory caused some of the students to pattern their
speech after his, sometimes in the personal mannerisms of his
private conversation, more often of his public utterances. They
would imitate the toss of the head, the deep bass voice, the
emotional crescendos and the dramatic diminuendos, his wide
range of tonal scale, his gestures, and the impression Wise gave
that his was the essence of prophetic thought since the days of
the Judges. All over America there soon flourished in the rabbinate a crop of miniature Stephen Wises. For decades, pulpits
across the country were occupied by rabbis imitating the Wise
manner as so many actors in a later decade were to bear the
mark of "The Method."

One day a young student preached on the subject "The
Prophetic Tradition of Judaism," imitating him so effectively that
Wise, too, was amused by the performance. Completing his pero-
ration, the boy declaimed: "And therefore, my colleagues of the
rabbinate, it is our bounden duty to maintain the prophetic tradition in Judaism, that prophetic tradition which began with
Isaiah and continues with Stephen Wise."

He sat down and looked eagerly toward Wise for the verdict.
Wise stood up, looked around the room, pretended to glower
at the perspiring student, while the class, too, waited with bated
breath. Then with a grin, Wise asked, "Why drag in Isaiah?"

Wise welcomed criticism and had the grace to read to the
class a letter of praise, ending with a warning from the correspondent: "And in closing, my dear Rabbi Wise, permit me to
say that I enjoy your addresses; but watch your Ego. Humility
is the greatest thing in life."

He was merciless with a student who tried to be an Emil

Hirsch of Chicago or a Henry Cohen of Galveston, imitating the cadences of these older men. He criticized the young man's exaggerated pronunciation, his reliance on a currently fashionable school of thought, and the use of polysyllabic words, strained epigrams, and sentimental religiosity. If the student, fresh from college, referred to *The Nation* and the *New Republic, The New Yorker, Harper's* or the *Atlantic Monthly,* Wise would ask, "When did you last read Maimonides? Or Spinoza? Or the pages of Josephus? They, too, had a word for our age."

He urged his students to visit the churches of the city: to go to Brooklyn and hear S. Parkes Cadman address a nationwide radio audience each Sunday afternoon from the Y.M.C.A. auditorium; to go down Fifth Avenue to the First Presbyterian Church and listen to the young Harry Emerson Fosdick. For a change of pace, he suggested Bishop William Manning at the Cathedral of St. John the Divine, but he warned them: "Remember, ye cannot serve both God and Manning." If they wished to hear other Anglicans, he referred them to his dear friend, the controversial Percy Stickney Grant at the Church of the Ascension, or the experimental Norman Guthrie at the Church of the Bowerie. Nor would it hurt them to observe John Roach Straton, the arch-Fundamentalist, or "Gypsy" Smith, the revivalist.

In every instance, however, he spoke of John Haynes Holmes as "the unmatched prince of the pulpit." Such positive praise from Wise helped to counter the negative words of Samuel Schulman at Temple Beth-El, who had circulated to clergymen of all denominations in New York City in December, 1922, a sermon-pamphlet in which he denounced John Haynes Holmes' teaching as "the greatest danger to the mass of Jewry in this great city." The J.I.R. students paid no heed to Schulman and en masse attended the Thanksgiving Union Services in Carnegie Hall where they could hear Holmes.

Holmes not only lectured to them in his course at the Institute but also spoke at Wise's birthday celebrations on March 17. Wise, now addicted to the use of green ink in honor of Saint Patrick, introduced Holmes each year with the love of a father and the affection of a brother. Holmes would respond with equally affectionate words and at one such luncheon predicted: "When, at the end of my earthly days, I am buried beneath the high altar of the Community Church, the inscription on my tomb will say, 'Here lies John Haynes Holmes: minister, hymn-writer, lecturer, editor, pacifist, social radical, and annual speaker at the birthday luncheons for Stephen Samuel Wise!' "

By the end of the Institute's first year, both students and faculty knew something historic had taken place. On Wise's forty-ninth birthday, in 1923, they gave him a surprise party and a group tribute:

> You have admirers everywhere; but we are amongst the most enthusiastic of them because the Institute has brought us so close to you and your work. We recognize in you the dreamer who can make his dreams come true, the practical idealist who has called many to righteousness and inspired an ever-growing band of workers to devote themselves to the good of their fellows.
>
> The Free Synagogue which you founded sixteen years ago in this city has indeed become a mighty force. But perhaps this Institute of Religion, your youngest creation, may be destined to fulfill a still higher purpose. We share your hopes that it may bring into existence many Free Synagogues, not slavish copies of the original Free Synagogue, but animated by the same spirit of free inquiry, of warm Jewish feeling, and of devotion to the cause of social regeneration.
>
> But, Dr. Wise, we not only admire you as an outstanding figure in Jewry; we love you as an affectionate and greathearted human being.

Among the faculty who signed were Richard Gottheil, George Kohut, Louis I. Newman, Sidney Goldstein, and Joshua Bloch; the students included Morton M. Berman, Philip S. Bernstein, Ralph Marcus, Irma L. Lindheim, and James Waterman Wise.

The dreams of the practical idealist had come true, and the Institute was growing. George Foot Moore of Harvard, one of the leading Christian scholars of Christian-Jewish relations and author of the classic two-volume *Judaism*, lectured that spring on "Hellenistic Judaism." Israel Abrahams came in the second semester, as he had promised; he captured hearts and minds so completely that Wise, who had insisted on remaining only the acting president until he found the right man for the position, made overtures to Abrahams to consider the presidency of the J.I.R. Harry Wolfson was to begin in the autumn as Professor of Philosophy and History; and Wise had the good fortune to have Henry Slonimsky resign from the Hebrew Union College and accept a chair in philosophy and psychology of religion. The Librarian was Joshua Bloch, later Director of the Jewish Division of the New York Public Library. Chaim Tchernowitz began to teach the Talmud and the Mishnah; and a little later the promising young historian Salo Baron started the American phase of his scholarly career.

Financial support came from many sectors of the Jewish community across the country, more than had been expected but still not enough. The Free Synagogue on the West Side and the Central Synagogue on the East Side voted to merge (a merger that lasted only two years) and pledged the sum of twenty-five thousand dollars annually for the Institute; in this arrangement, Wise was to be the rabbi with several associates, including Goldstein. Such a union was important not only for the J.I.R. but also for the future of Jewry in America. Wise wrote to Gershon Agronsky [Agron], formerly of Philadelphia and then a resident of Jerusalem: "I want to make clear to you something which I indicated in my address of Sunday morning at the first union service of the two congregations—namely, that the synagogue today affords practically the only Jewish contact of the American Jew. If that, too, is to be minimized, there will be no Jews in America."

His concentration on the Institute was briefly interrupted by a controversy about the American Jewish Congress. The Congress had received from President Obregón of Mexico an intimation that Mexico would be willing to welcome Jewish immigrants and provide them with land for an immigrants' colony. The Congress replied with a polite "No, thank you," thereby arousing the anger of Israel Zangwill. Zangwill, a pre-Herzlian Zionist but also president of ITO, the Jewish Territorial Organization which sought places other than Palestine as havens of refuge, blasted the Congress for its shortsightedness and ingratitude. In response, the Congress invited him to speak that October.

Zangwill came to New York and criticized the Zionists for their lukewarm loyalty to their objective, their inept leadership both in America and on the international scene, and their half-hearted interest in Palestine. The address "Watchman, What of the Night?" created a furor when it was delivered in Carnegie Hall and for weeks thereafter. Wise had been responsible for the invitation to Zangwill and, as president of the Congress, had to handle the hostile reaction from the crowd as well as the tumult in the newspapers of the following weeks. He tried to pacify the dissidents by reminding them that Zangwill spoke not for Israel but for Israel Zangwill only. The intense, kinetic Zangwill was astonished at the reaction to his address and not pleased by Wise's statements. They argued fiercely but parted as friends.

Another controversy arose over John Haynes Holmes' new book, *New Churches for Old*. Characteristically, Holmes inscribed one of the first copies, "To S. S. W.: Dearest of Friends—Noblest of Men," and sent it to Wise who accepted the gift with the kind of gratitude the two men had for such offerings of friendship. But Wise had to take issue because Holmes had stated in his book:

> For my part I would ask for nothing better than that Jews should remain Jews and Christians Christians, with a single exception that I would gladly have these two great branches of the human family come together in a closer affiliation of the spirit than they now enjoy.

He answered Holmes publicly in a sermon entitled "Can Jew and Christian Worship Together?" and pointed out what, he contended, Holmes had failed to see: worship was only a part of the life of Jews. Something more than that was held in common by Jews, namely, their Jewishness. Nothing in Jewish life, said Wise, could stand in the way of fraternal accord with the Christian. But this fraternity could be marred and perhaps even prevented forever by the Christlessness of Christendom and the un-Jewishness of the Jew. Each faith would have to be fully and truly itself before amity was genuinely possible.

Wise was sure that "the soul of John Haynes Holmes is aflame with passion for justice to the least of peoples, as it in truth must be for reparation and redress to one of earth's great and ancient peoples, such as is our own." He was certain that "John Holmes would no more think of attempting to convert or to proselytize Jews to any one of a hundred Christian sects than I would dream of moving his people to become disciples of Mohammed or the Buddha." Had this not been shown when, thirteen years earlier, Holmes had joined with him and Hall in union services where Jew and non-Jew had met in the spirit of common worship of the universal Father, but with no idea of merging or fusing into one group? Something more was required: the Christianization of Christendom. This, not Holmes' suggested hour of common worship, was the supreme need of the Western world.

Furthermore, Wise had to differ with Holmes on his view of Jewish history. Holmes had declared: "If the Jews in many places of the world had political and military power today, they would slay the Christians exactly as the Christians have been slaying them." This assertion Wise had to counter: "There is a Jewish factor in this problem after all; and Mr. Holmes, quite unlike himself for once, goes back to the Old Testament, which he finds full of stories of massacre and torment." With kindness and firmness, Wise denied Holmes' allegation: "Despite the catholicity and understanding of Mr. Holmes' spirit, he evidently has not been able to plumb the depths of Jewish forbearance and Jewish long-suffering, the inexhaustible and infinite capacity of the Jew for forgiving, loving, and even serving those who wrong him."

The dispute, widely publicized and discussed, was inconclusive; yet it was indicative of the fact that the two men could disagree, make their differences known in public, and not mar their friendship or the unique pattern of their parallel lives through the years. One thing was clear: Holmes wanted to help Jewry at this hour but Wise could not agree with his proposed remedy.

19. Righteousness as a Mighty Stream

*Yet I doubt not thro' the ages one
increasing purpose runs,
And the thoughts of men are widen'd
with the process of the suns.*
—ALFRED LORD TENNYSON, 1842

IN 1924, HOLMES WAS UNEQUIVOCAL in his support of Robert La Follette for the Presidency. As a delegate from New York City he attended the convention of the Progressive Party in Cleveland in July. He prepared, as rarely before, to make a fund-raising speech on the evening La Follette was formally to accept the nomination as the Progressives' presidential candidate. Just as Holmes neared the climax of his fund appeal and the ushers were readied to pass the baskets for the expected gifts, the eager La Follette, unrestrained by a major-domo or sergeant-at-arms, strode into the arena and onto the podium. Pandemonium broke loose and Holmes never finished. He was disappointed, but the finance committee of the party even more so. The lack of organization that fateful, futile night was characteristic of the Progressives during that apathetic campaign by all three parties as the electorate fatuously chose to "Keep Cool with Coolidge."

While Holmes made plans to campaign that summer and fall, Wise struggled to make a sound decision. A former Republican, he had been a supporter of the Democratic Party in the last three campaigns, the two for Wilson in 1912 and 1916, and for Cox and Roosevelt in 1920. Now he wanted to support and vote for a third party.

Late the previous winter, Wise had spoken on the Teapot

Dome and Elk Hill scandals, uncovered so effectively by Burton K. Wheeler's committee in the Senate; and he inveighed against "the Shame of the Republic." The only way to prevent further scandal, he said, was to form a third party. When the Committee of Forty-Eight in conjunction with the Farmer-Labor Party, aided the Conference for Progressive Political Action in calling a convention in Cleveland and asked Wise to take part, he parried and said that he might join later.

Meanwhile, his friends Governor Alfred E. Smith and Franklin Delano Roosevelt asked him to take part in the Democratic convention; and he consented to serve as an alternate delegate. It was a reluctant and almost recalcitrant Wise who accompanied the New York delegation into the sweltering Madison Square Garden for its sessions, which lasted many days. In his own mind he felt impelled to be present, if for no other reason than to fight the revived Ku Klux Klan, still in the ascendant in the Democratic Party. Smith, as a Roman Catholic, was anti-Klan; his arch-opponent for the nomination, William G. McAdoo, was not. An additional reason: the Democratic Party was the heir of Wilson's internationalism. This fact was underscored by the powerful speech given by the Cleveland attorney who had been Woodrow Wilson's Secretary of War, Newton D. Baker, in tribute to Wilson's memory and on behalf of the League of Nations. The Convention was stirred and Wilson's spirit seemed to hover above the assemblage for an instant; but the mood of the delegates was noninternational.

Toward the close of the sessions and before leaving for home, Baker sat at his desk in the Hotel Belmont on a hot July night and wrote Wise:

> Before I leave I want to send you just a word of grateful affection for all you have done and helped to do in these trying days. . . . No small part of my own confidence and comfort in all this struggle has come from the fact that you and others felt as I did about the rights and wrongs involved; and you helped to make the only difficult decision presented to me when you agreed that it would be better for the Cause of Peace to carry the protesting minority report to the floor of the convention. The event justified your judgment, but in so sacred

a cause I felt deeply burdened lest my own judgment might err. In many, in all ways, my dear Stephen, you have been a helpful friend here as always.

Wise was so dispirited by the convention that he left several days early to rejoin his family at Lake Placid and brood on what he should do. After considerable indecision he announced for John W. Davis. Had Smith been nominated, there would have been no doubt in Wise's mind; but now he gave Davis support that, at best, was halfhearted.

Newton D. Baker understood Wise's hesitancy and doubts; and in late July sent a note from Cleveland to convey his own certainties:

> He [John W. Davis] believes in the League [of Nations] and will, no doubt, say so which is a gain over the negations of Coolidge and La Follette. Davis is, as you know, immensely able and thoroughly high minded and unless all signs fail will pitch the campaign on a high scale. His defect is a lack of warmth and ardor. He reaches some places more slowly than more feeling people because he reaches them through mental operations alone, but he is liberal as compared with *either* of his opponents.

Baker was amused by an article Wise had written about William Jennings Bryan and the Nebraskan's dubious role as an elder statesman and advocate of compromise on the religious issue in the convention:

> That Mr. Bryan played the part of a prophet of Baal is a priceless characterization! He is an extraordinary man, with the light of battle in his eye and the lust of conflict in his soul, but I have reached a settled judgment that he has no moral convictions. . . . He has a simple conviction of the reality of God and the directness of his own relations to Him—but this has nothing whatever to do with any earthly matter and is separated by watertight doors from the other parts of his mind which he uses to think—or feel—about human affairs. As "a variety of religious experience" he interests me greatly, but not otherwise.

During those days Wise pressed Governor Alfred E. Smith to select Benjamin Cardozo and support him as a candidate for the

New York State Court of Appeals. Cardozo, a legal scholar with a flawless record at the bar, had overcome the taint of being the son of a man sullied by a Tammany scandal and, in Wise's eyes, was a great and good human being who would serve with distinction. "Al" Smith, a close friend of Wise's since the days of the Triangle Shirtwaist Factory fire in 1911, was reluctant at first but was finally won over. Cardozo was nominated on both party tickets and became Chief Judge of the Court of Appeals.

In the following year, 1925, Wise joined many friends of Holmes' in celebrating the centennial of the Church of the Messiah, now the Community Church of New York, and, at the anniversary dinner in the Aldine Club, was moved to declare himself completely in accord with Holmes' statement of faith in the future. Holmes had stated:

> After more than eighteen years of service in this church, with the growing realization upon me that I am moving on to middle years, I would speak this night one word of counsel which is somewhat different perhaps from that which I would have spoken at the start. Eighteen, sixteen, fifteen years ago that word would have been "courage," "determination," or some other term expressing exhilaration and the valor of victory. I hope that these words are still written upon my heart, for to my dying day I would be a fighter for the things I love. But I am now learning another, and perhaps greater word, and that is "patience." We can't do everything all at once. We can never hope ourselves to reach that goal for which we are striving. We must be satisfied with a few steps forward.

Both men believed in patient persuasion. At the request of the American Civil Liberties Union, they joined with other liberals in signing an appeal for pardon in behalf of Benjamin Gitlow. In a celebrated case involving this well-known Communist, the courts had convicted Gitlow under a New York State "criminal anarchy act" for publishing a subversive pamphlet and the Supreme Court had sustained the conviction. Their petition was in vain but their belief in freedom of utterance remained unshaken.

A few weeks later, Wise preached a sermon at Carnegie Hall one Sunday morning on "Jesus, the Jew," in connection with the newly published volume, *Jesus of Nazareth* by Joseph Klausner, and stirred up a controversy he did not desire at that particular time. He was astonished at the public reaction. Why should it be a sensation that a rabbi should speak on Jesus of Nazareth? It was not the first time he or fellow rabbis had done so. "The Christlessness of Christianity" had for years been his favorite sermon subject for Christians, especially before ministerial groups where he took special delight in jolting Christians about their lack of fealty to Jesus and his ethical teachings.

Only a year and a half before, a similar sermon of his on the same topic was quoted by a German newspaper and Wise was alleged to have spoken critically of Jesus and of Christians. Through Ismar Elbogen in Berlin, Wise authorized a statement that the publication of this mistaken report "constituted so foul a libel upon him that if it had been made in an American newspaper he would at once have sued." To Jacob Landau, editor of the Jewish Telegraphic Agency, which had carried the report, he protested the false quotations which "imputed to me a vulgar and ribald reference to Jesus." To both Landau and Elbogen, he wrote: "I never make any reference to Jesus save in the terms of that profound reverence which I feel for the spiritual character which is the possession of Israel and Christendom alike."

Wise could also have mentioned that when Harry Emerson Fosdick once invited him to address his congregation and a member of the audience asked Wise: "What do you think of Jesus?" he responded, "Jesus is my elder brother."

He was actually saying nothing new, for his audiences had heard such statements in one form or another in previous decades. In Portland in 1906 and in New York in 1916 he had discussed the relation of Judaism to other faiths and addressed himself to Jews deserting Judaism for Unitarianism. When referring to the Unitarian statement of faith as formulated by James Freeman Clarke, Wise cited the parallels to the House of Israel. Judaism, too, believed in "the fatherhood of God, the brotherhood of man, salvation by character." As for the Unitarians' fourth tenet, "the leadership of Jesus," Jews were "not blind to the radiance of that personality. To turn our back upon it, if we could, would be a stupid disavowal of our best. He is our own. He belongs in the eternal order of the Jewish prophets whose crown perhaps is radiant, uniquely benignant and beneficent. We accept his leadership, but not his unique leadership. There is only one leadership, and that leadership is vested in no man that has walked upon earth and that leadership belongs to God." Neither in 1906 nor in 1916 had this statement caused a stir.

Moreover, in 1916 at Carnegie Hall he had asked:

> What man, who thinks of the example of Jesus, can escape the mystery and the marvel of it, can resist its appeal? The great power of Christianity rests in that ethical and spiritual compulsion which that personality brought about. The Jewish position is as great and wondrous and appealing as is that radiant personality. That personality is not divine in any unique sense. We desire to emulate that high personality, but not to limit our emulation to and of that personality. The Jew recognizes, marvels at the radiance, the benignity of the personality of Jesus, the Nazarene Jew, but we do not class that personality by the side of God. God is One—unique, not humanly inimitable, but humanly attainable.

In the same vein he spoke in 1925, nine years later. He divided his address into four simple parts, each with what seemed to him an "undebatable thesis": (1) Jesus was man, not God; (2) Jesus was a Jew, not a Christian; (3) Jews have not repudiated Jesus; and (4) Christians have, for the most part, not adopted and followed Jesus, the Jew. By now Wise was a famous Zionist leader and Jewish spokesman, and his statement made headlines. Some Jews were angered by his insistence that Jesus should be accepted by Jews as an outstanding prophetic contribution to the ages, although the statement was not novel and had been made by many rabbis across the years. Other Jews were irked by the published statement of a Protestant ministerial association in Philadelphia that the preachers had welcomed the rabbi home to the true faith, Christianity.

The Yiddish press was up in arms; and Mizrachi, the Orthodox Zionist group, led the attack. Orthodox rabbis condemned Wise for his "heresy" and sought to expel him from the fold of Judaism, as they construed it.

Samuel Schulman of Beth-El agreed with the Union of Orthodox Rabbis in asking for Wise's resignation from the National

Chairmanship of the United Palestine Appeal. Otherwise, argued Schulman, if Wise were retained as chairman, "every dollar that will be given to this fund will be indirectly a support of his prestige and an endorsement of his methods and attitude in American Judaism." Schulman traced the controversy to the decadence in the Reform Jewish pulpit which "may be said to have become during the years a footnote to the footlights." He admitted that Wise preached his sermon "with passion and with eloquence" and added, "I might also say, with theatrical pathos." He characterized the utterance as "sensational . . . superficial, and . . . facetious." He deplored "the outbursts of the Rabbi of the Free Synagogue" and maintained that "to orate about Jesus . . . is indelicate and undignified and shows a lack of Jewish moral and spiritual virility." It was time, said he, "that a halt be called to the straining after sensationalism."

Schulman's attack caused Wise little concern, but he was worried lest the adverse reaction in the Jewish community at large destroy his effectiveness as head of the United Palestine Appeal. Owing to the urgency of Palestine's needs Wise had accepted the U.P.A. Chairmanship and set the goal for 1925–1926 at the unprecedented sum of five million dollars. The Appeal was in danger as the storm of protest in Jewish circles grew greater. Wise was concerned with saving the fund drive for the realization of Zionist dreams and the settlement of Jewish refugees. Consequently, he prepared to resign.

Nathan Straus turned the tide. He expressed his faith in Stephen Wise and gave six hundred and fifty thousand dollars as an additional contribution to the United Palestine Appeal. The gift surprised Wise and his associates by its suddenness and its size. After a long discussion, the executive committee of the U.P.A. voted overwhelmingly for Wise and informed him of their decision that his resignation would be declined. Wise was too moved to say more than the words, *"Ivri Anochi,"* a phrase from the Book of Jonah: "I am a Hebrew."

In that year, 1925, Holmes was busy each Monday at the luncheon meetings of the American Civil Liberties Union, which were concerned with the trial of John T. Scopes in Dayton, Tennessee. Scopes, a high-school teacher of science, had agreed to contest the Butler Act of the Tennessee Legislature which forbade the teaching of evolution. The A.C.L.U. promised financial help, legal advice, and publicity.

The American Civil Liberties Union was then in its fifth year and directed by Roger Baldwin. Its weekly meetings were chaired sagely by Harry F. Ward, Professor of Christian Ethics at Union Theological Seminary.

Another case, which absorbed the time left over from the Scopes trial, was that of Nicola Sacco and Bartolomeo Vanzetti, the two Italian workmen, a fish peddler and a shoe worker, accused five years earlier of having murdered a paymaster and his guard at South Braintree, Massachusetts. They had been indicted and convicted. But there was at the center of the matter a conflict of ideas. The murder charges were based on scant evidence and the guilt was apparently pinned upon them unjustly, although Sacco's innocence seemed not as well established as Vanzetti's; in reality, it became clearer each year that their radicalism had given them no chance for a fair trial on the charge of murder. The two men, it was proven, had evaded military service during the war and were avowed anarchists. There was little doubt in the minds of liberals and radicals, in America and throughout the world, who came to the men's support that Sacco and Vanzetti had been condemned for anarchism rather than for murder; the death sentence became a powerful symbol of a struggle to defend human rights and uphold justice. The court's verdict of guilty was sustained during these years while many organizations, chief among them the American Civil Liberties Union, clamored for a review of the Sacco-Vanzetti case.

Holmes, vice-chairman of the A.C.L.U. and a substitute in the chair for Ward during the latter's absence on lecture tours and a sabbatical leave, had practical means now to effect righteousness and affect the processes of justice. With his influence the A.C.L.U. was a powerful force in compelling the State of Massachusetts to review the Sacco-Vanzetti case. This work and his efforts on behalf of La Follette's Progressive Party candidacy gave the lie to the critics who accused him of being only an impractical idealist.

As a founder and former president of the Unitarian Temperance Society, Holmes considered the Eighteenth Amendment to the Constitution an admirable, long-overdue attempt to abolish the liquor traffic. He defended Prohibition in lectures and public controversies, particularly with Clarence Darrow, an ardent anti-Prohibitionist, as his opponent. In the last of a series of debates, Darrow drawled his points, as usual, with effective ease, while Holmes countered with all the eloquence at his command and ended with a stirring evangelical appeal for abstinence. Afterward, Darrow looked at him with his half-shut smiling eyes and said, "You can break, you can shatter the vase, but the preacher psychology still sticks around."

The "preacher psychology" had a difficult time with Holmes' idol, H. G. Wells. He had always felt drawn by the intellectual stimulus H. G. Wells offered but was repelled by his private life. During the first months of the Community Church in Boston, when Holmes began his once-a-month visits, he had to answer accusations about Wells' unconventional love affairs. In the summer of 1921, a year before he was received so cordially in Wells' London home, Holmes wrote to a Boston friend who was equally troubled by the Wells mode of life: "I believe that Mr. Wells is as honest as the stars, but all the same, if he is living this type of life, he is dead wrong, and he goes a long way toward knocking the bottom out of my faith." Holmes' reactions were strongly influenced by his ministerial attitudes and he therefore found the revelations "a great chasm of darkness in the record of this man's public service."

Yet he defended Wells, making sure, however, that he was not misunderstood. He was not condoning "sin" nor was he confusing public service and private life. He argued that the integrity of Wells' essential character and his right to be regarded as a leader of thought were established. At least Wells had uncovered with courage and candor the hypocrisies that prevailed in this intimate, intricately woven area of life. There was a certain honesty in his insistence on discussing the theme.

Yet Holmes was troubled about the element of concealment in Wells' double life. That was the worst thing:

> Personally I find the "free love" idea to be abhorrent, and I could have no place for it even in the furthest reaches of my

Utopian dreams. Social control of what is fundamentally a social phenomenon—i. e. relations between the sexes—is *basic*. But the "free love" idea is a way of life, all the same, and if a man believes in it and wants to live it, well and good! *But*, we have a right to insist, as an elementary principle of honesty and fair-dealing, that such a life shall be lived *openly*. My prime objection to the free lovers that I know is the deceit which they deliberately practice.

Five years later, however, he still had to defend Wells. His was not at any time an all-around admiration, for there was nothing profound in Wells, he confessed. The Briton presented no new truths and carried men through to no final conclusion. Nor was he a thinker in a scientific or philosophical sense. Yet he was a sensitive expositor of the contemporary world. With so active and fertile a mind, so inquiring and farseeing, he was, in Holmes' eyes, the most stimulating man writing in the English language. Nobody could set Holmes thinking so hard and fast as H. G. Wells and nobody's illumination of the scene seemed more helpful. From Wells, Holmes admitted, he received clarification of thought, lifting of emotions, and inspiration for fresh understanding and new progress.

Holmes' sharp defense of Wells verged on the contentious and friends in Boston asked him to be less sharp, more considerate in his approach. In his replies there appeared a certain irritation. He had been in New York almost twenty years and fatigue was wearing him down. In the winter of 1926–1927 he admitted to a friend:

> I am tired, dead tired, I'm beginning now to get so cross that I fear I shall be unfit to live with. But there is no chance for any let-up for the present. We are just now getting to the nervous climax of our plans for the new church and this is draining every nerve I have. Then people are dying and getting married and I am hustling all over town till it seems to me I shall drop. You really don't know what a wicked man I am, but I am—when I get tired.

The audiences at the Forum in the Community Church began to see this. He would be coldly brusque in the presence of bores and idle intruders, especially at the close of a long Sunday evening session when he yearned for his home in quiet Sidney Place in Brooklyn. His conduct of the Forum was that of a hard-boiled master in the art of handling audiences. He was impatient with windy, amateur orators on the floor and he told them to sit down when they went on too long. He became quite blunt if the Forum audience was impolite to a speaker who did not follow the particular approach fashionable at that time. When Manley Hudson of Harvard, an advocate of the League of Nations, spoke at the Forum, the audience attacked him. Holmes, though no devotee of the League idea, was determined that Hudson should have fair, polite treatment and referred to his congregation as "an audience and a mob."

Even in the Sunday services he had problems which taxed his patience. One Sunday morning a half-demented man arose in the balcony and interrupted the sermon to announce in a bold voice: "I am the Messiah!" Holmes paused for two seconds and then said, "Yes, I know you're the Messiah; but sit down now and see me after the service."

By the time his congregation prepared for the celebration of his twentieth anniversary in New York, Holmes had caught hold of himself and recovered his equanimity. He seemed to find a new strength as he was drawn into the textile strike in Passaic, New Jersey, and took an even more active part in the defense of Sacco and Vanzetti.

20. Despised and Rejected of Men

If it had not been for these things, I might have live out my life, talking at street corners to scorning men. I might have die, unmarked, unknown, a failure. Now we are not a failure. This is our career and our triumph. . . . Our words—our lives—our pains—nothing! The taking of our lives—lives of a good shoemaker and a poor fish peddler—all! That last moment belongs to us—that agony is our triumph.
—BARTOLOMEO VANZETTI, 1927

BY THE BEGINNING OF 1926, Holmes was compelled to make a number of personal and professional decisions. He and Madeleine helped their daughter Frances choose the University of Chicago for entrance in the fall; and they discussed with Roger his graduate courses at Harvard toward his doctorate. A small legacy to Madeleine allowed them to buy a permanent summer home on the Maine coast they had always loved. Through the following years, their Kennebunk Beach house between the Mousam River and the Atlantic Ocean became increasingly precious to them.

Exceeding all else in importance was the prospect of a new church. For four years, the congregation had met in the remodeled sanctuary; but now it was not large enough for Sunday congregations. The church had no reception room, no platforms or stage equipment, no lobbies or storage space, all of which were essential to a modern church. The nearby Church House was in bad repair and tight for space, hopelessly out of date; it offered no facilities for an adequate office staff, no opportunity

231

to expand activities. The property at 34th and Park was now valued at considerably more than a million dollars and the congregation was unwilling to build the conventional type of church which was all that its limited endowment funds could maintain. Holmes reminded the committee, meeting weekly to make plans for the future, that the real estate represented an enormous unearned increment and there lay upon them all the responsibility to use this wealth to benefit the community which had produced it. He described his vision of a church which would be a beacon of freedom, a building as prophetic of the future as cathedrals new and old were reminiscent of the past. He knew it also had to be equipped for modern use. If it was to be an assembling place for all sorts and conditions of men, to help them rest, worship, work, and experience a high fellowship, it would have to be built with both beauty and utility.

Months were consumed in committee meetings. A strong minority warned against over-building and insisted that the financial plan must be both secure and consistent with the ideals of the church. In the midst of these realistic discussions, going on endlessly from month to month, there was an awareness that the project had to be accomplished soon—but with care.

Meanwhile, Holmes took part, with Wise, in the 1925–1926 textile strike in Passaic. It was Justine Waterman Wise who involved them in it. Justine was now twenty-one and continuing with the interests she had had as an undergraduate at Bryn Mawr, Radcliffe, and Barnard. In her senior year at Barnard, she had conducted a survey for the Women's Division of the New York State Department of Labor to determine what happened to women industrial workers who had been injured and to decide whether adequate financial compensation had been awarded them.

In the fall of 1924, she and her friend, Bertha Paret, went to Passaic, a city with a large unorganized labor force and several of the largest woolen mills in the country, among them the Botany Worsted Mills and the Forstmann and Huffman Company. She found a job in a cotton mill and, under the name Justine Waterman, went to work as a quiller at eighteen dollars a week. In the winter of 1924–1925, she applied to their Central

Employment Bureau to seek work in a woolen mill. The Bureau, which had a well-organized spy system to prevent organization of the workers, informed her she could become a floor lady at twenty-two dollars per week. Ready to take the job, she was suddenly asked to leave town before she was arrested, because her real name had been discovered. Denied work in the woolen mill, she worked in a sweatshop, continuing her activities in adult education and research.

A year later, the strike in Passaic began. Justine came from New Haven, where she was attending the Yale Law School, to help organize the workers. The man who had spied on her came to her father at the Free Synagogue and confessed. He told the entire story, implicating the mill owners.

The mill owners had consistently paid a low wage. When Justine explained the problem to her father and to Holmes, she called it "a starvation wage" and accused the employers of looking upon the workers of Passaic as "a dull herd of 'foreigners,' mere cogs in a profit-making machine with the result of a ruthless and relentless system of exploitation." Wages had recently been cut again, wives and mothers had been forced to work at night while husbands and fathers worked the day shift, and the far-reaching espionage system intimidated the workers.

The mill owners had an excellent excuse for not negotiating because the strike was led by one Albert Weisbord, accused of being a Communist. Weisbord was chairman of a local committee of the Textile Workers whose letterhead was captioned: "The United Front of the Workers Against the United Front of the Bosses." To this, too, Justine had a response: "You will hear much of the menace of the violence of 'Reds' or Bolshevism, but it is Forstmann and Huffman, the Botany and their kind, that constitute the gravest menace to the peace and lawfulness of Passaic and of our country. No outside agitator, however radical, can be as menacing to the life and ideals of America as the interests which invoke our flag solely to protect their profits."

Justine sounded so much like Wise condemning Judge Elbert Gary in 1919 that her father was delighted. Wise sent a young Englishman, Basil Henriques—the director of St. George's Settlement House in London, whom he had brought from England to speak at the Free Synagogue and lecture at the Jewish Institute of Religion—to escort Justine to Passaic. When Henriques returned from the strikers' meeting, he reported: "Justine made such a speech to the strikers that you can retire, Rabbi." Wise proudly told his friends: "The New York papers were very full of it and pictured Justine as a most incendiary person with uplifted fists, smashing away in true Stephenesque fashion."

The American Civil Liberties Union moved in to guarantee the rights of freedom of speech and freedom of assembly. They were convinced that the strike was wisely conducted and that the strikers carefully avoided acts of violence and intimidation, in obvious contrast to the police who unlawfully interfered, broke picket lines, and forbade public meetings. In response to a request of the A.C.L.U. for speakers, Holmes addressed a meeting in Garfield, New Jersey; and a news photo in the *Herald Tribune* showed him before a cheering group of workers with his fists raised high as he gave a rousing speech. He brought relief funds, gathered at a large meeting in the Community Forum. Through him the American Civil Liberties Union was successful in circumventing the efforts of the police to invoke the riot act and prevent the assemblage.

Deeply stirred by the experience, Holmes wrote to Wise of his "pilgrimage to Passaic last week . . . a genuinely thrilling time. I have never seen a more wonderful spectacle than that of the discipline, courage, and cheer of the strikers. Under the most dire provocations—provocation which tested me to the breaking point—they were patient and uncomplaining. The meeting which I addressed gave me such a thrill as I haven't had in a dozen years."

Holmes confessed, however, that he was worried about the outcome: "The strikers talk bravely of going through the summer, but that's not going to be an easy job. It is a desperate thing to try to hold the attention and support of the general public over a prolonged period. I'm hoping therefore that your labors, Wise, and those of others along the line of settlement are going to produce fruit quickly."

The fruit did not come quickly, not before the winter of 1926–1927; but the labors were unyielding. Wise was constantly in touch with Father John A. Ryan of the National Catholic Welfare Conference and the Federal Council of Churches' representatives, Charles F. Macfarland and F. Ernest Johnson, as well as with Sidney Hillman of the Amalgamated Clothing Workers of America and William E. Borah, Senator from Idaho. Having aroused interest and concern on a national scale, Wise organized a committee of leading liberals to offer mediation; the strikers accepted, the employers declined.

Wise was disappointed, not half so much by the owners' rejection of the mediation proposal as by the ineffectual leadership of the United Textile Workers of America which he condemned as "hopelessly unseeing, sitting as tight as a medieval guild—a dreary and archaic crowd." William Green, Samuel Gompers' successor as president of the American Federation of Labor, reminded Wise that the United Textile Workers had autonomous authority in the A.F.L. and were in complete control of the strike, and that the A.F.L. must not "transgress upon the prerogatives of the authority of the United Textile Workers Organization." Wise, aided by his wife, gathered additional funds for relief for the workers and appealed to the A.F.L. for relief funds.

Wise and Norman Thomas arranged for a public meeting at the Y.M.C.A. to enable "Golden Rule" Nash of Cincinnati, well-known for his excellent employee relations, to speak to the strikers. The Y.M.C.A. yielded to pressure and canceled the arrangements, whereupon Thomas and Wise secured the Russian Church School Hall. At that meeting Wise attacked the Governor for his failure to intervene, and scored the churches, lawyers, and bar associations of New Jersey and of Bergen County. He accused the New Jersey police and judges of being "mill-controlled." Sheriff Nimmo of Bergen County had sent heavily armed police who had clubbed strikers into submission, arrested many, and forbidden picketing. The sheriff had boasted of having "broken the backbone of the strike"; and Wise, to the applause of the strikers, cried, "Oh, no, little Nemo, you have not broken the backbone of the strike. You have only defiled the order of the State of New Jersey. You have brought its name to shame."

While he was addressing the strikers in the Russian Church School Hall, Wise realized that Weisbord had not appeared, although he had been expected. A newspaper reported the next day that Weisbord's lieutenants decided it would be more prudent for him not to attend, an indication of their awareness of his controversial role. Wise had observed to the audience: "Weisbord may be politically a Communist, but he has lived by democracy! The officers of the law have talked justice and practiced violence."

But the going was slow. Months went by before a settlement was reached; and not until the following winter did Wise receive a telephone call from Norman Thomas, telling him that the strike had been settled and the workers authorized to return to work with freedom to organize a union. Wise then appealed again to the A.F.L. for funds to relieve the strikers' need for food and clothing.

Wise's relationship to the American Federation of Labor was one of more than merely good will on his part. The A.F.L. respected him; and when he requested a hearing, they granted it. While the Passaic textile strike was still in flux, he had asked William Green, president of the A.F.L., for the privilege of having the strike in particular, and laborers' rights in general, discussed before the Federation's meeting in Detroit. Why not select either a member of the proposed mediation committee or the entire committee? Green chose Wise.

When Wise arrived in Detroit in the early fall of 1926, he found the city embroiled in a controversy between the business community and the churches. At the instigation of James Myers, labor secretary of the Federal Council of Churches of Christ in America, and under the sponsorship of the Detroit Council of Churches, a number of labor leaders were scheduled to address congregations. President Green was to speak at the Y.M.C.A. in the closing event of this observance.

The Building Trades Association and the Chamber of Commerce opposed the move and called it a conspiracy to change Detroit into a "closed shop" city. The speakers, including Green, were labeled as un-American and un-Detroit. The Y.M.C.A., apprehensive about the success of its $5,000,000 fund-raising drive, rescinded the invitation to Green; and several of the ministers were ordered by their church boards to withdraw the scheduled appearance of the labor speakers. Only Reinhold Niebuhr, then of Bethel Evangelical Church, and Augustus P. Reccord of the First Unitarian Church did not capitulate.

Wise did not miss the opportunity to tell the A.F.L. convention that churches should not be chiefly "Sunday Clubs" of the foes of organized labor. He demanded that the religion of the prophets and of Jesus not be reduced to the level of a scab agency. He denounced the churches' cancellation of their invitation as "a tragic confession of fear that will justify the hundreds of thousands who hold that the church is one of the chief bulwarks of economic privilege."

Organized religion was not his only target. Wise took the occasion to criticize the leaders of the American Federation of Labor for their slowness in fighting for the organization of unskilled workers, especially for having been so laggard in supporting the Passaic textile workers. To the A.F.L., chronically afraid of forthright action and men with leftist views, Wise said that they too were victims of unjust methods used against the Passaic striker, the first weapon having been poison—namely, the charge that the workers were the agents of revolution.

It was owing in no small part to Wise's address that the Protestant ministers of Detroit opposed their enemies and accused them of improper intimidation of the churches. But there was a second result: the American Federation of Labor realized in greater measure its responsibility, from which flowed more direct leadership in the Passaic strike itself and an appropriation for relief funds, limited though they were. Wise suggested $50,000, but only $20,000 was voted.

That week, Eugene V. Debs died. Holmes was asked to officiate at the funeral. He wanted to go but was scheduled for a funeral in his own church. Rarely had he been in such conflict. Years later, in remembering his disappointment, he wished he had tried to secure a substitute for the local funeral and had gone to Indiana to help lay Debs to rest. Norman Thomas went in his place and gave the funeral oration.

The following Sunday Holmes discarded the sermon he had

planned. Instead he preached grandiloquently and quite un-
critically on Debs: "I like to think of him entering into heaven
and coming into the presence of the Lord Christ himself. I know
how the Lord Christ will receive him. He will stand, just as Debs
stood in his doorway in Terre Haute that happy day he welcomed me, with radiant smile and extended arms."

From his Boston outpost Holmes received a complaint: no
mention had been made there on any of the Sundays in late
October or early November by Clarence Skinner or himself of
Debs' death. Would he not repeat the Debs sermon when he came
in December? Holmes consented, grateful in the knowledge that
the congregation of the Community Church in Boston was
unique among American churches in protesting because the great
Socialist had not had honor paid him and insisting that due
tribute be given.

In 1927, their twentieth year in New York City, Holmes and
Wise joined in a cause they hoped would be successful but which
was destined to fail: their continuing defense of Sacco and Vanzetti. Both were convinced the men were innocent of the murder
of which they had been charged and were kept in prison solely
for their anarchist views. Hence, Wise's subject at the Free Synagogue, "Law Versus Justice in the Sacco-Vanzetti Case." Only
the previous week, he had spoken to faculty and students at the
Yale Law School. The lecture was arranged by one of Justine's
professors, Leon Tulin, who was soon to become her husband.

In July, Holmes was still hopeful about the fate of Sacco and
Vanzetti and told Mrs. Winslow, the secretary of the Community
Church in Boston, that he believed Governor Alvin Fuller to be
"an extraordinarily conscientious man and I will lay my bet he
will read every word of the record and work at the case day and
night for weeks. That's the kind of man he is. . . . I know that
Governor Fuller will never let those men go to the chair. I am
writing Governor Fuller today asking for an appointment next
Saturday or Monday. I feel no sense of urgency, as you seem to."

Mrs. Winslow's sense of urgency was justified, however. Although Governor Fuller responded courteously to Holmes and
scores of other influential people, he would not be moved. He
was even more adamant after his advisory committee confirmed
the sentence.

August 23, 1927, the day of execution, was at hand. No pardon
came from Governor Fuller's office, no recommendation from
Judge Webster Thayer that his "anarchistic bastards" be given
a commutation of sentence, no reprieve from the Supreme Court
or from Calvin Coolidge in the White House. At the midnight
hour, Holmes wrote the poem, "The Ballad of Charlestown Gaol,"
which Upton Sinclair included two years later in his novel,
Boston:

> There's a chair for you, Vanzetti,
> In the cold and empty room;
> A chair aloof and lonely,
> Like a spectre in the gloom;
> A chair with open arms and wide
> To welcome you to doom.
>
> They've made this chair, Vanzetti,
> Good men and strong and true;
> To manifest the will of God
> On poor men such as you;
> To show the Lord Christ lives again,
> And dies, the Lord Christ, too!

While Holmes and many liberals were intent on the Sacco-
Vanzetti case, Wise was also busy with Zionist affairs abroad
as the Zionist Actions Committee met in Basel. His mind was
really back in America, however, not only with the Sacco-
Vanzetti issue but also with the news that after many years
Henry Ford had repudiated the Dearborn *Independent* and its
defamatory articles on "The International Jew." Aaron Sapiro
and Louis Marshall had succeeded in securing a document apologizing for articles which had been reprinted by the millions and,
causing irreparable harm, were destined to be used in the 1930s
and 1940s by propagandists of Hitler's Nazism.

In the fall of 1927, Wise preached on the subject, "Henry
Ford's Retraction: Some Further Lessons," emphasizing that he
had not said "Henry Ford's Repentance" or "Henry Ford's Reparation," merely retraction. The damage had been done, Wise
lamented, for that summer he had seen cartoons in European
newspapers defaming the Jew. At bookstands in railway stations
in Switzerland, he had purchased *The Protocols of the Elders*

of Zion, which would most likely not have been published had the Dearborn *Independent* not been given free rein by Ford. Wise took the opportunity of berating "a lamentable habit of the American people—that of assuming that a man's success in any field guarantees the infallibility of his judgments and the inerrancy of his acts in all fields." But he added, "God pity and forgive Henry Ford! God keep America true to the American hope of good will and brotherhood among men!"

In the fall of 1927, Wise's activities were as involved and complex as ever. A typical week of Wise's commitments, entered in his desk calendar for the year 1927, reflected the many interests that kept him busy. On a Sunday morning in Carnegie Hall in November, he discussed Judge Ben Lindsey's proposal for "Companionate Marriage," opposing it and yet dealing sympathetically with Lindsey's effort to combat a growing divorce rate and find a basis for successful marriage. In the afternoon, Wise spoke to the Cranford Community Forum in New Jersey on "The Best and the Worst in American Life," and that evening took part in the Community Church Forum on "Directions in American Life."

The following morning, November 21, he had conferences with Salo Baron on the J.I.R. program of Jewish studies and with engineer Julius Fohs of Texas on geology and prospects for oil in Palestine; and, in the evening, attended a dinner meeting at the Savoy Plaza arranged by his associate, Sidney Goldstein, on behalf of the Social Service Division of the Free Synagogue.

Tuesday's schedule included a fashionable wedding, after a meeting of the Free Synagogue's Women's Organization; luncheon at the Harvard Club with Louis Cornish, executive vice-president of the American Unitarian Association; several callers at his study, including Mrs. John Foster Dulles, to discuss community problems; and a dinner at the Yale Club given by Henry A. Atkinson for the Committee on Religious Rights and Minorities, concerned with the uncertain future of Rumanian Jewry.

Wednesday's meetings began with a conference in the office of Judge Julian Mack on Zionist affairs, about which he had conferred at length on several occasions during previous weeks with Louis Lipsky; then followed an afternoon session at the Bankers'

Club with the Board of Directors of the Hebrew University in Jerusalem. In the evening he attended two dinners, the first at the Commodore Hotel under the auspices of the Church Peace Union and the World Alliance for International Friendship Through the Churches to discuss another project of Henry Atkinson's, "The World Congress of Religions on Behalf of Peace"; the second dinner at Sherry's, at the invitation of Maurice Wertheim, to plan the work of the Jewish Agency for Palestine.

The next morning, Thanksgiving Day, he joined Holmes in their annual union service of the Free Synagogue and the Community Church in Carnegie Hall, an enterprise now in its tenth year.

By Friday, he was ready for a long weekend of speaking. He took the noon train to Jamestown, New York, to speak that evening on Henry Ford. After a night on the sleeper to Chicago, he arrived on Saturday afternoon and in the evening gave his address to the Chicago Culture Club on "The Best and the Worst in American Life." On Sunday morning he exchanged pulpits with the young rabbi, Louis Mann. While Mann spoke in New York at the Free Synagogue, Wise addressed thirty-five hundred people at Temple Sinai on the popular subject of the hour, "Do We Need a New Religion?" Separating wheat from the chaff, he asserted that the abiding values of Judaism would, if freshly interpreted, make a new religion needless. He discussed Henry Ford's "retractions" at Temple Sinai's famous Forum on Sunday afternoon and then was driven forty miles north to Wilmette for a public lecture in the evening.

Early Monday morning, he rode down to Evanston and spoke to twelve hundred students at Northwestern University's convocation on the subject, "The College Student in America." After lunch at the Standard Club in the Loop, he discussed the future of the Jewish Institute of Religion with community leaders, then took the train to Milwaukee to participate in a debate on Zionism.

Such a Herculean schedule rarely tired Wise in those years of his greatest strength. The strain seemed only to make him stronger, for like Antaeus he took strength from his touch with the earth. To be with the people gave him the power he needed for his work. On the train he would rest a while and then write notes for future speeches, intermittently scrawling letters to Louise.

Wise's sermon subjects in that year, 1927, included such diverse topics as "Different Types of Anti-Semitism," a new variation on an old theme; "What Good Is Prayer?" a perennial topic on which he felt deeply and spoke powerfully; "Is Suicide Ever the Way Out?" a fashionable subject in any age or nation; and "Does God Need Man or Man Need God?" "You Gentiles and I, the Jew," prompted by his affirmative response to Maurice Samuel's biting book, *You Gentiles,* gave him a chance to say much in criticism of Jewish pretensions and Gentile arrogance. Portions of these lectures and sermons were given again in synagogues and churches, at public forums and in college assemblies, usually to overflow audiences.

Central to all his interests was his ministry at the Free Synagogue. No matter how far afield his Zionist and community activities took him, the home base for his work was the Free Synagogue. He centered his attention not alone on his preaching, important though that was, nor even on the Social Service Division, but on the educational activities as well. Newspaper photographs often showed him at a Seder helping the Jewish children, with their Christian guests, both white and Negro, read the Haggada and asking the age-old question: "Why is this night different from all other nights?" There were many unpublicized days when he would have charge of the confirmation class which, because of his full schedule, would have to meet early Saturday morning or late Sunday afternoon. Whenever possible through the years, he would be present at the confirmation exercises and deliver the address to the confirmands. At funerals and weddings of congregation members, he officiated whenever possible.

On an average of every two or three years he was able to take an ocean voyage. This would give him needed rest and time to read, walk the deck, meet famous personages, write letters, and make plans for next year at the Free Synagogue and the Jewish Institute of Religion. On his return voyage from Europe in 1927, he prepared to join Holmes in the campaign to outlaw war.

21. Learn War No More

> ... the natural bond
> Of brotherhood is severed as the flax
> That falls asunder at the touch of fire.
> Lands intersected by a narrow firth
> Abhor each other. Mountains interposed
> Make enemies of nations who had else
> Like kindred drops been mingled into one.
> Thus man devotes his brother, and destroys.
> —WILLIAM COWPER, 1780

IN THE FIRST WEEKS OF 1928, Holmes singled out four major
interests on which to concentrate in the next year: a shift in his
emphases and responsibilities at the Community Church, the
Outlawry of War campaign, the presidential contest between
Herbert Hoover and Alfred E. Smith, and preparations for an
extended journey to Palestine.

The previous November, John Herman Randall, his associate
for eight years, resigned to become president of the World Unity
Foundation; and Joseph Ernest McAfee, director of Social Service
for the previous four years, assumed some of the tasks. Holmes
took back into his own hands many duties of which he had
formerly been relieved: administrative details, sermons every
Sunday (except the month's first Sunday, reserved for Boston),
and regular programs before the Women's Federation and the
Friday Night Social Club. He gave up all outside lectures, except those around New York and Boston, and remained in the
city. For his occasional absences, he provided distinguished guest
preachers: William Lyon Phelps of Yale; Lewis Browne, author

of *This Believing World;* Bishop William Montgomery Brown, a heretic of the Episcopal Church; and Reinhold Niebuhr, recently appointed to Union Theological Seminary. He invited stimulating speakers for the ever popular Sunday Evening Forum, men like Scott Nearing, Clarence Darrow, Lincoln Steffens, and Stephen Wise. He supervised the work of the educational department which presented lectures by Joseph Wood Krutch on the contemporary drama, Harry Overstreet on social psychology, Will Durant on philosophy, and Count Hermann Keyserling (in his initial appearance in America) on the institution of monogamous marriage and its future.

More pressing, however, was the question of a new church. During 1927, construction had seemed imminent. Blueprints were prepared, contracts drawn up, and hopes raised; but uncertainty about the kind of church and disagreement among the committees postponed the decision. Holmes tried to see a silver lining, claiming that the delay was not without its advantages to all concerned and no waste of time and energy had been involved. The new church would be a better church for every moment of seeming inaction, and the results worth waiting for. But disappointment prevailed throughout the congregation.

Among his outside interests, the campaign for the pact to outlaw war took precedence. From the time Salmon O. Levinson introduced his idea in the *New Republic* in March, 1918 (when John Dewey quickly seconded the motion), Holmes remained in constant touch with him. The archives of Levinson include many folders of letters from Holmes as well as from those to whom Holmes commended the project: David Starr Jordan, John Dewey, and Stephen Wise. The most persuasive proponent was Charles Clayton Morrison, editor of the influential *Christian Century.* In the early 1920s, Holmes had introduced Levinson to Morrison; and from that time on, they all worked closely together.

Holmes was almost as indefatigable as Morrison in defending Levinson against friends who accused him of overestimating the potential of this brain child and of being bitter and intolerant about the League of Nations. Holmes, himself, had no faith in the League. Yet the ease with which he consigned the League to oblivion was almost as blithe as the simple solution of the outlawry program: "As an institution, war is outlawed . . . specifically condemned, repudiated, cast aside as a recognized and legal method of settling disputes. As nations participate in war, they are resorting to a method of settling a dispute which is criminal under the international law of peace, and thus they are themselves criminal nations."

The idea was not new, but Levinson had given it a liveliness and an urgency which advocates of earlier generations had not been able to achieve. In the pages of *Unity, The World Tomorrow,* and *Christian Century,* supporters pressed for the four major objectives of Levinson's proposal: nations must unite in (1) preparing and adopting an international code of law, including (2) a declaration that war, as a crime, would be punished by the law of the nations; (3) founding a court to interpret and enforce such international law, a court more powerful than the World Court; and (4) depending on public opinion to sustain the power of that tribunal.

By 1923, Holmes was heartened by Levinson's success in inducing Senator William Borah of Idaho to introduce the resolution on the outlawry of war in the United States Senate. A year later, church bodies and international organizations began to adopt resolutions on the matter; and a conference, convened by Raymond Robins, Sherwood Eddy, and Kirby Page, succeeded in combining the peace efforts of pro-League and anti-League groups so that all united on a platform advocated by *Unity* and its editor, Holmes.

When Foreign Minister Aristide Briand of France and the American Secretary of State, Frank Kellogg, signed the treaty to outlaw war on August 27, 1928, Holmes was certain that something new had taken place. Here was a turning point in human history. By the time he hailed the great event with a special sermon in early October the fifteen original signatories had been increased to thirty-five and included the Soviet Union. "The caravel of peace is now launched on the great ocean of human affairs," he asserted. "Now at last, after all the centuries of agony and fear, the blessed ship is on the tide." But it was not yet really a ship, only a hull, said Holmes, a beautiful hull—symmetrical, buoyant, perfectly balanced: "The mast has to be hewn and stepped, the rigging to be woven and put in place, the canvas to be cut and sewn and bent to the yards, the rudder to be shipped, and a crew to be disciplined and trained."

Encouraged by the signing of the treaty and impelled by his hatred of war, Holmes composed an Armistice Sunday sermon for November 11 that ranked among his most powerful. Entitled "The Unknown Soldier Speaks," the sermon, delivered in university chapels in subsequent years and reprinted many times in religious and pacifist journals, told of an imaginary visit to the Tomb of the Unknown Soldier in Washington, with the Unknown Soldier throwing out his arms in agony and crying, "How long, O Lord, how long before mankind shall see that war is the blackest lie in hell?" To Holmes there appeared the scene of the Crucifixion; and through the silence, far away, as though drifting across the seas of time from an eternal past, there came familiar words, "My God, my God, why hast Thou forsaken me?"

The close of Holmes' sermon, reflecting a pacifism he equated with liberal Christianity and Socialist allegiances, described their final words and parting:

> The Soldier spoke. . . . It was like the voice of St. Michael to the hosts of heaven.
>
> ". . . There is a grave," he said, "that no man knows, not in the earth, for it is lost, but in the heart, where it may be found, the grave of him who said: 'Love your enemies, bless them that curse you, do good to them that hate you, and pray for them that despitefully use you and persecute you; that ye may be the children of your Father Who is in heaven, for He maketh his sun to rise on the evil and on the good, and sendeth rain on the just and on the unjust.'"
>
> The great words died away, like organ tones. The Unknown Soldier was looming tall and beautiful, like an angel.
>
> "These are the heroes," he said, very gently. "Their graves are the holy ground of earth. Here build your altars of faith and hope and love, and here let the people worship and bow down, and find Great Peace."
>
> The voice of the Soldier was silent. His glowing body began to fade. Suddenly he was a shadow again, and the shadow a darkness. I was alone. The wind was cold upon me, and I shivered. Then I seemed to start, and wake, as though from

sleep. It was the draught from that open window in my room.
I arose to shut it, and my book tumbled noisily to the floor.
What was it I had been reading, as I sat down here in this
chair, and looked out over the city, and thought of the Unknown Soldier far off there on the hill? Oh, yes—a book of
poems! And here was the open page—and two short stanzas.
I must have been pondering them as I fell asleep:

> Who goes there,
> In the night,
> Across the wind-swept plain?
> *We are the ghosts of a valiant war,*
> *A million murdered men.*
>
> Who goes there,
> In the dawn,
> Across the sun-swept plain?
> *We are the hosts of those who swear,*
> *It shall not be again.*

In that same month, November, 1928, Holmes learned that
implementing the pact was more difficult than talking about it,
especially since its ratification by the U.S. Senate was paired
with the adoption of a large navy bill. Should he and his peace-
minded friends oppose the navy bill as a matter of consistent
pacifist policy and thus endanger the outlawry of war pact?
Would the navy bill perhaps nullify the pact? Or could the navy
bill, reduced in importance by President Calvin Coolidge's statement that the ships provided for in the bill need not be built,
be considered a great pacifist triumph? Since the navy bill was
an inevitable hangover from the old era out of which the Kellogg-
Briand Pact was now taking mankind, might it not be accepted
until the Kellogg-Briand Pact was ratified, extended, completed,
and firmly established? Holmes and his friends could at least
agree on one thing: no let-up in arousing public opinion against
increased armaments and in favor of ratification of the outlawry
of war pact.

In the presidential election of 1928, Holmes decided to cast a
protest vote, supporting Norman Thomas on the Socialist Party
ticket. He would not think of voting for Herbert Hoover because
this meant a continuation of Harding-Coolidge policies, and they

were odious to him. As for Alfred E. Smith, this was impossible, for Holmes, a lifelong Prohibitionist, could not support a "Wet." Norman Thomas was running for the first time on the Socialist slate and revealed abilities as a campaigner; he had not the slightest chance, however, lacking the drawing power of Debs in 1912 and 1920, or of La Follette for the Progressives in 1924.

To Holmes the choice was not of great moment. For *Unity*, he performed the dutiful task of gathering four articles on why the respective authors would vote for Hoover, Smith, Thomas, and William Z. Foster of the Communist Party. Holmes' wife joined by his brother Hector and his sister Marion, were planning to vote for Smith; and Madeleine teased him by affixing a large rotogravure picture of the happy warrior to the bedroom wall facing Holmes' bed. When urging friends to vote the Socialist ticket, Holmes said that if all "good people would vote for Norman Thomas, he'd get a vote that would shake the nation, and the world!"

Wise wanted to see a Roman Catholic elected, if for no other reason than to break the boycott of a candidate because of his religion. He believed in Al Smith as a spokesman for a more liberal element in the Democratic Party and as a foe of the Ku Klux Klan. Earlier in the year, in an address on "The Religion of the President and the Spirit of America," Wise asked that not only Roman Catholics be considered eligible for the Presidency but Jews as well. He foresaw the bitterness of the summer and autumn, a bitterness which Holmes did not anticipate, and insisted there be no religious test for a presidential candidate. He deplored the "whisperings of an unholy conspiracy," the reprehensible effort to promulgate an unwritten law that neither Catholics nor Jews could be eligible for the highest office of the land.

Through Wise at this time came an opportunity for Holmes and his wife and son to learn more than they already knew about the Jews of Palestine. From Nathan Straus, who had been captivated by Holmes' personality and his extraordinary way with words and ideas, came an invitation for John and Madeleine to visit Palestine. Wise, serving as intermediary for Straus, suggested they go early the following year (1929) and arrive shortly before January 31, Straus' eighty-first birthday. Then Holmes, as a Christian, could join with a Jew and a Moslem in dedicating the Nathan and Lena Straus Health Center in Jerusalem. Holmes arranged for a ten-week absence from the church.

To prepare for the trip Holmes read extensively, but confessed to some bewilderment at the complexity of the Zionist issue and the many-sidedness of the Jewish community both in America and abroad. He liked the spirit of the book Louise Waterman Wise had translated from the French, Aimé Pallière's *Unknown Sanctuary*, and felt a kinship with this Christian who had traveled to a land sacred to Christians and found himself converted to both Judaism and Zionism along the way.

He was also intrigued by another, quite different, book, written by one "Analyticus" and entitled *Jews Are Like That.* "Analyticus" had composed character sketches of, among others, Henry Morgenthau, Louis D. Brandeis, Felix Adler, Louis Marshall, Nathan Straus, and Stephen Wise. When Henry Morgenthau read the acid treatment of himself, he wrote to Wise and asked if he knew the identity of the author. Wise told Morgenthau he did know but the publisher, Brentano's, had requested him not to disclose the man's name. The evasion was truthful enough but of no avail, for soon it was revealed that "Analyticus" was James Waterman Wise.

To Holmes, who knew all the men personally, the most illuminating section of *Jews Are Like That* was the chapter about Wise. With due respect, even praise, for his father's ability as a fighter, zeal as a prophet, and fearlessness as a public figure, the son-author remarked: "Wise's written oratorical style is as bad as the best of George William Curtis. He has an almost pathological addiction to antitheses, a delight in epigrams which borders on the abnormal, and when conscious of himself and of his flawless oratorical manner, he is at his worst."

In a sermon, "Dare Jews Criticize Jews?" Wise praised the book's "refreshing newness" and called it "an honest, sincere and courageous book, though not without mistakes, and possessed of the merit of being the first attempt in Jewish life in America of giving an unsparing and true appraisal of important Jews—or of those Jews who think they are important."

By this time Holmes had grown to be something of an authority on Zionism. He knew that, in the American Jewish community, a fierce battle raged between Zionists on the one hand and, on the other, many leading philanthropists—among them Julius Rosenwald, Louis Marshall, and James Rosenberg, who were willing to spend a minimum of five million dollars to help colonize Russian Jews in the Soviet Ukraine and the Crimea, rather than in Palestine. The controversy was complicated by the fact that the leading Zionist of the world, Chaim Weizmann, was trying to persuade Marshall and his friends to accept representation as non-Zionists in the Jewish Agency for Palestine. Wise had opposed the Ukraine project, partly because he considered it anti-Zionist but mostly because it would aid the Soviet policy of opposition to Zionism.

Holmes found that when attacks came from outside the Jewish community, the rival factions within Jewry could close ranks and attain a strength like that of the ancient Maccabees; but otherwise there were a quarrelsomeness and divisiveness among Jews, as in other groups that seemed unified to outsiders, which sapped their strength and dissipated their effectiveness.

He experienced a sense of relief, therefore, when he went to Washington to be briefed by Justice Brandeis in his home in late December. All day, they sat in Brandeis' tiny study, scarcely larger than a clothes closet, with Holmes' chair perched in the hall outside, while the nonobservant Jew spoke of the Holy Land the Hebrew prophets had loved so dearly many centuries earlier and had prophesied would one day know the Return of its People.

22. They Shall Repair
the Ruined Cities

And the land that was desolate shall be tilled,
whereas it was a desolation in the sight of all
that passed by.   —EZEKIEL, 36:34

WHEN HOLMES LEFT FOR PALESTINE in early January, 1929, he
had disposed of some literary chores. One assignment was completion of his yearly allotment of a dozen brief biographies for
the *Dictionary of American Biography,* published over a period
of years under the auspices of the New York *Times* and the
American Council of Learned Societies. Holmes enjoyed the
work, for the men and women of whom he wrote included many
with whom he had co-operated or contended in the struggle for
religious and social liberalism: Helen Frances Garrison Villard
and Anna Garlin Spencer, Josiah Strong and Charles Henry
Parkhurst, Jacob August Riis and Percy Stickney Grant. Another
commitment was his introduction to Mahatma Gandhi's autobiography, *The Story of My Experiments with Truth,* scheduled
to be published later that year.

By late January, Holmes, accompanied by his friend, Judah
Magnes, was roaming Palestine, sometimes by motorcar, often
on horseback. Jerusalem was the base of operations. From there,
he made side trips to all the historic places, interviewed rich and
poor, professional men and women, laborers, *chalutzim* [pio-
neers] in the communal settlements, Jews and Arabs, Christians

and Moslems, officials in Zionist agencies, and administrators in the British Mandatory Government, most notably the High Commissioner, Sir John Chancellor.

Sir John was not sanguine when he talked with Holmes about the prospects of rebuilding Palestine. The land was really much too arid and desolate, he said. Others shared his pessimism. A British official appraised Tel Aviv, now twenty years old and a noisy, sun-beaten, jerry-built city, as "a boom town." It really had no future: "The people live by taking in one another's washing. It has no basis of industry or civic life. It has had one collapse. The next one will end it." One official foresaw only failure for the *kibbutzim:* "The agricultural colonies are all sentimental nonsense. The Jews naturally belong in cities; they can't maintain themselves upon the land."

As for the Zionist Movement itself, another official said, "It is in the hands of paid officials who go to Zionist congresses and bargain for their own support. A few years more and the bottom will drop out from under them. The second generation of settlers here in Palestine will get tired and refuse to work any more; the Jews abroad will get tired and refuse to give any more. And that will be the end."

The impatience and contempt of the British with whom he spoke were reflected in the remark of a snobbish undersecretary, who said to him in a clipped English accent, "These Arabs, you know—well, they are gentlemen and one can invite them to one's table. But the *Jews!*" By a gesture of the hands the Englishman emphasized his disdain.

Consequently, Holmes was not impressed by British rule. Unlike many pro-Zionists, both Jewish and non-Jewish, he did not consider the advent of Great Britain in Palestine in 1917 the greatest development of the Zionist Movement. There was no question that the paved roads and improved sanitation came from the British. General conditions of law and order stood in sharp contrast to the corruption and chaos of Palestine's four centuries under the Ottoman Empire, but Holmes had grave reservations about the Mandatory officials and their intentions. He felt that they had done little to advance the purposes of the Zionists; their power and pride, self-interest and procrastination

were nothing but disturbing elements. He did not believe that
the Balfour Declaration was entirely altruistic, for it had been
issued by Britain more for military advantage in the Great War
than to aid a minority. Arthur James Balfour was not deeply
interested in the aspirations of the Zionist Movement.

"Why do you revere this man? Why do you hang his picture
on the walls of your homes?" Holmes asked the Jews. "The very
name Balfour should be enough to stir doubts and conjure
fears. This man never had an unselfish emotion in his life and
never anywhere served a great humanitarian cause. He has been
consistently cynical in his statesmanship. The common man,
Gentile or Jew, has never existed for him except as a nuisance
or occasionally as a danger. He would harry the Jews of Palestine today as ruthlessly as he harried the patriots of Ireland
yesterday, if they disturbed the interests or threatened the peace
of British rule. To think of this man sharing the hopes of the
Jews for Zion, or serving these hopes as incidentally they serve
the Empire, is utterly fantastic. Nothing I see in Zion so disturbs
me as the elevation of 'bloody Balfour' as a patron saint of Zion."

Holmes' Palestinian friends responded that England has always been the best friend the Jew has ever had.

"That England was the center of liberalism during the nine-
teenth century," Holmes replied, "and did advance the idea of
equal rights for Jews wherever they lived, I grant you. The
British government did intervene on behalf of Jews in North
Africa and Eastern Europe when they were subjected to per-
secution and pogroms. It's true that Great Britain has less anti-
Semitism by far than Russia, but the British still look upon the
Jews of Palestine as just one more 'white man's burden'!"

Also disquieting to Holmes were the poverty and ignorance of
the Arabs. Here was a burden to both the English and the Jews.
Holmes could not fail to agree with Judah Magnes of the Hebrew
University and Henrietta Szold of Hadassah that it was a mission
of the Jew to elevate the status of the Arab.

In fact, they believed Palestine should be a Jewish-Arab state
with equal populations of Jews and Arabs; thus they differed
radically from political Zionists. The problem of how an equal
balance of population would be maintained, especially with the

high birth rate of the Arabs and the Jews' introduction of modern medicine from the West which lowered the Arabs' infant mortality rate, was not, however, easily to be solved.

Toward the goal of Jewish-Arab friendship, Holmes thought the Hebrew University might make a major contribution. It offered education to Arabs too, although few Arabs had as yet ventured to register.

Magnes led Holmes around the new campus on the brow of Mount Scopus, and introduced him to scholars from a dozen different countries, who were establishing themselves in fields of Hebrew letters and comparative religion, science and archaeology. Standing in the open-air amphitheater and looking out to the Dead Sea and the Hills of Moab in the distance, Magnes expressed his hope that someday an Israel Symphony Orchestra might give concerts there. Holmes looked out to the hills in which the body of Moses had been interred, where "no man knows the place of his burial to this day," and grasped the meaning of Asher Ginsberg's [Achad Ha-am] plea for "a University which, in the very beginning, will endeavor to become the true embodiment of the Hebrew spirit of old and shake off the mental and moral servitude to which our people have been so long subjected in the Diaspora."

Holmes was repelled by the commercialization of Christian holy places. The reputed sacred sites were doubtful in origin. Solomon's Stables were neither Solomon's nor stables; had he not looked on two sepulchers of Christ, three gardens of Gethsemane, and several graves of Moses?

The Jewish holy places intrigued him more when, after his trip to Damascus which left him unimpressed, he visited Safed, "the city set on a hill which cannot be hid." Here he entered the center of Jewish learning and piety, synagogues where services had been held for centuries without a break.

Particularly impressive to him was a pilgrimage to the Bahai shrine in Haifa. He stood before the graves of the founders and prophets, Abdul Baha and Bab, on the slopes of Mount Carmel, and Baha O'Llah in the Bahai Garden of Acre. To Bahai friends in America he described the tall cypresses and verdant gardens: "Here, appropriately, was not darkness, but light; not gloom, but glory. Those prophets' shrines are truly among the sacred spots of earth. There have been few in any age to compare with them in point of insight, vision, lofty thought, and noble speech. Were it possible to stand by the grave of Jesus, I felt I should be moved in this same way."

The faith of the pioneering Jews in their country's future was the most compelling fact of his entire trip. Standing on a hill from which he could see swamps being drained, crops sown, and trees planted, Holmes noted bleak hills to his left and remarked to his guide, "Look at those mountains. There's nothing you can do with them."

"Those hills," his companion answered, "were once beautiful with figs and olives. We shall make them beautiful again."

"How can you possibly do that?" Holmes asked him.

"We shall terrace them," his companion replied, "as they were terraced in the old days. Those slopes are not merely sand and rock. There is soil there still. And the soil that has been washed away into those valleys, we'll carry back, basket by basket, shovelful by shovelful, until the hills are green again."

"You can't do that," Holmes cried, "not in a hundred years!"

"What's a hundred years in the life of the Jew?" was the answer, the bravest words Holmes heard in Palestine.

On one notable occasion Holmes joined the pioneers in founding a village. In mid-February he was invited to take part in the explorations for water at a new settlement called Nathanya in honor of the American benefactor, Nathan Straus. Holmes was driven some thirty-five kilometers north of Tel Aviv along the coastal road and found a handful of workers gathered before their huts amid the wind-swept dunes. Standing with him atop the bluff overlooking the Mediterranean, they shared their dream of transforming this desolate prospect into a seaside city flanked by orange groves and new industries. Holmes listened patiently, if a bit skeptically, to their ambitious plans and then watched them dig for a spring. Suddenly, the fresh water gushed from the sandy earth, and whatever doubts about Nathanya's future lingered in his mind changed to certainty. When the settlers asked their American visitor to be the first entry in Nathanya's guest book, Holmes wrote: "Like Columbus, I am the first visitor to look upon this fair land."

For Holmes, his wife, and their son, the weeks in Palestine

had few lost moments or wasted motions. There was not a single closed door during the entire stay—quite a different experience from Holmes' Russian trip in 1922, when gates were barred and tongues guarded. In Palestine, he moved as though in a blaze of light.

He met Communists. They were not, as in the Soviet Union, in the majority nor in power, but were a small, seemingly insignificant, yet potent and dangerous, minority. He found them among the workers and the tribesmen, among the Jewish zealots and the Arab fanatics who considered it a pious duty, a patriotic obligation, to stir up trouble between Jews and Arabs. He called them "children of chaos in their deliberate campaign of agitation."

At the end of February, Holmes presented his convictions at a press interview in Jerusalem. The New York *Times* correspondent, Joseph M. Levy, prepared a long dispatch and mailed it to New York. When Stephen Wise opened the *Times* on March 17, the Sunday morning of his fifty-fifth birthday, he found a four-column feature headed:

SUCCESS OF ZIONISM A MATTER OF TIME

Dr. Holmes Tells Factors Which Would Bring Victory to the Cause in Palestine—Many Difficulties Exist—Land Itself, Government and Arab Relations Must be Improved, New York Minister Says.

Holmes' extended report ended with a Social Gospel assertion: "Here, as nowhere else, the Kingdom of God is possible, and the building of that Kingdom is the task of today and not of tomorrow."

He promised that, when he returned home, he would "plead with all men, Jews and Gentiles, to give to this cause as never before," a promise he kept in the following months, as he spoke many times in the spring of 1929. Christians, accustomed to anti-Zionist reports from returning missionaries, were now to receive a new slant; Jews, jaded by the old story from their own, would now listen eagerly, opening their pocketbooks and writing checks as had the philanthropic Nathan Straus in earlier days.

When Holmes and his wife were met at the pier in New York by the church staff on the eve of Palm Sunday, he was both pleased and disappointed by the news they brought. His pleasure came from their report of the warmhearted reception given Reinhold Niebuhr, his guest preacher on six of the ten Sundays he was absent.

The disappointment, deep and painful, stemmed from the disclosure that nothing had been done about the church building. Negotiations for builders and financial transactions had collapsed and in his annual report that summer Holmes had to confess that all was confusion. At his urging, however, negotiations began again; and, by fall, architect and trustees, bankers and lawyers seemed ready to proceed with the building of a combination church-and-apartment hotel at Park Avenue and 34th Street. Although a sense of expectancy now stirred within the church, inaction persisted.

After a whirlwind three months of speaking on the Eastern Seaboard and out in the Midwest during the spring of 1929, Holmes left for his vacation and set to work on a book he planned to develop from the twenty long articles he had written over as many weeks for publication in *Unity*. The book would be called *Palestine: Today and Tomorrow—A Gentile's Survey of Zionism*.

In the midst of his writing, the Arabs in Palestine attacked the Jews; and the British imposed, belatedly and ineffectually, harsh military means to stop the "troubles." After momentary dismay and a halt to his writing, Holmes continued with scarcely a change, save to add some footnotes deploring the riots, criticizing the British, and condemning Arab violence. By late autumn, after helpful critiques from both Stephen Wise and David de Sola Pool, Rabbi of New York's Spanish-Portuguese Synagogue, the book was published. It received uniformly good reviews with one major exception. In *The World Tomorrow*, Harry Emerson Fosdick complained that the book, while beautiful in diction and incisive in observation, showed that Holmes had fallen prey to Zionist propaganda.

Holmes' pro-Zionism was not, however, marked by anti-Arab polemics. His was a cultural Zionism, not merely a nationalistic hope: "I have aligned myself with those who look to Zion as fundamentally an ethical and spiritual phenomenon, and find its destiny in a deliberate surrender of the 'things of this world' to those high ideals of the Law which are Israel's unique and precious contribution to mankind. In the new Zion, as not in the old, the prophets and not the kings must prevail."

His qualified Zionism and identification with Judah Magnes' bi-national point of view impelled Holmes to defend Magnes' efforts to effect reconciliation between Arabs and Jews in Palestine. The same Joseph M. Levy who had interviewed Holmes for the New York *Times* in Jerusalem arranged for Magnes to meet H. St. John Philby and exchange opinions about the possibility of peace. The time seemed propitious, since the riots had been quelled and Arab resisters had retreated, though in sullen anger and with the resolve to return again for successful warfare against their sworn enemies, the Jews. Philby was now negotiating with the Arabs, but as a "British agent" without either portfolio or official appointment. He had been the British emissary to Ibn Saud in the Great War and was at the time unofficial adviser to Saud, who was then King of Arabia; he had been political secretary in Iraq and, as a British resident in Transjordan, had adopted Mohammedanism as his faith.

After conferring with Philby, Magnes issued a statement to the New York *Times*, always his major avenue of approach to the American public, and supported Philby's proposals with minor modifications. Essentially, he agreed with Philby that the Mandate for Palestine should be altered and the Zionists' objective of a Jewish State with a Jewish majority relinquished.

Only three weeks earlier Magnes had delivered a Balfour Day address in Jerusalem and asked for a peace in Palestine based upon the faith of one faction in the other. That address, the Philby proposals, and his own amplification caused a hue and cry for Magnes' resignation from the chancellorship of the Hebrew University. American Zionists, among them Wise as a chief opponent of Magnes, raged at Magnes' "wretched, misbegotten pamphlet" and berated him as a dissenter. Nathan Straus told Wise: "The present head of the University has done all Jews an irreparable harm. I don't claim to be a prophet, but

I feel sure he will make himself out to be a martyr, unless he is removed immediately. He is a disgrace to the entire rabbinate of the world."

In an America stunned by the stock market crash of late October and November, the Zionist storm was scarcely noticeable; but Holmes noticed it. In early December, he received an inquiry from Jacob Billikopf, a social worker of Philadelphia and a relative by marriage of Magnes' asking him for his opinion of Magnes' Jerusalem pleas for amity between Palestinian Jews and Arabs. Holmes replied he had thought intensely about the address and was profoundly moved by it. He had this to say to Billikopf:

> Wholly apart from all questions of practicability and inner Zionist politics, I think that Magnes' speech was one of the greatest things that I have ever read in my life. Everything else aside, it was heroic to the point of sublimity. It fairly makes me tremble to think of the courage that it took for Magnes to get up in Jerusalem in the midst of such a crisis as prevails at this hour and speak those words. Every word of that address was prophecy in the truest and highest Old Testament sense.

But there was more than heroism and prophecy, said Holmes; Magnes had risen to an even higher level:

> . . . It is my own humble opinion, from the standpoint of my study of the Palestine situation, that Magnes' address represented true statesmanship. I know of no other possible solution of the present Zionist problem but the one which he marked out.

Holmes had something else on his mind that he did not hesitate to share with the Philadelphian:

> I regard it as a scandal of the first order that so many of the Jews of this country should now be baying like wolves on Magnes' track. My God, is it possible that the Jews of today, after all their centuries of tragic history, can't recognize one of their own prophets when he rises up among them? . . . Magnes is the greatest prophetic spirit in the world of Jewry today. He ranks in my mind with Jeremiah. . . . My prayer is that the Jews are not going to rend Magnes today as they did Jeremiah yesterday.

As the ire of Israel abated and the issue receded in importance, Holmes' friends, both Jews and non-Jews, saw in his pro-Zionism the affirmation of an idealism akin to that of his colonial ancestors and stated by him in these words:

> What we see in Palestine is a deep-founded full-rounded civilization, reared in an inhospitable country, amid a primitive people, by the labor of men's hands and the sacrifice of their heroic hearts. It needs but the presence of a determined mind, a courageous heart, an idealistic spirit, to make this country an experiment station for the ills of man. Here in this adventure is the dream of a society of justice, righteousness and peace. I know of nothing in history to compare with it, unless it be the early settlement of New England.

23. All We Like Sheep Did Go Astray

Because of the magnitude of the disorders God gave this age a violent physician.
—ERASMUS, 1524
(Concerning Martin Luther)

IN THE WINTER OF 1929–1930, shortly after the stock market tumble signaled the outward collapse of an economic system which had previously shown signs of inward instability, John Haynes Holmes reassessed himself and his church.

He had been in the ministry for more than twenty-five years, almost twenty-three of them in New York; but in this, his fiftieth year, he found his strength not as inexhaustible as before. He wrote: "I used to denounce evil much more than I do now, and I am ashamed to have to confess it. In those days, like every young man, I was all ablaze with the fire of prophecy, and did some preaching, I think, that was worthwhile. Today the fires are burning low and only a cataclysmic event, like that of the recent crash in Wall Street, can stir them anew." Hence his sermon in mid-December of 1929, "Stock Exchange Gambling, Stop It! How?" which recommended federal investigations to be followed by federal regulation of exchanges.

As for his home life, Holmes was as contented as on the day of his marriage in 1904. At their silver wedding anniversary, three months after returning from Palestine, the Holmeses congratulated themselves on the happinesses of twenty-five years. Their children were now grown and educated. Roger was studying for his doctorate and a career in teaching philosophy, while Frances, after her years of study at the University of Chicago

261

and at Radcliffe, was planning to marry Morris Lovejoy Brown of Boston the following spring. Apart from some minor operations and lesser illnesses, John and Madeleine Holmes could be grateful for good health.

In the church, the major problems were still financial obstacles and the committee's indecision. Despite his disappointment, he knew that the Community Church, by its service to the community, could lay just claim to its name. For a time in the mid-1920s it had seemed as though the congregation were going to be mostly proletarian, but now a number of professional and mercantile members provided a balance. "The Homestead," a gift from Victor and Minnie Olsa of their farm in Putnam County, gave to many who otherwise would never have known it a camp and conference experience; Holmes was president of its board of directors. The consultation service, counseling the mentally disturbed and finding jobs for the unemployed, grew in scope.

At the close of 1929, an anonymous gift made possible twelve successive lectures by Alfred Adler, the psychoanalyst, and every evening the church auditorium was filled. Police reserves kept the crowd in line and handled the disappointed who had to be turned away.

Interest was high whenever Holmes preached on psychology and marital problems. The three best-attended services in one year were when Holmes preached on "Bernard Shaw and the Role of Asceticism," "Havelock Ellis and the Art of Love," and "Bertrand Russell and the Experiment of Freedom." From his own counseling and reading, he concluded that the psychology of the relations of men and women, either in marriage or out of it, were vital to human happiness; and he looked forward to the time when there might be a special clinic for marriage counseling and planned parenthood, a hope achieved four years later by Abraham and Hannah Stone. In a letter to a young couple who had come to him for advice and help, he wrote: "There are two deep-down, fundamental things that wreck marriages: (1) sex maladjustment and (2) money, by which I mean debt and the worries, bickerings, and dissensions that accompany debt. . . . In the early days when I talked with unhappy husbands and wives, I used to fumble around a good deal. Now I move quickly and with precision—I always ask, first, about sex and then about money affairs. Nine times out of ten if it isn't one, it is the other."

The church was used to capacity throughout the week. On Sunday the program was full and no space was left. After the morning service came an afternoon meeting, under McAfee's informed direction, to discuss current events; and in the twilight hour, there would be quiet readings from classical or modern poets, often with a visiting poet as the reader. Following a social hour came a dinner in the Church House where people met in an informal manner; and the Community Forum in the evening and its subsequent discussion hour brought large crowds, the largest of any forum in New York. The array of outstanding speakers included Maurice Hindus on Soviet Russia, Maurice Samuel on conditions in Palestine, S. K. Ratcliffe on England under Ramsay MacDonald, and Professor Gaetano Salvemini on Italy under the rule of Fascism.

Yet the ever-present financial problems of the church gave Holmes the feeling of quicksand under his feet. The business depression began to create economic insecurity.

An additional vexation was the municipal chaos caused by the antics of New York's "playboy mayor," James J. Walker. To oppose Walker and Tammany's civic corruption Holmes supported Norman Thomas as a candidate for the mayoralty and served as chairman of the Non-Partisan Committee on behalf of Thomas.

Marxism, too, was on the rise. One of the best correctives for it, in the view of Stephen Wise, was Zionism. He wrote to Ismar Elbogen in Berlin, like most liberal Jews of Europe an anti-Zionist:

> Forgive me for saying that I am afraid that you are a little too cynical about your daughter's passionate enthusiasm with respect to Palestine. You speak of Zionism and Bolshevism as though they were equally dubious, if not dread, alternatives. Surely, that is not true. I find that Zionism lifts up the hearts of our young people and exercises an enriching influence over their lives. What Bolshevism means to the Jewish people of Russia, it is not necessary to discuss.

Yet it was necessary to discuss Bolshevism, especially with his students at the Jewish Institute of Religion. Some of them seemed unaware of Judaism's capacity to provide a vital, dynamic faith that could counter the devil-may-care faithlessness of their contemporaries, challenge Marxism as a philosophy and communism as an economic solution, and complement the idealism of Zionism.

So he spoke to them at his birthday dinner in the spring of 1930. In the afternoon he had taken part in a debate on religious persecution in the Soviet republic and was astonished that, in the large gathering, each antireligious reference made by other speakers was greeted with applause, every derisive allusion to organized religion in general and personal religion in particular was cheered, mostly by the younger Jews. In his casual response, he talked at first in bantering fashion, then shifted from badinage to a higher level:

> These young people, alas and alack, take the same position with regard to our simple ethical and spiritual heritage that the Soviet Government takes with regard to that mass of superstitions and mummeries known yesterday as the Orthodox Greek Church. We are not a people of mummeries. We are a people of vitality. We are a civilization. Ours is a spirit. But that spirit in form is a living, deathless brotherhood. And I, for my part, cannot understand how young Jews can listen patiently to any words that place Judaism among obsolescent and perishable things.

In the kind of clarion speech which brought many men into the Jewish ministry, Wise concluded: "If I were twenty-six instead of fifty-six, oh, how I would rejoice in the clear call and summons to you young men to be watchmen upon the tower of Israel, who, if you do your duty truly and without fear, will never have the blood of your people upon your head."

In 1930, he began to discern the historic pattern of Zionism in relation to the British Empire. Each year during the previous decade, he had become increasingly critical of the British and now was forced to an onslaught more direct than ever before. In his book, *The Great Betrayal*, he judged the British Mandate as utterly bankrupt.

One reason for his sharp judgment was that, when the British sent Sir John Hope Simpson to Palestine to confer with the High Commissioner, the Foreign Secretary, Lord Passfield (Sidney Webb), had reassured a Labor member of his Commission, Harry Snell, that the report would not be hostile. When Stephen Wise invited Snell to address a meeting of the American Jewish Congress in Washington, Snell recalled his assurances in London and repeated these to the Congress delegates. Though a dissenting member of the John Hope Simpson Commission, Snell was convinced that "the essential instruction in the Mandate is to secure the establishment of the Jewish National Home." If there were contradictory phrases in the instructions, they would appear to be only precautionary, purely subordinate.

The day after his speech, Snell was astounded, as were the delegates to the Congress, to read that the Hope Simpson Report had gone in the other direction and planned to curtail Jewish aspirations in Palestine to an even greater extent.

The nervous strain was too much for Wise. He could not sleep. His doctors ordered him to take a long rest, but he could not until he had written down the main points for his book and given Jacob de Haas an outline. De Haas, a veteran Zionist and biographer of Theodor Herzl, became coauthor and prepared a draft.

Two weeks later Wise was well enough to add his own insertions to the introduction and main body of the book. He wrote his own *J'Accuse*: "I, for my part, am ready to charge the officials of the Palestine administration, alike in London and Jerusalem, with having so bedeviled the situation as to deepen Arab-Jewish differences, which at the outset were superficial. Statesmanship with goodwill could easily have composed the situation that Colonial Office bureaucracy with ill intent has done everything to confound."

To his congregation and to lecture audiences, to Zionist rallies across America and at the seventeenth Congress in Basel, Wise spoke in these terms: "We are not beggars gathered together to plead, but sons and daughters of a great people, assembled . . . to make solemn protest against a wrong that is and against a greater wrong that threatens the Jewish Homeland in Palestine.

Britain cannot afford to violate her pledge to the Jewish people. No nation is great enough to be free to do wrong. England deals with us as though we were a small people, but we represent the supreme moral values of the world, which in part are become incorporate in the life of England."

Jewry was now threatened by a greater danger abroad, the rise of Hitler. To Elbogen in Berlin, Wise wrote, "I can well imagine in what a state of uncertainty things are in your country. We have a horror of the possibility of Germany surrendering, even though for a short time, to Hitler."

Conditions in Germany, anxiety about British policy in Palestine, worsening economic conditions in America, and the inability of the Hoover administration to bring aid to the unemployed made Wise believe it imperative to issue a publication which would be independent and forthright, inclusive and incisive in presenting the truth about these situations. When his son, Jim, suggested founding a magazine, Wise encouraged him. The weekly, *Opinion: A Journal of Jewish Life and Letters,* published its first issue on December 7, 1931.

In *Opinion,* John Haynes Holmes began his feature, "Through Gentile Eyes," regretting again the persecution of the Jew by Christians. He wrote that if he were a Jew, he would be a Zionist, try to be himself, try to live his own life and thus unite himself with the life of humanity at large, and seek to achieve his own racial and religious goals, in fulfillment of the dream of a humanity redeemed and a world set free.

Speaking at the commencement exercises at St. Lawrence University, where he was awarded an honorary degree in June, 1931, Holmes shared the platform with two of the foremost capitalists in America, Owen D. Young, president of General Electric and chairman of the board of trustees of the University, and Andrew W. Mellon, the Pittsburgh financier and Secretary of the Treasury under Harding, Coolidge, and Hoover. Holmes compared the world of 1931, twelve years after the Treaty of Versailles, with the world he knew when he graduated from college, twelve years before the opening of the Great War:

> My world, a generation ago, believed in capitalism, and saw the permanent success of capitalism in substitution of surplus for

deficit. Your world today is fearing the collapse of capitalism, for we have discovered that an economic system which solves the problem of production but is unable or unwilling to solve the problem of distribution, contains within itself the seeds of destruction.

I entered a society thirty years ago which was undisputed master of the earth. Our money was triumphant at home and was swiftly completing triumphs abroad. You are entering a world, where, for the first time, a competitor of our western society has suddenly appeared. I am referring of course to Russia, which is the most momentous and portentous phenomenon of our day. I believe that our world is not large enough to contain these two systems, and that one will either destroy or absorb the other.

He therefore welcomed any idea which would challenge the existing order and was sympathetic with any revolt against it that would seem to be intelligent and beneficent. Paying no attention to Young or Mellon, he urged his young hearers to be rash and not prudent, bold and not timid.

What seemed to be revolutionary to some, seemed to others, notably the Communists, reactionary. Holmes called himself a radical, especially a religious radical, but he had been caustic in denouncing social radicals, listing their sins as arrogance or pride, dogmatism, intolerance, uncharitableness, and unbrotherliness. As a consequence, apparently, the Russians denied him an entrance visa for the Soviet Union. Holmes, who had been accused for almost fifteen years of being a Red, now found the door closed to the Red Utopia. Eventually, however, the visa was granted, in great measure due to the intercession of Anna Louise Strong, editor of the Moscow *Daily News* (the English language newspaper).

The following winter Holmes celebrated his twenty-fifth anniversary at the Community Church. He compared himself at fifty-two with the young man of twenty-seven, "much soberer than he was before, infinitely more patient and compassionate, and, if the truth be told, far less of an optimist. He no longer has the easy confidence and bright hope for the future that he once had. He sees dark days ahead—at the best, a long struggle, sustained at bitter cost and cruel sacrifice, for a world which shall at last know justice and find peace; and, at the worst, a collapse of our age, which shall bring . . . another thousand years of darkness."

"One of the most poignant disappointments and even griefs of my life," he said, "is that of the intellectual radicals whom I know and work with outside the church, and whom I value among my closest friends and associates, hardly one of them ever shows his face inside the doors of my church. . . . I say nothing about this, because I think I understand—the church has completely dropped out of the lives of these people. But why shouldn't they recognize what I am trying to do and endeavor at least to establish a new kind of church?"

When the invitation came to give a liberal-radical interpretation of his views in a course at the New School for Social Research, he spoke on "The Future of Religion." He noted with approval the three main trends of the time: increasing secularization, the autonomy of ethics and a resultant independence of ethics from religion, and the distintegration of religion under the impact of the physical or natural sciences ("In the conflict between religion and science during the last four hundred years . . . the outcome is perfectly plain: the victory of science on every battle field where the issue with religion has been joined"). As for Christianity, the broom swept clean: "The traditional thought-content of Christian theology is as unreal to scientists as the Lost Atlantis or the Islands of the Blest."

But could not something abide? If religion, all religions, were disintegrating, would not such a process prepare the way for religion in a more perfect sense? The outlook for the future meant that there would be no gods, no churches, no Sundays, no Bibles, no prophets nor saviors nor messiahs, and no religions —merely religion. There would be no sects nor denominations; all would be parts of the one inclusive whole, the divine brotherhood of humankind. The world would become one great temple, and man one great family, and all true life divine. That far he had never gone before and never would again.

During these days a book appeared bearing the title of one of his most popular sermons, *The Sensible Man's View of Religion.* Eugene Exman of Harper and Brothers began publishing a series of sermons by famous ministers, each book of ten best sermons selling for one dollar; and at his invitation, Holmes brought together ten of his best, including "The Unknown Soldier Speaks," "Is the Universe Friendly?" "Sex: Are There Any Standards?" Exman made the book unique by asking Stephen Wise to write an introduction; thus this book, out of the whole series of some thirty-six issued one per month over three years, was the only one introduced by a rabbi. Wise wrote:

> In the case of John Haynes Holmes . . . every word he speaks is charged, when not surcharged with the dynamic of an uniquely vivid and vibrant personality. . . . Somehow the miracle of the preacher is renewed in these pages. . . . I have heard many things said of Mr. Holmes, but never once that the author is "sensible," whatever that may mean. Sensitive, understanding, genuine . . . utterly compelling as none other in the American pulpit, we have in these sermons and addresses something priceless, a fragment of an incomparably rich and significant personality. John Haynes Holmes does many things well, identified as he is with many great causes. But he does nothing so well as he preaches. Here he is at his best, a torch bringing light as do few men in any generation, a kindling flame to multitudes who gladly sit at the feet of this prophet and feel themselves blessed.

Holmes had the opportunity in turn to express his own appreciation at Wise's twenty-fifth anniversary when he told the congregation of the Free Synagogue: "You know that he is the greatest orator of our time, and the outstanding moral and spiritual leader of the age . . . the 'great American preacher' of this hour!"

Turning to Wise, he addressed him directly:

> My dear friend of the many years we have known together in this city, my beloved colleague in the ministry, my sustained comrade on a road that has been long and at times very hard, my master in speech and spirit beside whom I have been glad to walk that I might learn and understand, I find it an altogether characteristic thing that you should have invited me to come to this place today and share in the joy of this anniversary occasion. For of all the things that I have learned of you through

the lovely years we have had together, I have found nothing more distinctive than the fact that whatever you possess you have been quick and eager to share with others. The talents of your mind and the sympathy of your heart you have always poured out on your friends. The books of your library which are dear to a man next only to the children of his own flesh, you have taken and placed in the library of your Jewish Institute of Religion for the use of professors and students. Your money, richly earned by your incomparable abilities, you have lavishly given to causes so notably served by your incomparable zeal. Your life through all these years, in sweat and tears and blood, you have laid here upon the altar of humanity.

In these times, shifting so swiftly and unpredictably, the two men came closer together. These were dark days and were to become even darker for both men on the international scene and at home. For two years, Wise's son-in-law, Leon Tulin, had been wasting away from leukemia and he died in the fall of 1932. Wise worried about the nation's worsening depression, the ever longer bread lines, the growing number of unemployed, Hitler's bid for power, but to see Justine grieve cut deepest into his heart.

Now, more than ever before, he needed to be sustained by the Rock of Israel. He had given help to thousands in their sorrow, had spoken such words of comfort not long before at the funeral of Nellie Cardozo, sister of Benjamin Cardozo, that the bereaved Justice had written: "As I look back on the ceremonies of yesterday afternoon, and think of them in the more tranquil hours of today, it seemed to be the most beautiful that I have ever heard. You said the right thing with such grace and delicacy and charm. It was a prose poem. I knew it would be, or at least I thought I knew, and I was right." In the following months, he gave so much strength to Benjamin Cardozo that, for the rest of Cardozo's life, the jurist told friends only Wise understood the depth of his grief and saved him from insanity. Now Wise, and his friend Holmes, brought comfort to a beloved daughter.

24. A Little Man in the Big City

How long are we going to be amused by this little man? —JOHN HAYNES HOLMES, 1931

BY THE CLOSE OF 1929, Tammany Hall was firmly entrenched in power. Mayor James J. Walker had been re-elected in the November election over his chief opponent, Fiorello H. LaGuardia; in fact, Walker received more votes than all of his rivals combined. The Non-Partisan Committee to Elect Norman Thomas as Mayor, headed by John Haynes Holmes, was disappointed by the tepid response to its candidate.

In early December a meeting of the Board of Estimate was announced for the thirtieth of the month, when several bills would be considered to increase the salaries of the comptroller and president of the Board of Aldermen from $25,000 to $35,000, those of each of the five borough presidents from $15,000 to $20,000, and that of the Mayor from $25,000 to $40,000. Members of the board were forbidden by law to increase their own salaries; but they might do so for their successors in office, even if they were themselves the successors.

Stephen Wise decided to fight the move even though he knew his efforts were probably doomed. He let loose his first blast of opposition in a speech before the Alpha Mu Sigma fraternity at the Hotel Pennsylvania on December 22 and denounced these salary raises as "vulgar common graft." Remembering his own part in the campaign in the fall, he remarked, "When I think of what has been happening in the political life of our city in the last few days, I cannot help wondering at my moderation in my speeches for Norman Thomas in the last campaign."

A week and a day later, Wise was present in the crowded meeting room of the Board of Estimate when Mayor Walker announced that he would sign the bills insuring the large increases. Wise asked for the floor and denounced the action as "a morally unfit thing to do . . . lamentable and abhorrent."

Wise continued: "This is the easiest money about which I have ever heard, within the limits of the law, coming to a group of men who presented themselves for election seven weeks ago and who never, as far as I know, hinted in the remotest way the possibility of their proposing any such self-rewarding legislation."

"You can go further there, Dr. Wise," interposed Mayor Walker. "There were seven men at that time who had never even thought of it, to say nothing of even hinting at it. If those seven men were invited to do that by an eighth, was it an abhorrent thing to do? With that conclusion, we disagree."

"Yes, I still declare it is an abhorrent thing to do," answered Wise. "The seven proposed beneficiaries might still have said to 'the playboy' who proposed the measure: 'We are very grateful to you, but we must add in Biblical language, "Is thy servant a dog that he should do this thing?" ' "

At this point, gasps were heard throughout the chamber. Walker lamely defended the move as not "immoral and unfair" and said he would not veto the bill.

Wise had lost a battle but not the war.

By the autumn of 1930, the investigations led by United States District Attorney Charles Tuttle and the first investigation carried on by Referee Samuel Seabury, appointed to the post by the Appellate Division at the request of Governor Franklin D. Roosevelt, disclosed abundant corruption and chicanery in the politics of the city of New York. John Haynes Holmes was convinced that he should now join the protest.

In October, Holmes preached on "The Shame of Mayor Walker's New York: A Plea to My Fellow Citizens" and asked the congregation to join him in protest to the governor of the state, the several district attorneys, and all proper officers in authority "to use their every power under the law to expose and punish the wickedness in high places which is now sapping the life of our city and betraying the welfare of its people."

Holmes indicted the city administration and accused James J. Walker of neglecting his office. First, the Mayor, often sojourning in Atlantic City or Palm Beach, Southern California or some European spa, rarely attended to his duties. Second, Walker acknowledged responsibility to Tammany Hall and admitted in his campaign for re-election that fall that he turned to the Tammany leader, John F. Curry, for both guidance and control. Third, he was indifferent to any moral corruption in the city and greeted specific data with wisecracks, defending himself because he had not witnessed the reported bribery or visited the houses reputed to be of ill fame.

Now it was time, Holmes said, for a leader to arise and for charter reform to be undertaken as in Seattle and Cincinnati. Would not the congregation therefore adopt the resolution appealing to

> our fellow-citizens in New York, more especially to financiers and business men, to lawyers, physicians and educators, to the pastors of our churches and the rabbis of our synagogues, to social workers, labor leaders, and all other leaders of public opinion, to join us in an organized movement for the revision of our municipal charter, to the end of delivering our city from political control and establishing it upon a non-partisan and scientific basis of administration? We, citizens of New York, do pledge ourselves this day to the single and loyal service of this great cause, that our city may at last become a safe abode of happy people and a monument to the integrity and security of our free democracy.

After Holmes finished reading the resolution from the pulpit, the congregation rose spontaneously and, in an unusual act for a church service, responded with applause; then they bowed their heads for the benediction which consecrated them to its fulfillment.

Into Holmes' office, not long afterward, came Norman Thomas and Paul Blanshard to discuss implementing Holmes' suggestions for a new organization to deal with the city's affairs and to channel its citizens' protests. As Holmes had served as chairman

of the Non-Partisan Committee the previous fall of 1929, would
he now serve as chairman of a newly organized City Affairs
Committee? John Dewey had consented to be a vice-chairman,
as he had also been in the Non-Partisan Committee; and Norman
Thomas and Francis J. McConnell, Bishop of the New York
East Methodist Conference, would be joined by Stephen Wise
in the other vice-chairmanships.

Holmes and Wise both agreed and the City Affairs Committee
began its work with offices adjoining the League for Industrial
Democracy of which Thomas was then executive director. From
that time on, Holmes and Wise worked as a team, signing almost
all documents as chairman and vice-chairman, and proving to be
superior to the usual figureheads of such organizations in their
degree of participation and in their willingness to take responsibility for significant action. In the course of time, except for the
formidable letterhead listing some of the 1,500 outstanding
citizens in New York in the organization, the bracketing of
Holmes and Wise signified the City Affairs Committee.

The two men knew that this program would be unsuccessful
if they did not work in close relationship with the Citizens'
Union, headed by Charles Burlingham, "the first citizen of New
York City" and lay leader in St. George's Episcopal Church.
Promises of help came too from the City Club and its president,
Richard S. Childs, and from the New York Committee of One
Thousand of which William J. Schieffelin was the chairman.

Prestigious names and a group of supporting organizations
were not enough, however. The City Affairs Committee needed
specific data. Holmes and Wise had to rely upon their researchers,
Paul Blanshard, Henry Rosner, and E. Michael White. Aided by
Norman Thomas who was fully conversant with the political
affairs of New York, these three staff members prepared informative summaries of the city's problems. Their research revealed the
facts behind the steep rise in the cost of land, the exorbitant
profits made by selling plots for public enterprises, and the
special privileges granted. They built a strong case against Tammany Hall, despite obstacles placed in their way; but it was
more difficult to make Mayor Walker the target. He was guarded
by various circles of associates who were beholden to him for

their own profits, gained by fee splitting, patronage favors, and inside knowledge on real estate transactions. They were an outer rampart and gave the Mayor protection. To make matters more difficult, neither Governor Franklin D. Roosevelt nor his associates in Albany were inclined to give the City Affairs Committee encouragement or co-operation.

The Committee planned to present its charges first to the Governor, and then to appeal publicly for action by him and by the legislature. Meanwhile, the Mayor continued his visits to the night clubs and speak-easies of New York, usually in the company of the actress Betty Compton.

The Republicans in the New York State Legislature pushed through a bill authorizing an investigation into certain phases of the New York City government; and Governor Roosevelt reluctantly signed the bill, thus providing funds to carry on a second Seabury investigation. In reply to charges made by the City Club, the Governor ordered an investigation of the District Attorney's office and turned again to Judge Samuel Seabury, appointing him counsel for the committee of inquiry, to be known as the Hofstadter Committee.

By mid-March of 1931, the City Affairs Committee was ready to file formal charges against Mayor James J. Walker and to list specific counts. When the document was ready, Blanshard and Rosner checked it once again to make sure there were no errors. Then Holmes and Wise requested the opportunity to present the document to the Governor.

When the two men arrived at the home of Sara Delano Roosevelt, the Governor's mother, on East 65th Street, the maid led them up the broad stairway to a salon which had been transformed into a study-and-reception room. The Governor received them with reserve. There was a chill in the air.

Both Holmes and Wise were unusually subdued. Holmes made the briefest of presentation remarks and gave the document to Roosevelt who accepted it with curt thanks and said he would read it as soon as he had an opportunity. They prepared to leave, for there was nothing else to say. As they started toward Roosevelt to shake hands and say good-by, he said crisply, "I have listened to you. Now you sit down and listen to me."

Then he proceeded to lecture Wise about a letter the rabbi had sent to the Executive Mansion in Albany protesting an appointment to a judgeship. His voice, harsher and more cutting than its wont, lashed at them, especially at Wise. The rabbi, accustomed to telling Alfred E. Smith how and why he felt about controversial issues or appointments, remained silent. He was not cowed, merely astonished. Roosevelt talked sharply for more than a half hour. Finally, he finished and dismissed them.

Wise, mystified and smarting from the attack, did not see his critic in person again for five years until a reconciliation in 1936 brought him into Roosevelt's second presidential campaign. Holmes was so hurt and amazed at the Governor's spleen that he always remembered the evening with distaste and never again had any regard for Roosevelt.

The Governor sent a copy of the charges to Mayor Walker with a request for a reply. Then he waited. While he did so, Tammany Hall warned the Governor that if Roosevelt referred the charges against Mayor Walker to the Legislature's Special Committee for General Inquiry into New York City Affairs and its counsel, Judge Seabury, his action would be considered an unfriendly act. Roosevelt did not move.

Walker filed his answer, denying the charges, and in his reply stooped to repeat the caustic comments made about Stephen Wise by Mayor William J. Gaynor twenty years earlier: "He is a clergyman, and it is always a painful sight to see a clergyman with no charity or truth in his heart or soul. All-sufficient insufficiency; self-sufficient Rabbi Wise! He thinks he is pious, but he is only bilious. He is a man of vast and varied misinformation, of brilliant mental incapacity and of prodigious moral requirements."

Walker summed up: "Need I add a word to this picture?"

Roosevelt's answer was to dismiss the charges made by the City Affairs Committee against Walker. He rejected the Committee's request for a rebuttal.

The Hofstadter Committee, led in its inquiry by Judge Seabury, did better, however. It took damaging testimony, uncovering more graft and misappropriation of funds than had been expected, even by the men lodging charges in the initial briefs.

The facts pointed more and more to Walker as the key person, and he began to show signs of restiveness. Even then he claimed that a Republican conspiracy was being prepared against him. The Governor's continued silence helped him.

When Holmes returned from his trip to Europe in the summer of 1931, he launched an attack on Walker. Both the *Times* and *Herald Tribune* devoted an entire column to Holmes. He was news, not only because he had been with Gandhi on many occasions in London, but because he, the pastor of a leading church in New York, was also chairman of the City Affairs Committee. His first comment to reporters in the ship's salon was to criticize Mayor Walker's European "circus trip" of that summer: "There is no question but that the Mayor received gorgeous entertainment, but to me it was terribly tragic that at a time when Europe is cracking up on the edge of an abyss he could indulge in ease and comfort and display. It was Nero fiddling while Rome was burning. I frankly do not believe that the Mayor was even aware of the tragedy that was going on around him."

At a Carnegie Hall meeting that spring Holmes had referred contemptuously to the "small little man" and predicted: "It is altogether probable that when the lid, now being pried up with such enormous difficulty, has at last been lifted and the loathsome mess of corruption which festers beneath has been revealed to the light of day, the citizens of New York will rise up in their wrath and smite the persons responsible for the conditions which disgrace us. I shall myself not be at all surprised if in the end we see Mayor Walker driven from office under the whip lashes of the outraged conscience of the people."

Judge Seabury bored steadily in and by the end of 1931 had prepared two large volumes of evidence which he sent to the Governor. Roosevelt, as before, made no comment. On January 6, Roosevelt received a telegram from Holmes and Wise, demanding that the letter from Judge Seabury to the Governor be released to the press. Roosevelt replied that the Seabury letter could not be released until the attached transcript had been carefully examined. He reminded them tartly that, as Governor, he had many constitutional duties to fulfill and he attended to matters in their order of importance. He hoped they would perceive "the spirit of courtesy in which this letter is written," leaving the inference to be drawn that their telegram had been anything but courteous.

The Governor's reluctance to move swiftly and the spectacle of his keeping a weather eye cocked on Tammany, in view of the presidential election of the following November, infuriated Wise. He would not listen to his old friend, George Foster Peabody, who, though no longer a Democrat, considered Roosevelt the only possible choice to oppose Herbert Hoover in the fall.

Wise knew that Roosevelt needed Tammany; New York's 94 votes were an important element in the Governor's securing the requisite 770 votes for the nomination at the Democratic National Convention. Roosevelt's unwillingness to antagonize the men of the Wigwam caused Wise to tell Peabody that he would not support Roosevelt. Could not Peabody see that he was being "grossly misled by the personal charm and winsomeness of a pseudo-liberal who has not given an iota of support and furtherance to any efforts to cleanse this politically filthy and corrupt city in which we live?" Roosevelt had done nothing on behalf of unemployment insurance. He had no deep convictions about social justice and would, if power were given him, be ready to compromise.

In brief, Wise wrote Peabody, Roosevelt was "one of the great and grievous disappointments of my days. Hoover promises little and does little. Roosevelt will promise very much, almost anything, and will do exactly as Hoover has done, without the frankness of Hoover as the representative of a system to which you and I can certainly give no more than the most partial and most grudging assent."

Peabody tried to reason with him, but Wise considered the issue closed. With a sharpness never known before in their relationship, he told his friend that nothing "would be gained by the continuance of our correspondence."

Wise wanted action and Albany would not meet his demands. Why couldn't Albany respond as quickly as Washington did when Wise pressed a matter? On January 13, 1932, the day Governor Roosevelt's chiding letter reached the studies of Holmes and Wise, Wise was in Washington attending a dinner

where five senators and fifteen members of the House of Representatives had gathered to hear him and Bishop Francis J.
McConnell urge them to support old-age pensions. During the
dinner hour the conversation centered not on the topic of the
evening but rather on the announcement that day of the resignation from the Supreme Court of Associate Justice Oliver Wendell Holmes, Jr. The men discussed the available men from whom
President Hoover might choose Holmes' successor. Virtually
everyone present considered Benjamin Cardozo the best qualified.
To Senator Brookhart of Iowa, Wise suggested that Senator
William E. Borah of Idaho would be the most suitable man
to recommend that Hoover name Cardozo. Wise remembered
that Borah had bitterly opposed Brandeis' nomination to the
Supreme Court in 1916 because the lumber interests of Idaho
hated Brandeis and his fellow conservationists, and that, in later
years, Borah regretted his stand. Three days later, Wise received
a telegram from Borah: "Am anxious to see Judge Cardozo advance to the Supreme Court. Can we help cause along? Confidential."

A month after the appointment, Justice Brandeis wrote Wise
a note about several matters and at the close added: "We are
very happy over the Cardozo nomination." In mid-March, Wise
and Borah sat together in the Supreme Court chambers as Cardozo was inducted as the newest Associate Justice.

On March 25, 1932, Holmes and Wise, on behalf of the City
Affairs Committee, asked the Governor to remove Sheriff James
A. McQuade of Kings County for the same cause that impelled
the Governor to oust Sheriff Thomas M. Farley on an earlier
occasion and reminded the Governor of the reasons he had given
at that time: "Public office should inspire private financial integrity . . . for there is a requirement that where a public official
is under inquiry or investigation, especially an elected official,
and it appears that his scale of living or the total of his bank
deposits far exceed the public salary he is known to receive, he,
the elected public official, owes a positive public duty to the
community to give a reasonable or credible explanation of the
source of his deposits, or the source which enables him to maintain a scale of living beyond his salary."

Their letter so irritated Roosevelt that he wrote a long answer to the two men, released it to the press, and announced he had denied their demand and their earlier request that he use his "utmost interest and influence to induce the surrogate of Queens County to dismiss John Theofel, Chief Clerk of the Queens Surrogate Court and Democratic leader of Queens County." Roosevelt told Holmes and Wise that their request was refused because "you seek to establish a new form of government, utterly repulsive to the representative form under which we live."

Once more he proceeded to lecture them: "Let me tell you two gentlemen straight from the shoulder that I am becoming convinced from your letters that corruption in public office and unfit servants in public office are both far less abhorrent to you than they are to me. A rushing into print early and often with extravagant and ill-considered language causes many of our decent citizens to doubt your reliance on law, on order, and on justice."

With the news on the front page and the entire text on inside pages, reporters turned to Holmes and Wise for their comments. Holmes was out of town and thus not available for an interview; but Wise promptly answered for them both: "Dr. Holmes and I will probably make a joint reply tomorrow to the exquisitely courteous communication of Governor Roosevelt. Not being candidates for political office, high or low, our statement will be made without regard to electoral or any other kind of votes."

In a few days the two men had prepared a long letter which they sent to the Governor and then released at a mass meeting called by the City Affairs Committee. The Holmes-Wise letter was read aloud and then Holmes explained that there was "only one reason for the letter from Roosevelt: it was inspired by a violent hatred of those who dared to expose the political criminals upon whom the Governor depends to make him President of the United States."

Wise, in turn, kept the audience of one thousand persons constantly laughing with his jibes at the Governor and concluded by asking: "Would you like to see in the Presidency a man as merciful to wrongdoing, as lenient to corruption as Roosevelt has proved himself to be?"

By this time, Franklin Roosevelt had endured enough. The following Saturday, reporters reached him in his home at Hyde

Park and sought his reaction to the meeting and the two men. Roosevelt rasped over the telephone: "If they would serve their God with as much zeal as they seek to serve themselves, the people of the city of New York would be the gainers."

After Roosevelt was nominated as the Democratic choice for the Presidency at the Chicago convention in July, 1932, he ordered Walker to appear at public hearings in Albany. On August 11, the hearings began. Now Walker squirmed. It was clear that he had no defense. His charm was of no avail. By the end of August he knew the game was up. He resigned his position and, with funds hastily gathered from his hidden resources, prepared to leave for Europe. Taking Betty Compton with him, he sailed into exile.

When Franklin Roosevelt was elected President in November, 1932, Wise and Holmes were ready to forgive, if not to forget. Both of them had supported Norman Thomas for the Presidency but now sent a conciliatory letter to the Executive Mansion in Albany:

> Dear Governor Roosevelt:
> We feel that we wish to tender you our congratulations and good wishes upon your triumphant election to the Presidency. We hope that the years will abundantly vindicate the judgment of the American electorate and that you may rise to the unique opportunity of service which that election affords you. We trust that, whatever have been the differences between us with regard to civic affairs, you may feel free to call upon us for whatever service it lies within the power of American citizens to render to their government and President.

A few weeks later, the President-Elect replied in friendly fashion:

> My dear Dr. Holmes and Dr. Wise:
> That is a mighty nice letter of yours and I honestly appreciate the spirit in which it was written. Some day I should much like to talk with both of you because I am confident that your ultimate objectives and mine in the cause of better government are the same. I have never differed with you in that objective, though, as you know, I felt very strongly that you were using methods last year which would hurt rather than help the ob-

jective. If you will let me, I will gladly talk over with you my reason for feeling this.

Wise and Holmes never accepted the President's invitation to talk things over. Wise did not see him until three and a half years later, and Holmes' path never crossed Roosevelt's again. During these crowded months Holmes found an island of refuge in the work he did in preparing for the Oxford University Press *The Heart of Scott's Poetry*. This anthology, including a scholarly critical introduction, was compiled to commemorate the one hundredth anniversary of Sir Walter Scott's death.

Scott's work had always given Holmes perspective. Some might have accused him of escapism, but he knew that each summer when he read anew some of the Waverley novels, he found a balance amid his activism. Now Scott meant even more to him as the world he had hoped to see remodeled in the form of H. G. Wells' visions and Romain Rolland's idealism seemed headed for destruction. As he turned the pages of Scott's beloved prose and poetry, he yearned for the simpler life of the Victorian era, delighted in looking upon himself as a nineteenth-century liberal, but realized that, in his fifty-third year, he had need of something more resilient and lasting than Victorian virtues.

In the Walker case he and Wise had tasted victory, but the world facing them in 1932–1933 was forbidding and forlorn. Dismay and defeatism were the prevalent mood of the time.

In the spring of 1933, *Vanity Fair* put its spotlight on Wise. A double spread featured pictures of Carl Sandburg, "An American Genius"; Somerset Maugham, "An Englishman of Genius"; Robert M. Hutchins, "The Youngest National Oracle, Now of the University of Chicago"; Fiorello LaGuardia, "Little Flower, Preparing to Run for Mayor of New York"; and Dr. Stephen S. Wise, shown in a stern Steichen portrait: "The Rabbi—Leader of American Protests Against the Hitler anti-Semitic Campaign—with his leonine head, a voice of thunder and the strength of an ox." In the years ahead, as the world crises deepened, he and Holmes would need that strength.

V. Along the
Autumnal Slope

(1933–1949)

If toward the Infinite you would stride,
Then walk within the finite on every side.
—GOETHE, 1820

25. *The Years of the Locust*

> *In the midst of all the wrongs and sins of our day, the crimes of men, society, and state, amid popular ignorance, pauperism, and war, and slavery, too—is the church to say nothing, do nothing?* —THEODORE PARKER, 1846

WISE AND HOLMES were now popular public figures. In 1933, a Broadway comedy, *She Loves Me Not*, highlighted this fact. At one point in the play, the managing editor of a tabloid cleared his cluttered desk and shouted directions at reporters on various telephones. To one he said, "Call Rabbi Stephen Wise and get a statement." To another he cried, "Get John Haynes Holmes on the phone and have him dictate a paragraph!"

Both men found increasingly serious problems in the trend of events. The possibilities of peace had begun to diminish in recent months and the general feeling of hopelessness in both America and the rest of the world made it necessary for them to rethink their faith. Holmes could not see his way clear to sign the "Humanist Manifesto" circulated by Charles Francis Potter, founder of the Humanist Society in New York. When asked why, he responded that while he did begin his religious thinking with man rather than with God and might therefore start from a humanist point of view, human experience sent him toward God.

Wise called Holmes "the most religious of the humanists and the most humanistic of the religionists" and found the proof of this oft-quoted sentence in the early spring of 1933. When Wise announced a protest march and rally against Hitlerism, Holmes

asked if he might take part. The rabbi had planned for only
Jewish leaders and their organizations to participate. A crowd,
many thousands strong, gathered at Columbus Circle and then
marched down Broadway as far south as Union Square. At the
head of the throng with Wise was Holmes. No other Christian
took part. No bands, no flags, no drum majors and parading
horses. There were instead thousands upon thousands of Jews,
and Holmes, walking silently block after block. This was the first
large-scale protest against Hitler.

When Stephen Wise went to Europe that summer he wanted
to consult with Ambassador William E. Dodd in Berlin, but was
warned that it would be wiser for him not to enter Germany.
He could, however, go to Vienna. There he visited Sigmund
Freud. Wise liked to tell how in the course of their conversation
Freud and he discussed the question of who were the five most
important Jews in the world. "Well, you, of course, Dr. Freud,"
said Wise, "then Albert Einstein, Chaim Weizmann, Justice
Brandeis, and probably Henri Bergson."

Whereupon Freud asked: "And what about Stephen Wise?"
"Oh, no, no, no, no," answered Wise.

Freud took the ever-present cigar out of his mouth and said,
"You know, I would have believed you if you had answered 'no';
but, my dear Dr. Wise, I don't believe you when you answer,
'no, no, no, no.'" Wise thanked him for the psychoanalysis given
without charge.

Wise was deeply troubled when he learned President
Roosevelt had told Ambassador Dodd that, though there was no
question "the Germans are treating the Jews shamefully, yet
this is not a governmental affair. We can do nothing except
for American citizens who happen to be made victims. We must
protect them, and whatever we can do to moderate the general
persecution by unofficial and personal influence ought to be
done." To Wise this was too little.

From the Soviet Union came different tidings, for Justine,
touring Russia, was sending enthusiastic letters to him in Europe.
Wise answered: "I get a curious impression, i.e., curiously
mixed, as we read and re-read your letters, as of a very old
and forgotten world—Ivan's and Catherine's and Peter's—and

of the newest of worlds yet to be. Don't think, dear child, that I am indifferent to all the fascinating and thrilling things that you have written about the land you are visiting. We can only hope that we shall be able to appropriate the best of that new order without losing some of the very precious things which still obtain in the old."

But then preoccupation with the fate of Jews in Europe absorbed him:

> I'm sick over what I have seen and heard in Paris and London. Our "progress" is back to Hell! Oh, what we hear and read from unimpeachable sources from day to day about Germany! According to every worthwhile authority, Jewish and Christian, the Jews of Germany are finished and their only recourse is "*heraus*." Did you know that Germany has introduced the head-man's axe—as another token of return to medievalism? Stories that are told to us by lawyers, doctors, artists and composers are too awful to repeat. Oh, how I'd love to fight against it— with all my heart. I can't write more tonight. I'm tired and the back of my head hurts a lot, ever since the talk with the refu- gees. Once more, Justine, I am afraid I shall not be interested in anything more as long as this lasts, and it threatens to last for two or three or four years.

When he returned to America in the early autumn, he ap- pealed to Christians as well. Harry Emerson Fosdick heeded his plea for a Christian reaction and called together a group of New York's leading ministers. Meeting in the Fosdick apart- ment in Knox Hall at Union Theological Seminary, the group listened to Wise, intently yet incredulously, as he said, "The modern Haman who has set out to destroy the Jewish race is a world menace, forasmuch as he has enslaved and degraded Germany. A mighty nation is in chains and who dares to dissent or protest? The racial fanaticism of the Hitler Reich may be a most immediate and deadly peril to us Jews, but it is no less truly a threat and a danger to all races and to all nations. The query is, which will be the next race to be proclaimed inferior, debased and debasing? It may be Czechoslovakia, or Poland, or France. Only one thing is certain, namely, that the most vulner- able of the neighbors of the Reich will be singled out for doom."

In later years the men remembered his saying, "The Jew may be hurt first. It is the very heart and fabric of Christianity that will ultimately, has indeed already, come under attack." Yet that night, many thought him unbalanced, intemperate.

Wise's demands were few. First, there must be unity among Jews. Secondly, there should be a boycott against German goods—"an honorable, peaceable weapon of self-defense of Jews under attack everywhere by Hitlerism." And thirdly, there should be the opening, to some extent at least, of the doors of the United States to Jewish refugees.

All through that fall, winter, and following spring, he could think of little else. Fortunately, his sense of humor did not desert him. The Marx brothers had then become popular comedians on the screen, and his colleague at the Free Synagogue, Sidney Goldstein, asked him if he planned to see their newest movie. Wise answered, "Why should I? We've just had a meeting of the J.I.R. faculty."

On his sixtieth birthday in 1934, Wise told a reporter of the New York *Evening Post* that "Hitlerism means war. I do not believe that either my country, or the great countries of Europe, England, France, Italy, are doing what they can in order to prevent Hitlerism bringing about a war which, if it comes, whether we like it or not, whether or not we have part therein, will for a thousand years impair, if not invalidate, the texture of civilization."

Louise, after her husband's birthday celebration in 1934, phrased the problem more poignantly in her diary:

> What days of celebration! What testimony to his public acts and words—how glad we both should be—and yet this year of Nazi terror has so saddened and wearied us we can hardly think of our own cause with gratitude. And yet how grateful I must be and truly am for all that has been mine and still is—through his unfailing love and the benediction of his life companionship. No woman has ever been more blessed!

Wise was saddened because, in the face of "Hitler's Satanic resolve to destroy the Jewish people, I find a minimum of understanding of the gravity of the situation on the part of the

[American] Jews, for they are blind and obtuse as were the German Jews up to the hour of the disaster."

When Wise openly opposed Father Charles Coughlin and his anti-Jewish broadcasts from the Shrine of the Little Flower in Royal Oak, Michigan, he was astonished to discover that among the hundreds of letters written by listeners to the Free Synagogue, nine tenths of them in favor of Coughlin, many were from Jews. The Jewish opponents could not, however, match the "Christians" who called Wise a "Christ-killer" and an "anti-Christ" for attacking Coughlin. One, in Holmdell, New Jersey, wrote: "You are trying to confuse the public. You are twisting Father Coughlin's speeches. All Americans should thank God for Father Coughlin." And another said: "It's about time you quit criticizing Father Coughlin. The shoe is on the other foot. You are stirring class hatred. If there are five Jewish crooks for every Christian crook, that is your duty as a rabbi to try and correct it."

Wise tried to refute them: "I am not at all persuaded by what you say. I consider him a most menacing figure. Everything that I see and hear about Coughlin confirms my impression that, although nominally a liberal and anti-wealth and pro-social justice, if he persists as a national figure, I have no doubts that the Church will ultimately take him off. He will lend support to the pro-Fascistic, anti-liberal anti-radicalism in America." Seven years had to go by before Wise was proven correct. Coughlin continued his anti-Jewish innuendoes and was close to the isolationist forces; only in 1942 did the Roman Catholic Church finally forbid his radio broadcasts.

Wise continued to place his faith in the unity of the Jewish people, both in America and throughout the world, and in the ultimate victory of Zionism. Not without opposition from the more wealthy, cautious circles in Jewry, he pressed for a meeting of a World Jewish Congress. In hours like these, Wise could say wryly, "Where two Jews are assembled, there are three opinions."

In the summer of 1935, he experienced several depressing weeks in Europe; and then he took a long trip to Palestine, where he found his belief in the Zionist movement and its accomplishments reinforced. The will-to-do was there, both among the recent immigrants and among the settled villagers and pioneers.

Wise heard promising reports. David Ben-Gurion, then head of the Jewish Agency, impressed him with information on the steady development of the land, showed him the settlements of new refugees in the communal villages, and spoke of the plans of the Haganah's self-defense movement. Henrietta Szold, then seventy-five years old, introduced Wise and his wife to the work of Youth Aliyah, the organization for the resettlement of Jewish children from Germany, which she had established the year before.

In Europe there had been only despair; here was growth. On the Continent, they had found hatred and distrust, anti-intellectualism and anti-Semitism, even more virulent than Herzl had predicted forty years earlier. Yet here was the Old-New Land of Herzl's vision. Wise described its flowering as the result of an "investment no greater than that of the combined Jewish golf clubs of America."

Wise wrote to members of the Free Synagogue: "Let no one ever again say in my presence, 'The Jews are incapable of collective, sustained, and selfless effort.' I have looked upon the results of that effort and I have never been prouder of my fellow Jews than I am at this hour, having seen what all of us together, Zionists, have done."

To his children, however, he admitted his concern for the future: "The tragic Jewish inferiority complex is operant everywhere and they may be mowed down by the scythe of British sharpness and ruthlessness. Here are terrible dangers. Our representatives are unequal to the burden of countering a rotten, unfriendly government."

While in Palestine he and Louise received word of Justine's appointment as Justice of the Domestic Relations Court in New York City. To Lewis Browne, his former student, he wrote: "I suppose you know that I am the father of a judge, and a darn good judge at that! She is doing a superb job in the Children's Court." And to Ruth Mack Brunswick, daughter of Judge Julian Mack: "Young Stephen [Justine's six-year-old son, Stephen Wise Tulin], whenever his mother speaks sharply to him, addresses her sarcastically, 'Yes, your Honor.'"

Before Stephen Wise returned to America, John Haynes Holmes had gone to Europe and spent a crowded month in the Third

Reich of Hitler. He returned with apprehensions and fears, not only for Germany but for Western civilization. He now agreed with Wise that Hitler would be a deadly and dominant force for years to come. He was haunted by the conviction that "the Jews of Germany are doomed." Holmes found that the Jews were like criminals condemned to execution, allowed to exist for only a while in their death house, destined to be excluded from all phases of German life without a chance for a reprieve. There was no dissenting voice and the conclusion was repeated by Nazis and anti-Nazis, German functionaries and American journalists. Only by getting the Jews out of Germany, Holmes argued, would there be any chance of Jewish survival. Boycotts were essential, but more urgent was the work of immediate rescue on a wholesale basis. While Holmes prepared articles and addresses on the German visit during his trip back across the Atlantic in August, 1935, his thoughts were occupied by the threat of war, for Mussolini had announced his intention of annexing Ethiopia.

On a voyage home, four years earlier, Holmes, partially inspired by the power Gandhi showed at the Round Table Conference in London, had sketched an antiwar play. The invasion of Manchuria by Japan, the failure of the League of Nations to prevent annexation, war preparations by Germany and Italy had impelled him to complete a workable draft during summer vacations. One late August afternoon in 1934, he came from his study to the living room of the Kennebunk Beach house and triumphantly announced to the family, "I've finished it! I've finished it!"

"What have you finished?" asked Frances.

"The play," cried Holmes. "I've completed it! It's all done!"

"Yes, all done except to find a producer, a theater, a cast, and an audience," Madeleine reminded him.

"Well, I think it has possibilities," Holmes countered. "I'll tell you what I'm going to do. If this play is ever produced, I'll divide the royalties four ways: quarter shares will go to each of us— to you, Madeleine; to Roger and Louise [Roger's wife]; Morris [his son-in-law] and Frances; and the last one-fourth to myself. All right?"

The skeptical family thought it a fair and generous arrangement and then dismissed the play from their minds. But by the next summer *If This Be Treason,* on which Holmes was assisted by a co-author, Reginald Lawrence, was given its first week's tryout at the Westport Country Playhouse. The summer audience liked it well enough and the Theatre Guild announced it as the first play of the 1935–1936 season.

On the early autumn evening of the Broadway première the family strolled on the sidewalk outside the theater during the intermission. When they had all reassembled in their box seats, Madeleine noticed that her husband had not returned. When he still did not come back after ten minutes, she sent Morris Brown out to find him. Morris could not locate him in the theater and went out into the lobby. He saw the apprehensive playwright walking up and down on the sidewalk nervously clasping and unclasping his hands. It took persuasion to bring him back to his seat.

The first-night audience, as well as those of the subsequent six weeks, cheered the play. They applauded the impassioned speeches of the pacifist American President and hissed the equivocating Japanese leaders. At the close, Holmes and his co-author, Reginald Lawrence, responded to the cries of the audience for "author, author!"

The critics, however, did not like it, as Morris and Frances Brown learned to their disappointment when, after walking for hours in Times Square after the opening-night performance, they bought the early editions of the morning newspapers. The New York *Times* and New York *Herald Tribune* strongly voted no. Brooks Atkinson admitted that *If This Be Treason* was exciting in its implications and conceded that the play was "worth doing, seeing and discussing," but termed it a "mad, idealistic melodrama, not a suave and silken theatre bauble, for from the intellectual point of view it oversimplifies an enormously complicated problem and from the artistic point of view it is trash." The *Herald Tribune's* Percy Hammond called it "a greasy extravaganza, loud, boisterous and unreal, a bad and blowsy play about a good idea, which, although produced under the Vatican auspices of the Theatre Guild, is as impious a desecration of the theatre as Broadway has ever reveled in and proves that Dr.

Holmes, known in pulpit circles as one of the most ardent of the dominies, belongs in the Church rather than in The Music Box."

Peace lovers wrote Brooks Atkinson and Percy Hammond to castigate the unfriendly reviews. Lillian Wald considered Mr. Hammond's criticism "flippant and totally lacking in respect to the message, to the theatre and to the office, out of tune and of no value."

Hammond was so harried that, in a Sunday column, he pleaded: "I wish the infuriated pacifists who threaten to tar and feather me, to ride me on a rail, to shoot me at sunrise and hang me from a sour-apple tree, would confer with Dr. Holmes before they do so. He, like the gentle Galilean, will whisper 'peace!' to them and instruct them to let me go."

Brooks Atkinson wrote a rebuttal review in the *Times* and called the solution of the play highly improbable: "Although it enkindles the imagination of its audience by the recklessness of its thought, it is, as a theatre production, as imposing on the stage as a Tammany Funeral."

To the *Times* Holmes wrote a long letter defending his stage President's attempt to make peace with Japan. He cited copious historical references to rulers of ancient and modern times who had performed similar acts and argued that he and Lawrence had sought to show how governments could "help and not thwart the people's desire for peace; if any government did half as much for peace as every government now does for preparedness, propaganda and patriotism for war, it might achieve peace. What would happen if an American President were doing as much for peace as an Italian Premier, let us say, is now doing for war?"

The exchange of letters and the pacifists' publicity did not draw a larger audience. Wise wrote Holmes that he had recommended *If This Be Treason* to his congregation on two separate occasions and had publicized it in *The Free Synagogue Bulletin*. Pacifist groups did their best to foment interest, but the play did not last. It grossed $8,000 the first week, $7,300 the second. Every seven days a small royalty check came to Holmes. Following his advance of $500, the first week's net enabled Holmes to give his wife her quarter share and to send similar eighty-four-cent checks to Roger and Frances. His instructions to them and their spouses: "I must insist, that the condition of this gift, now and later, is that the money is not to be spent in riotous living. I shall be very much displeased if you use this money to buy a Packard car, or for any other extravagant and unnecessary purposes. I believe it wise, perhaps, for you to tuck this money away as security in your old age and this first check will give you a grand start. Your loving Father, J. H. H."

During this same period, Wise was having trouble with his plans for the World Jewish Congress meeting in the summer of 1936. Opposition came from some of the most influential Jews in the United States, most of them either leaders or members of the American Jewish Committee, among them Roger W. Straus, James N. Rosenberg, and Felix Warburg.

Wise's opponents claimed that such a meeting in Geneva would create only confusion in the minds of both Jews and non-Jews; furthermore, it would impede the work of existing organizations in America and abroad. The Jews of Germany and Russia would not be able to attend or participate; the majority of Jews in England and France would probably not take part; and in the United States many important groups, such as the B'nai B'rith, the American Jewish Committee, and the National Council of Jewish Women, united in opposing the movement. Conditions in Palestine, they claimed, inflamed by renewed riots between Arabs and Jews and repressive measures by the British, would make the meeting inadvisable.

Wise and Louis Lipsky, president and vice-president respectively, of the American Jewish Congress, insisted that the World Congress be held. The Nuremberg Laws, with their severe repression of the German Jews, made the meeting imperative, they argued.

James Rosenberg sent Felix Warburg a draft letter asking Herbert Lehman, then Governor of New York State, to bring his influence to bear on Wise. But Warburg vetoed the approach to Lehman: "I will do nothing about Herbert Lehman. I think that, so long as he is in office, he should not be asked to take part in any activity that is connected with Jewish politics. If he were urged by somebody else and would ask me if he should take a hand in this, I should advise him not to do so, because Wise is so indiscreet. . . . He would be only too happy to state that 'even the Governor was importuned' to block his Jewish Congress."

The World Jewish Congress meeting in Geneva succeeded in some ways and failed in others; and Wise returned to the United States as president of the Congress, ready to take on three additional responsibilities: the editorship of *Opinion*, a case of father succeeding son; the presidency of the Zionist Organization of America; and the effort to help Franklin Roosevelt win his second term as President.

Wise's political mutation since 1932 was surprising to many. Friends in Washington and Boston had acted as intermediaries and reconciled Wise with the President. Wise wrote to Emanuel Neumann, a Zionist leader then in Tel-Aviv: "I went to Hyde Park last Monday and saw the Country Gentleman who lives there. I am giving this whole month, night after night, to out-of-town addresses for F.D.R. I think the outlook is good."

Wise's change of heart about Franklin Roosevelt came in part from his awareness of the achievements of the New Deal: the conservation program, the regulations of the Securities and Exchange Commission, the preliminary plans for Social Security, the comprehensiveness of the National Labor Relations Act, and the effectiveness of the Public Works Administration. Wise was impressed by another factor: Roosevelt's seemingly successful intervention with the British against restrictions on immigration into Palestine.

Wise was quite aware that Holmes might be puzzled by his sudden shift of position and he therefore wrote a long letter to his friend:

> I wanted to write to you, not once but twenty times in the last weeks, chiefly because I wanted you to know of my meeting with the President. A number of my friends, knowing particularly that it was my duty to support Roosevelt against the Al Smiths, Raskobs and the DuPonts—Felix Frankfurter particularly, I fancy, after hearing an address by me at Ford Hall—brought it to the attention of the President, that despite his bitter attack on us, I was giving my full moral support to the

Administration, despite its obvious shortcomings and its multitudinous defects.

Wise knew that Holmes, like himself, had not forgotten the tensions between them and Roosevelt in 1931 and 1932:

> It was not easy to go there, for no man of importance in public life has ever attacked us as he did. Still, I could not permit personal rancor or resentment on my part to stand in the way of giving my support to him who, after all, has dared to do that which the Liberty League folk so savagely resent. There was no reference to the past in our conversation. We resumed where we had left off before the break. I am perfectly sure that the President will be eager to see both of us again whenever we are ready for a visit.

Wise had a more important motive in visiting the President:

> It may have been, dear Holmes, that I would not have accepted his invitation to go to the White House, despite my resolution giving him the uttermost of my support against those who would if they could destroy him, had it not been for my feeling that I might help him to see the light and the right about the Nazi situation. Excepting for Frankfurter and Brandeis, he has been surrounded by timorous Jews. Can't I see you soon and tell you more about things? I really was sorry for the President. He is not being fought for the things that are wrong but for the things that you and I believe to be right. He has not quite wholly been converted from his faith in the present social system. But the reactionaries may yet achieve even that notable victory.

The following summer Wise planned to attend a meeting in Europe of the Jewish Agency for Palestine. An important reorganization was to take place, and Felix Warburg, no longer opposed to him, planned to be present. Wise cabled Chaim Weizmann: "Warburg as you know utterly devoted to cause Palestine upbuilding. He will stand with us under all contingencies."

When Wise collapsed from fatigue that summer of 1937, Warburg wrote sympathetically: "I cannot say that I am astonished because the strain under which you put your constitution with your great activity is very apt to affect you—and, as always, these attacks come at the most inopportune moments." Warburg had been concerned about the opposition of Palestinian Jews to the partition of Palestine and apprehensive of their socialist leanings. Yet he reassured Wise: "I certainly will let no personal likes or dislikes stand in the way in regard to reaching some sort of agreement abroad, but I don't like to ride in motor cars without brakes and driven by people who talk with both hands and therefore may get the car off the track."

When Wise, late that summer, prepared his New Year's message, he looked back at the good things that had happened —his recovery of health, Justine's marriage in the spring to the New York attorney Shad Polier, the increased support of his work by Jewry in the United States and abroad. He wrote Felix Warburg: "I think you are to be congratulated upon what was achieved. It was high sportsmanship and more than sportsmanship to accept that resolution [to contemplate the establishment of a Jewish State in Palestine]. You have moved us to proclaim throughout the world that we expect the British Government to help us negotiate with the Arabs. It is a moral achievement of no mean order."

By that autumn, Holmes, still the pacifist, was deeply troubled about the Spanish Civil War, while Wise, because of his own personal convictions and his closeness to the Loyalist cause through his son's work, supported it wholeheartedly. Holmes told Wise of his letter to Upton Sinclair expressing disagreement not only with the Rebels but also with the Loyalists:

> There was a real democratic issue in Spain in the beginning, but this has been lost completely in the progress of a war which should never have been begun. I interpret the Spanish situation now as nothing but a fight between Communism and Fascism, and this does not stir my interest. I am still a pacifist, and from this pacifist point of view a civil war is only worse than a nationalistic war. I think the issue of democracy disappeared from that fight some time ago—the parallel with the World War in this regard is positively terrifying! Here we are, in the good old fashion, asked to plunge into one more struggle to make the world safe for democracy, and I see no reason why I should be fooled today on that issue any more than I was 20 odd years ago. If we want to plunge into a fight between Fascism and

Communism, well and good; let us say so. But what galls me
is this latest attempt to propagandize the American people into
another war to save civilization.

In a sermon, "Spain! Is Armageddon Coming?", Holmes deplored the "sinister element . . . of the active intervention of
Soviet Russia to match the intervention of Italy and the German
Reich" and regretted that "in Spain today, there is no longer
an open and honest fight between two groups of Spaniards
for the control of their own country, but an undisguised and
shameless struggle, on Spanish soil, with the Spanish people, men,
women, and children, as helpless victims, between two alien
movements for world supremacy." He sorrowed over "the hesitancy and weakness of the democratic powers in the face of the
most awful crisis which Europe has seen since the dread days
of August, 1914."

By the close of 1937 it was clear to both men that the world
had changed greatly since they began their ministries in New
York thirty years earlier. Early in 1938, when Wise presented
Holmes to his congregation at the thirty-first anniversary celebration, he wrote a few notes to guide his words: "Some men
great in one thing—Christian relations, or Negro, or free speech,
or civic life, or Palestine, or India. He great and serviceable
in all. Men speak of prophetic eloquence. What is it—this divine
afflatus? Seeking truth and uttering it without fear or reservation.
When the rest of us succumbed, he was true in the day of war.
God give us men—a time like this demands. God has given us
one man, and his name is—Johannan [Hebrew: 'The Lord is
gracious']. The grace of God is on his speech and on his soul.
The eloquence of a life. What he says—he is and does!"

26. And Darkness Fell

*The earth was corrupt in God's sight and the
earth was filled with violence.* —GENESIS, 6:11

BY THE SPRING OF 1938 the Nazis had effected their long planned
Anschluss with Austria and Hitler triumphantly entered Vienna.
Now the *Führer* turned his eyes on Czechoslovakia and promised
that with the settlement of the Sudetenland issue he would
"make no more territorial demands." In the summer, as Hitler
became more bellicose and threatened military action, Holmes
was touring Europe with his daughter Frances and trying to
enjoy his visit like an average tourist. He and Frances visited
famous sites in France, Switzerland, and Great Britain. Holmes
was such a knowledgeable guide that Frances wrote her mother:
"Traveling with Father is like traveling with a history book!"
Soon Madeleine received worried notes from her husband and
daughter, but in spite of the danger of war they would not alter
their plans for a mid-September arrival in New York.

As Holmes and his daughter sailed across the Atlantic to
America, Wise wrote him on August thirty-first:

> We sit here in pained anxiety about the news from London,
> Paris, Berlin and Prague. Sometimes it seems as if war might
> come at any hour, but I somehow have the feeling that Roose-
> velt's threat and England's sometime firmness may yet avert the
> worst, although, unlike you, I confess I do not know what the
> worst is. Let me get a glimpse of you, brother of the flesh and
> spirit alike!

Their paths did not cross until later in the autumn; Wise wrote Holmes again in late September when Chamberlain and Daladier signed the agreement with Hitler and Mussolini at Munich; Wise surmised that Holmes' pacifism would lead him to a different interpretation of the appeasement moves and to think this was in truth "peace in our times." He tried to describe his unhappiness to Holmes:

> You may not feel as I do, but to me this is one of the saddest days of history. It does not mean that England and France are opposed to war. It means that they ignominiously surrendered to Hitler or that together with Hitler and Mussolini they may do battle against Stalin. This is capitalism's betrayal of every human hope! It is one of those tragic days of all human history. I feel as my forefathers must have felt on that day in the year 70 which witnessed the destruction of the Temple. Human liberties are fled, democracy is a sham, standards have gone, the moral realm of mankind is laid waste. God help us!

A few days later Wise wrote him again: "I know you will feel that we have been saved from the horror of horrors which is war"; while Wise shared that feeling, he had to point out that "the evil day has only been put off." He explained why he was so apprehensive:

> The representatives of the two democracies have sat in conference with the two cruellest, foulest dictators of earth. They have yielded. Germany threatened to march October first. England and France did not stop her or stay her march. But to the crime of invasion they lend the august sanction of the democratic powers. And all this is done in the absence of Czechoslovakia and without her consent!

Holmes would understand the parallel he was drawing.

> Jesus at least had the dignity of being crucified in his own presence. Czechoslovakia was crucified in her absence by the Judases who betrayed her to the Pontius Pilates of a new day.

In his grief over the annexation of the Sudetenland by Nazi Germany, Wise planned to speak his mind:

> I shall in my first Sunday address call it "Dishonor Without Peace." My heart is broken over the end of a great and noble

democracy. Don't think we have escaped war. We have war without sacrifice. We have victory with shame!

On November 9, 1938, a night of terror broke out in Germany. When Ernst vom Rath, Third Secretary of the German Embassy in Paris, was shot by a sixteen-year-old Jewish boy, Herschel Grynszpan, the Nazis used the incident as an excuse to launch a long-planned pogrom. Hundreds of Jewish shops and dwellings were set on fire and utterly destroyed. Synagogues all over Germany were burned, then pillaged. Over 20,000 Jews were arrested, many killed or seriously injured. After this "Crystal Night," grimly foretold by the "Horst Wessel" song of the Nazis, Wise admitted to Holmes, "For the first time, I am afraid. I have an undefined dread that 'Hitler the madman and cripple-minded Goebbels' may call for a widespread massacre."

Amid his darkness of despair, Wise found some light and hope in Holmes' writings in *Unity* and *Opinion*, and his printed sermons and new books. Wise had a fraternal pleasure, as well as a professional's pride, in the book of Holmes' accumulated articles from *Opinion*, called *Through Gentile Eyes*.

Holmes also had issued his most searching book in many years, *Rethinking Religion*, which was based on a series of weekly lectures on radio station WQXR. In *Rethinking Religion* Holmes followed the theme of John Dewey's Terry Lectures at Yale, *A Common Faith*: the essence of religion was not revelation of some divine disclosure but man's normal experience in the realms of nature and human nature. To him, the living witnesses of true religion were Albert Schweitzer in Africa, Toyohiko Kagawa in Japan, and Mahatma Gandhi in India, "widely different in manifold aspects of their lives but all saints in the utter dedication of their personal lives, prophets and heroes in their far-visioned ideal of human redemption."

Holmes was still "rethinking religion" with his congregation in their temporary meeting place at Town Hall. The new apartment-hotel at Ten Park Avenue had been constructed, but he and the congregation did not yet have a church building. Town Hall was less bizarre than a theater but not a sanctuary. Louis Mayer's sculptured heads of Emerson and Lincoln on the platform were the only tangible reminders of the old home at 34th Street and Park Avenue.

The property on that prominent corner had been saved from foreclosure by the legal talents of Salmon O. Levinson and George E. Moesel. Each year had been something of a crisis; and, by 1938, when forty thousand dollars was needed, Wise asked if he might help. Contributing generously on his and Louise's behalf and gathering from friends other sizable checks, he sent them to Holmes.

The property was saved by these and many other such gifts, but additional funds were needed if a church building was to be erected. Wise, a master at securing funds from friends and supporters of every good cause, suggested giving a testimonial dinner for Holmes. Why not celebrate his fifty-ninth birthday with a fund raising event? A committee set to work. On November 29 at the Hotel Astor, Holmes found many of his old friends on the dais: Wise and his wife, Levinson and his wife, John Howland Lathrop of Brooklyn's Unitarian Church of the Saviour, Mayor and Mrs. Fiorello LaGuardia. Johanna M. Lindlof, a member of the New York Board of Education, was chairman of the dinner.

Lathrop said that "John Haynes Holmes begins where the rest of us leave off." Haridas T. Muzumdar, speaking for Gandhi, nominated Holmes for the Nobel Peace Prize. The representatives of organized labor and of the National Association for the Advancement of Colored People honored him. Mayor LaGuardia praised him for his work on behalf of better city government.

Then came Wise, who harked back to their joint labors in liberal religion, politics, the N.A.A.C.P., civil liberties, trade unions, the editorial tasks of *Opinion*, and Zionism. Finally he came to the point:

> Tonight we go into the era of blueprints of the Community Church and in order to prove to you that I am not a regenerate Christian but merely an unregenerate Son of Abraham, I say to you now: let us tonight build one story of the Community Church—tonight before he leaves. What is the use of leaving this prophet homeless any longer? You, in your day, have the privilege of building a House of God that shall go down in

history as the home of a man of God whose name was John. Tonight let us see to it that some part of what he has merited from the city, from the races, from the life of the nation, that some part of that he shall attain. Let us enshrine him long decades before he becomes a memory.

Later in the evening Wise was discouraged by the slow response to the fund appeal and returned to the platform to help anew. Adept at gathering money, he came back to the microphone and said: "Madame Chairman, you may be a great educator, but you are a poor beggar. If I were standing here I would ask at once not who is going to give, but who is going to be the next giver. Not many can give five thousand dollars. Don't be too gentle— don't be too refined about it. Insist upon every one." Wise then announced a gift from his own congregation of a dollar per family —or nine hundred dollars.

The next morning Wise was still so exhilarated by the previous evening that he wrote Holmes:

> I cannot begin the day's work without telling you of my great joy in the celebration of last night which I think must have touched your heart, even though you turned it off as humbly and handsomely as you did. It was a great outpouring of friendship and love, and it shows that a man's best work is not done in vain, and that a life greatly and selflessly lived does make its appeal, even to frozen or petrified New York.

As for the gift from his congregation, Wise was aware that it "will not be much, but the spirit is fine; and it becomes a matter of precedents, and indeed of communal history, when a synagogue deliberately sets out to help in the building of a Community Church." Though ten years were to elapse before the Community Church had its building, this encouragement now heartened Holmes.

These were, however, gloomy days for Wise as he tried to alleviate the suffering of his people in Europe. As he ended his terms as president of the Zionist Organization of America and as chairman of the United Palestine Appeal, Wise was troubled about the growing numbers of Jewish refugees pouring out of Germany and the difficulty of placing them. He was further burdened by the impossibility of opening wide the gates of Palestine to Jews fleeing the Hitler terror; now the British seemed bent on making the aperture even narrower. At this time, as in the previous several years and on into the nineteen forties, Wise signed innumerable affidavits pledging his own guarantee that the refugees whose entry into the United States he sponsored would not become public charges.

Adding to his anxieties was the fact that attendance at the Free Synagogue had begun to diminish. When Holmes complained that at the Community Church the attendance was alarmingly low, Wise wrote him:

> You did not touch bottom on Sunday. It was I who dropped lower than the cellar. The attendance was 500 so I beat you by 100, while Emmett Fox [a popular preacher in New York] gets them. I know why he does and we don't. He puts people at ease, makes all sorts of quieting, soothing, reassuring promises. We cannot. We have our honest doubts, and the world for a time seems hell-bound, and we cannot conceal it from ourselves or from those to whom we minister. Tell them, as Fox does, that all is right with the world, and they will come crowding to you and smile with you and cheer you. But heaven knows I don't want them to come to me on those terms. We cannot pour molasses over cannon-balls and bombs in order to make them palatable.

Among the "bombs" was the British White Paper then in preparation and intended to limit drastically Jewish immigration into Palestine in the following years. As a member of the Jewish Agency for Palestine, Wise prepared to leave for Britain and conferences on the problem. His premonitions were not happy: "We know we are going to be bamboozled. I know that England is about to fool us to the top of her bent. But what can we do about it? If we poor Jacks withdraw from the Conference with the Arab Kings, the world will say we are afraid to meet with them. We have got to take our chance, though it is a rotten chance."

The conference was no different from what had been expected. From it came not only the Arabs' refusal to sit at the same table with the Jews, but also the announcement by Colonial Secretary Malcolm MacDonald that immigration to Palestine was to be limited to seventy-five thousand over the next five years and then would cease completely unless the Arabs consented to its continuance—a most unlikely possibility.

Five weeks later, Wise returned on the M.S. *Champlain.* From Holmes came the following note:

> Welcome home, and comfort to your spirit! I feel as though you were returning from the saddest mission of your life, but I know you are not accepting defeat, and I am confident that you will find all about you sympathy to lift your heart in this dire but not irreparable tragedy which has befallen Zion. Along with my compassion for Jewry and my contempt for the Empire, I feel a profound sense of outrage for Christendom, which is equally betrayed with Zion in this dreadful decision to return the Holy Land to the Arabs. This morning I sent letters to [Samuel McCrea] Cavert and [George A.] Buttrick, in a desperate endeavor to get the Federal Council to act in the name of Christian churches and the clergymen in this country.

Wise replied:

> I have had a heart-breaking experience, but I am going to try to share what Brandeis yesterday called, my own "invincible optimism." I have learned a few things in England—chiefest, perhaps, not to grow down-hearted. Let me see you very soon. It will be a joy to have a word with you.
>
> What wonderful letters are those that you have written to Cavert and Buttrick! All I can say is that your appeal to them is worthy of you. I can think of no higher praise.

Both Wise and Holmes knew that though Cavert, the general secretary, and Buttrick, the president of the Federal Council of Churches of Christ in America, might be sympathetic, the Council as an organization could do little. Not only was it a federation of different denominations which would find it difficult to effect unanimity; but there was neither an informed conscience nor even a deep desire to act in this regard. Most of the men who might be relied on as supporters had scant knowledge of the issues at stake and were hesitant about committing themselves. Furthermore, the missionary forces in Christendom were of no disposition to let Palestine be granted to the Jews as a Jewish state. Their own friendship with the Arabs, their stake in the missionary enterprise in Arab lands, and a subtle, well-hidden anti-Jewish feeling led most missionaries to seek the destruction of Zionist hopes. The influence of this group within the ranks of Protestantism was not inconsiderable.

By the time Holmes turned sixty in 1939, the war had begun in Europe and he wrote letters to friends to bolster them in their pacifism. Such pacifists as John Nevin Sayre, Kirby Page, and A. J. Muste stood firm with him, but Albert Einstein, a pacifist since World War I, had joined the ranks of those supporting the war. So had Wise, who had given many indications of moving in that direction. In the spring of 1938, Wise had vigorously opposed the proposed amendment to the Constitution by Representative Ludlow which would have forbidden the Congress to declare war until a popular referendum in the nation had approved. Wise predicted it might "prove to be democracy's supreme gift to the Fascist powers, for Ludlow and his supporters may not understand it, but it is such parliamentary ineptitude which accelerated the death of most parliaments."

The *Christian Century* asked a number of eminent men—Harry Emerson Fosdick, Reinhold Niebuhr, Francis J. McConnell, Charles P. Taft, and Holmes, among others—to answer the question, "If America Enters the War, What Shall *I* Do?" In his article, Holmes reaffirmed his views of the past and stated simply that, first, he would not support his country if it went to war, even if Hitler ran roughshod over all the earth, for he did not look upon Hitler "with the eyes of so many of my contemporaries—as a unique embodiment of wickedness, a monster intruded upon the earth like Satan come from Hell. To me, Hitler is all that is horrible, but as such he is the product of our world, the veritable incarnation of our nationalistic, capitalistic and militaristic era. Whatever is worst in our civilization seems to have come to a vile head in him. He is our own sins sprung to life, to confound us, scourge us and perhaps destroy us."

Secondly, there was the challenge not of this war but of war itself; and if America went to war against Germany or Japan, he would not support it, for like the early Christians and later

Quakers, he was opposed "to all war, to war as an accepted method of settling disputes between nations, to war as an established institution and practice of arms, to war as a weapon either of aggression or defense."

The alternative to war? This answer he gave to both Jews and Christians.

To the Jews, he wrote in *Opinion* that they should follow Jeremiah who had been a pacifist in the dreadful period when Jerusalem was besieged by Nebuchadnezzar. In his mind the Jew had been the supreme pacifist of history and had endured without striking back, had died without resisting. They, in Holmes' reading of history, had set the noble pattern of meeting violence and hatred with patience and forgiveness. With this pacifist interpretation of their past, Holmes urged the Jews not to deny their own witness in this dread time. They should not emulate the Gentiles who had sought a spiritual assimilation by worshiping at the pagan altars of Mars and neglecting the altar of their own true God. The Jews were, after all, human and such a trend was understandable; but nonetheless the tendency was pitiable, for when Jews became as other men, the world would lose its finest spiritual heritage.

For Christians, he wrote *Out of Darkness*, a book dedicated to his "Beloved Comrades in the Fellowship of Reconciliation." He spoke of the need for remnant groups of the Spirit to be "sacred vessels containing the bread and wine of God's living presence among men." *Out of Darkness* received excellent reviews from his fellow pacifists and strong dissent from the non-pacifists; it went into several printings. Essentially, his viewpoint was catastrophic:

> Unless war is abolished, nothing else whatsoever seems worth doing. Why strive for the maintenance of civil liberties, when all liberties may be swept away in a single night for the advent of war? Why establish the high standards of labor on the farm and in the factory, when all social standards may on the instant be swallowed up in the maw of war? Why fight for the conquest of disease, the abolition of poverty, the health, happiness and prolongation of human life, when life may be seized by war, and by some hideous cataclysm of nature and cast to the lowest

depths of misery and death? Why struggle and sacrifice to make this world a decent place to live in, when war may suddenly make it a veritable sink-hole of indecency? Why foster learning and culture, work for progress and enlightenment, when war lurks in the shadows to cast us into the black pit of barbarism? Why walk in the way of love, when war has the right, on any pretext, at the beck of any premier or president, to command us to walk in the way of hate?

When Norman Thomas spoke at one of the America First meetings, Holmes gave the invocation. Anyone working for peace was an ally; but he could not join the America First movement because he was at variance with its isolationism as well as in direct opposition to its overtones of anti-Semitism.

Within a few weeks the die was cast, for, as his play had predicted, the Japanese attacked in the Pacific.

On the Sunday after Pearl Harbor, December 14, 1941, he again expressed opposition to war and presented his open resignation to the chairman of the Board of Trustees to be acted upon, if and when the trustees felt his presence would be embarrassing to them or the church. Of course, the resignation was not accepted.

Not all Holmes' friends favored his stand. Many Christians and Jews, with whom he had been close, now disassociated themselves from him. At the Community Church in Boston the reception was no longer so friendly, as he wrote to a Chicago friend: "I am terribly worried about the church, as it seems riven in twain by the impact of the war situation. I understand that finances are very bad this year, and certainly the temper of the church is distressing. I preached a pacifist sermon there last month, and I never would have known it was my old congregation, as questions were hostile, and many of the people angry. I wonder—will the church we founded in the spirit of pacifism so many years ago now fail us? I can't and won't believe it, and I try to remember how dreadful are the times and how hard it is for those who have not lived through one war to understand this one."

A half year later, he confessed he had "been sorely disappointed over the Community Church in Boston this year. . . .

I have had no such experience in my own church in New York. . . . Deep down in my heart is the thought that twenty years of training ought to do something for a congregation. But it seldom does, not at least in war time, when every standard of sanity disappears and every law of goodwill is promptly repealed. This perhaps is the basic horror of war—these spiritual casualties, which wreck the inner life more terribly than the outer world itself."

He reported to Wise that the reception in some Jewish communities had been unfriendly—places like Indianapolis, Rochester, and Cleveland, where he had always found audiences receptive even to his most outspoken words. Now they were hostile and did not invite him; or, if he were invited, the invitation would later be canceled. It had even been implied that he was anti-Semitic.

Wise sympathized, despite his own pro-interventionist views. The best evidence of his oneness of spirit, if not of mind, was the answer he gave Franklin Delano Roosevelt when the President's Advisory Committee on Political Refugees met at the White House. After having discussed the refugee problem for an hour with awareness and understanding, the President turned to Wise and said, "Can't you do anything with John Haynes Holmes? What's the matter with him?"

Wise answered, "John Haynes Holmes believes that war is the greatest of evils. He obeys his conscience and his God in opposing war under any and all circumstances."

The President laughed and said, "Well, that's all right. So do I—BUT . . . !"

When America sent troops to Europe and the Far East in 1942, Holmes wrote Mrs. Wise in answer to a note of hers, "I cannot see where we gain anything by adding the horror of war to the horror of Hitlerism."

Wise retorted,

> Have we added the horror of war? Did we wage war on Austria, Czechoslovakia, Poland? Have we set out to wage war upon Japan, or did we try to make peace with Japan in the decentest way? Hitler has permitted his horrors of war upon lesser people to culminate in a world war against Freedom and Democracy.

The loss of human freedom, the cancellation of Democracy for five hundred or a thousand years are greater evils than the evil of war in which we resist the forces of evil, or assist them by non-resistance. I wish I could see eye to eye with you, or what would be better, I wish you could see eye to eye with me.

One of the things on which they could see eye to eye was the need to maintain civil liberties; and Holmes had, on an earlier occasion, given Wise a blow-by-blow account of the struggle within the American Civil Liberties Union in 1940 when Harry F. Ward resigned as chairman and Holmes succeeded him. Communism was the issue. Several members of the board were pro-Soviet and had either joined the Communist Party or were so sympathetic to it that they adhered undeviatingly to its line. Often the meetings became chaotic. After the Nazi-Soviet Pact of 1939, a demand was made for the expulsion of a Communist Party member, Elizabeth Gurley Flynn, who had been a board member of the A.C.L.U. for many years.

Holmes' attitude against any "United Front" had been stated earlier. In 1937, he described the Soviet purges as massacres "horrible beyond description." In *Unity* he had written: "If this be the new Utopia of the future, God save us all!" He had repented of any kind of fellow-traveling in the late 1930s and freely admitted: "We liberals . . . accepted covertly, if not openly, the most dangerous and ultimately disastrous idea that can lodge within the human mind, namely that the end justifies the means," and regretted having "defended, or at least apologized for, evils in the case of Russia which horrified us wherever else they appeared."

At the historic A.C.L.U. meeting in 1940, Elizabeth Gurley Flynn refused to resign and a debate began that lasted from late afternoon until the middle of the night. The vote was nine to nine. Holmes, as chairman, had to cast the deciding vote: he voted that she resign.

Not long before, John Dos Passos, the novelist, had written to him and emphasized the need for an immediate change of personnel in the American Civil Liberties Union. Dos Passos argued that despite its "enormously valuable work . . . I don't see how men who have been able to swallow the intellectual absurdities and the moral indecencies of the Communist innocent front can be of any further use to the defense of American democracy." Holmes and the Board of Directors agreed.

In the winter of 1941, he lost his valued friend Salmon Levinson. Holmes, joined by Rabbi Louis I. Mann and Dean Charles Gilkey, conducted the funeral service in the Bond Chapel of the Divinity School on the campus of the University of Chicago. All three told of Levinson's contagious enthusiasm and driving idealism.

Holmes spoke of Levinson's varied roles as world citizen, leader in good causes, and counselor of governments and statesmen, but most of all as a friend who "came to me in an hour of dire extremity . . . and through the sacrifice of unstinted time and strength, unmeasured labor and incredible patience, and the vast skill and knowledge of his profession, all freely offered 'without money and without price,' through a period of four years and over a distance of a thousand miles, saved me and my church from irreparable ruin."

He asked the congregation:

> Do you remember the passage in John Bunyan's *Pilgrim's Progress*, where is described the death of Mr. Valiant-for-Truth? Bunyan tells how Mr. Valiant-for-Truth was suddenly taken with a summons, [and] . . . when he understood it, he called for his friends and said: "I am going to my fathers . . . My sword, I give to him that shall succeed me in my pilgrimage, and my courage and skill to him that can get it. My marks and scars I carry with me, to be a witness for me." A great company of men and women followed Mr. Valiant-for-Truth to the river, and he entered the dark waters and passed through. And when he emerged, all "the *trumpets sounded for him on the other side!*" Listen! Can you not hear them now, those trumpets on the ramparts of God's city, sounding their silver song as for a king come back victorious from the wars?

27. Haman Redivivus

> *My tears have been my meat day and night,*
> *while they daily say unto me, where is now*
> *thy God?*   —PSALMS, 42:3

IN 1942, AMERICA WAS AT WAR and beginning to feel, especially on the seas, the deadliness of German military supremacy; the Russians appeared to be defeated by the Nazi armies besieging Leningrad and moving steadily toward Moscow. The British had apparently lost most of North Africa; and the Middle East, especially Palestine, was in jeopardy. The cause of the United Nations seemed on the verge of disaster.

Wise did not want Holmes to think that he had succumbed to despair:

> I do not lose faith—my faith that we will, in part because of these awful sacrifices, march on to a decenter, juster and, it may be, a warless world. Faith, as we both know, isn't a thing to be reasoned about. One has it, or one has it not. You and I both have it. Both of us see the divine, even from far off, toward which all creation moves, though it moves haltingly, painfully and, perhaps it must be so, sacrificially.

For a number of weeks they were not in touch with each other, not because of any disagreement on war and peace but rather because their lives were so inordinately full of activity. In midsummer while on his vacation, Holmes had a long letter from Wise apologizing for the gap in their correspondence: "I do not know what has come over me, but I cannot write letters. I am ashamed to think that I haven't written to you before this, but it has not been possible. I haven't been in the spirit or mood for writing to anyone, not even to you, dearest and best of friends."

Wise then explained his long silence:

> I have had the unhappiest days of my life. Please remember, dear Holmes, that in addition to all your suffering over everything connected with the war, I have something more, namely the uniquely tragic fate of my people. You will be tempted at once to ask, why do I think of it as "uniquely tragic"? "Is it any worse than the fate of the Czechs or Yugoslavs or Poles?" Yes! Think of what it means to hear, as I have heard, through a coded message—first from Geneva, then from Berne, through the British Foreign Office—that Hitler plans the extermination at one time of the whole Jewish population of Europe; and prussic acid is mentioned as the medium.

Four weeks earlier Gerhard Riegner, Director of the Geneva office of the World Jewish Congress, had heard from a German industrialist visiting in Switzerland of Hitler's plans to exterminate some 4,000,000 Jews in Nazi-occupied countries by deporting them to concentration camps in eastern Europe and exterminating them in gas chambers and crematoria. Riegner had evidence that mass deportations from Czechoslovakia and France were already under way. He gave the information to the American and British consulates in Geneva and asked that the Americans inform Wise as the president of the World Jewish Congress and that the British tell Sidney Silverman, member of Parliament and chairman of the British section of the Congress.

Riegner waited for word to come from either New York or London. Frantically he inquired again and was told by the American consul in Geneva that the State Department considered the information not authentic, certainly unsubstantiated, and was therefore not inclined to deliver the message. Eventually the British Foreign office conveyed the message to Silverman who in turn transmitted it to Wise. The next day Wise went to Washington and conferred with Sumner Welles, then Undersecretary of State, who asked him to say nothing until he could confirm the reports.

In the next two months Riegner had confirmation that his

information was sound and that the mass extermination had begun; once more he sent details through the Berne legation. Welles
telegraphed Wise to come at once to the State Department. In
Welles' office Wise heard words he never forgot: "I regret to
tell you, Dr. Wise, that these documents I hold in my hand, and
which have come to me from our Legation in Berne, confirm
and justify your deepest fears." Wise then read that two or three
million Jews had already been killed and that the Nazi regime
planned to destroy the remaining Jewish population of Europe.

The documents were stamped with the red seals of diplomatic
protocol. To Wise their color suggested the blood of his people.

Welles said to him, "For reasons that you will understand,
I cannot give these to the press, but there is no reason why you
should not. It might even help if you did."

Wise called a press conference and gave out the information.
It confirmed the suspicions aroused by the scant reports hitherto
available.

Wise then reminded Holmes in a letter that if men who had
"some spiritual and moral power had moved America and Britain
and France really to intervene in behalf of the slain innocents,
war might not have come. These things have led to war; they
have not come out of the war. Moreover, Jews, unarmed and
defenseless, have been unable to do anything for themselves;
and the world has done little, if anything, for them."

Wise apologetically added: "I don't want to preach at you.
I don't want to turn my heart inside out, but I am almost
demented over my people's grief."

One evening, Holmes read articles by James G. McDonald,
former League of Nations High Commissioner for Jewish Refugees, and J. B. Oldham, British churchman and editor of *Christian Newsletter,* and was so aghast at their description of the
Jewish tragedy in Europe that he wrote Wise: "When I got
through, I felt as though my blood was congealed and was no
longer moving in my veins. Do you remember my prophecy in
1933, that in twenty-five years there wouldn't be a Jew alive in
Germany? How little I realized at that time how far short of the
horrid reality my prophecy would fall, that the limit would be
ten or twelve years and not twenty-five, and that the area of

extermination would not be Germany but most of the continent of Europe. God, how much longer can we survive?"

In early December, Wise attended a meeting at the Hotel Statler in New York called by a group of Christians, led by Henry A. Atkinson, Reinhold Niebuhr, S. Ralph Harlow, Francis J. McConnell, and Holmes, to found an organization of Christians to deal with the problem. To this group, known as the American Christian Palestine Committee, Wise outlined the needs of the Jews and their claim to Palestine. The Committee determined to interpret to the Christian community the plight of the Jews of Europe, press the U.S. Government to urge British revocation of their 1939 White Paper limiting Jewish immigration to Palestine, present the achievements of Jewish settlers in Palestine, and enumerate the historic ties and international commitments promising a Jewish state in Palestine.

Wise was depressed and more burdened with his people's fate than before. He continued to receive word from Riegner through the State Department of the wholesale slaughter of Jews by the Nazis. Suddenly the State Department officials stopped the messages from Riegner for the incredible reason that public protests might increase if such reports continued.

Wise found that the State Department committed an even more serious crime than withholding information, when the possibility of rescuing Jews was ignored and concrete proposals to save them were allowed to atrophy through sheer inaction. In early 1943 Wise had heard from Riegner that if funds were sent into Switzerland, about 70,000 Jews in France and Rumania could be rescued and an additional group of Polish Jews moved to Hungary where extermination had not yet been started by the Nazis. If the money were deposited in Switzerland in the accounts of certain officials from Nazi-occupied Europe who were willing to co-operate, and if the funds were held until after the war, this plan could be achieved. In July, 1943, Wise went directly to the President and presented his plan for gathering such funds and sending them through the World Jewish Congress to be placed in escrow with the American legation at Berne. Wise pointed out to Roosevelt that the sums thus made available would not be payable until peace had been declared and then added significantly, "Our armies will see to it that these Nazi mercenaries shall not live to reap the benefit of their hostage-holding, blackmailing plan."

Roosevelt's reaction astonished and delighted Wise: "Stephen, why don't you go ahead and do it?"

Wise replied that he had not felt free to discuss the matter with Henry Morgenthau, Jr., the Secretary of the Treasury. Roosevelt immediately picked up the telephone and spoke with Morgenthau, "Henry, this is a very fair proposal which Stephen makes about ransoming Jews out of Poland into Hungary."

When Morgenthau received further details in the letter Wise wrote Roosevelt, he sent it on to the State Department where Cordell Hull, the Secretary of State, gave his assent.

There for some unknown reason the process stopped. Not until the following winter did the State Department issue instructions to grant a foreign funds license to Riegner in Geneva. Five months had gone by since the President of the United States, the Secretary of State, and the Secretary of the Treasury had given their full approval. Wise was in anguish as he thought of the hundreds of thousands of lives which might have been saved.

He had additional anguish from causes which were even more irksome than the delays of officialdom; for on the one hand he had to counter extremist statements on the part of the most zealous of the Zionists, and on the other hand to deal with outright opposition to his program among the Jews.

Wise knew the importance of having a united Jewry. To bring about such unity, he helped in the organization of the American Jewish Conference which met in the late summer of 1943 under the cochairmanship of himself, Louis Lipsky, and Henry Monsky, president of B'nai B'rith. The Conference, representative of American Jewry, adopted a resolution asking for a Jewish Commonwealth in Palestine. The American Jewish Committee then withdrew, to the disappointment of the conveners of the Conference. The B'nai B'rith remained in the Conference only by dint of Monsky's statesmanship and on a basis of specific reservations.

The Conference signified to government circles and international leaders that American Jewry was united in asking for a homeland for the Jews. Wise himself was certain that "within five years, or perhaps it may be sooner, there will be a free and democratic Jewish Commonwealth in Palestine." Many of his friends thought him rash and his enemies considered him insane.

Heartened by increasing sympathy in the non-Jewish community, especially among many Christians whom he knew personally, Wise felt that in the following years Christian support would increase. At the moment he took courage from the reports from Europe of Christians who had sacrificed their lives to defend Jews and endangered their very existence by housing Jewish refugees. The King of Denmark was courageous enough to say that, if the Jews of Denmark were compelled to wear a shield of David on their left arm, he, too, would wear one.

Wise was hopeful—and not without reason:

> It may be that, after the war, we shall have the joyous surprise of finding that here and there in many places, there are groups of Jews, though in the aggregate inconsiderable, who will have survived, chiefly because of the tender solicitude and courage and charity of Christian neighbors, men and women who have hidden Jews away, who have placed them in cellars, who have enabled them to disguise themselves in order to escape the Gestapo, who have helped them to live in the secret places of forests and have done this at greatest risk.

To free Wise for Zionist work, which, in his seventieth year, became more urgent and more burdensome, the trustees of the Free Synagogue granted him a leave of absence for the duration of the war. He would preach only during the High Holy Days— and once a month, if he desired. His associates, Sidney Goldstein and J. X. Cohen, as well as a rabbi-preacher soon to be called, would divide the duties of the active leadership of the congregation among themselves. By the spring of 1943, Wise found the third man, Edward E. Klein, who had been a student of his at the J.I.R. and would come from his post as director of the Hillel Foundation at the University of California in Berkeley. A year later, Wise confided to Holmes his hope that Klein would ultimately become his successor.

In almost the same week, Holmes gave Wise a similar confidence; he had set his heart on having as his successor a young

318 RABBI AND MINISTER

man named Donald Harrington. A graduate of Antioch College, the University of Chicago, Meadville Theological School, and the University of Leyden, Harrington was well known as a pacifist, a social liberal, and minister of the People's Liberal Church of Chicago.

Wise was busy as cochairman, with Rabbi Abba Hillel Silver of Cleveland, of the American Zionist Emergency Council. During the late spring and summer of 1944, both of them, Democrat and Republican, worked with the platform committees of their parties to insert a Palestine plank.

Of Wise's presentation in Chicago before the Democratic Committee, a non-Jewish reporter wrote that it was an occasion "with an aura of intense drama, which found not a few moist eyes in the audience, as a venerable Jewish rabbi last night pleaded, as did Moses: 'Let my people go!' It was one of the most brilliant of Rabbi Stephen Wise's addresses and the intensity of the delivery was seen."

Wise's request was granted; the plank in the platform called "for the opening of Palestine to unrestricted immigration and colonization and its establishment as a free Jewish Commonwealth." Now Wise campaigned actively for Roosevelt's fourth term and gave one of his most persuasive talks at the Ford Hall Forum that fall. He was certain that Roosevelt was in earnest when he promised to exert all pressure possible to assure a Jewish state.

At the Jewish Institute of Religion in 1944, Wise could spend only two or three hours per day because of other commitments; but in these he autographed copies of his new book, *As I See It*, a collection of essays and editorials from *Opinion*; recommended young graduates and men in active ministries as candidates for the chaplaincy; arranged for the Rabbi of Temple Israel in Boston, Joshua Loth Liebman, to discuss religion and psychiatry under the Charles W. Eliot Lectureship, which resulted in the best-seller *Peace of Mind*. It was then, too, that Wise opened negotiations for a merger of the Institute with the Hebrew Union College in Cincinnati.

More than four years would elapse before the J.I.R.-H.U.C. merger was consummated, but the long, tedious meetings began

with Wise a reluctant yet convinced participant. The feeling
between the two institutions was no longer one of rivalry; but
certain sacrifices, Wise knew, were inevitable. The spiritual and
intellectual flavor of the Institute could easily be lost, as well
as its status as a New York institution, wholly autonomous and
independent of the Cincinnati school. In addition, the Institute
would no longer be able to serve so effectively as a seminary
for two sectors of American Judaism—Reform and Conservative
—and might have to become a Reform Judaism school as was the
Hebrew Union College in Cincinnati. Yet Wise felt that he could
not undertake the task of securing the funds needed to assure the
future of the Institute and that despite the losses, it was necessary
to achieve the merger.

The close of the year was brightened for Wise by Roosevelt's
victory at the polls; but it was darkened by military reverses
of the Allies in Europe, as well as by a personal tragedy and
a conflict of views with Abba Hillel Silver which led to Dr.
Silver's resignation from the cochairmanship of the Zionist Emergency Council.

The personal grief was the death of Justine's newborn son,
Michael. In October, 1944, Wise wrote her from West Lafayette,
Indiana, at a time when it appeared that Michael would still live:

> This is the first time I have written to you since dearest Michael
> came. You know without any word of mine how I feel about
> him and you—all of you. By a veritable miracle you were saved
> in a moment of gravest peril. The miracle may be renewed for
> you and Shad and that ineffably precious baby. I did not de-
> serve the miracle—tho Mother's love did—but you, my child, do,
> you who have been consideration and sacrifice and tenderness
> to others even when undeserved. We just will not let him go.
> Your deserving will be his ransom.

Within a short time, Michael died. Wise's sadness was helped
by his constant joy in Justine and Shad's son Jonathon, then
three years old.

At the end of the year, the conflict between him and Silver
became so intense that the Silver group attacked him: "All too
often Dr. Wise treated the Zionist movement of the United
States as a piece of personal property and has bitterly resented

any new leadership which threatened his monopoly." Wise restrained himself to the simple reply of two sentences: "As far as Dr. Silver's personal attack upon me is concerned, I have had and I shall have no controversy with him. The American Zionist Emergency Council has, by its acceptance of his resignation, passed judgment upon the issue involved."

This dispute was not resolved until the following summer when, for a period of a few more months, unity was re-established in the Zionist Movement. Wise and Silver once more became cochairmen and Wise could say resoundingly, "The American Zionist Movement is not so much 'united' now as it is *re-united.*"

By May of 1945, the Allied military forces were on their way to final victory against Germany and as they reached the concentration camps, the full story began to be known. Wise learned that the symbol for hope from the outside world in the concentration camps of Europe was the code word "Stephania." His name had become a synonym for hope among tens of thousands of displaced Jews, those fighting underground and those rotting in the death camps. When a letter from a desperate Jew in Europe was addressed, "Rabbi, United States," the post office knew who was meant and forwarded the letter to Stephen Wise.

After Franklin Roosevelt died in April, 1945, Wise went to Washington to meet the new President, Harry S. Truman. Wise found him not as talkative as Roosevelt nor as winsome, but willing to listen, eager to learn. A few years later Truman said, "I was for a Jewish Homeland then and I am for it now. I could foresee difficulties in the way of establishing that homeland, but no difficulty was as great as the moral disgrace of failing to establish it."

The joy of victory in Europe—and three months later in the Far East—was marred for Wise when he attended the World Zionist Conference at Queens College in London and realized painfully that the meetings took place, as Chaim Weizmann observed, "in the shadow of the greatest catastrophe in Jewish history, for the powerful Jewish community of the past is now broken." When Wise gave a eulogy in honor of Franklin Delano Roosevelt, the assembly arose in spontaneous tribute. He assured them they could place their faith in Truman, just as the British delegates were told they could trust the newly elected Labour Party in Great Britain, the successor government to Churchill's. Misgivings lingered in his mind, however, and these he conveyed to Holmes in letters.

It was not the first time that year that he had done so, for earlier in the spring, after spending a fortnight in San Francisco as a member of one of the delegations of nongovernmental organizations represented at the Conference for the United Nations Charter, Wise became dubious about the proceedings. When Holmes told him of his own doubts, Wise responded, "I feel as you do about San Francisco. It is chiefly an attempt to secure the gains of the war. Britain is bent upon remaining an empire; Russia desires to become a mighty empire; and we are wobbling between the two, not quite an empire, but insistent upon getting things which will involve us in all sorts of trouble."

When in the early autumn the British Labour Party was ready to go back on its 1944 resolution to establish a Jewish National Home, Wise was again alarmed and wrote Holmes:

> I do not like to write as I do, but you will understand, perhaps almost better than any of us, that England is about to commit a great wrong—the England that you have never quite trusted, the England that I have been foolish enough to trust throughout the years. After six million of my people have been slain, one and a quarter to one and a half million remain homeless on the European continent, afraid to return to Poland, for they rightly dread pogroms, with only one place to which to go—Palestine. Lift up your voice on their behalf and let your trumpet tones demand justice for the Jew.

Holmes lifted up his voice on November 2, 1945, the twenty-eighth anniversary of the Balfour Declaration. By that time, Britain's intentions were clear: the Labour Party planned to do nothing to implement its Palestine promises.

Holmes was suspicious not only of Britain's intentions but America's as well. He had been stunned by the magnitude of America's "sin" in dropping the atomic bomb on Hiroshima and Nagasaki. He warned against the bomb and its use, for, as he wrote in *Fellowship*, the bomb's potential was beyond all imagination. The secret of the bomb could not be kept, and there was no evidence in the history of human nature that man could be trusted with such great physical power. Now he pleaded for a sovereign government which would unite mankind and abolish clashing interests among the nations.

Though his life was now quieter than Wise's, Holmes was still tormented by the need to raise funds, an unpleasant task for him but necessary if the church was ever to have a permanent home. His conscience was, as always, outraged by continuing wrongs done by man to man, and he spoke out against them. In that summer of 1945 the Meadville Theological School awarded him the degree of Doctor of Divinity, *honoris causa:*

> John Haynes Holmes, spiritual son and heir of Theodore Parker, living exponent of the prophetic conscience, courageous in utterance and in battle, devoted to study and a minister's learning, reformer, successful dramatist, author, writer of hymns that sing beyond the years, gentle to men, terrible against wrong, king of the American pulpit.

28. Perfidious Albion

> S.S.W.: *"Mr. President, you have not a drop of non-British blood in your veins, for you are English, Scotch, Irish; but you do not seem to trust England. I, on the other hand, son of Abraham, have only Jewish blood in my veins and not one drop of British blood; but I trust and revere England."* Woodrow Wilson: *"Rabbi, I know my family better than you do."*
> —CONVERSATION IN THE WHITE HOUSE, 1915

STEPHEN WISE, COMPLAINED *Liberal Judaism*, could talk of little else than Zionism in the months of America's adjustment to peace. His preoccupation was especially evident in the winter of 1945–1946 at a convocation at the Hebrew Union College in Cincinnati, when Henry Morgenthau, Jr., and Wise received honorary degrees and addressed eight hundred guests. Morgenthau described the dangers facing the world because of Allied vacillation in policies for occupied Germany. Wise said that he had no intention of making a Zionist speech; but he soon yielded to the temptation before this captive audience, few of whom were Zionists, many non-Zionists, and a sizable number anti-Zionists. The editors of *Liberal Judaism* commented: "The impression among his hearers was prevalent that he missed a rare opportunity to cement firm friendship between the J.I.R. and H.U.C., which had chosen to recognize his over-all services by an honorary doctorate."

Yet Wise could think of nothing but Zionism. He still smarted from the rebuke of Britain's Foreign Secretary, Ernest Bevin,

323

who sneered at the Jews' desire to be "at the head of the queue." The Labour Party had persuaded the American Government to join with the British Government in still another investigation, the Anglo-American Committee of Inquiry on Palestine, which was scheduled to begin in January.

Only a month later, Wise was in Washington to give testimony before this Committee. He told its six American and six British members that he appeared with very great reluctance, for the facts were well known with regard to Palestine and the status of the Jews, so well known that another inquiry was superfluous; yet a stern sense of duty impelled him to appear. The American chairman of the Committee, Judge Joseph Hutcheson, broke in to say, "May I with the greatest deference to your point of view remind you, sir, that history records that the impact of the same facts is different at one time than at another?"

Wise knew that the Committee would visit the displaced persons' camps in Europe and then move on to the Middle East to hear the conflicting claims of both Jews and Arabs. Thus he limited himself to a presentation of the historic homelessness of the Jewish people and their plight in modern Europe. He described Zionism as "an historical continuum, to use that awkward Latin term which has come to us through German metaphysics: there has never been a time in the nineteen and more Christian centuries during which there has been an abandonment or a waiver in relation to Zionism on the part of Jews."

In his closing words, he hoped he would "be forgiven if I say to you that the Christian world suffered six millions of the people of Jesus of Nazareth to die, to die in the most awful way. You will forgive me if I say, as I close, that the Christian world owes the Jews some reparation, I think a great measure of reparation. We have blessed the Christian world; we have given the Christian world its holiest treasure. The Christian world, if Christian it be, cannot do less than say to the Jewish people, 'You have labored, you have grieved, you have suffered, you have long been injured. Palestine shall be yours.' "

Each member of the Committee rose and, taking his hand, thanked him for his presentation. An Orthodox rabbi called out, "It was a *Kiddush ha Shem* [a sanctifying of the Holy Name]!"

Eliahu Epstein [Elath] of the Jewish Agency for Palestine, later to become ambassador from Israel to the United States, and in 1949, ambassador to Great Britain, said to him, "Your seventy years were a preparation for this hour." And his grandson, Stephen Wise Tulin, who had skipped school to hear him, came up to give him a hug that rejoiced his heart.

There were tears in the eyes of the Committee members. One correspondent wrote: "With his grey mane and strong, worn face, he seemed an aged lion, rousing himself for a heavy effort. He spoke with characteristic and commanding dignity. 'A great gentleman,' was one British Committee member's comment in the hall afterwards."

Wise wrote to his wife, "The Lord was with me."

Wise arranged for what turned out to be the most effective testimony on the part of Christians. He had telephoned Reinhold Niebuhr to come to Washington to testify, although he had been warned that the docket was full. Wise hoped someone might not appear and Niebuhr could then substitute. His hope was not in vain. Niebuhr's chief, Henry Sloane Coffin, president of Union Theological Seminary in New York City and an adamant anti-Zionist, did not show up for his place on the program; Niebuhr took the time and testified cogently. The members of the Committee were visibly impressed.

While the Committee carried on its extended study in subsequent months, the pressure of the refugees for immigration mounted and the patience of the Palestinian Jews dwindled. Outbreaks of violence and terrorism in 1946 came to a climax in the bombing of the King David Hotel and caused John Haynes Holmes, pro-Zionist but also propacifist, to write Wise in alarm and protest. Wise responded:

> I agree with you that there are disturbing things happening in Palestine, but it is Britain that is responsible for violence. The government that prevents Jews from entering into Palestine is guilty of violence, most especially seeing that those who choose to enter are the survivors of the Hitler horror.

Holmes was not entirely convinced. There was logic in what Wise had said, and he acknowledged the legitimacy of many points in Wise's rejoinder; but still he made a plea for restraint:

> I have your letter, and hasten to say that I agree in spirit with
> all that you say about the immigration problem in Palestine.
> When I deprecated the resort to violence in that country, I did
> not have in mind at all the defiance of the White Paper and the
> righteous attempt to get Jews into the Holy Land. The Jews
> would indeed not be worth their salt if they bowed in abject
> surrender to the situation created by the White Paper. Here
> they are vindicating their right, and themselves suffering and
> not practising violence. What I had in mind in what I wrote you
> was the resort of the Jews in Palestine to terrorism, the organi-
> zation of their terrorist movements, their gathering of arms and
> recruiting of military forces, their agitation for a *de facto* govern-
> ment, etc. etc. I believe these methods are not only wrong, but
> are disastrously futile. They can lead only to disaster. Gandhi
> has shown the way. For a quarter of a century he has opposed
> violence, and organized his movement of a non-violent basis,
> and now, as the reward of infinite patience and heroic resolution,
> independence is coming to India. This is his hour of triumph,
> and his the victory.

Wise reflected anxiety to such an extent that Louise wrote him
a word of caution: "Be careful of your precious health and
strength, so we and the causes that need you may have all that
you are and do for years to come. Try to speak more calmly,
darling. Lately I have felt you are consumed by excitement and
passion. Believe me, dearest, your words will mean all the more
if you are strongly deliberate; and quiet strength will add to
your vitality in every way. Now my lecture is done, Dodi [be-
loved]. Please heed it for my sake."

He tried to take her advice; but the causes were many, almost
too many. He took part in long meetings for the planned merger
of the Jewish Institute of Religion and the Hebrew Union College; he went to Washington regularly as a member appointed
by President Harry S. Truman to the Commission on Higher
Education and convened with such men as Bishop G. Bromley
Oxnam, Monsignor John A. Ryan, and Harvard's James Conant;
he spoke to the Congress of Industrial Organizations in Atlantic
City; he planned for meetings of the Zionist Executive and the

World Zionist Conference in Basel in the winter of 1946–1947, and the World Jewish Congress in Geneva in 1948; and he began to gather funds for the building of the sanctuary at the Free Synagogue, postponed for more than a quarter of a century since the "million-dollar bonfire" of his steel strike sermon of 1919.

In the summer of 1946, Louise Waterman Wise was awarded the Order of the British Empire, for she had campaigned actively for aid to Britain before America's entry into World War II and welcomed many thousands of British soldiers from every part of the Empire to the Congress Houses during the war years. She refused the award and wrote the British Ambassador:

> I must with regret decline the appointment because of my deep unhappiness over the conduct of the British Mandatory Government with respect to the Jewish people in Palestine. A mandatory government should act as a trustee for the well-being of the people. The British Mandatory Government has not from the beginning borne itself as a trustee, and its recent conduct in imprisoning some of the leading members of the Executive of the Jewish Agency for Palestine, its imprisonment of hundreds, perhaps even thousands of Jewish settlers in Palestine, and, above all, the ruthless conduct of its representatives with respect to the Jewish settlement, have so pained me that I cannot with self-respect accept any appointment or distinction of the British government.

Wise made headlines when it was learned that his application for a visa to Palestine had been denied. No reason was given, although ample cause for British reluctance to issue visas was evident in the outbreaks of violence in Palestine that summer.

In the same week, rising above the question of British injustice to the Jews in Palestine, he asked for American aid to Britain. The British Government was hard pressed by commitments throughout the entire Empire; struggling with an inflation created by six years of war and its first year of postwar life, it appealed to the American Government for a loan of four billion dollars. Some American Zionists and several Jewish leaders felt the time was ripe for a *quid pro quo* if the British received such a loan. Why should there not be a demand for the fulfillment of promises about Palestine? Why could not the British help Jewish refugees establish themselves as settlers in Palestine and ultimately aid in the formation of a Jewish state? Wise was not interested in using the loan to the British as a lever for Zionist objectives and he pressed for the loan which was soon granted by the United States Congress.

Later that year Wise and the other members of the Zionist Executive of the Jewish Agency met with officials of the British Colonial Office. Chaim Weizmann reminded the British Colonial Secretary of Wise's support of the loan; and, in the presence of Ernest Bevin, Wise commented that he had "acted with true Christian charity the day after I was denied a visa to Palestine by your Government."

In the fall it was apparent that three months of intense activity would precede a return to Europe, this time for the World Zionist Congress in Basel. During those autumn months, he made a long trip to the West Coast, accompanied by David Petegorsky, executive director of the American Jewish Congress. Louise came to the train and urged Wise to remain unperturbed by attacks from opponents. Then she turned to Petegorsky and mournfully told him how much she would miss her husband. She said, "David, my advice to young girls would be, 'Don't marry the man you love.'"

In early 1947, he was so disillusioned that he withdrew from any office in the Zionist Movement and again went his own way, at the very hour younger men were leading to victory the cause he had helped inaugurate and had nurtured for almost half a century. These were difficult times, for the tides of opinion in Zionist circles began to run against him, but also because he lost a dear friend and associate in the American Jewish Congress, the brilliant Alexander Pekelis, whose plane crashed in Shannon on the return flight from Basel.

His physical energy was cut down by visits to his physician for X-ray treatments after which a forty-eight-hour period of rest was often essential. His spleen was three times its normal size; and a double hernia was inoperable, because of the danger of profuse bleeding resulting from polycythemia from which he had suffered for sixteen years, without the knowledge of even his closest friends.

He needed the encouragement Holmes gave him on his arrival home from Europe:

> I have just read in the papers this morning the announcement of your return yesterday on the "Queen Elizabeth," and I count this a welcome opportunity to respond to the lovely letter you wrote me when you sailed away on this mission to Basel. You must have had a strenuous and exciting time, for the conference was momentous. I can guess how you feel about some of the things done and not done, but I gather from the reports that there was a magnificent spirit of determination in the gathering, and a power of utterance which was remarkable. Amid all the turmoil and terror of this hour, I cannot but feel that some measure of justice for Zion is on the way. The great cause will win out in the end.
> Welcome home!
> With affectionate greeting to Mrs. Wise and yourself, and all best wishes for the New Year.

For both men, the new year of 1947 was to bring both triumph and tragedy.

29. Gandhi's India

*If I believed in the "'Second Coming,'" as I do
not, I should dare to assert that Gandhi was
Jesus come back to earth. When I think of
Romain Rolland, I think of Tolstoi. When I
think of Lenin, I think of Napoleon. But when
I think of Gandhi, I think of Jesus. He lives
his life; he speaks his word; he suffers, strives,
and will some day nobly die, for his kingdom
upon earth.*   —JOHN HAYNES HOLMES, 1921

IN THE WINTER OF 1946–1947 John Haynes Holmes was invited
to travel to India. An old friend and member of the Community
Church, Taraknath Das, conveyed the invitation on behalf of the
Watumull Foundation. Holmes was to lecture in the leading Indian universities, travel throughout the land, and meet its political leaders, especially Gandhi and Nehru, the latter for the first
time.

Holmes was dubious. How could he get away for that length
of time? He had too many other responsibilities to handle and his
strength seemed inadequate. Would travel conditions be satisfactory? For that matter, would the church let him go? Das and
he soon worked out the plan. Consultation with church officials
showed that they considered the invitation an honor to their
minister as well as to them. Holmes could delegate responsibilities to Donald Harrington, his associate minister, and leave with
no anxiety on that score. What was more appropriate than for
him to visit the land of which he had spoken and written so much,

see Gandhi again, and return to America with a new interpretation of India?

Holmes' enthusiasm for the trip grew now that the invitation was enlarged to include his son Roger, due for a sabbatical semester from his post as professor of philosophy at Mount Holyoke College. In earlier years, he might have been more apprehensive about leaving the country for five months without keeping his hand at the helm of *Unity*. But he was no longer the editor-in-chief. During a long debate at the close of the war, he had been deposed from the position because the nonpacifists on the editorial board refused to accept his pacifism as a major theme in the editorial policy presented by *Unity*. The magazine began in 1946 to publish his writings less and less and to become once again a denominational journal of regional coverage.

To Holmes there was something ironic in the fact that his pacifism, influenced so greatly and reinforced so mightily by Gandhi, had caused him to lose the position he had accepted in succession to a pacifist, Jenkin Lloyd Jones.

Holmes enjoyed a restful summer in Maine, and then left for Europe on the *Queen Elizabeth*. After a brief time in London, depressing and threadbare after the war, he and Roger started their grueling journey by plane through the Middle East, a trip marred by engine trouble and long delays along the way. They arrived in Bombay two days behind schedule and utterly fatigued. Government officials and a score of reporters were there to greet them at the airport and encircle their necks with garlands of flowers.

Immediately they were busy. The first day they were given a reception by the Mayor of Bombay; the next day, by the President of the Provincial Congress. The third day, Holmes spoke at a mass meeting in celebration of Gandhi's birthday. Held on the open sands by the sea along the Marine Drive, the rally was attended by more than 100,000 people. Such crowds, such emotions Holmes had never known before.

In Delhi, their quarters were in the sumptuous home of Dr. Bhatnagar, an eminent scientist and scholar, across the road from Nehru's house and around the corner from Gandhi's residence. The day Holmes met Nehru for the first time and saw Gandhi again was, as he wrote Madeleine, "in some ways the greatest day of my life."

They found Nehru burdened with gigantic problems. Sleepless and worn, he could pay little attention to them when they were his guests at luncheon. All efforts to draw him out in conversation failed, until Roger turned the conversation to philosophical idealism; and Nehru picked it up spiritedly.

In the late afternoon, Holmes spent a half hour with Gandhi in their first meeting since London sixteen years earlier. He found the Mahatma sitting cross-legged on his immaculate white mattress, surrounded by pillows and cushions. Gandhi seemed troubled by a slight cough; yet he wore nothing more than his loincloth and a light shawl draped about his shoulders and chest. As always, there was the ineffably lovely smile and the gift of making a guest feel at ease.

While Roger took a photograph of the two talking together, Holmes appraised Gandhi anew. He found him heavier than in London in 1931, his flesh firm and glowing with health. Only the voice was weak and there was difficulty in hearing him. He had been deeply saddened by the riots and massacres in recent weeks following the partition of India. There was no bitterness or despair in what he said. He seemed to Holmes greater at this hour than ever before; still simple and humble, brave and dauntless, and yet, single-handed, quieting the people of India.

That evening Holmes and his son attended the regular prayer meeting where about five hundred people gathered before Gandhi's lodgings. The Mahatma prayed with them, read from scriptures and talked briefly. If it had not been for electric lights and the microphone, Holmes thought, the scene would have resembled that of Jesus surrounded by his disciples as described in the New Testament.

Ambassador Henry Grady welcomed Holmes at the Embassy but urged him to cancel the trip and go home. Riots were increasing. Transportation was impossible; the country was torn in two. As ambassador he could not guarantee their safety. To come so far and now cancel the arrangements seemed unwise to Holmes. He decided to stay. He and Roger did their share of waiting for arrangements to be completed and train schedules to be restored, but soon they were able to keep to their original schedule.

Holmes endured the heckling of Communists at student rallies and the polite, persistent verbal nudges of orthodox Christians. He was struck by the pride that aristocratic Indians took in prison sentences they had served during the British rule, amazed at the enormous gap between India's oceans of poverty and its tiny islands of culture and wealth.

In Benares he found the most complex contradictions in India. Here were the modern and the ancient, the home of a famed university and the center of illiteracy, the Holy City where corpses were placed in the Ganges to spare them the fate of retribution in their reincarnation and where the living went to bathe and be purified amid fetid air and unclean waters. Here were the worst and the best in India: ignorance and learning, superstition and culture.

In one of the most thrilling experiences of his life he was led in an academic procession by Sri Sarvepalli Radhakrishnan, Vice-Chancellor of the University. Clad in colorful hoods and scarlet robes striped with gold, the gift of the University, Holmes marched with his colleagues past the impressive buildings on a new campus eight miles from the city. As the man who had discovered Gandhi for America and interpreted him most effectively, Holmes received the degree of Doctor of Humane Letters.

Above and beyond all else on the journey was his impression of Gandhi's influence. When at the age of seventy-eight, Gandhi walked hundreds of miles into the countryside, his mere presence pacified the multitudes. To Holmes, the only parallel was the attitude of America toward Lincoln and the reverence of Christianity for Christ.

The independence of the new India was still so novel and exciting to Holmes that he could not see in true perspective the extent and the limits of Gandhi's spiritual and political power. At this critical moment in India's emergence as a free nation, Gandhi was a link between the past and the future, between ancient and modern India. As the vast land struggled out of its traditional milieu, Gandhi's idea of village self-sufficiency, his abhorrence of the introduction of the machine, and his ethics of nonviolence began to lose their relevance. In the eyes of many of

Gandhi's closest friends and associates, the independence of India had turned out to be the culmination of Gandhian ethics.
To Holmes it was the high-water mark of the peaceful approach
to national rivalries. He felt that he could not have chosen a
more significant time to visit Gandhi's India.

In his conversation with Gandhi at the close of his stay, he
was gently chided because he had traveled by plane and train
and not by the traditional Indian method of bullock cart. But
Holmes preferred the more modern mode of transportation.
If ever he admired Gandhi for his tenacity and sympathy, his
resilience and equanimity, it was on this trip. Even by using
every modern conveyance, he found it to be the most exhausting
journey he had ever known, both physically and spiritually.

Honored at every turn with lavish quarters and full reporting
in the newspapers, large crowds and luncheons with such personages as Lord and Lady Mountbatten, Holmes was at times
exultant and at other times unutterably depressed. There was too
much of everything: poverty, filth, throngs, receptions, teas, dinners, meetings, and acclaim. He longed for home.

His homesickness was most acute on Christmas Eve in Bengal
when he visited the school founded by Rabindranath Tagore and
was given the room where Tagore had lived. At the Christmas
service he tried to express his awareness of the debt America
owed India's two greatest men, Tagore and Gandhi. He told of
Tagore's visit to America in 1916, when the princely poet was
greeted as a recent Nobel Prize winner, and recalled the treas-
ured afternoon of quiet, lofty conversation they had in a New
York hotel room; he remembered the unique contribution Tagore's mystical faith had brought to an acquisitive American
society. And as for Gandhi, seeing him again and talking to him
was like meeting Christ.

The trip back to America was not without its drama and humor.
The War Department would not clear America's prize pacifist for
entry into Occupied Japan and appeals to General Douglas Mac-
Arthur brought permission too late. Yet a mechanical breakdown
in the airplane provided him with two days and a half in the land
from which he was barred, but with no tourist privileges.

In Hawaii he had a welcome rest; but he knew this was the last long trip he would ever take. When he returned to New York, utterly spent, he rested briefly and began to prepare articles, sermons, and lectures about his journey. Strength came back slowly to his travel-worn body, much more slowly than ever before.

Predominant in his messages was a tribute to Gandhi. Someday, he said, the world would exalt Gandhi; but little did he know how soon this would take place.

On Sunday, January 25, he preached on his visit to India and asserted: "So great is the reverence for the Mahatma that no one can even imagine violence done before him!"

Yet five days later, a fanatical Hindu killed Gandhi. Like millions of others throughout the world, Holmes was deeply shocked. Now "the hope of the world" had gone.

On Sunday, 1,700 people crowded into the Community Church. Holmes read for the first lesson Part XII of the Bhagavad-Gita:

> Tell me, O Lord, which of those who worship and serve Thee, with earnest minds well mastered, serve Thee most worthily and best? . . . Verily, I say unto thee, that he is very dear and near to Me, who harboreth no malice or ill will to any being or thing; who is the friend and lover of all nature; who is merciful, free from pride and vanity and selfishness; who is undisturbed by pleasure or pain, being balanced in each; who is patient under wrong and injustice, and who is forgiving, contented, ever devout, with mind, senses and passion that are under control, and whose mind and understanding is ever fixed upon Me.

For the second lesson he read from Matthew Arnold's "Balder Dead" and he concluded with George Santayana's sonnet: "With you a part of me hath passed away. . . ." The congregation sang Gandhi's favorite hymn, Frances Ridley Havergill's

> Take my life and let it be,
> Consecrated, Lord to Thee.

Holmes noted in his eulogy that if Gandhi had been assassinated thirty, twenty, or even ten years earlier, the news might have been buried on an inner page of the newspaper. He spoke of the contrast between former years when Gandhi was unknown and this day when the mightiest empire in the world had been humbled by his "crazy doctrine of non-violence." He drew a contrast between the time the world had laughed when Winston Churchill called Gandhi, in scorn and contempt, "a half-naked fakir," and this hour when the world revered him as "The Great Soul."

When Stephen Wise heard of Gandhi's death, he told his congregation that Friday night at the Free Synagogue:

> Only twice before in a long life have I quoted the Homeric phrase, 'The sun has perished out of the heavens,' for the first time in 1904, when the mournful tidings came that the most completely prophetic and Jewishly creative figure of a thousand years, Theodor Herzl, had passed; for the second time, on the afternoon of April 12, 1945, when America and indeed the whole world were stunned into silence and, after that, into tears, when word came that Franklin Delano Roosevelt had ceased in every sense to be mortal. And now for the third time when I learned that bullets of violence had overcome the supreme figure of non-violence in our century.

Gandhi fell, said Wise, because "he was too much a *bar shalom,* a son of peace." Gandhi would become, he declared, "one of the supreme figures of a millennium, for he had, by the force of his moral genius, effected that which only the most terrible of internecine wars could and would have brought about, namely, the manumission of the great Indian people and their partition into two relatively peaceful states."

Knowing how critical Wise had been of Gandhi in the past and how grave had been his reservations even to that day, Holmes cherished the tribute. He had thought of Wise all during his trip to India, but particularly on two occasions. The first was on November 29, his own sixty-ninth birthday, when the news came of the United Nations' decision to partition Palestine into Jewish and Arab states. The second was two weeks later when Holmes had gone to the American Express Office in Calcutta for his mail and opened a cable informing him that Louise Waterman Wise had died.

30. Let My People Go

> *He shall cause them that come of Jacob to take root:*
> *Israel shall blossom and bud, and shall fill the face of the world with fruit.*
> *The wilderness and the solitary places shall be glad for thee.*
> *The desert shall rejoice, and shall blossom like the rose.* —ISAIAH 27:6, 35:1

IN THE FALL OF 1947 Stephen Wise could see that his wife was beginning to weaken. Though fragile through all her life, she had adhered to a schedule of work heavier than two or three women, even of her ability and strength, might have undertaken.

Louise's public activities were still as wide-ranging as ever. The Child Adoption Committee of the Free Synagogue had now, more than three decades after its establishment, a large staff and an ever greater demand for homeless children to be placed in childless homes. Her newly organized American Committee for the Rehabilitation of European Jewish Children sought shelter and friendship for homeless, friendless youth; and she did not hesitate, while thanking Christian families for tending refugee Jewish children during the war, to rebuke Christian leaders, especially Roman Catholic prelates, for trying to proselytize on behalf of the Church among these orphans of the storm. The American Jewish Congress Women's division, which she had founded, became effective in demanding for Jews and all minorities the human rights and basic dignity to which every man and

337

woman is entitled. She continued her work at the Congress Refugee Houses, furnishing them and supervising them personally so that newcomers might know friendship and kindliness during their first months in a new land.

But Louise Waterman Wise was no longer strong. She tired more quickly. At this time she would occasionally, very occasionally, take brief naps and rest periods, and welcome, as she wrote to Stephen, a Gandhi-like day of silence; but the signs were unmistakable.

Even until a week before her death, she maintained the steady pace: visiting department stores to select blankets for her "guests" at the Congress Houses, chairing meetings many hours in length, speaking on a nationwide radio network, and wondering to Stephen why people wanted to hear her. She followed closely the United Nations debates during October and November on the Palestine Partition Plan, and encouraged her husband to carry on his work without interruption.

On Thanksgiving night, Wise left for a trip to Chicago with some misgivings, for Louise was obviously not well. Yet she admitted neither pain nor weakness and urged him to go. It was a difficult trip, for he too was unwell. A long, enjoyable conversation in the Pullman compartment with his son-in-law, Shad Polier, about new plans for work together in the American Jewish Congress and projects for its work in the field of civil rights gave him heart; and a barbiturate, which he rarely used, eased his pain and allowed him to sleep for a few hours.

On Friday, the twenty-eighth of November, he had all-day meetings on Jewish affairs, in the midst of which he found time, as always, to write Louise and Justine long letters on stray pieces of paper and telegraph blanks; and then a Friday evening service at the Temple in Glencoe.

On Saturday evening, a great mass meeting of Jews, planned months before, coincided with the day of the victorious vote at Lake Success. When Wise heard of the vote in favor of the partition of Palestine, he interrupted the proceedings to announce the UN's decision.

On the way back to New York he experienced something of a triumphal tour. After talks at Northwestern University in

Evanston and in Chicago and Detroit, he returned to New York and spoke to his own congregation on "What May We Expect of the New Judea?" and also continued his biweekly visits for X-ray treatments.

By the end of the following week, Louise had tired so much that her family called the doctor, who indicated the end might be near. Her heart, having poured out energy in abundance for others, now began to falter. Fortunately, she suffered no pain and talked quietly with her son and daughter.

By Monday, December 8, his wife's condition became so serious that Wise canceled engagements for that day. He did not attend a scheduled luncheon of her favorite organization, the Women's Division of the American Jewish Congress. Nor did he attend meetings of the executive council of the Free Synagogue or the steering committee of the Congress in the late afternoon and early evening. He informed Nahum Goldman that he could not accompany him to meet with the Soviet UN delegate, Andrei Gromyko, to discuss, on behalf of the Jewish Agency for Palestine, implementation of the UN Partition Plan for Palestine. He canceled his acceptance of an invitation from Albert Einstein for dinner in Princeton the following evening, but summoned the energy to address several hundred people of the Social Service Division of the Free Synagogue and then, at Louise's urging, boarded the train for Princeton to address a meeting of the Hillel Foundation.

He returned home after midnight to find Louise desperately ill. She died during the night.

Telegrams, telephone calls, and letters began to pour in. The family had known that she was loved and honored, but such love and esteem had not been given to her even during an honor-filled lifetime. Most moving were tributes of her "guests," both past and present, at the Congress House. From Dr. Eric P. Mosse, whom she had helped bring to America:

Dear Dr. Wise:
. . . I cannot forget, how my belief in human kindness and decency, shattered through my experience in Germany, were restored the first time, when I saw, how this old, lovable and humble great lady walked through the streets herself to get me

some desk, etc., to get me the chance to work. There was no secretary, no phoning, but doing the things *herself*. It was a tremendous lesson to me I'll never forget.

From Ernest Kahn, another whom she had aided:

My wife, myself and our little daughter . . . will never forget the impression this great and gracious lady made upon us when she personally visited us in our room speaking to us in such a nice and comforting manner and even giving our little girl a doll. She knew how to handle human beings and to help them keep their self-respect. Her memory is a blessing to mankind.

And from an Associate Justice of the Supreme Court:

I will never forget the lovely visit I had with your dear wife at the dinner last spring. . . . The thing that touched me most deeply was the great tenderness with which she spoke of you. So I know what great joys and heartaches you two have shared together and I know how deep the sorrow of this dark hour is.

—William O. Douglas

A long cable had come from Calcutta; over and over again Wise said to his children, "If only Holmes were here, if only Holmes were here."

David Petegorsky of the American Jewish Congress was chosen by Wise to deliver the eulogy at the memorial service in the Free Synagogue. He told how Louise Waterman Wise "witnessed the triumph of many causes—in American democracy, in human rights, in Jewish life. Her encouragement to and faith in the man at whose side she stood, her unflagging faith in the just and the right, her imperviousness to the attacks of the skeptical and the faithless, were the major elements in victory."

To Petegorsky, as to thousands of others, her selflessness was paramount:

Louise Wise was one of those rare persons whom one had to meet only once. To be touched only lightly by her, to listen to a word from her, to witness a single one of her acts was to see, as if in a flash, the very essence of human goodness and beauty and dignity. And because her words and her acts touched so many people in all lands and of all kinds, her inspiration and her example were so far-reaching and extensive. That is why her sainted memory, like her consecrated life, will continue to serve as an abiding inspiration for good and for justice to countless men and women everywhere.

The day after the funeral Wise returned to Dr. Keen for still another X-ray treatment. Then after several days of mourning, he went to Atlantic City with Justine to rest.

In too few days he returned and started again on a round of meetings and appointments. With Fanny Korn, a devoted friend who had worked closely with Louise at Congress House and helped him in many difficult tasks, he planned a hostel for youth in Jerusalem as a memorial for Louise. With Joseph Levine, one of the few still-living founders of the Free Synagogue and a key board member of the Jewish Institute of Religion, he conferred about the merger with the Hebrew Union College in Cincinnati. With Joseph Schwartz of the American Jewish Joint Distribution Committee he discussed relief measures for refugees detained by the British Government then, and for another fifteen months to come, on the island of Cyprus. With Edward Kiev he planned the expansion of the J.I.R. library. With Otto Nathan he arranged Albert Einstein's public appearance at the Free Synagogue. With Arthur Lourie and Moshe Shertok [Sharett] he anticipated the part to be played by the Jewish Agency in the establishment of a Jewish State the following spring at the expiration of the time allotted by the UN for the transition of the Mandate.

There were letters by the hundreds to be written. Each sympathy note or telegram he answered personally. He carried on a long correspondence with Nelson Glueck, his successor as president of the soon-to-be merged Hebrew Union College-Jewish Institute of Religion, and set dates for inaugural sessions in the fall.

Wise still had his problems with his fellow Zionists. In fact, Zionism seemed never to be without problems. The Zionist Organization of America was about to celebrate the fiftieth anniversary of its founding by Richard Gottheil and Stephen Wise in 1897. A Victory Dinner was planned in honor of Abba Hillel Silver of Cleveland for his important part in the proceedings on Palestine at the United Nations. The Zionist officials did not invite Wise. Their rebuff came within a fortnight after Louise's death.

Holmes, responding to Wise's sadness, visited him on several occasions and wrote him as often as possible. Wise, in answer to one of these letters, said: "I am still miserable and just out of bed. I have had two weeks of it now. I have never been well since Louise left me. I do not know that I ever will be."

On May 16, Wise attended a Victory Rally at Madison Square Garden. Twenty thousand had seats and more tens of thousands waited in the street outside. Israel had been established on Friday, the fourteenth, for the fifteenth, the date set by the UN, was the seventh day of the week, the Jewish Sabbath. What had been planned as a possible protest meeting against inaction by the United Nations now hailed the *fait accompli*. When Wise appeared on the platform, the audience applauded, exceeding the tribute to all other Zionist leaders.

Wise now resumed writing his long-planned and often-postponed autobiography, *Challenging Years*. Though he suffered from his illness and was still involved in an unbroken round of meetings, weddings, funerals, and sermons, and in writing for *Opinion* and the *Congress Weekly*, he worked each morning on his book. He wrote in small, almost crabbed style, line upon line so close that his secretaries could scarcely decipher the script. Events of the past flowed in upon him and caused his aching arm to protest at the swiftness with which it had to move across the desk. Sometimes the memories came so fast he had trouble keeping them separate and maintaining chronological order. The early days in New York and the first parish in Portland took second place. As the prophetic passion came to the fore, the priestly function receded in importance. Historic events, not his personal life, took precedence.

He interrupted work on the autobiography to write an editorial for *Opinion*, after having taken part in the dedication of Holmes' Community Church, now at last completed: "Great preacher though Holmes be, he is far more than a preacher of matchless eloquence. He has for more than four decades been guide, friend and inspirer to all the people irrespective of race, creed or color and has made the Community Church the spiritual and moral abode of men irrespective of creed or color or national origin, to all of whom he stands as a veritable apostle of faith in what God is and of what man, unshackled, may become."

He was reluctant to tell Holmes that life had begun to go downhill; yet, in a letter a few weeks later, he admitted: "I cannot help saying to you, as one of the oldest and dearest of my friends, that the passing of Louise makes it much more difficult to go on with any real joy or zest, though my children are devoted and the grandchildren are a delight to my heart."

In the summer of 1948, he accompanied Shad Polier and David Petegorsky to the World Jewish Congress meeting in Geneva. After resting aboard ship, he composed the foreword for *Challenging Years* at Montreux. Looking out upon the waters of Lake Geneva, he saw the Castle of Chillon and wrote: "I remember that we were never, not even in our darkest years, like him who regained his freedom with a sigh. Jews are regaining their freedom with exaltation. We believe that such freedom will result in a nobler Jewish people—it may be in a more free and just and peaceable world."

For the first time, he was attending an overseas gathering of such size and importance without Louise by his side. He knew it would be the last time he could be present at a World Jewish Congress meeting and, in his concluding address to the Congress, bade it farewell.

During the following autumn and winter his strength waned. He still spoke and wrote, sometimes recovering his former vigor swiftly, miraculously. He effected the merger of the Hebrew Union College and the Jewish Institute of Religion and became president emeritus; he launched a number of fund-raising drives on behalf of Israel; and he moved from his old apartment to the Hotel Delmonico at 59th Street and Park, to be near Justine.

He wrote to Albert Einstein, Felix Frankfurter, and countless old friends. He composed blistering editorials against anti-Zionists in Jewry and Christendom. And he pondered the destiny that had made him an American Jew:

> I am a member of the earliest of the earth's great people to emerge from darkness and to dwell in the light. If I were born

over again, I would beseech that I might be born an American Jew, not unburdened by the prejudices and discriminations which bear down upon my people and yet strong enough to lighten in some degree the burden of my fellow Jews, far from the heights of Messianic realization and yet not without faith that though the promised things of truth and brotherhood tarry, they shall yet come, still struggling to proclaim the unity of the Godhead, and yet certain that out of the unity of mankind the wider faith would grow.

31. The Lion and the Lamb

The value of any man's ministry is, or ought to be, gauged by the power with which he has furthered the loyalties, deepened the sincerities, kindled the aspirations, magnified the enthusiasms which together are little less than the whole of life. Whatever helpfulness and heartening and upliftment a man brings to his fellow men is decisive of the value of his ministry; and these things are unascertainable, and even if ascertainable, are too sacred for speech. Then, too, he, who tonight ends his ministry among you, owes an accounting not to you but to Him, Whom he has sought to serve in serving you. —STEPHEN S. WISE, 1906

EVEN IN THE LAST WEEKS of his life Stephen Wise was a Lion of Judah. Through the battle-worn body coursed a new strength. He reared the scarred head, set anew the grim jaw, and attacked again on platform and in print.

In the pages of *Opinion*, he published in the next to the last month of his life an answer to the anti-Zionist American Council for Judaism, and their speaker at a meeting in New York, Henry Sloane Coffin, who held "Zionism responsible for the 'all-time low of Christian prestige throughout the vast Moslem world of three hundred and fifty million.'"

In his alliterative style, Wise called the charge "palpably and pitiably untrue." The real culprits, he maintained, were the Mandatory Government of Great Britain, as well as the anti-

Zionist Christians represented by Coffin, who "have shown little concern for the liberation and benefit of the Arab serfs other than to share with them the truths of Christianity." As for the "so-called American Council for Judaism, a minority within a minority," he had only contempt: "Unless it wish to sever itself from the body and soul of the Jewish people, [it] has no right to offer a platform for an impoisoning declaration against the Jews of America and the State of Israel. We know well the world will never identify these cowardly persons with the heroic enterprise of the Jewish State. These, whether they hire or are hirelings, have chosen the ignoble way of self-obliteration at a time when self-redemption lay within their unheroic grasp."

He could still give blows to the Republicans, among whom he had many years earlier counted himself but against whom he now contended. Five weeks before his death, he was given the 1949 Award of Merit of the Decalogue Society of Lawyers in Chicago for his "courageous leadership in defense of the civil rights and human dignity of every man in the land." When he rose to respond, his reserves were drained and his voice quavered. As the audience responded to his quips, he became stronger. He began to tell of meeting President Roosevelt when he was on a bear-shooting trip in the Northwest and of how he had told him about his father, Aaron Wise, who had chosen America as a homeland ten years before becoming an immigrant. Roosevelt had responded, "Then, rabbi, your father was an American even before he came to this land." Wise realized that many in the audience might think he was referring to a more recent Roosevelt and hastened to add: "This was *Theodore* Roosevelt. After all, Franklin Roosevelt never had time to shoot bears. He was too busy shooting Republicans!" When the audience applauded, Wise boomed out with all his former power, "The trouble with Franklin Roosevelt was that he didn't shoot enough Republicans!"

He also challenged the Roman Catholic hierarchy, members of which had, in referring to "atheistic Russia," alluded to what seemed to be an inevitable conflict between the Soviet Union and the nations of the West. His hand shook as he composed a statement to issue to the press, deploring what appeared to be a call for war on the part of some Roman Catholic leaders. There had been many times in his life when he had wanted to challenge the Roman Catholic church which had so often been in positions of power in lands where Jews had suffered persecution, but he had refrained for fear of possible retribution against them. Now, he felt, he must speak out since the peace of the world was involved.

On March 17, twelve hundred people came to the Hotel Astor for the seventy-fifth birthday dinner. Among the many speakers was, of course, Holmes. Aware of Wise's illness and weakness, Holmes, nearing his own seventieth birthday, read aloud a poem of both congratulations and encouragement. Of its six stanzas, three stood out:

I ponder well the time when you were young,
And lifted high a sword of living flame;
You spoke with roll of thunder on your tongue,
And God's own angels gathered where you came.

A rapt Isaiah again, you heard God's word,
"Whom shall I send, My purpose to fulfill?"
And straight and tall, you stood before the Lord,
And cried, "Send me, to do Thy perfect will."

The years have flown—God's banner droops and dips,
And you are weary from the ceaseless fight.
But still the living coal burns on your lips,
And high the sword is pointed to the light.

When Wise responded, his hands trembled as they held the manuscript. He read from the handwritten pages, an expedient to which he had rarely had to resort. Slowly and eloquently he listed what seemed to him achievements in his life, but coupled with them unattained objectives. Foremost among the latter was the defeat of forces opposed to the enhancement of man's dignity and freedom. Those hostile forces, still arrayed against him and his, seemed sometimes more formidable than ever. Yet if granted the time, he would struggle against them. Rising to a new pitch of emotion and bringing the audience to its feet in acclaim, Wise concluded: "I'll fight! I'll fight!! I'll fight!!!"

As his family helped him put on his overcoat and scarf, Wise, worn and spent, turned to Holmes and said, "I should never have tried it, Holmes. I should never have tried it."

Yet later that month he tried still another foray. He went to Boston for a first look at the newly founded Brandeis University and accompanied its president, Abram Sachar, on a tour of the campus in Waltham. It is reported that at a faculty luncheon that day when he sensed tension over the question of salaries, Wise took out his wallet and passed around the pictures of his six grandchildren: Jim's three children—Stephen, Halie, and Debbie—and Justine's three—Stephen, Trudy, and Jonathon. Then he smiled and said: "Gentlemen, you see how many grandchildren you can carry in your wallet, if you don't care about money."

At Ford Hall Forum, where he had first appeared forty-one years earlier, Wise chose as his subject, "My Challenging Years: A Seventy-Fifth Birthday Anniversary Address" and spoke as a father to his children: "I have lived to see the Jewish State. I am too small for the greatness of the mercy which God has shown us." Many in the audience wept. Ford Hall had always had a quasi-religious atmosphere but that Sunday night of March 27, it was more genuinely religious than in all its history, for at the close Wise did something he had never done there before: he gave the benediction in Hebrew.

He returned to New York, went to his physician and said, "Now I'm through. Put me in the hospital." To Justine, speaking in Los Angeles, he wrote, "In a few moments I shall go to the Lenox Hill [Hospital] to get well. Don't worry, speak as you did at F. S. [Free Synagogue]. These two days of rest have helped me not a little. So I'll gain a lot to finish the book and be at Nyack in August!"

Nyack and the chance to rest at the weekend home of Shad and Justine were not to be, for he did not return from the hospital. He was operated upon, but the doctors said they could do little. Each day his vitality ebbed.

Stephen Wise Tulin flew in from Oberlin for a last visit. The grandfather and grandson talked of philosophy, books, Steve's courses at Oberlin, and his plans to study law. Wise gave the boy his briefcase to use at Yale Law School where his father

had taught and his mother had studied. Jim's son, Stephen
A. Wise, gave a blood transfusion when the doctors prescribed
one.

His pain became so intense that the doctor prescribed seda-
tion. Wise, awakened by a noise in the street, emerged from a
coma and startled the nurse by asking her name and thanking
her for having done so much to make him comfortable during
these last days.

In the library of the Jewish Institute of Religion that year, one
of Wise's students had chanced upon a sermon his teacher had
preached at the Free Synagogue at the end of World War I,
thirty years before.

> The adventure of death . . . differs not from any other adven-
> ture of life save that we face the uncertainty of our adventure
> thereunto not being free to choose the hour of the inevitable
> rendezvous. I never resort to the soothing commonplace—what
> all men have endured, we, too, may safely adventure. Rather
> do I ask—who amongst us would wish to escape the greatest of
> adventures? Life is no more truly my birthright than it is my
> right to know that I am about to set forth when the hour strikes.
> As for another, let the adventure of death signify hope unaltering
> and love unafraid; as for self, mine cannot be less than courage
> unequaling and trust unafraid.

Such courage and trust were Wise's. With his two children
at his side, he spoke to them gently and without fear. "Take my
hand, darlings. I am entering the Valley."

Wise had instructed his family that, when he died, they should
look in his wallet for a letter he had prepared some days earlier.
Jim and Justine found:

> I am not tearful or maudlin as I write this, but I am so wretched
> that I would be insensitive and stupid not to write as I do.
> When something happens to me, Ed [Klein] knows about the
> things I prefer for the Service.
>   Ed, of course, is to have charge of the Service, whether at
> the Synagogue House or in Carnegie Hall, where I preached for
> thirty years and with which I became associated during the
> stronger years of my life—or, best of all, in the new building.
>   In view of the large part which The [American Jewish] Con-

gress and Zionism have had in my life, I think that, just as in the
case of Mummie, I would like Dave [Petegorsky] to speak the
word of farewell if he were equal to it. Dave has grown very
dear to me. He knows what it is that I most deeply care for:
the state of Israel and freedom and justice for Jews everywhere.
If an address is to be made, it shall be made by Dave. He has
become very dear to me and he is a loyal and faithful comrade.

I would like a prayer or the reading of a poem by my beloved
friend, Holmes.

You won't see this while I am alive. When you do see it,
I beg you to understand that my release, whenever it comes, is
a great mercy. I am far from well and comfortable. As you
know, I hate to leave you both and Shad and Helen and my
precious grandchildren, but I feel the time is drawing very near
for me to go Home. If God wills, it will mean the reunion of my
spirit with that of Mummie's and you know that I want my dust
to be placed in the niche wherein she lies.

All love forever to you who have taken such wonderful care
of me and will do so, to my end, whenever it is to be. You will
love and care for each other.

Into the Hand of God I commend my spirit. May He continue
to vouchsafe me His grace and mercy.

The next day, April 20, the front page of the New York *Times*
stated: "Wise Lies in State at The Free Synagogue." Lines began
to form early in the day along West 68th Street to Amsterdam
Avenue and over to Columbus Avenue. Thousands of people
gathered to walk into the Free Synagogue and pass by the casket.
They came down the slightly sloping aisle of the sanctuary to
the altar, flanked by United States and Israeli flags, where pulpit
and altar rails were draped in black. Beneath the glass cover of
the casket lay Wise in his customary black broadcloth suit with
a white shirt and black tie. The coffin was, on his instruction, of
plain pine in accordance with the Jewish tradition that required
all men to be equal in death. The only floral piece was a single
spray of daffodils, placed on the coffin by Jim who had picked
the flowers early that morning from his garden in Ridgefield.
The face that had been so grim and determined in his wrath
against injustice was now placid and calm, serene and almost
childlike. In a single afternoon seven thousand five hundred
people, whites, Negroes, and Orientals, stopped by his casket

and either mutely or audibly echoed the gnarled charwoman who walked at the head of the line after an all-day wait on the street and said "God bless his soul."

The telegrams and letters at home piled high. The first expression of sympathy came from the Union of Sleeping Car Porters.

The New York *Times* carried three columns of tributes to Wise, many from groups he had helped to found and foster. Among the many little paragraphs of tributes in the "Deaths" column was a statement from the Armenian Church of North America, signed by its Bishop and the Diocesan Council, expressing "sorrow and a deep feeling of loss for a great humanitarian and friend of the Armenians who will never forget the zeal and the courage with which he drew the attention of the American people to the plight of Armenians after the First World War and was one of the initiators of the great work of relief."

On the afternoon of April 22, three thousand people crowded into Carnegie Hall and fifteen thousand stood outside in a pouring rain. Loud-speakers carried the service.

Edward Klein read Psalms Ninety and One Hundred and Forty-four, and Holmes read from John Milton's "Samson Agonistes" and Matthew Arnold's "Rugby Chapel." Wise's colleagues, Sidney Goldstein and J. X. Cohen, participated; and David Petegorsky gave the eulogy.

Holmes remembered the day of the funeral: "I looked about me and saw the great throng of men and women crowding that vast auditorium as a full tide filled with the sea and I whispered to my soul, 'They knew him for his greatness.' Then the service was done and we marched on to the rain-swept streets and saw crowds of patient witnesses, waiting mile after mile 'through storm and flood,' to pay their last honor to the dead and again my soul whispered to itself, 'These knew him and loved him for his goodness.'"

The funeral entourage left 57th Street and the police gently parted the crowd. Enroute to the cemetery the procession rode through Harlem where thousands upon thousands of Negroes stood on the sidewalks to bid Wise farewell.

Holmes could say, as David said of Jonathan, "I am distressed for you, my brother. . . . Very pleasant have you been to me; your love to me was wonderful, passing the love of women."

32. The Last Puritan

The years will not be many before my powers as a preacher will abate. Then I shall retire— I hope without waiting to be told. I shall take no other church, for I shall want to live to the end with this church, like my wife, as my only love. Rather shall I seek some quiet refuge where my books and pen may be my only solace, and, when I do not read or write, dream happily of the days we had together. And I shall smile at follies, and no longer weep at failures, remembering only how much forgiveness I have had at your good hearts. And I like to think that, in those days of tender recollection, I shall not be ashamed of the record we have written. For whatever the chances and changes of our lot in a world of wild despair, we have striven steadfastly to be "not disobedient unto the heavenly vision."
—JOHN HAYNES HOLMES, 1932

WITH MOHANDAS GANDHI DEAD in January of 1948 and Stephen Wise in April of 1949, John Haynes Holmes had lost two of his chief springs of inspiration and he felt his time for retirement had come. There was no need for "waiting to be told." The only person who told him anything was Madeleine; when asked, she said his seventieth birthday, November 29, 1949, seemed to her a suitable date.

Fortunately, he still had his family intact. Now he could devote more time to his children, Roger and Frances, and his grandchildren, Adria and Janice Holmes and David and Alison Brown. The relationship with his associate, Donald Harrington, was the warmest and most satisfying he had experienced with any colleague and he watched the church flourish under the younger man's leadership.

In the winter of 1948, when almost all of his contemporaries had retired from active careers—save those hardy perennials, Norman Thomas and Roger Baldwin—his doctor warned him he could no longer continue at even the reduced pace of the recent years. On the trip to India a strange tremor had appeared in his hands and limbs, and after his return, physicians diagnosed these as signs of Parkinson's disease.

In the fall of 1948 he had attained his cherished wish, that of completing and dedicating the new edifice of the Community Church. For the first time in seventeen years the congregation had a permanent home on the old site. Some members complained because there was no room for storage and inadequate space for the growing church school, the first time in his memory that the Sunday School had flourished.

The auditorium—or "sanctuary," as some of the oldsters still liked to call it—was all he had ever desired. The seating accommodations, retaining the dignity of a pew, were individual seats with deep indigo-blue cushions in oak frames and carried bronze memorial plaques, many of them in memory of the liberals and radicals with whom he had worked across the years. The church auditorium had no altar; and, in place of a reredos, the architect had designed a marble backdrop nine feet in height and thirty feet in width to serve as a background for the oak pulpit. The Sunday that Holmes asked for the gift of a pulpit in memory of Gandhi, he was startled when a visitor from India came to him immediately after the service and pledged the needed sum.

To Holmes the new building's red brick walls, unbroken surfaces, and straight lines had a chaste beauty wholly in keeping with the lofty purposes of the Community Church he emphasized in the dedication sermon: "Like a school, a library, a museum, this church should exist for the general betterment of the community, for I conceive of a church as a public institution which belongs to all the people and may be used by all the people."

One pew was dedicated to him in the church he had sought so long; and the rebuilt adjacent building on East 35th Street, used for parish-house purposes, was to be named the John Haynes Holmes House.

In the spring of 1949, after he had announced his resignation effective November 29, the congregation of the Community Church did not hesitate to choose Donald Harrington as successor. The unanimous vote was cast on the day of the tenth anniversary of his marriage to Vilma Szantho, first woman to be ordained to the ministry in central Europe.

On the last Sunday in November, 1949, Holmes gave the congregation "An Account of My Ministry" and welcomed his successor to an office "abundantly earned and abundantly deserved." Turning to Harrington, Holmes said, "Don, this is a solemn moment in my life. I am surrendering, on the eve of the Psalmist's span of years, my most precious possession. Like Cornelia, the Roman matron, who, when asked to show her jewels, presented her two sons, Tiberius and Gaius, so I present my jewels, this congregation, which I can keep no longer. It is grievous for me to give these people up. But my comfort is that I am placing them in your tender and loving care."

Turning then to the congregation, Holmes concluded, "So does life run its blessed course, with no regrets, but always with exceeding great joy."

But it was not good-by. Holmes stayed on in retirement and extended his ministry to other areas. He was to write more hymns, additional articles and book reviews, sermons and books. Living in an apartment on the fifteenth floor of Hotel Ten Park Avenue and going each day to his study on the eleventh floor, he continued to work. Often he was needed for funerals and weddings; the families first "cleared" with an understanding Harrington and then asked Holmes to officiate.

He wrote more books. To Gandhi he paid tribute in *My Gandhi*, modeled after William Dean Howells' *My Mark Twain*. Then he set to work on his autobiography, *I Speak for Myself*. From 1952 until 1958, he wrote and rewrote. Although his infirmities increased, owing to the spread of Parkinson's disease, the manuscript went well.

The writing was interrupted in the summer of 1953 by an attack on him from the House Un-American Activities Committee. Releasing uncorroborated testimony by four former Communist Party officials, who underwent no cross-examination and never confronted the men they accused, the Committee, in part encouraged by Senator Joseph McCarthy, included Holmes among those who were said to have helped the Communist Party infiltrate American churches. The accused persons were neither heard by the Committee nor even notified of the accusations.

Holmes was alleged to have been named, along with Stephen Wise and Judah Magnes, in testimony said to have been given primarily by Benjamin Gitlow, who for ten years had been a member of the Communist Party, U.S.A., and at one time served as its general secretary. Ironically, this was the same Gitlow whom both Holmes and Wise had sought to have Governor Alfred E. Smith pardon almost thirty years earlier.

Holmes, shaken, but not for long, answered the Committee's ill-considered, baseless charges:

> I am primarily concerned at this moment in protecting the beloved names of Rabbi Stephen S. Wise and Dr. Judah L. Magnes from the vile charges brought against them, since they are dead and cannot therefore speak. From intimate contact with these great rabbis through more than forty years, I know and can testify without reservation that Wise and Magnes were absolutely innocent of the offenses alleged.
>
> As for myself, I view the attacks upon me with contempt. They are as ridiculous as they are false. I am led to set against them the conduct of my forty-four years as a minister of religion in New York City. If the record and reputation of those years cannot save me from irresponsible assault, then am I indeed the unhappiest of men.

The National Association for the Advancement of Colored People and the American Civil Liberties Union immediately refuted the Committee's accusations; and Holmes' Board of Trustees responded bluntly and forthrightly in his defense.

Bishop G. Bromley Oxnam, who had been subjected to similar unjust and inaccurate charges by a Congressional committee that year and had successfully refuted his accusers and their accusations in a dramatic confrontation in Washington, deplored the fact that the testimony had cast suspicion on three great religious leaders, two of whom could not answer because they were dead. Oxnam wrote in his *I Protest:*

> The nation possessed no more distinguished and devoted re-
> ligious leaders than Dr. John Haynes Holmes, Rabbi Stephen S.
> Wise and Rabbi Judah L. Magnes. . . . Rabbi Wise was a
> patriot and a great humanitarian, the friend and adviser of
> American Presidents, a man internationally known and respected,
> a religious leader loved by Christian and Jew alike. . . . Would
> that the practices of this Committee might be subjected to the
> devastating logic of Rabbi Wise's towering intellect and the
> nation once again hear his courageous and prophetic voice, and
> feel again the power of his personality. It is such as he who will
> save us from the practices that threaten the free way of life.

Some weeks later Benjamin Gitlow wrote a letter to the Peek-skill (N.Y.) *Evening Star* to say: "The charge was not made that these men were ever Communists or members of the Communist Party."

Yet such false accusations reflected the temper of America at the time, a temper which disturbed Holmes, for it was indicative of a tide of reaction against the religious and social liberalism of the previous generations, especially of the half century of his own active ministry. Such reaction he found as well in theological circles in the obscurantism of "neo-orthodoxy" and the current revival of Calvinism. Like his friend Halford Luccock of the Yale Divinity School, he deplored "the poison gas of Continental theology." Holmes termed it "speculation run riot with the human mind, fancy making folly of the phenomena of life, a reflection of man's despair, yet unreal and unimportant."

Remaining a theist and rejecting nontheistic humanism, Holmes invoked his belief in both God and man: "In man is the highest expression of the Godhead and in the exaltation of man the all-sufficient revelation of the Most High." Saddened to think that men were now living in an age of denial and doubt, he condemned the neo-Calvinists

> as presenting the worst instead of the best in human nature,
> for to them man is a monstrous creature. He knows his sinful

condition, and knows, also, his utter inability to do anything about it. The result is an incurable wickedness which overcomes all virtue. It is damnation come again, with our World Wars the dreadful witness of man's plight. That a theology of this kind can long survive is not to be believed. It may seem to flourish for a time, especially under conditions such as prevail today. It may leave in its wake a litter of queer and sterile faiths, as witnessed by the poisonous cult of Immoralism. But in the end the true spirit of man will assert itself and save the world anew.

When, in 1958, he was reminded by a friend of the tenth anniversary of Gandhi's assassination, he said he felt that "the greatest thing that has happened since Gandhi's death is the work of Martin Luther King, who has taken the whole law and gospel of Gandhi's teaching and proved its worth anew."

In his eighth decade, awards came to him from a wide variety of organizations: the Stephen Wise Free Synagogue, Congregation B'nai Jeshurun, the American Civil Liberties Union, the League for Industrial Democracy, the Fellowship of Reconciliation, the National Association for the Advancement of Colored People, the Congress of Industrial Organizations, the American Unitarian Association, the American Christian Palestine Committee, and many others.

Of all the awards and prizes one was lacking: an honorary degree from Harvard University. Other colleges, universities, and seminaries (the Hebrew Union College-Jewish Institute of Religion, St. Lawrence, Meadville, Rollins, Benares in India) had honored him, but not his alma mater, save by the invitation to give the 1946 Ingersoll Lectures on "Immortality." Friends who asked the Harvard administration that he be considered received only a polite acknowledgment. No reasons were ever given for the failure of Harvard to honor one of its most distinguished graduates; but some hazarded the guess that perhaps Charles W. Eliot had been irritated by Holmes' pacifism, A. Lawrence Lowell angered by his defense of Sacco and Vanzetti, and James Conant nettled by Holmes' attack on the scientist's secularism and lack of interest in the Divinity School. Holmes rarely admitted the disappointment, but it hurt.

He knew his days of preaching and speaking were over; seldom was he persuaded to enter a pulpit. On one occasion, in 1956, he returned to the chancel to attend the ordination and installation of his grandson David Brown as minister of the Unitarian Church in West Upton, Massachusetts. He and Donald Harrington left after church on a Sunday afternoon and drove from New York. Delayed by the Thanksgiving weekend traffic, they arrived at the New England church and found the Unitarian congregation, which had been waiting for an hour, singing the stirring Lutheran chorale, "A Mighty Fortress Is Our God." As an antidote to the Reformer's motif, Holmes' hymns were sung. At the close of the service he pronounced the benediction, a prayer of his own composition.

Now life was quieter. True, the correspondence was still heavy, but the pressure was no longer intense. He received twenty-five to thirty letters a day; and, of course, every one had to be answered. Later in the day would come a rest period and time for reading. He still balked at the afternoon rest period: "Why should a man rest? Daytime is for wakefulness, not sleep."

As his illness became worse, the once lithe and straight body became bowed. The swift, sure walk became unsteady. On several occasions he fell, often suffering bruises that lingered or wounds that bled. Then, in March of 1959, co-ordination suddenly failed; he fell directly against the edge of the stair that separated the entrance hall from the living room. He had escaped disaster on sea and land, had seemed to have guardian angels hovering about him for almost eighty years; but now he broke his hip in his own apartment. In the hospital, the doctors drugged him, set the hip, and warned the family he might not last long. The news spread. Letters and cards by the hundreds streamed in and each was carefully acknowledged, this time by his secretary. Yet he rallied because there was always the Maine Coast for the summer. He wanted to get back to Kennebunk Beach. This hope held until early June when the doctor ordered: "No summer in Maine!"

In New York he stayed for one of the hottest summers the city had ever known and with no relief from the air conditioner he

could not abide: "Artificial and noisy and uncomfortable." Not
at all like Kennebunk Beach.

He had, however, another medicine, a new book on which he
began to work. For many years he had written hymns, many of
them outstanding. When hymnals were revised, the best remained; the excellent became the permanent.

Henry Wilder Foote, an astute judge of hymns for the free
church and the Social Gospel, urged Holmes to gather his best
and add explanatory paragraphs. The Beacon Press in Boston
gave him a contract; and, in the torrid summer of 1959, Holmes
wrote brief, almost too brief, paragraphs about the dramatic
circumstances that led to their composition, of the creative
process that enabled a man to write lines congregations wanted
to sing.

The Collected Hymns of John Haynes Holmes was published
in time for the 1960 May Meeting of the American Unitarian
Association in Boston, the conference which completed the
thirteen-year period of negotiations to unite Unitarians and Uni-
versalists. The audience listened to Donald Harrington hail "a
new world faith," taking its place alongside Protestantism,
Catholicism, and Judaism: "We are not less Christian but more."

Holmes' darkest day was May 28, 1961, when Madeleine died.
That morning he had been taken by wheel chair to help Donald
Harrington unveil the fourteen-foot statue of the prophet Isaiah,
designed by the sculptor Moissaye Marans. Placed on a pedestal
twenty-five feet above the pavement outside the Community
Church, the towering statue dominated the entrance to the
church on East 35th Street near Park Avenue. In the evening,
almost as though she knew something meaningful and important
for Holmes had now been taken care of and her responsibility
thus fulfilled, Madeleine, ill for only a few days, quietly passed
away.

A year later, John Haynes Holmes joined his children, Roger
and Frances, in dedicating a marble tablet in her memory in the
lovely Memorial Chapel of the Community Church, wrote a
special hymn for the occasion, and helped to prepare the inscription:

RADIANT WITH GOODNESS AND GENEROSITY
ZESTFUL IN LIVING
COURAGEOUS IN TRIAL
NONE KNEW HER BUT TO LOVE HER
NOR NAMED HER BUT TO PRAISE

Uneventfully and irenically, he now lives in retirement, still the Puritan without the Calvinist theology. He retains dignity. He has a high sense of personal responsibility: attention to details, punctuality, preparation of long and thoughtful letters with exactitude of diction. He maintains a stalwart independence of thought and will not succumb to the passing enthusiasms of the hour, whether humanism or existentialism, eclecticism or cynicism. Steadfastly he opposes smoking and drinking. He deplores the fact that the machine age robs life of the personal element and suggests that Gandhi was right in opposing the evil trend of the machine.

At heart he is still the New Englander: rigorous in his thinking and ethical code, convinced that God moves in both nature and history and that men are made for destinies higher than those upon this earth.

In these final years, during his lingering illness, he has often recalled lines he wrote a half century ago, words that keep his hope aglow:

From Life to Death!
An eager breath,
A battle for the true and good,
An agony upon the rood;
A dark'ning of the light—
And night!

From Death to Life!
A peace from strife;
A voyage o'er an ocean wide
That moves from shore to shore its tide;
A passing of the night—
And light!

Postscript: John Haynes Holmes did not live to see a finished copy of this book, for he died on April 3, 1964, the very day the first copies came off the printing press.

Acknowledgments and Sources

I AM INDEBTED TO THE LIBRARIES OF: the Meadville Theological School, Chicago, Ill.; Union Theological Seminary, New York, N. Y.; The Congregational House, Boston, Mass.; Hebrew Union College-Jewish Institute of Religion in New York City and Cincinnati, Ohio; New York State Education Building, Albany, N. Y.; and to the New York City Public Library; Boston Public Library; Lucy Scribner Library, Skidmore College, Saratoga Springs, N. Y.; Crandall Library, Glens Falls, N. Y.; and Hillview Library, Diamond Point, N. Y.

To my wife, Phyllis Gierlotka Voss, I am grateful for encouragement and guidance; she aided me in many ways.

To Justine Wise Polier, James Waterman Wise, Frances Holmes Brown, Roger Wellington Holmes, Edward E. Klein, and Donald Szantho Harrington, I express my thanks for their constant interest and the loan of important documents.

I deeply appreciate assistance across the years from Benjamin Abrams, the Mayer family, Charles Rosenbloom, Meyer and Hy Sobiloff, Dewey Stone, and Jack Weiler.

Corrections and suggestions have been given by June Rossbach Bingham, Dorothy Boggs Bolton, Stanley F. Chyet, Gerold Frank, S. Michael Gelber, Sonja Petra Karsen, Abraham I. Katsch, A. William Loos, George E. Moesel, Sulamith Schwartz Nardi, Joseph Saidel, Judd L. Teller, Carlyn Voss, and Daniel Day Williams.

Files of correspondence with Rabbi Wise and Dr. Holmes were made available by Felix Frankfurter, Frederick Hankinson, Harwood Hill, Edith Lovejoy Pierce, the late Henrietta Posner, Flora Schneider, Upton Sinclair, Philip Slomowitz, Mortimer Smith, Ida Sturtevant, Henrietta Van Buskirk, and Gertrude Winslow.

Over many years I have talked about these two men to a host of friends, several of whom are no longer alive; and the memory of the stimulating conversations and correspondence impels me to thank at least these: Robert Adamson, Melvin Arnold, Roger Baldwin, Philip S. Bernstein, Joseph S. G. Bolton, Sherwood Eddy,* Frederick May Eliot,* Harry Emerson Fosdick, Felix Frankfurter, Herbert

Friedman, S. Ralph Harlow, Edward Kiev, John Howland Lathrop, John Howard Melish, William Stuart Nelson, Reinhold Niebuhr, David Petegorsky,* Charles Francis Potter,* Bernard G. Richards, Eleanor Roosevelt,* Joseph Shubow, Norman Thomas, Paul Tillich, and Harry Wolfson. None of these friends should be held accountable for errors in fact or judgment which may persist in this book.

To Gail Donovan, Irma Fisk, Hazel Ridout, and Marion Snyder, I am grateful for typing drafts of the manuscript.

I am indebted to the Yaddo Corporation of Saratoga Springs and to its executive director, Elizabeth Ames, for the opportunity to work in the quiet and solitude of that beautiful retreat.

As I look back over the twelve years since this project was conceived, I sympathize with James Boswell who finished his volumes on Samuel Johnson and mused in his foreword:

> The labor and anxious attention with which I have collected and arranged the material . . . will hardly be conceived by those who read them with careless facility. The stretch of mind and prompt assiduity by which so many conversations were preserved, I myself, at some distance of time, contemplate with wonder; and I must be allowed to suggest, that the nature of the work, in other respects, as it consists of innumerable detached particulars, all which, even the most minute, I have spared no pains to ascertain with a scrupulous authenticity, has occasioned a degree of trouble far beyond that of any other species of composition. Were I to detail the books which I have consulted, and the inquiries I have found it necessary to make by various channels, I should probably be thought ridiculously ostentatious.

There are, however, certain books and periodicals, which deserve mention, especially for those who may want to carry the inquiry further. A listing of these follows.

PROLOGUE: IN THE BEGINNING

The details of Stephen Wise's debut at the Hudson Theatre were provided by his friends and family, his autobiographical *Challenging Years* (New York, 1950), and various contributors to *The Diamond Jubilee Journal* (1949), "dedicated to Dr. Stephen S. Wise on the occasion of his 75th birthday." The descriptive information concern-

* Deceased

ing John Haynes Holmes' first Sunday in New York was derived from personal interviews with him, several autobiographical sermons during the intervening decades, and from his autobiography, *I Speak for Myself* (New York, 1958). Additional items of interest concerning the city and its events have been found in issues of the New York *Times* of those weeks in the winter and spring of 1907.

1. THE GOLDEN DOOR

The biographical data concerning Wise in this and subsequent chapters are available in (1) *Challenging Years* and the "Biographical Note" by Justine Wise Polier and James Waterman Wise in the opening pages of that book, (2) the foreword by them in their compilation of *The Personal Letters of Stephen Wise* (Boston, 1956), and (3) personal notes found among his papers after his death in 1949. Of Aaron Wise, his son, Stephen, wrote movingly in *What I Owe My Father,* edited by Sidney Strong (New York, 1930).

2. "CHAI" MEANS EIGHTEEN—AND LIFE

The eighteen-year-old Stephen Wise was described as a promising pulpit orator in a news item of the *American Israelite* on November 22, 1892. Biographical data concerning Rabbi Adolf Jellinek and his contemporaries, as well as of many of the Jewish leaders mentioned in this book, may be found in *The Universal Jewish Encyclopedia* (New York, 1939). The spiritual leader of Congregation B'nai Jeshurun for the forty years from 1920 to 1960, Israel Goldstein, presents the history of the synagogue and its rabbis in *A Century of Judaism in New York* (privately published in 1930, with foreword by Cyrus Adler).

3. BASEL, LOUISE, AND THE NORTHWEST

Herzl's *"Wenn Ihr wollt ist es kein Märchen"* is a quotation from his novel *Altneuland, [Old-New Land]* (1901). William James of Harvard wrote an appreciation of Thomas Davidson in an article in *Memories and Studies* (Boston, 1911); and Morris R. Cohen, one of Davidson's disciples, composed an informative sketch about him for *Cyclopedia of Education,* Vol. II (New York, 1911). The letter from Thomas Davidson to Felix Adler, and many other items used in this and subsequent chapters are in the Stephen Wise Archives at Brandeis

University, Waltham, Massachusetts. Here may be found the news clippings concerning Wise's Zionist activities and the Cooper Union meetings of February, 1900.

4. EMANU-EL REJECTED

Not only the New York *Times* but also Wise's letters to relatives and his own recollections, especially in *Challenging Years* and *The Personal Letters of Stephen Wise*, provide material for this account. To secure a balanced picture of Louis Marshall, a principal figure in this episode, the reader should consult the two-volume work, *Selected Papers and Addresses of Louis Marshall*, edited by Charles Reznikoff (Philadelphia, 1957). Wise respected Marshall's sterling qualities: "I can forgive Louis Marshall almost anything because he is such a good Jew!" The quotations are excerpts from Louise's letters to Leo and Jennie Waterman, and from Stephen Wise's sermons in bound editions of printed sermons entitled *Beth Israel Pulpit* and available in the Library of the Hebrew Union College—Jewish Institute of Religion, 40 West 68th Street, New York, N.Y.

5. DREADING TO LEAVE AN ILLITERATE MINISTRY

The biographical material was assembled from the sources used for the Prologue and from personal interviews and correspondence with John Haynes Holmes and members of his family. The lives of Theodore Parker, Minot J. Savage, and other eminent Unitarians in this and later chapters are described in *Heralds of a Liberal Faith*, edited by Samuel Atkins Eliot (Boston, 1910, Vols. I, II, and III; and 1952, Vol. IV). *Theodore Parker: Yankee Crusader* by Henry Steele Commager (Boston, 1936; second edition, Boston, 1947, 1960) is still the most felicitous biography of the man Holmes called "the greatest religious figure in nineteenth-century America." Francis Greenwood Peabody's *Reminiscences of Present Day Saints* (Boston and New York, 1927) and Van Wyck Brooks' *The Flowering of New England: 1815–1865* and *New England: Indian Summer 1865–1915* are helpful for vignettes of leading lights of that era and region (New York, 1936 and 1940).

6. DANVERS AND DORCHESTER

The incidents of these three years (1904–1906) were culled from both published and unpublished portions of John Haynes Holmes' autobiography, *I Speak for Myself*, and supplemented by personal interviews with him. Louis M. and Helene S. Hacker's *The Shaping of the American Tradition* (New York, 1947) gives the important selections from Josiah Strong's *Our Country* and from scores of other significant documents in American history over more than three centuries. The bound copies of the "Weekly Calendar" of the Third Unitarian Society of Dorchester, Massachusetts, and of Holmes' first book of sermons, *The Old and the New*, are in the possession of the Community Church of New York City, 40 East 35th Street, New York 10, N. Y. The definitive work on Robert Collyer is, of course, *The Life and Letters of Robert Collyer*, the two volumes by John Haynes Holmes (New York, 1917). Some of the same material in much briefer form is to be found in *The Messiah Pulpit* of 1912–1913 (December 8); 1913–1914 (December 7); and 1914–1915 (April 11). The *Year Books of the Church of the Messiah* from the years 1907 to 1915 contain many references to Dr. Collyer and his work.

7. YOUR YOUNG MEN SHALL SEE VISIONS

In the Jewish Publication Society edition of the Bible (to which Stephen Wise contributed the translation of the Book of Judges), the epigraph from the Book of Joel is cited as chapter three, verse one. Material for this chapter was provided by (1) interviews with Dr. Holmes whose memories from a half century ago are startlingly clear; (2) recollections of the Wise children, James and Justine, of their parents' recounting of those days; and (3) thoughts expressed in *The Free Synagogue Pulpit* and *The Messiah Pulpit*, as well as in Wise's letters to the congregation of the Free Synagogue and Holmes' annual reports to the Church of the Messiah during the years 1907–1910. The data and quotations are taken from documents available at the Stephen Wise Free Synagogue, *The Synagogue and Social Welfare* by Sidney E. Goldstein (New York, 1956), and from the 1907–1908 *Year Book of the Church of the Messiah* and *The Messiah Pulpit* of 1908–1909. Further information about the development of the Social Gospel on the lives of its principal figures may be found in *The Early Days of Christian Socialism in America* by James Dombrowski (New York, 1936); *American Protestantism and Social Issues: 1919–1939* by Robert Moats Miller (Chapel Hill, 1958); *The Rise of the Social Gospel in American Protestantism* by C. H. Hopkins (New Haven, 1940); *The Course of American Democratic Thought* by Ralph H. Gabriel (New Haven, 1940); *The Genesis of the Social Gospel* by

C. C. McCown (New York, 1929); and *The Background of the Social Gospel in America* by Visser t'Hofft (Haarlem, 1928). The purpose and program of the Ford Hall Forum are described in *Democracy in the Making*, a symposium edited by George W. Coleman (Boston, 1911), and in *Challenge of the Forum* by Reuben L. Lurie (Boston, 1930).

8. A SOCIAL GOSPEL

The epigraph by Walter Rauschenbusch at the beginning of this chapter is taken from the preface to his *Prayers of the Social Awakening* (Boston, 1910). The *Year Books of the Church of the Messiah* (*1907–1918*) and the *Year Books of the Community Church* (*1919–1930*), as well as *The Messiah Pulpit* (*1907–1918*) and *The Community Pulpit* (*1919–1949*), contain the data and dates, comments and convictions of John Haynes Holmes noted in this chapter. A sympathetic, often adulatory, treatment of Holmes' thought may be found in Robert Hendrick Budrie's *An Examination of the Religious Presuppositions and the Ethical and Social Concerns of John Haynes Holmes as Revealed in his Writings* (New York, Union Theological Seminary, dissertation on behalf of a degree for Master of Sacred Theology, 1956). A scholarly work on the precursors and contemporaries of Minot Savage and Robert Collyer is *Yankee Reformers* by Arthur Mann (Boston, 1954); the extensive bibliography in this lucid volume lists a legion of books about social settlements and the social reform movement of the time.

9. I, THE LORD, LOVE JUSTICE

The Herbert Croly quotation is taken from his book *The Promise of American Life* (New York, 1909). The founding of the National Association for the Advancement of Colored People is described in *The Walls Came Tumbling Down* by Mary White Ovington (New York, 1947) and *Fight for Freedom* by Langston Hughes (New York, 1962); various publications of the N.A.A.C.P., 20 West 40th Street, New York, N.Y.; *The Quest for Social Justice: 1898–1914* by Harold Underwood Faulkner (New York, 1931); and *The Muckrakers* by Arthur and Lila Weinberg (New York, 1961). The *Year Books of the Church of the Messiah* for 1909–1910–1911 and the engagement books from the study of Stephen Wise give the schedules of the men for those days.

10. TO PUBLISH GOOD TIDINGS

The quotation by William James at the beginning of this chapter is on page 91 of *The Varieties of Religious Experience* (New York, 1902). The letters objecting to Holmes' department, "The Modern Church," are on pages 61, 87, and 105-106 of *The Unitarian Advance*, Vol. I, No. 3 (New York, November, 1910). The background of the Social Gospel is given in the books cited for Chapter 7. The two most significant works of the movement are Walter Rauschenbusch's *Christianity in the Social Crisis* and *Christianizing the Social Order* (New York, 1907 and 1912, respectively). The union services of the Free Synagogue, the Church of the Divine Paternity (Universalist), and the Church of the Messiah (Unitarian) are described in *The Unitarian Advance*, Vol. II, No. 5 (January, 1912), pp. 139, 140, 164. The story of Convocation Week at the Meadville Theological School is told on pages 228-229 of *The Unitarian Advance*, Vol. I, No. 7 (March, 1911); and the several quotations from Holmes' addresses, as well as the critical comment about his book, *The Revolutionary Function of the Modern Church* (New York, 1912), are found in subsequent issues of *The Unitarian Advance*. The experiment at the Labor Temple in New York City, appreciatively yet critically appraised by Holmes, is described by its founder Charles Stelzle in his autobiography, *A Son of the Bowery* (New York, 1926). *The Triangle Fire* by Leon Stein (New York, 1963) tells the story of that tragedy, as do also accounts in the New York *Times* of March 26, 1911, and following days. Two contemporary books, dealing with more recent years but giving excellent background for this chapter, are the Robert Moats Miller volume on *American Protestantism and Social Issues,* mentioned earlier, and *The Protestant Search for Political Realism, 1919-1941* by Donald Burton Meyer (Berkeley and Los Angeles, 1960); other valuable interpretations are *We Are Not Divided* by John A. Hutchison (New York, 1941) and *The Decline and Revival of the Social Gospel* by Paul Carter (Ithaca, 1956). The work of liberals and radicals in the first part of the twentieth century has been described by many participants: Charles Edward Russell, *Bare Hands and Stone Walls* (New York, 1933); Ida Tarbell, *All in the Day's Work* (New York, 1939); Frederic Howe, *The Confessions of a Reformer* (New York, 1925); Upton Sinclair, *American Outposts: A Book of Reminiscences* (New York, 1932); Oswald G. Villard, *Fighting Years* (New York, 1942), etc. The incident of Justice Hughes' asking

Stephen Wise to release the statement to the press is described in Vol. I (p. 300) of *Charles Evans Hughes* by Merlo Pusey (New York, 1951) and in the New York *Times* of June 21, 1912.

11. IF I FORGET THEE, O JERUSALEM

The various references to the Free Synagogue were found in articles in the New York *Evening Post* and New York *Sun* during those years, especially the article in the New York *Evening Post* for Saturday, September 4, 1915, as well as a special publication by the Free Synagogue of "Reports Read at the Seventh Annual Meeting, April 7, 1914 and Addresses Delivered at the Seventh Anniversary Celebration, Carnegie Hall, May 3, 1914." The story of how John Haynes Holmes wrote his greatest hymn, "The Voice of God Is Calling," is told in his autobiography *I Speak for Myself* (New York, 1958). Further information about Judah L. Magnes is available in *For Zion's Sake* by Norman Bentwich (Philadelphia, 1954). Many sidelights on Stephen Wise from 1913–1917 are to be found in *The Personal Letters of Stephen Wise* (Boston, 1956). Other matters are dealt with in several chapters of his autobiography *Challenging Years* (New York, 1949). A critical but appreciative treatment of the American Jewish Committee was written by C. Bezalel Sherman, in the *Jewish Frontier* of April, 1957, while two enlightening articles about the origin of the American Jewish Congress, "Birth of Congress" and "Forty Years Ago: Birth of the American Jewish Congress," both by Bernard G. Richards, are to be found in the *Congress Weekly* of December 20, 1948, and November 24, 1958, respectively. The account of Henry Morgenthau's address, "Palestine and Zionism," was taken from *The Day* for June 23, 1916. References to the Church of the Messiah and to Holmes' activities are found in the *Year Books of the Church of the Messiah* from 1913 to 1917.

12. WHY DO THE NATIONS RAGE?

The epigraph by Walter Rauschenbusch is an excerpt from his prayer against war in *Prayers of the Social Awakening* (Boston, 1910). Data for this chapter are to be found not only in the books and periodicals mentioned earlier—John Haynes Holmes' *I Speak for Myself, The Unitarian,* and *The Unitarian Advance, Unity,* the *Christian Register,* and the New York *Times*—but also in *The Conscientious Objector in America* by Norman Thomas (New York, 1923); *Preachers*

Present Arms by Ray H. Abrams (New York, 1933); *New Wars for Old* by John Haynes Holmes (New York, 1916); *The Fight for Peace* by Devere Allen (New York, 1930); and a Bachelor of Divinity thesis (1948), by Kenneth Jackson Smith, entitled *John Haynes Holmes: Opponent of War* and available at the Meadville Theological School, Chicago, Ill.

13. A HOUSE OF PRAYER FOR ALL PEOPLE

The credo about "The Church Universal" by Keshab Chandra Sen is quoted by Lewis Mumford in his *The Conduct of Life* (New York, 1951). The activities and writings of John Haynes Holmes during these years are described in the many references to him and articles by him in the pages of *The World Tomorrow* and *Unity*, as well as in the *Year Books of the Church of the Messiah* and various sermons in *The Messiah Pulpit*. The decisive meetings at the time of Holmes' call to the Abraham Lincoln Centre in the winter of 1918–1919 were described by Holmes and several people who were present, especially Marion Snyder, a member of the church. Oswald Garrison Villard's comments on Stephen Wise's wartime employment are in his autobiography, *Fighting Years;* and Wise's story of those days is to be found in his *Challenging Years.* Upton Sinclair's critical treatment of organized religion, *The Profits of Religion,* was published in 1918, and John Haynes Holmes' letter to him about the book was loaned by Indiana University's Lilly Library.

14. AS OF RIGHT AND NOT ON SUFFERANCE

The title of this chapter is an oft-quoted phrase in the 1922 White Paper on Palestine issued by Winston Churchill as Colonial Secretary. The assurance to Stephen Wise by Woodrow Wilson was recalled by Bernard G. Richards, a member of the delegation of the American Jewish Congress to the White House on March 2, 1919, and is recorded in an interview by the Oral History Research Office at Columbia University. It is to be found in a slightly different version in *Challenging Years* by Stephen S. Wise. The Zangwill proposal was set forth in an exchange of correspondence between him and Lucien Wolf in December, 1918. The dates and conversations of Wise in London and Paris in late 1918-early 1919 are to be found in his own personal notes, as well as in memoranda prepared by him and by his associates as reports to colleagues in America.

15. THE LABORER IS WORTHY

Wise's sermons were published in *The Free Synagogue Pulpit.* In 1920, the Inter-Church World Movement published its *Report on the Steel Strikes of 1919,* and, in 1921, the same publisher, Harcourt, Brace & Co., issued a sequel: *Public Opinion on the Steel Strike.* The Iron and Steel Institute attacked the report in *An Analysis of the Inter-Church World Movement Report on the Steel Strike* (New York, 1923). Valuable interpretations of the *Report* of the Inter-Church World Movement were published in the *Christian Century, Nation, Christian Advocate, Survey, New Republic,* etc., in 1920 and 1921.

16. WHAT DOTH THE LORD REQUIRE OF THEE?

The quotations from the letters of Stephen Wise come from *The Personal Letters of Stephen Wise* and many unpublished letters, as well as from his other books, particularly *How to Face Life* (New York, 1915) and *Child Versus Parent* (New York, 1922). Some of the problems Wise had to face in the Jewish community are listed with a mordant pen by Maurice Samuels in *You Gentiles* (New York, 1924) and *Jews on Approval* (New York, 1932). The plans of the Free Synagogue for 1921–1922 were described in an article by Stephen S. Wise in the *Jewish Tribune* and by adjacent news items in the issue of April 15, 1921. The letter to Zona Gale was loaned through the courtesy of the Wisconsin Historical Society, Madison, Wisconsin. Holmes' religious outlook of that time is described in his books, particularly *New Churches for Old* (New York, 1922) and several sermons, especially "Jesus, the Revolutionist" (November, 1920) and "What God Means to Me" (March 1921), and in his chapter, "A Struggling God," in a symposium, *My Idea of God,* edited by Joseph Fort Newton (Boston, 1926).

17. WHO IS THE GREATEST MAN IN THE WORLD?

The quotations about Mohandas Gandhi were taken from "Who Is the Greatest Man in the World Today?" a sermon of April 10, 1921; "I Meet Gandhi," a sermon delivered October 11, 1931; and various sermons through the intervening years, including "The Dilemma of the Moral Life" (1931). Additional sources were Holmes' autobiography, *I Speak for Myself* and his book, *My Gandhi* (New York,

1953), dedicated to "Jawaharlal Nehru, Friend and Follower of Gandhi, Greatest and Noblest of Modern Statesmen." The article by Gilbert Murray, "The Soul As It Is," is to be found in the *Hibbert Journal*, Vol. XVI, No. 2, pp. 191-201. Stephen Wise's criticism of Gandhi's views on Zionism was published in the *Jewish Chronicle* (London), October 30, 1931. His address when the Community Church awarded its medal to Mahatma Gandhi was printed in *The Community Pulpit*, No. 18, April 24, 1932.

18. HE HATH HOLPEN HIS PEOPLE ISRAEL

The various letters quoted in this chapter were either in the Stephen Wise Archives at Brandeis University, Waltham, Massachusetts, or in the American Jewish Archives at the Hebrew Union College-Jewish Institute of Religion in Cincinnati, Ohio. Information concerning the founding of the Jewish Institute of Religion in New York City and Wise's relationship to it was given by letters, articles, and conversations with many of his former students. The sermons by Stephen Wise referred to were in *The Free Synagogue Pulpit*, Vol. VI (1921–1922), Vol. VII (1922-1923), and Vol. VIII (1926-1927). Other books of interest for this chapter are two biographies by Norman Bentwich, *Solomon Schechter* (Philadelphia, 1938) and *Judah L. Magnes* (Philadelphia, 1954), and the biography *Israel Zangwill* by Joseph Leftwich (New York, 1957).

19. RIGHTEOUSNESS AS A MIGHTY STREAM

Many items in this chapter come from correspondence in the files of Stephen Wise and in *The Personal Letters of Stephen Wise*, as well as in the files of the Hebrew Union College-Jewish Institute of Religion; letters loaned by Mrs. Gertrude Winslow, secretary of the Community Church of Boston for many years; and the *Year Books of the Community Church* of New York for 1924 and 1925. The controversy about Wise's sermon, "Jesus, the Jew," is described in his *Challenging Years* and more detailed information comes from the New York *Times*. The activities of the American Civil Liberties Union and its involvement in the Scopes trial, as well as in the Sacco-Vanzetti case (dealt with further in Chapter Twenty), are described in *Education of an American Liberal* by Lucille Milner (New York, 1954); *Trial by Prejudice* and *Let Freedom Ring* by Arthur Garfield Hays (New York, 1928); *Six Days or Forever?* by Ray Ginger (Boston, 1958); *The Case of Sacco and Vanzetti* by Felix Frankfurter (Boston, 1927); and

The Legacy of Sacco and Vanzetti by George Louis Joughin and Edmund M. Morgan (New York, 1948). Among the many books on Prohibition and the Eighteenth Amendment one still stands out: *Pressure Politics* by Peter H. Odegard (New York, 1928). The shifting scenes in American life of that time are portrayed by John Higham in *Strangers in the Land* (Brunswick, New Jersey, 1955).

20. DESPISED AND REJECTED OF MEN

The letters by John Haynes Holmes to Mrs. Gertrude Winslow were loaned by Mrs. Winslow. Many other items came from the files of Stephen Wise and John Haynes Holmes, James Waterman Wise and Justine Wise Polier. The correspondence and newspaper clippings, especially from the New York *Times*, New York *Herald Tribune* and New York *Graphic*, as well as the correspondence with labor leaders William Green and Sidney Hillman, Senator William E. Borah, and various churchmen were found in the files of the late Stephen S. Wise; additional sources were Wise's personal letters to his family. The American Federation of Labor convention of October, 1926, in Detroit is described in articles of that time in the *Nation* (Vol. CXXIII, pp. 387-388); *Christian Century* (Vol. XLIII, pp. 1292-1294); *The World Tomorrow* (Vol. IX, pp. 216-218); as well as in such books as *Religion in Our Times* by Gaius Glenn Atkins (New York, 1932), *The Protestant Search for Political Realism* (1919–1924) by Donald Burton Meyer (Berkeley & Los Angeles, 1960), and *Courage to Change* by June Rossbach Bingham (New York, 1961). Wise's sermon "Henry Ford's Retraction: Some Further Lessons" is No. 4 in Vol. VIII of *The Free Synagogue Pulpit* (1927–1928). Two of the most informative books about the so-called "Protocols" are *An Appraisal of the Protocols of Zion* by John S. Curtiss (New York, 1942), sponsored by a committee of historians including Carl L. Becker of Cornell, Sidney B. Fay of Harvard, Dixon Ryan Fox of Union College, Carlton J. H. Hayes of Columbia, William L. Langer of Harvard, Allan Nevins of Columbia, and many others, and *The Learned Elders of Zion* by Pierre Charlex, S.J. (with an introduction by William Granger Ryan), in *The Bridge*, a yearbook of Judeo-Christian Studies, Vol. I (New York, Seton Hall University, 1955).

21. LEARN WAR NO MORE

The salient facts about Holmes' church through these years are found in the *Year Books of the Community Church* for 1927, 1928, and 1929; and the details of the campaign for the Outlawry of War Pact in a number of volumes: *The Outlawry of War* by Charles Clayton Morrison (Chicago, 1927), *S. O. Levinson and the Pact of Paris* by John Stoner (Chicago, 1943), *The Fight for Peace* by Devere Allen (New York, 1930), and various issues of *Unity* and *Christian Century* from 1918 to 1928. Holmes' sermons through the years, especially, "August 28, 1928: A Turning Point In History" and "The Unknown Soldier Speaks," preached in October and November of 1928, are to be found in *The Community Pulpit* of 1928–1929. The poem quoted in the latter sermon is by Thomas Curtis Clark. His letters to Mrs. Gertrude Winslow from 1918 to 1928 reflect his thinking about the Pact and the League of Nations, as well as the presidential election of 1928. James Waterman Wise's *Jews Are Like That* by "Analyticus" (New York, 1928) contains his character sketches of Jewish leaders in America at that time. Aimé Pallière's *Unknown Sanctuary* was translated by Louise Waterman Wise and published in New York in 1928. The sermons of Stephen Wise, which gave his views on religious requirements for candidacy for the Presidency and on his son James' book, are "The Religion of the President and the Spirit of America" (*The Free Synagogue Pulpit*, No. 7, 1927–1928), and "Are Jews Like That?—Dare Jews Criticize Jews?" (*The Free Synagogue Pulpit*, No. 2, 1929–1930).

22. THEY SHALL REPAIR THE RUINED CITIES

The major source of information for this chapter is the series of Holmes' articles over an extended period in *Unity* in the late winter and spring of 1929 and his book *Palestine: Today and Tomorrow* (New York, 1929). Additional material is in the 1929 *Year Book of the Community Church* of New York. The story of Judah Magnes' 1929 mediation efforts is told in greater detail in Norman Bentwich's *Judah L. Magnes.*

23. ALL WE LIKE SHEEP DID GO ASTRAY

The epigraph by Erasmus was quoted by Philip Melanchthon in his address at the funeral of Martin Luther in 1546. The quotations from letters to and from both Wise and Holmes are made possible by the loan of such letters by their families. The statements by Holmes on his twenty-fifth anniversary were included in an interview in the New York *Herald Tribune*, published Saturday, January 23, 1932. The various sermons quoted were from *The Free Synagogue Pulpit* and *The Community Pulpit* during the years 1929 to 1932. The address at the St. Lawrence University Commencement in June of 1931 was printed in the *Christian Leader* (Vol. XXXIV, No. 26), June 27, 1931. The lecture by Holmes at the New School for Social Research on "The Future of Religion" is from *Religion Today: A Challenging Enigma,* edited by Arthur L. Swift (New York, 1933), and *The Sensible Man's View of Religion* by John Haynes Holmes published by Harper and Brothers in 1932. Stephen Wise's and Jacob de Haas' *The Great Betrayal* was published in New York in 1930.

24. A LITTLE MAN IN THE BIG CITY

The information about New York City politics in the 1920s and preceding decades is given in *What Is the Matter with New York?* by Norman Thomas and Paul Blanshard (New York, 1930), *Tammany* by Alfred Werner (New York, 1928), *The LaGuardia Years* by Charles Garrett (New Brunswick, N. J., 1961), and *The Man Who Rode the Tiger* by Herbert Mitgang (Philadelphia and New York, 1963). The New York *Times,* and New York *Herald Tribune* and the New York *World-Telegram* of those years tell the story of Mayor James J. Walker and his problems. The personal files of Stephen S. Wise and John Haynes Holmes, as well as those of the City Affairs Committee, describe the struggle these men had in seeking the ouster of Mayor James J. Walker. The reference to Wise in *Vanity Fair* is quoted in *Vanity Fair,* edited by Cleveland Amory and Fredrick Bradlee (New York, 1960). Interesting but not appreciative references to Wise and Holmes are made in *Beau James* by Gene Fowler (New York, 1949) and *A House Is Not a Home* by Polly Adler (New York, 1953).

25. THE YEARS OF THE LOCUST

The material for this chapter was gathered from sources mentioned before, as well as from the correspondence of the men made available at the American Jewish Archives of the Hebrew Union College-Jewish Institute of Religion in Cincinnati, Ohio. In addition, articles from *Opinion* during these years were helpful, especially one by Henry Smith Leiper describing the meeting at the home of Harry Emerson Fosdick. Dr. David Randall of the Lilly Library at the University of Indiana in Bloomington, Indiana, provided letters from Holmes to Upton Sinclair.

26. AND DARKNESS FELL

The fifty-ninth birthday dinner for John Haynes Holmes at the Hotel Astor is described indirectly by the speeches and introductions contained in a stenographic transcript of the proceedings. The work and thought of both Holmes and Wise are reflected in the correspondence of the two men during these days, an exchange of letters which became more frequent in their later lives, as well as in Holmes' letters to Mrs. Winslow of the Community Church in Boston and Wise's to his family. The *Christian Century* for 1939 and 1940 contains the articles by Holmes and the many others asked to contribute to the series on "If America Enters the War, What Shall I Do?" Holmes' book, *Out of Darkness,* was published by Harper and Brothers in 1942. The dramatic and historic anti-Communist struggle in the American Civil Liberties Union is given an extended treatment in Lucille Milner's book *Education of an American Liberal.* Both Holmes and Roger Baldwin furnished additional details.

27. HAMAN REDIVIVUS

The source material for this chapter was found in many of the publications and books listed before, letters and clippings from the files of Wise and Holmes and such magazines as *Opinion, Unity, Fellowship,* and *Life.* The statement by Harry S. Truman about his support of Zionism was given in an address, "Salute to Israel," before the Jewish National Fund on May 9, 1962.

28. PERFIDIOUS ALBION

The 1915 conversation between Wise and Wilson in the White House is related in *Challenging Years.* The editorial comment in *Liberal Judaism* about Wise's visit to Cincinnati is in the issue of January, 1946. The quotations from Stephen Wise's testimony before the Anglo-American Committee of Inquiry on Palestine are taken from a transcript of the official minutes, made available by the American Jewish Archives of the Hebrew Union College-Jewish Institute of Religion in Cincinnati. The newspaper account describing Wise's appearance before the Inquiry Committee in Washington was written by I. F. Stone of the Washington Bureau of *PM,* January 9, 1946. The report of the President's Commission on Higher Education was published by Harper and Brothers in 1950. The exact quotation of Louise Waterman Wise's letter to the British Ambassador, declining to become an Honorary Member of the Most Excellent Order of the British Empire, Civil Division, was printed on pages 94-95 of *Legend of Louise* by James Waterman Wise (New York, 1949).

29. GANDHI'S INDIA

The material for this chapter comes from letters John Haynes Holmes and Roger Holmes sent to their family, articles Roger Holmes wrote for the Holyoke *Transcript,* and sermons delivered by Holmes on his return, "My Visit With Gandhi" and "My Adventures With Religion in India," as well as his book *My Gandhi* (New York, 1953).

30. LET MY PEOPLE GO

Stephen Wise's sentences about the Castle of Chillon are taken from *Challenging Years* (New York, 1949). The eulogy by David Petegorsky at the funeral of Louise Waterman Wise was published in the January 9, 1948, issue of *Congress Weekly,* Vol. XV, No. 1. The various letters from which quotations were taken are in the files of Justine Wise Polier.

31. THE LION AND THE LAMB

The quotation at the opening of the chapter is taken from Vol. III of the *Beth Israel Pulpit* (1906). The editorial by Stephen Wise about Henry Sloane Coffin and the American Council for Judaism is in the March, 1949, issue of *Opinion,* Vol. XIX, No. 5 and is entitled, "The Ignoble Way." News items concerning Stephen Wise's illness, death, and funeral are in the New York *Times* of April 18-April 23, 1949.

32. THE LAST PURITAN

The material for this chapter was secured mostly from personal interviews and correspondence with John Haynes Holmes over many years, as well as from newspaper clippings of the time and various issues of the *Community News.* The quotation by the late Bishop G. Bromley Oxnam is on pages 97 and 98 of his book, *I Protest* (New York, 1954).

Writings of Stephen S. Wise

The Improvement of the Moral Qualities (translation from the Arabic and exposition of an ethical treatise of the eleventh century by Solomon ibn-Gabirol), 1901.

An Open Letter to the Members of Temple Emanu-El of New York, 1906.

Child Versus Parent, 1922.

How To Face Life, 1924.

The Great Betrayal (with Jacob DeHaas), 1930.

Never Again (edit.), 1943.

As I See It, 1944.

Challenging Years, 1949.

The Personal Letters of Stephen Wise (edited by Justine Wise Polier and James Waterman Wise), 1956.

Contributor to the symposiums *What I Owe My Father,* edited by Sidney Strong, 1930; *We Believe in Prayer,* edited by Sidney Strong, 1930; and many others.

Forewords and prefaces to *Old-New Land (Altneuland)* by Theodor Herzl, translated by Lotta Levensohn, 1941; *The Immortal Adventure,* by Irma Lindheim, 1928; *Franklin Delano Roosevelt: The Tribute of the Synagogue,* edited by Max Kleiman, 1946; and many others.

Contributing editor of *The New Palestine* and *Opinion;* founder and editor of *Opinion;* founder and contributing editor of *Congress Weekly;* contributor of articles, essays, sermons, and book reviews to many magazines and newspapers.

Sermons bound in printed copies of *Beth Israel Pulpit* (1902–1906) and *The Free Synagogue Pulpit* (1907–1949).

Writings of John Haynes Holmes

The Revolutionary Function of the Modern Church, 1912.
Marriage and Divorce, 1913.
Is Death the End?, 1915.
New Wars for Old, 1916.
Religion for Today, 1917.
The Life and Letters of Robert Collyer (Vols. I & II), 1917.
Readings from Great Authors, 1918.
The Grail of Life, 1919.
Is Violence the Way Out?, 1920.
New Churches for Old, 1922.
Patriotism Is Not Enough, 1925.
Palestine Today and Tomorrow, 1929.
The Heart of Scott's Poetry, 1932.
The Sensible Man's View of Religion, 1932.
If This Be Treason (a play in collaboration with Reginald Lawrence),
   1935.
Through Gentile Eyes, 1938.
Rethinking Religion, 1938.
Out of Darkness, 1942.
The Second Christmas and Other Stories, 1943.
The Affirmation of Immortality, 1947.
My Gandhi, 1953.
I Speak for Myself, 1958.
The Collected Hymns of John Haynes Holmes, 1960.

Contributor to the symposiums *What I Owe My Father*, edited by
Sidney Strong, 1930; *My Idea of God: A Symposium of Faith*, edited
by Joseph Fort Newton, 1926; and others.

Introductions to *America Arraigned* by Lucie Trent and R. Chey-
ney; *Youth and the Singing Shadows* by B. D. Allinson; *The Social
Evolution of Religion* by George Willis Cooke; *Life of Jesus* by Ernest

Renan; *There Is a Psychic World* by Horace Westwood; *Letters to a Disciple* by Mohandas Gandhi, and many others.

Contributing editor of *The Unitarian* (1907–1910) and *The Unitarian Advance* (1910–1917); contributing editor of *The World Tomorrow* (1917–1934); contributing editor of *Unity* (1910–1919) and editor (1919–1945); contributing editor of *Opinion* (1931–1956); contributing editor of *Fellowship* (1943–1957); author of articles, sermons, and editorials from 1904–1957 in *Christian Register, Christian Leader, Christian Century, Survey, Survey Graphic, Century, North American Review, Atlantic, Nation, New Republic, Progressive, Newark Journal, Saturday Review,* etc.

Regular contributor of book reviews for many years to *Books* of the New York *Herald Tribune* and to many other periodicals.

Sermons bound in printed copies of *The Messiah Pulpit* (1907–1919) and *The Community Pulpit* (1919–1949); occasional contributor to *The Community Pulpit* from 1950–1957.

Index

Abraham Lincoln Centre, 154
Abrahams, Israel, 211, 216-17
Adler, Cyrus, 50
Adler, Felix, 42, 43
American Civil Liberties Union, 183, 223, 226-7, 234, 310
American Council for Judaism, 345-6
American Jewish Conference, 316-17
American Jewish Congress, 131, 135, 163, 167, 169-70, 176, 217-18, 294
American Union Against Militarism, 141, 142-3
American Unitarian Association, 148, 149-50, 152
Anglo-American Committee of Inquiry, 324-5

Badger, George, 108
Baker, Newton D., 221-2
Baker, Ray Stannard, 97-8
Baldwin, Roger, 183
Balfour Declaration, 136-7
Beth Israel (Portland, Oregon), 46ff., 56ff.
B'nai Jeshurun (New York), 36, 37
Brandeis, Louis D., 131-2, 170, 250
Broadway Tabernacle, 173
Brown, David, 358
Brown, Harvey Dee, 154, 172
Brown, Morris Lovejoy, 262
Butler, Nicholas Murray, 21, 144

Cardozo, Benjamin, 120, 222-3, 270, 279
Central Synagogue, 217
Channing, William Ellery, 21
Church of Eternal Hope, 80
Church of the Messiah, 19-20, 75, 84-6, 90-1, 125-6, 132, 138, 144-6, 150, 151ff., 223
City Affairs Committee, 273ff.
Cohen, J. X., 317
Coleman, George W., 92
Collyer, Robert, 21, 75, 86, 95-6, 114, 126, 127-8, 148
Community Church of Boston, 174, 238, 308
Community Church of New York,

157ff., 191, 194, 201, 223, 231-2, 262-3, 267, 301-3, 308, 353, 354, 359
Community Forum, 173, 229-30, 234, 263
Coughlin, Charles, 289
Crothers, Samuel McChord, 68, 70

Darrow, Clarence, 228
Davidson, Thomas, 43-4
Debs, Eugene V., 159, 160, 237-8
Demarest, Clifford, 157
Douglas, William O., 340
DuBois, William E. Burghardt, 102

Eddy, Sherwood, 201
Elbogen, Ismar, 224
Eliot, Charles William, 106
Eliot, Samuel A., 148, 150
Emanu-El, Temple (New York), 18, 52, 53ff.
Ethical Culture Society, 42, 105, 173
Exman, Eugene, 268-9

Fellowship of Reconciliation, International, 140-1, 152
Fenn, William Wallace, 70
Flynn, Elizabeth Gurley, 310
Forbes, John P., 71
Ford, Henry, 239-40
Ford Hall Forum, 92
Fosdick, Harry Emerson, 287
Free Synagogue, 18, 19, 27, 58, 79ff., 99-100, 103, 104-5, 127, 137, 139, 150, 189, 209, 212, 217, 242, 304, 317, 349, 350
Frankfurter, Felix, 163
Fuller, Alvin, 238-9

Gandhi, Mohandas K., 198ff., 251, 330ff.
Gary, Elbert, 177, 178, 179
Goldstein, Sidney, 99, 100, 134, 317
Gompers, Samuel, 176
Gottheil, Gustav, 33, 54
Gottheil, Richard, 32, 36, 42, 44
Great Synagogue (Vienna), 34
Green, William, 235, 236-7

381

Hadassah, 130
Hale, Edward Everett, 69-70
Hall, Frank Oliver, 109-10
Harnack, Adolf, 200
Harrington, Donald, 318, 353, 354, 358, 359
Haynes, John Cummings, 64-6, 69, 70-1, 75
Hebrew Union College, 210, 318-19, 341, 343
Hebrew University (Jerusalem), 254
Henriques, Basil, 233-4
Herford, Travers, 211
Herzl, Theodor, 40-1, 45, 50-1
Hirsch, Emil, 80, 98-9
Hirsch, Solomon, 48
Hitler, Adolf, 285ff.
Hodgkin, Henry, 140
Holmes, Alice Haynes, 63-4, 71
Holmes, Frances, 84, 231, 261-2
Holmes, Hector McIntosh, 64
Holmes, Madeleine Hosmer Baker, 69, 71, 189-90, 231, 359
Holmes, (Marcus) Morton, 63-4, 71
Holmes, Marion, 64
Holmes, Roger, 74, 261, 331ff.
Hudson Theatre, 17-19, 21, 79, 80
Hughes, Charles Evans, 105, 122-3

Jacobs, Henry F., 36
Jellinek, Adolf, 33ff.
Jewish Encyclopedia, 51
Jewish Institute of Religion, 209ff., 318-19, 341, 343
Jewish Publication Society, 42, 49-50
John Haynes Holmes House, 354
Jones, Jenkin Lloyd, 108, 154

Kahn, Ernest, 340
Kellogg-Briand treaty, 245, 247
Kendall, Edith, 94
King, Martin Luther, 357
Klein, Edward E., 317
Kohler, Kaufmann, 47
Kohut, Alexander, 33

La Follette, Robert, 220
League to Enforce Peace, 141-2, 144
Lee, Roger, 71

Levinson, Salmon O., 154, 244-5, 311
Liebman, Joshua Loth, 318

McAfee, Joseph Ernest, 243
Magnes, Judah L., 258-9
Manning, William T., 144
Marshall, Louis, 54, 55, 56, 167-8, 170
Meadville Theological School, 112
Melish, John Howard, 114
Moore, George Foot, 216
Morgenthau, Henry, 79-80, 81, 135-6
Morrison, Charles Clayton, 244-5
Mosse, Eric P., 339-40
Mott, John R., 140
Murray, Gilbert, 198-9

National Associaton for the Advancement of Colored People, 102-3
Nehru, Jawaharlal, 329, 331ff.
Neubauer, Adolf, 33, 35
New Amsterdam Theater, 173
Newman, Louis I., 209
Niebuhr, Reinhold, 257, 325
Nielson, Francis, 140-1
Niles, David K., 92

Ochs, Adolph, 122-3
Oldham, G. Ashton, 144
Opinion, 266, 295, 301, 307, 342, 345
Oxnam, G. Bromley, 355-6

Parker, Theodore, 38-9
Parkhurst, Charles, 21
Passaic textile strike, 232ff.
Peabody, Francis Greenwood, 73, 122, 180, 278
Petegorsky, David, 340-1, 350
Philby, H. St. John, 258
Polier, Justine Wise. See Wise, Justine
Potter, Charles Francis, 285

Randall, John Herman, 172, 174, 243
Riegner, Gerhard, 313-14, 315-16
Rodeph Sholom (New York), 28, 35

Roosevelt, Franklin D., 275ff., 295-6, 309, 318, 319
Roosevelt, Theodore, 122, 125
Rothschild, Lionel, 165

Sacco-Vanzetti case, 227, 230, 238-9
Sachar, Abram, 348
Savage, Minot, 21, 22, 65-6, 70, 71, 85, 89
Schechter, Solomon, 50
Schiff, Jacob H., 110-4, 130-1
Schulman, Samuel, 81, 111, 178, 215, 225-6
Scopes, John T., 226-7
Seabury, Samuel, 272ff.
Seligman, James, 54
Settlement House, 79
Shippen, Rush, 70
Silver, Abba Hillel, 319-20
Silverman, Joseph, 54
Simkhowitch, Mary Kingsbury, 94
Sinclair, Upton, 132-3, 160-1
Skinner, Clarence R., 174
Smith, Alfred E., 221-3, 248
Snell, Harry, 265
Stelzle, Charles, 113
Stoll, Carl, 194
Straus, Nathan, 226, 248-9, 255
Strong, Josiah, 71-2
Szold, Henrietta, 42, 50, 130

Taft, William Howard, 125-6, 144, 149-50
Techmon (Haifa), 130-1
Third Religious Society and Third Congregational Church (Dorchester, Mass.), 70ff.
Town Hall, 301-2
Triangle fire, 114-16
Truman, Harry S, 320-1
Tulin, Leon, 238, 270
Tulin, Stephen Wise, 348-9

Un-American Activities Committee, 355-6
Union of American Hebrew Congregations, 210
Unitarian Church (Cambridge, Mass.), 68
Unitarian Church (Danvers, Mass.), 68-9

Unitarian Fellowship for Social Justice, 91
United Palestine Appeal, 226
Unity, 190, 197, 200, 201, 245, 257, 310, 331
University Settlement, 43

Voss, Carl August, 148

Waldman, Morris, 99
Walker, James J., 271ff.
Warburg, Felix, 294-5, 296-7
Ward, Harry F., 183, 310
Warren Goddard House, 94
Waterman, Jennie, 83
Waterman, Leo, 83
Weisz (Wise), Aaron, 27ff., 37
Weisz, Joseph Hirsch, 28, 29, 53
Weisz, Sabine de Fischer (Farkashazy), 28
Weisz, Sarah, 28
Weizmann, Chaim, 166
Welles, Sumner, 313-14
Wells, H. G., 193-4, 228-9
Wilson, Woodrow, 121-2, 123-4, 125, 136, 139ff., 160, 162-3, 166-9
Wise, Ella, 29
Wise, Ida, 28
Wise, Isaac Mayer, 33, 41
Wise, James Waterman, 27, 29, 50, 113, 175, 349, 350
Wise, Justine (Polier), 27, 50, 232-3, 290, 297, 319, 349
Wise, Louise Waterman, 27, 42ff., 55, 57, 81, 142, 249, 288, 326, 327, 336, 337ff.
Wise, Otto, 28, 46
Wise, Wilma, 28
Wood, Henry Wise, 140
Wood, Ralph, 58
World Jewish Congress, 294-5, 313, 315, 343
World Zionist Conference, 320-1, 328

Zangwill, Israel, 217-18
Zionism, 40ff., 127ff., 163ff., 205, 217-18, 226, 239, 248-50, 251ff., 263, 318ff., 323ff., 341-2
Zionist Organization of America, 295

ABOUT THE AUTHOR

Carl Hermann Voss, a graduate of Union Theological Seminary in New York City and the University of Pittsburgh, also pursued further study at Yale University and the University of Chicago and is an ordained clergyman.

Part of his career has been devoted to the parish ministry, and he has also occupied executive and editorial positions in national and international religious organizations. Among other institutions he has taught at the New School for Social Research, Skidmore College, and the Theological School of St. Lawrence University.

He has received many honors, including the Honorary Fellowship of the Hebrew University of Jerusalem and the National Brotherhood Award of the National Conference of Christians and Jews. He has been a resident scholar on behalf of the NCCJ at the Ecumenical Institute for Advanced Theological Studies at Tantur in Jerusalem and the Centre for Postgraduate Hebrew Studies at Oxford University.

Author of eight books and editor of two series, one in the humanities, the other on religion, Dr. Voss is currently engaged in research on a new book.

His wife, Dr. Phyllis G. Voss, is a psychologist and an associate professor at the University of North Florida. They make their home in Jacksonville, Florida.